DATE DUE			

TEACHING WORD RECOGNITION SKILLS

compiled by Mildred A. Dawson

Reprinted from the Publications of the
International Reading Association
Newark, Delaware 19711

INTERNATIONAL READING ASSOCIATION OFFICERS

1973-1974

President   MILLARD H. BLACK, Los Angeles Unified School District, Los Angeles, California

President-Elect   CONSTANCE M. McCULLOUGH, California State University, San Francisco, California

Past President   WILLIAM K. DURR, Michigan State University, East Lansing, Michigan

DIRECTORS

Term expiring Spring 1974

William Eller, State University of New York, Buffalo, New York

William J. Iverson, Stanford University, Stanford, California

Eunice Shaed Newton, Howard University, Washington, D. C.

Term expiring Spring 1975

Harold L. Herber, Syracuse University, Syracuse, New York

Helen K. Smith, University of Miami, Coral Gables, Florida

Grace S. Walby, Child Guidance Clinic of Greater Winnipeg, Winnipeg, Manitoba

Term expiring Spring 1976

Ira E. Aaron, University of Georgia, Athens, Georgia

Lynette Saine Gaines, University of South Alabama, Mobile, Alabama

Tracy F. Tyler, Jr., Robbinsdale Area Schools. Robbinsdale, Minnesota

* * *

Executive Secretary-Treasurer   RALPH C. STAIGER

Assistant Executive Secretaries   RONALD W. MITCHELL
JAMES M. SAWYER

Business Manager   RONALD A. ALLEN

Director of Research   STANLEY F. WANAT

Journals Editor   LLOYD W. KLINE

Publications Coordinator   FAYE R. BRANCA

* * *

CONTENTS*

---

*The articles in this volume have been reprinted from the following International Reading Association publications: Proceedings of the Conventions, *The Reading Teacher,* *Handbook for the Volunteer Tutor,* and *First Grade Reading Programs.* Original source is cited at the beginning of each article.

INSTRUCTION IN SPECIAL ASPECTS OF WORD RECOGNITION

ARTICLES PARTIALLY RELATED OR VERY GENERAL

The International Reading Association attempts, through its publications, to provide a forum for a wide spectrum of opinion on reading. This policy permits divergent viewpoints without assuming the endorsement of the Association.

INTRODUCTION

TEACHERS are perennially interested in articles concerned with the word-attack skills. In recent years, this interest seems to have increased as certain linguists have applied their knowledge of the nature of language to the phonology of words. While sounding out words is only one of several aspects of word recognition, almost all of the pertinent articles published by the International Reading Association have dealt directly with phonics, to the neglect of structural analysis and contextual clues. This volume, therefore, gives chief emphasis to phonics as a means of analyzing words.

There are five parts in this volume. The first is comprised of a single article that gives an excellent overview of the field of word recognition. Part II includes a dozen recent articles that present the overall general program of word analysis and the policies that underlie it. Part III contains articles dating back to 1963 when *The Reading Teacher* published the pioneer article by Clymer in which he reported on the comparative utility of phonic generalizations in the primary grades. Nine of the remaining articles similarly evaluate certain phonic elements and the generalizations concerning them. Two discuss rules that deal with accent on syllables and their effect on the pronunciation of words.

Part IV is concerned with such special aspects of word recognition as sight vocabulary, sensory cues, visual discrimination, contextual clues, and—of course—phonics. The articles differ from those in Part III in that they more narrowly deal with particular aspects of word recognition and are more concerned with methodology in certain instances. Three surveys of innovative approaches to reading, such at i.t.a. and "words in color," are included.

Certain articles were found to be only partially pertinent to a volume dealing with word recognition. These are listed in a general bibliography in Part V. The reader is advised to look up those articles that promise additional and desired information.

MILDRED A. DAWSON
Compiler

PART I: Overview

Dr. Singer has written an overview with excellent coverage, great clarity, and creditable organization. While his article is intended for the paraprofessional who is tutoring children or adults, it is fully as valuable for a teacher or supervisor who wishes a clear-cut overview of the entire field of word recognition.

Teaching Word Recognition Skills

Harry Singer*

TO TEACH WORD recognition, the tutor should know some principles of teaching word recognition, have an idea of a sequence of it, and learn some basic techniques for teaching it. In each of the remaining sections of this chapter are practical suggestions to use in teaching word recognition.

Principles of Teaching Word Recognition

1. Proceed from the familiar to the unfamiliar a step at a time. Although there may be some disagreement, the following is an example of a sequence going from the familiar to the unfamiliar: learning names for actual objects, associating a name with a picture of an object, recognizing a name in print in conjunction with a pictured object, and finally recognizing the printed word alone. In this sequence, one goes from a sensori-motor-perceptual type of experience to symbols to represent the experience. For example, from a name of a live dog, to the name for a picture of a dog, to recognition of the printed word "dog" alone.

2. From *dependence* on the tutor to *independence*. To follow this principle, first tell the student the whole word, then give hints, and finally let the student figure out the word from the variety of techniques he may have learned. Thus, at first the tutor tells the student that the word is "dog." Next time, the tutor gives the individual clues to help the student figure out the word clues, such as, inferring from the context (a picture context or a sentence context or both), "The _____ said, "Bow wow." Or the tutor gives the direction to sound out the word, a task which implies, of course, that there is for the particular word a one-to-one sound-symbol correspondence. But, this approach does not work for all words in the English language. For example, it works for "dog" but not for "right."

3. Teach the individual a variety of ways of recognizing words. Indeed, each technique of word recognition breaks down or is inadequate because no one technique applies to all words in the English language. The skilled reader must learn to use a variety of techniques, and he must also learn to shift appropriately from one to another. For example, he might use phonics to sound out "cat." But, in addition to sounding out c-a-t, he must also synthesize or put the sounds together to get the whole sound of "cat" which he then

*Handbook for the Volunteer Tutor, 1969, 46-59.

recognizes as a familiar word. In contrast, individuals, except in a classroom, never hear anyone point to the actual object and say that's a "c-a-t" (usually pronounced "cuh-ah-tuh").

Phonics or one-for-one sound symbol correspondence might work for "cat" but not for "right." If the individual tried to use phonics on "right," it would come out "r-i-g-h-t." No matter how many times the individual letters were sounded out, the word wouldn't come out "right." To make the word come out "right," the individual would have to shift to another one of several techniques; he could use context plus the initial consonant to infer the word, as in the following sentence:

<blockquote>After the boy answered the question, the
teacher smiled and said, "That's r_____."</blockquote>

Or he could have been taught the initial consonant (through such words as red, row, run) and the phonogram, ight through such words as light, fight, night. By substituting the initial consonant, "r," he would get the word "right." Another way of recognizing the word is by using a combination of phonics and knowledge of silent letters, ri(gh)t. The student who has learned a variety of approaches can then be flexible in recognizing words. If one approach doesn't work, he could switch to another. He is likely to do so not only if he knows a variety of approaches but if he is also continuously testing his solution against the criterion of meaning or asking himself, "Does this word pronounced this way make sense?"

4. Introduce new words and new techniques gradually and with adequate repetition so that the learner has a growing feeling of mastery. The basal readers or textbooks used in the primary grades for developing word-recognition skills provide for about ten repetitions of a newly introduced word and five repetitions of previously introduced words. It is estimated that the average individual requires about 38 repetitions to recognize a new word quickly and accurately.

5. Use an interesting way of having individuals practice recognizing new words. The most interesting way is to have the individual do a lot of reading in which he is likely to use the new words. The basal readers follow the introduction of new words with a story in which, by design, the new words appear several or more times. High interest, but low-level difficulty reading material is likely to contain words that the tutor is trying to get the student to learn.

A list of words that most pupils should know by the third grade has been constructed by Dolch who discovered that these words accounted for about 75 percent of all primary words and 50 percent of all adult words. The Dolch Readers and other materials published by the Garrard Press systematically use this vocabulary.*

---

*Basic Sight Words, Garrard Press, Champaign, Illinois. This word list can also be found in M. A. Tinker and C. M. McCullough, Teaching Elementary Reading (2nd Ed.). New York: Appleton-Century Crofts, 1962, 550-551.

The Reader's Digest Reading Skillbuilder** is another set of high-interest materials which start at a low level of difficulty and increase in difficulty. Together these two sets of materials would be very useful in teaching older individuals whose interests are more mature but who for one reason or another have not learned how to read or how to read as well as they should.

6. If the individual needs drill on recognition of words, try to provide it in a variety of ways. One technique that works well is to have the individual make up sentences using the word. Copy down the sentences and have the individual read them. Then cut up the sentences into words and have him recognize the individual words. Then have him group common initial consonants or common sounds in these words. Or he might group common syllables or prefixes and suffixes. He might also search through magazines for illustrations for his words.

7. A student's knowledge of progress is extremely important. Two techniques that can be utilized for concretely showing progress are 1) making a file of new words and 2) constructing a cumulative chart.

The card file might show the word in a sentence on the front with the word in the corner divided into syllables and perhaps even dia-critically marked. On the back of the card, the word would appear in isolation. The individual could test himself by looking at the back of the card to see if he knows the word in isolation and checking himself to see if he was right by reading the sentence and using context clues to check himself. For young children, pictures might also be used to identify the words.†

The cumulative chart could be kept daily or weekly. Below are examples of these charts:

Daily—to indicate immediate consequence of practice in recognizing new words.

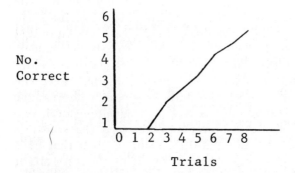

**Educational Division, Reader's Digest Service, Pleasantville, N.Y.
†The Garrard Press's "Popper Words" is based on this principle.

Weekly or monthly—to indicate cumulative number of new words learned.

Cumulative
No. of New
Words

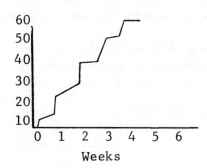

Weeks

8. In each lesson, try to maximize the probability of success. Individuals who have experienced failure are extremely sensitive to further failure. One strategy to attain success is to start by having the student tell a story. (See Chapter V for a detailed explanation of the language-experience approach.) Or, if the individual prefers, have him relate the activities for the day or tell an anecdote. Copy down the story and teach the individual to read the story. First, go over the story and have the individual identify words he doesn't recognize. Then, teach these words, which will be put into the word file and plotted on the chart. Then, have the individual read the story. Next, cut up a copy of the story into sentences and have the individual reassemble the sentences. Then, cut the sentences into words. Again, have the story reassembled. Then, have the individual use the words to make up new sentences.

9. From the very beginning, consult with the student's classroom teacher, provided that the individual is still attending school. The tutor might get from the classroom teacher valuable suggestions and even materials for helping the individual. In any case, the tutor and the classroom teacher should be working together to help the student. If the teacher or the student wants the tutor to help with the daily assigned lesson, the tutor could use the above principles with the assigned materials. Helping with the daily lesson is a short-range strategy that might pay off equally as well as a developmental, systematic program, provided the discrepancy between the student's assignment and his level of reading ability is not so great that he is overwhelmed by too many new words to learn. If so, the tutor might have to concentrate his efforts upon the long-range strategy of taking the individual back to a level where he can be successful and starting a developmental reading program at that level.

10. For developmental or corrective reading instruction, it is necessary to follow *a sequence for teaching word recognition*. There are several logical sequences that could be used, but no one of them can be said to be *the* sequence to follow. The following is one sequence:

A Developmental Sequence of Word Recognition

(A list of materials for teaching each of these aspects of word recognition can be found at the end of this section.)

Approximate Grade Level

1	Sight words
1–2	Initial consonants
	Final consonants
	Consonant digraphs (ch, th, wh, sh)
1–2	Consonant blends (fr, sl, cl, pl - - and those needed)
	Advanced consonant digraphs (qu, nk, ng); variants (s, es, ed, ing)
	Silent consonants
	Contractions
	Simple structure of sentences and punctuation markers for speech patterns, such as use of commas, periods, question marks.

Approximate Grade Level

2	Vowels
	Long and short sounds
	Vowels in phonogram ("r<u>igh</u>t, m<u>a</u>k<u>e</u>, etc.")
	Simple suffix (farm<u>er</u>)
	Rhyming endings
	More complex sentence structure and punctuation markers
3	Syllabication
4	Prefixes, suffixes, roots
5	Accent and dictionary work

Types of Word-Recognition Techniques

The types of word recognition techniques can be grouped into three somewhat-overlapping categories: predominantly visual clues, emphasis on meaning, and mainly analytical procedures.

Predominantly Visual Clues

1. *Picture aids.* Printed words are often learned by their association with pictures. For identifying nouns, pictures can readily be

found in magazines. For other categories of speech, such as verbs and adjectives, cartoon strips can be used. A variety of ways of illustrating various parts of speech may be found in a small pocketbook, *English Through Pictures*.* (See list of references.) This pocketbook may also be used for teaching English to bilingual children by having the children act out the sentences as they read them.

2. *Sight words* or "instant" recognition of words. Through recognition of the same words in a variety of situations, individuals build up a sight-word vocabulary. This vocabulary increases as the individual matures in reading. Eventually the skilled reader recognizes all words at sight or recognizes them so rapidly that he becomes almost oblivious to the process because it occurs so quickly and so effortlessly. Two procedures can be used for developing sight words:

(a) *Flash cards*. This procedure has already been discussed in the section on principles of teaching word recognition. It's a useful technique but should only be used for a short period of time because boredom sets in rapidly. However, there are a variety of techniques for making such exercises interesting, such as having the student use the words to construct sentences.

(b) *Easy reading*. Seeing the same words in a variety of stories is the most interesting and best way of teaching sight-word recognition. A list of interesting, yet easy-to-read books for older children and adults are listed in Chapters VIII and IX.

Whether a book is easy depends on how well the person can read. The rule of thumb is that if the individual has difficulty with more than one or two words per hundred, it's not an easy book for him. Whether a book is interesting, of course, depends upon the interests of the reader. For determining whether any book is easy, but interesting, the best procedure is to have the individual select the book himself and try it out.

Emphasis on Meaning

1. *Context clues*. This technique consists of using a sentence to help the individual infer the meaning of the unknown word and then to think of the word itself. By looking at the initial consonant and other parts of the sentence, the individual is employing a very powerful combination of word-recognition techniques. The teaching procedure calls for constructing a sentence in which the unknown word is omitted or all but the initial consonant is omitted. Then the individual reads the sentence and tries to infer the unknown word. These sentences may be placed on cards with

---

*I. A. Richards and C. M. Gibson. *English Through Pictures*. Pocketbooks, 1953.

the missing word on the back so that the flash-card technique can also be used and the cards then filed as tangible evidence of achievement. The tutor can teach the individual to recognize and use these clues whenever they appear in stories, and the tutor can also use this approach in giving hints for recognizing new words. Examples* of various types of context clues follow:

(a) *Definition.* The unknown word is defined. "Tom liked to ride on the last car on the train. The last car on the train is the c _ _ _ _ _ _."
(caboose)

(b) *Experience.* The individual can infer the word from his experience. "Betty was going to grow her own flowers. In each row, she placed s _ _ _ _ _."
(seeds)

(c) *Contrast.* The unknown word is opposite in meaning to known words or phrases. "She missed the noises of the big city. On the farm it was very q _ _ _ _ _."
(quiet)

(d) *Familiar expression.* The unknown word is part of an idiom or everyday expression. "To his surprise, the big man was as g _ _ _ _ _ as a lamb."
(gentle)

(e) *Summary.* The unknown word sums up the ideas in the preceding sentences. "First, Tom saw the riders rope the steers. Then he laughed at the cowboy clown on his horse. Then he watched the cowboys race around the ring. Tom had a lot of fun at the r _ _ _ _ _."
(rodeo)

(f) *Reflection of a mood or situation.* The unknown word explains the mood of the story. "After a few days away from home at camp, she began to miss her family, her dog, and her friends. She was h _ _ _ _ _ _ _."
(homesick)

2. *Compound words.* Words which represent the combination of two words may be recognized when separated, and the meaning of the two words gives the meaning of the combined word. At the primary grade level, such words as "summertime" and "fireman" can be recognized this way. One technique is to have each part of the compound word on a separate card and bring the two cards together so that they appear to make one word. Or, the two parts of the word can be underlined separately, e.g. <u>fire</u> <u>man</u>.

---

*C. M. McCullough. "The Recognition of Context Clues in Reading," *Elementary English Review*, 22 (1945), 1-15. Adapted with permission of Dr. McCullough.

Analytical Techniques

Structural and phonetic analysis are the two major types of analytical techniques.

1. Included in structural analysis are the following:
   a. Compound and hyphenated words (by-product).
   b. Root words and their variants which include the various endings to indicate tense and number, such as "rush" and "rushed," "boy" and "boys."
   c. Contractions, such as "didn't."
   d. Syllabication, the parts of a word which may or may not represent meaning components, such as prefixes or suffixes, but do represent boundaries between sequences of sounds in a word.

Structural analysis in this section will emphasize syllabication. In general, a word has as many syllables as heard vowel sounds. To teach syllabication, do the following:
   a. Pupil and tutor should first pronounce the word carefully.
   b. Identify the number of heard vowel sounds.
   c. Group about five words together that fit a principle of syllabication. Teach the pupil to divide each word into its syllables. Have the pupil then try to formulate the rule. Then have him supply or search for words that fit the rule. After he has learned the following rules, he can then classify new words according to the rules. Remember, this technique requires a thorough understanding of vowel sounds and consonants if it is to be successful.

Rules for Syllabication

(Many students have difficulty with this. Use only when applicable.)

1. If there is only one heard vowel sound in a word, the word is monosyllabic and, therefore, cannot be further divided. Examples: late, night, trees.
2. In words containing two heard vowel sounds, when two consonants are together in the word with vowels on either side, the word is usually divided between the consonants. Examples: af ter, but ter, bar gain.
3. Affixes (prefixes and suffixes) usually form a separate syllable. Examples: unhappy, lively. (Note: "ed" is usually only a separate syllable when preceded by "t" or "d" as in "wanted" and "needed." When preceded by other consonants, "ed" does not form a separate syllable as in "called," "rushed," "liked," etc.)
4. If there is one consonant between two vowels in a two-syllable word and the first vowel sound is long, the long vowel usually

ends the first syllable and the consonant begins the second syllable. Examples: la dies, po lite. (The first syllable is called an "open" syllable.)

5. If there is one consonant between two vowels in a two syllable word and the first vowel is short, the consonant usually ends the first syllable and the second vowel sound begins the second syllable. Example: cam el, mag ic. (First syllable is called a "closed" syllable.)

6. Compound words are divided into their component parts. Examples: high way, rail road, snow flake.

7. "Le" endings are special cases. If the word ends in "ck" when "le" is taken off, then "le" is a separate syllable. Examples: crackle, pickle. In all other words, "le" takes the preceding consonant. Examples: eagle, candle.

8. For words which contain more than two syllables, follow the former principles, proceeding from the largest to the smallest division of the word:

   a. Inspect for compound word. Example: steel worker, kinder garten.

   b. Take off affix: worker, kinder garten.

   c. If one or more of the parts have more than one heard vowel sound, determine whether vowel sounds are long or short. Then divide into open and closed syllables, as in kind er gar ten.

   d. Inspect for special "le" endings.

Phonics

"Sounding out" words or the application of phonetic principles to the recognition of new words is useful for about 80 to 85 percent of words. One procedure for applying phonics or relating sounds to letters is the following:

   a. Group known sight words with a common consonant or vowel. For example: can   cut   car

   b. Have individual read each word to make sure each word is a known sight word.

   c. Have pupil notice the initial letters of the words are alike and the initial sounds are alike. Tell the pupil the name of the letter (small and capital letter).

   d. To test whether pupil has learned the sound for the initial consonant, have the pupil give additional words with the same initial sound. If he gives the following words, form them into two columns:

cold	kite	city
cup	kit	cent
cap	kind	

   e. In the preceding examples, point out

1. some words have the same sound-letter correspondence.
2. some words have the same sound but a different letter, and
3. some words have the same letter and a different sound.

This discovery will help the pupil limit his generalization and perhaps will help him become flexible in shifting from one sound-letter correspondence to another in recognizing words.

f. Pupils can also learn phonograms the same way:

came	night
game	right
tame	light

After reading through the list of words with a common phonogram, have pupils supply or search for additional words with the same phonogram. (See list of references for sets of phonograms.)

g. With knowledge of consonants and phonograms, pupils can figure out new words by means of consonant substitution. For example, the pupil who knows "tell" and "sell" and the initial consonant "b" can then figure out the new word "bell."

h. Although pupils can and do learn to read by implicitly using rules, it may help to know the rules. To teach them, proceed in the following way. Teach inductively by presenting words that illustrate a vowel principle, and then teach deductively by stating a vowel principle and having words categorized under that principle. One can teach the following vowel and consonant rules:

1. Long vowel sounds are usually the names of the vowel letters, as in āte, ēat, īce, ōpen, ūse, or as in the following sentence:
   A sweēt, nīce, ōld ūnicorn.

2. When two vowels are together in a word, the first is usually long and the second is usually silent, as in āid, ēast, trīed, bōat, rūeful.

3. However, there are many exceptions to the preceding rule, particularly when the first vowel is followed by "u," "o," and "i." Examples: haul, caught, good, spoon, broom, said, oil.

4. In words containing two vowels, one of which is a final "e," the final "e" is usually silent and the preceding vowel is usually long. Examples: āte, sēe, īce, nōte, ūse.

5. Single vowels followed by "l," "r," or "w" usually have a blend sound. Examples: talk, ball; car, far; saw, raw.

6. When "y" ends a word that has no other vowel, then "y" has the sound of long "i." Examples: my, try, sky. If "y" ends a two-syllable word, it frequently has the sound of long "e." Examples: merry, scary, surely. If "y" is

preceded by another vowel, there is a different sound for both. Examples: they, boy.

7. Consonants are sometimes silent or not sounded. Examples: lamb, night, ghost, hour, know, pneumonia, island, buy, wrote. These silent consonants must be learned as sight words. That is, an individual has to learn that in certain words, there are one or more consonants that are silent. This condition is frequently true for words beginning with "kn" (know, knife), words that have "gh" in them (light, night, right), and words ending in "mb" (lamb, thumb, limb). Although silent consonants make phonics inapplicable to many words, silent consonants are important for word recognition, particularly for discriminating homonyms (words that sound alike but are spelled differently), such as "buy "and "by," "two and "to," "know" and "no." If words did not have silent letters in them, one would have to use some other clues, such as diacritical markings for determining pronunciation. For example, try to read this sentence in which the silent letters have been omitted: "We caut eit fish at eit this morning and at them at nit." This sentence with the silent letters in reads: "We caught eight fish at eight this morning and ate them at night."

Cautions in Teaching Word Recognition

1. Proceed only as rapidly as the student can be cumulatively successful. Whether teaching new sight words, a new structural analysis technique, or a new phonic principle, provide sufficient practice and use of the new instruction in various reading situations so that the pupil does not get overloaded with too much too quickly. Some students need a slow rate of learning, and others can have a faster rate of learning. Sometimes the same student can learn some things slowly and other things quickly. One has to judge what is the best pace or rate of learning for the student. Begin each session with a review of the instruction of the previous session; then after the pupil demonstrates he remembers what he was taught, go on to new instruction. If the student doesn't remember, then have a quick review of the previous instruction before going on to new instruction. But, be sure to evaluate your rate of instruction to determine whether it fits your student's rate of learning. If you can, keep a graph or chart of the rate of instruction.

2. Plan each lesson carefully. Make sure you know what you want your student to accomplish at each session. A brief outline of the lesson will help. A typical lesson might include the following.

   a. Review words.

b. Introduce new words (print word in sentence) and discuss them to get pronunciation, ways of recognizing word, word meaning, and similarity to previous words and experiences associated with the word.

c. Have the student recognize new words in a variety of sentences.

d. Make a card (for card file) for each new word.

e. Make an experience chart (see Chapter IV) using the new words or read a story containing the new words.

f. Try to arouse curiosity for reading the story by having the student formulate questions about the story from knowing its title or from looking at the illustrations. If the story has questions at the end, at times let the student read the questions first. Then read the story. Later, let him predict in advance what the questions are when he reads the title of the story. The eventual objective is to get him to formulate questions as he reads and thus read to answer his own questions. This process will make him an *active* reader.

g. Have the student reread story into a tape recorder and then listen to the playback. Let him evaluate his own performance.

h. Teach a new word-recognition skill and have the student practice the skill in an interesting way.

3. Try to work with the student at least twice a week. At first, do not require him to do anything outside of the tutoring session. As he becomes successful, he will ask to take home books or he will begin to bring books, new words, or materials to the session. Gradually you might begin to assign homework. Be sure, though, that the student knows how to do the homework. If he is to read a book at home, he should know practically *all* the words in the book. As he learns ways to recognize new words, he can be given books with new words which he can attack using skills he has already learned in the tutoring session.

4. As much as possible, plan and evaluate with your student. Find out what he thinks his difficulty is, how he is trying to solve it, how he tries to read, and what he would like to learn. Make the process of teaching and learning a mutual situation in which both you and your student are working together to achieve a common goal.

Selected References to Teaching Materials and Teaching Aids

Word Recognition Materials

(For a more complete listing, see Chapters VIII and IX)

Basic Sight Words. Champaign, Illinois: Garrard Press.

Breaking the Sound Barrier. New York: Macmillan.

English Through Pictures, I. A. Richards and C. M. Gibson. New York: Pocketbooks.

Eye and Ear Fun, Book 4, Word Independence in the Middle Grades, Clarence R. Stone. St. Louis: Webster. A complete sequence of word-recognition techniques and exercises from letter names and sounds to word meaning analysis, using prefixes, suffixes, and roots.

Phonics in Proper Perspective, Arthur W. Heilman. Columbus, Ohio: Charles E. Merrill, 1964. General instructions on teaching phonics, includes techniques and exercises for teaching consonant sounds, vowel sounds, syllabication, and accent.

Phonics Skilltexts. Columbus, Ohio: Merrill.

Phonics We Use. Chicago: Lyons & Carnahan.

Phonics and Word Power, My Weekly Reader Practice Books. Columbus, Ohio 43216: Education Center. Workbook-type materials designed for grades 1–3. Ranges from instruction on initial consonants to syllabication.

Reading with Phonics. Philadelphia: Lippincott.

Speech-to-Print Phonics, Donald D. Durrell and Helen A. Murphy. New York: Harcourt, Brace & World.

PART II: General Program and Policies

This part of the reprint volume affords a general view of a program in word recognition, extending from the early elementary school years through college. Expert analysis of research findings to date is provided by Wittick and Aaron as a means of validating desirable policies and of deciding which policies to avoid or eliminate. Robinson and Brzeinski give good advice on the desirable time to initiate instruction in word recognition skills, while Piekarz and Durkin give knowledgeable warnings based on common sense as well as their thorough acquaintance with research findings. Seymour makes clear the difference between phonics and the linguistic approach to beginning reading in terms of phonology.

Why Not an Intensive-Gradual Phonic Approach

CAROL K. WINKLEY*

AS ONE attempts to discuss the familiar, age-old topic of phonics, there is a temptation to presume that there is, or ought to be, some sane solution to the controversy that has raged in recent years and reached new heights with the publication of Chall's (1967), *Learning to Read: The Great Debate*. As Artley (1967), Strang (1968), and others have professed, it is doubtful that a topic so basic to "breaking the code" should become a subject for any more than thoughtful, well-designed, and impartial research as well as careful and discerning analysis of the process involved.

EXAMINATION OF THE PROBLEM

Evidence from research certainly supports the practice of teaching sound-symbol or phoneme-grapheme relationships. However, an examination of research—whether it be that summarized by Chall (1967), Gurren and Hughes (1965), Weintraub (1966), or others—seems to raise more questions than it answers.

It has not shown why so many pupils fail to acquire a workable technique for decoding written language when Austin and Morrison (1963) found that 95 to 99 per cent of the elementary schools participating in their survey reported that phonetic analysis was taught in grades one through six, and when such leaders in the reading field as Bond, Fay (1968), and Durrell (1969) believe that phonics is actually over-taught. In addition, research has not provided conclusive evidence concerning the specific phonic generalizations that actually prove to be most helpful to pupils faced with the task of unlocking unknown words. Word counts have been made by Clymer (1963), Emans (1967), and others to determine the "utility" of certain principles but it is not known whether their findings bear any relationship to children's actual utilization of the principles when they are engaged in the act of decoding unfamiliar words.

It appears, though, that the most important question that remains unanswered today pertains to methodology—what is the best, most efficient procedure for teaching pupils the relationship that exists between the sounds of the spoken language, with which they are familiar, and the symbols used to represent that language when it is recorded or written? At the same time teaching "reading

*The Reading Teacher, 23 (April 1970), 611-617, 620.

for meaning," an issue about which there should be no debate, has become hopelessly entwined in the controversy.

In an attempt to shed some light on the problems involved in teaching pupils the phoneme-grapheme correspondence characteristic of the English language, three questions will be considered. First, why is phonic instruction so ineffective in our schools; second, how can phonics be taught efficiently; and third, what method of instruction appears to be dictated by a careful analysis of the process involved.

REASONS FOR INEFFECTIVE PHONICS INSTRUCTION

Several years of in-service training of reading teachers, first as a reading consultant and now as a college instructor of graduate students, have convinced the author that the average teacher of reading does not know as much phonics as the average third-grade pupil. On a test of phonic knowledge, administered to forty teachers enrolled in a graduate level course at Northern Illinois University, the mean score was ninety out of 110 possible points, or about 82 per cent mastery. Reviewing several similar studies of teachers' knowledge of phonic skills, Spache (1964) concluded that "the average teacher is not thoroughly trained in phonics in college reading courses." It is even questionable whether the college instructors themselves know the phonic principles one might expect to be taught in elementary school classrooms. This fact seems to support Austin's (1961) contention, following her surveys reported in *The Torchlighters* and *The First R* (1963), that the place to begin, if we are to improve the reading skills of children, is with thorough and intensive training of college instructors of teachers of reading.

Since college professors frequently offer time limitations as their excuse for not teaching phonic generalizations more thoroughly, Marion Hull, who is involved in pre-service as well as in-service training of reading teachers at Northern Illinois University, has prepared a program for self-instruction of phonic principles. Entitled *Phonics for the Teacher of Reading*, this 116-page booklet, providing immediate feedback regarding the accuracy of responses, can be completed by a student or teacher in approximately five hours of independent work. Among the phonic principles taught are 1] the twenty-five consonant phonemes (voiced, unvoiced, and nasal) with a discussion of other graphemes representing each sound and other phonemes represented by each grapheme; 2] the nineteen vowel phonemes including the long sounds, short sounds, other single vowel sounds, diphthongs, and digraphs;

3] vowel clues; 4] syllabication principles; and 5] accent generalizations.

It can be argued that in order to read the literature with any
degree of understanding teachers need to know the definitions,
concepts, and principles presented. However, it is extremely doubtful that they should all be taught to children. For example, is it
really essential that children know the difference between voiced
and unvoiced consonants? Must they learn the definitions of phoneme, grapheme, digraph, diphthong, etc.? Should they be expected
to recall when the inflectional ending "ed" forms a separate syllable
and when it is pronounced with the preceding syllable? These
concepts are of interest to teachers studying the characteristics and
consistencies of the English language but they probably would be
of little or no value to a pupil wishing to use his phonic knowledge
to figure out an unfamiliar word. There is a desperate need for
well-controlled studies which will provide evidence regarding the
specific phonic concepts actually helpful to pupils attempting to
identify words.

In addition to deficiencies in teachers' knowledge of phonics,
another possible explanation for the ineffective teaching of phonics
in many classrooms is that it is not being taught efficiently. Lacking
complete understanding of what they are attempting to teach,
teachers are "belaboring phonics to death" by teaching concepts
and understandings that the children have already acquired. This
leads to the second question, "How can phonics be taught efficiently?"

PRETESTING TO INCREASE EFFICIENCY OF TEACHING

It appears reasonable to say that knowledge of a phonic
principle cannot be considered acquired by any pupil until he
can use it to identify unknown words to which it is applicable.
This is the true purpose of teaching phonics. It can, therefore, be
assumed that children go through various stages or reach various
levels of understanding concerning any phonic generalization. The
job of the teacher then becomes one of finding out where the
"breakdown" is for each and every child who is unable to apply a
particular generalization. A pre-test consisting of ten steps is
recommended as a useful procedure for identifying the starting
point for teaching any generalization. Although it is commonly
done, teachers should not go back to the auditory discrimination
step, for example, and use games and various auditory exercises
to help pupils discriminate one sound from another unless the

child's knowledge has not progressed beyond that stage.

The following steps are proposed for pre-testing of children's knowledge of any phonic principle. The steps are continued until the teacher locates the level at which each child demonstrates successful achievement. Because pre-testing begins at the highest level and procedes to successively lower levels of mastery, the first pre-test step is numbered *Step 10* (which coincides with the number of the related teaching step.)

Step 10: Present unknown words, to which the principle is applicable, and ask the pupil to pronounce each word. When testing a pupil's knowledge of consonant and vowel sounds, phoneme substitution in known words can be utilized.

Step 9 : Ask the child what phoneme the grapheme represents in isolation.

Step 8 : Have the pupils write the letter that stands for a specified sound heard in words as they are pronounced by the teacher.

Step 7 : Ask pupils to select the letter, for which they see a visual representation, which stands for a particular sound heard in the name of a pictured object.

Step 6 : Several words are presented from which the pupils are asked to select the one(s) in which a particular sound appears.

Step 5 : Several letters are presented from which the pupils select the one that represents a particular sound in a word pronounced by the teacher.

Step 4 : The pupil is asked to name the letter(s).

Step 3 : As the teacher pronounces several words, the child is asked to select those which contain a particular sound heard in a word.

Step 2 : The child is asked to isolate a particular sound in a spoken word.

Step 1 : The children are asked to locate a certain symbol appearing in several written words.

There appears to be a logical progression of skill development illustrated in these steps that are necessarily pre-tested in reverse order. No "diagnostic" test, presently on the market, is constructed in such a way that it identifies the level at which a child's skill breaks down in relation to any phonic generalization nor even whether a usable knowledge of the principle has been acquired by a child. Thus, responsibility for pre-testing and interpreting the results falls squarely on the classroom teacher.

Certain adaptations of these steps will be necessary to pre-test knowledge of vowel principles, syllabication, and accent clues. It is possible to simplify the pre-testing process by testing at alternate steps or even every third step. Nevertheless, the judicious use of this procedure of pinpointing children's starting levels in learning phonic generalizations should go a long way toward obviating the practice of overteaching phonics.

AN INTENSIVE-GRADUAL PHONIC APPROACH

If the hypothesis is accepted that the use of pre-testing as a diagnostic procedure will, in turn, improve the efficiency of phonic teaching, a method of instruction can be examined which is based on the assumption that the teacher has knowledge of each pupil's starting level for the generalizations she plans to teach. Because children's levels of progress will differ, individualized or small-group instruction will be required. Each child will need to be "plugged in" at the appropriate level (the lowest level at which the child makes any errors or where he is unsure of his responses) and be taught by successive steps until he reaches the level at which he can identify unknown words either in isolation or in context. In addition, he must learn a "plan of attack" for words that turn out to be exceptions to the principle being taught.

Using an inductive approach, leading from the known to the unknown, children can be taught any phonic principle as soon as they have in their sight vocabularies three of four words to which that principle applies. If one endorses a synthetic method of phonic analysis, no knowledge of sight words is needed and a deductive approach is dictated whereby the teacher presents the "rule" which children are expected to apply in their attack on unknown words.

An analytic method of phonic analysis, termed "gradual" by Gurren and Hughes and "intrinsic" by Chall, is recommended in this article for the following reasons:

1. It permits reading to be taught from the very beginning as a thought-getting process. The child's first encounter with the "code" is for the purpose of expressing and/or securing ideas or meanings.

2. The content of reading materials need not include nonsense words or nonsense stories necessitated when phonic principles are taught first and then used as limiting factors in the choice of vocabulary.

3. Unknown words can be identified quickly and efficiently since letter-by-letter sounding is not required. The pronunciation of consonants in isolation is unnecessary, thereby eliminating the unavoidable addition of an "uh" or schwa sound to each consonant phoneme as it is sounded when a synthetic method is employed.

4. Phonic principles are applicable to multisyllabic words, making it possible for children to readily identify the longer words met at the intermediate grade levels.

5. It lends itself to an intensive treatment to the same degree as a synthetic method. An analytic method is characterized by a *gradual* introduction of phonic principles as readiness is

established and a need exists for pupils to learn them, but this does not prevent an *intensive* teaching of the principles once they are introduced.

How does the analytic method work? In order to ensure complete mastery of a phonic generalization, twelve steps, the first ten of which correspond to the pre-testing steps described earlier, are recommended:

1. Teach the children to recognize the grapheme, representing the phoneme, as it appears in words and other printed material.
2. Help the child to hear and isolate the individual sound as it is heard in a word pronounced by the teacher and repeated by the child.
3. Teach the children to recognize the sound each time it is heard in a word pronounced by the teacher. Have the children indicate in some way the words in which the sound is heard.
4. Teach the letter name. Durrell's continual insistence of the value of teaching letter names is based on the fact that the sound represented by the letter is heard when the names of twenty-two of the twenty-six letters of the alphabet are pronounced. In addition to the five vowels that stand for their letter names when they represent their long sounds, Durrell has identified eight long "e" consonants (b, c, d, g, p, t, v, and z) six short "e" consonants (f, l, m, n, s, and x), two long "a" consonants (j and k), as well as "r", whose names, when pronounced, contain one phoneme that each grapheme represents.
5. Teach the children to recognize the grapheme that stands for a particular sound heard in spoken words.
6. Have the children identify words containing the grapheme representing the specific sound heard in a spoken word.
7. Show pictures of objects whose names begin with the particular phoneme(s) being learned. Teach children to select the grapheme representing each particular phoneme. Now the child does not hear the sound but must "think" it in order to select the correct visual symbol.
8. Have the children write the graphemes representing particular phonemes heard in words pronounced by the teacher. Now, the visual symbol is not seen and the children must recall it in order to match it with the auditory stimulus. The children should, at this point, be led to make a generalization regarding the phonic principle. Based on the examples presented, what "clue" would help them with the sound if they came to a word they didn't know?
9. Have the children recall words which contain the sound represented by the grapheme. List them on the board so that the sound-symbol relationship can be reinforced.
10. Provide practice in phoneme substitution or applying the clue to unknown words in isolation. Start with known words if using phoneme substitution. Have children "think off" a particular phoneme and "think on" the sound represented by the letter being substituted. If a vowel principle, syllabication clue, or accent generalization is being taught, the children should be helped to apply the clue to unknown words.
11. Since context reading provides an additional help and is our ultimate goal for using word recognition skills, practice should be provided in identifying unknown words appearing in sentences and paragraphs.
12. Teach children a procedure for identifying words that are exceptions to the clue taught. Since the reader does not know a word is an exception when he meets it in his reading, he will first apply the clue he has learned. If he doesn't recognize the word as one in his speaking vocabulary, he should be taught to try other sounds. It is hoped that he will ultimately derive the correct

pronunciation. If not, he should be taught to use the dictionary. Whenever a word pronunciation does not "trigger" meaning, the dictionary becomes the last resort.

It is important that any principles or clues taught for use in single syllable words will also be applicable in multisyllabic words. When unknown words of more than one syllable are met, the children must be taught clues for dividing words into syllables as well as generalizations for determining which syllable is accented. There is a definite need for teaching accent generalizations since the vowel principles are applicable in accented syllables only. The vowel sound in the unaccented syllable can be expected to be that represented by the schwa symbol (ə) or a short "u", and occasionally by a short "i" sound.

COMPARISON OF ANALYTIC WITH SYNTHETIC APPROACH

Although the research reviewed by Chall (1967) and earlier by Gurren and Hughes (1965) was admitted to be "shockingly inconclusive" (Chall), the conclusion was reached that a "code-emphasis," "systematic," or "intensive" approach, which was really a synthetic method, produced results superior to those of methods comparable to the one described previously. What is a synthetic method? It is an approach whereby children are taught to sound letters and letter combinations singly and then blend these individual sounds to form a word. For example, children would sound the word "tent" as "tuh", "e", "n", "tuh", since they had previously learned the sound represented by each letter ("t" says "tuh", for example.) By an analytic method, the generalization is made that the letter "t" usually represents the sound heard at the beginning of the key word "top." In attacking the word "tent" the child would be taught to recall a known word resembling this word—"went," perhaps—then "think off" the "w" and "think on" the "t" of "top"—making "tent".

There is no logical reason that an analytic method, which has been termed a "meaning-emphasis," "intrinsic," or "gradual" approach, can not and should not also be an intensive, systematic code-emphasis approach. Although it must necessarily be gradual in its introduction of phonic principles, this fact does not preclude an intensive attack on teaching the clues, once they are introduced.

CONCLUSION

It is recommended that teachers, thoroughly knowledgeable

regarding clues to phoneme-grapheme relationships, first pre-test to determine their pupils' levels of understanding of phonic generalizations, and then begin at the point of breakdown to teach by a systematic inductive approach those generalizations for which the children already know a few sight words. This analytic method has undoubtedly failed to demonstrate superiority over synthetic methods in some studies chiefly because it has been poorly taught. This proposed code-meaning emphasis approach, introduced gradually and intrinsically as a part of the overall reading program, should be taught systematically and intensively. It is hypothesized that such an approach would go a long way toward solving the decoding problems of readers of all ages.

REFERENCES

Artley, A. Sterl. Significant issues in the teaching of reading. In J. E. Frost (Ed.) *Issues and innovations in the teaching of reading.* Glenview, Ill.: Scott, Foresman, 1967. Pp. 192-194.

Austin, Mary C. *The torch lighters: tomorrow's teachers of reading.* Cambridge, Mass.: Harvard University Press, 1961.

Austin, Mary C., and Morrison, C. *The first r: the Harvard report on reading in elementary schools.* New York: Macmillan, 1963.

Chall, Jeanne. *Learning to read: the great debate.* New York: McGraw-Hill Book Co., 1967.

Clymer, T. The utility of phonic generalizations in the primary grades. *The Reading Teacher,* 1963, *16,* 252-258.

Durrell, D. Assuring success in beginning reading. Paper presented at the First Conference of the Illinois Reading Council, Normal, Illinois, March 22, 1969.

Emans, R. The usefulness of phonic generalizations above the primary level. *The Reading Teacher,* 1967, *20,* 419-425.

Emans, R. When two vowels go walking and other such things. *The Reading Teacher,* 1967, *21,* 262-269.

Fay, L. The classroom teacher as an innovator/experimenter in reading. Paper presented at meeting of Northern Illinois Reading Council, DeKalb, Illinois, October 15, 1968.

Gurren, Louise, and Hughes, Ann. Intensive phonics vs. gradual phonics in beginning reading: a review. *The Journal of Educational Research,* 1965, *58,* 339-346.

Hull, Marion A. Phonics for the teacher of reading. DeKalb, Illinois: Northern Illinois University. *(Unpublished programmed text)*

Spache, G. D. *Reading in the elementary school.* Boston: Allyn and Bacon, Inc., 1964. P. 283.

Strang, Ruth. How successful readers learned. Paper presented at Second World Congress on Reading, Copenhagen, Denmark, August 2, 1968.

Weintraub, S. A critique of a review of phonic studies. *The Elementary School Journal,* 1966, *67,* 34-40.

The Role of Phonics in Teaching Reading

JACK BAGFORD*

IN THE PAST, there has been much controversy among teachers concerning the value of phonics to the teaching of reading. Some have argued that phonics has limited usefulness because of the relatively unphonetic character of the English language; others have felt that such knowledge is not only a useful but necessary part of the reading program. Fortunately, there are now some limited agreements about the use of phonics in the teaching of reading.

There is no longer any serious doubt about *whether* phonics content should be included in the reading program; teachers and reading specialists almost universally accept it as an indispensable tool for teaching children to read. Disagreements concerning phonics are still very much in evidence, but they have now centered largely on questions of 1) how phonics should be presented, 2) what content should be included, and 3) when should it be emphasized. Though space will not permit a penetrating analysis of these questions, an attempt will be made to raise some basic issues regarding the manner in which these questions may be answered and to provide reading teachers with guidelines for action until results of research and practice answer them more adequately.

How should phonics be taught

Historically, there have been several different approaches to the teaching of phonics. In recent decades it has been customary to categorize them into two main types, analytic approaches and synthetic approaches.

The *analytic approaches* to teaching phonics are those approaches in which the teacher first teaches a limited number of sight words, possibly 75 to 100, and then teaches the reader to utilize these known words to infer letter-sound associations for unknown words. In presenting phonics analytically, a teacher might teach a number of sight words, including, for example, *bat, bill,* and *bug.* Then by *analyzing* the words and noting that they all begin with the same sound, the students learn the letter-sound association for *b.* Subsequently, when unknown words such as *basket, bitter,* and *bundle* occur in his reading, the student will know the *b* sound and will thus have a clue to help him identify the words.

The *synthetic approaches* to teaching phonics are those approaches in which the teacher first teaches the sounds which certain letters represent and then teaches the pupil to combine (or synthesize) the sounds into words. Following one of the synthetic approaches, a teacher would first present the sounds represented by the printed form of the letters: for example, *p* usually sounds like *puh; a* sounds like *a;* and *t* sounds like *tuh.* When the sounds are blended, the word is *pat.* Later on, when the student meets words like *pen* and *pig,* he will know that they begin with the *p* sound and thus he will have a clue to their identification.

Since the early 1930's, those who fa-

*Reading and Realism, IRA Proceedings, Vol. 13, Part 1, 1969, 82-87.

vored analytic approaches have been in the majority, but there has been continuous support for the synthetic approaches. Recently, since linguistic scholars have focused attention on "breaking the code" as the prime emphasis for early reading instruction, the synthetic approaches have gained remarkably in their popularity. Beginning with the Boston studies in the mid-fifties (7) and continuing with the Sparks-Fay study (11), the Bear study (3), the Bliesmer-Yarborough study (4), and the USOE First and Second Grades Studies (8), evidence has been presented to support the contention that synthetic approaches provide a more rapid start in reading than analytic approaches do.

Chall (5) recently presented a convincing case for those reading programs which make use of the synthetic approaches. Under a grant from the Carnegie Foundation, she has made a searching analysis of the major research findings related to problems of beginning reading instruction. One of her major conclusions was that "code emphasis" approaches (synthetic approaches) proved superior, at least in the primary grades, to "meaning emphasis" approaches (analytic approaches).

There does appear to be some question about whether early gains made by synthetic approaches can be maintained as the children progress through the reading program (11). Further longitudinal research is needed on this very important point, but one would think that intermediate grade teachers and curriculum workers could find ways of maintaining reading gains achieved by primary grade teachers, almost regardless of the manner in which the gains were achieved.

This assumption, however, may be entirely contrary to fact. Children taught by synthetic methods may over-learn some word-analysis habits which later militate against reading growth; they may learn to concentrate so intently on word analysis that attention to meaning is impeded; they may acquire habits that slow down the reading rate and thus make it difficult to comprehend rapidly; they may grow to believe that reading is a process of drill on seemingly meaningless sounds and thus grow to dislike reading. If in their zeal for phonics mastery, primary grade teachers have overemphasized habits that will need to be unlearned at a later date, then it does seem probable that children taught by the more moderate or the more analytic approach would become the better readers.

With present knowledge teachers still must rely somewhat on their own judgment about what is best. It is comforting to note that children do learn to read by any of several methods. At this point in time a reasonable course seems to be 1) teach letter-sound associations relatively early in the reading program with a synthetic emphasis while at the same time considering interest and comprehension as prime goals and prime guides for teaching procedures, and 2) after the child has progressed sufficiently in his word recognition ability, shift the emphasis rather rapidly to comprehension while at the same time trying to foster high interest in reading.

What phonic content should be taught

Through the years much information has been compiled concerning speech sounds and their written representations. It is a generally accepted fact that some of the information is helpful in teaching reading and some of it is not. In fact, this matter is implied by the way phonics is defined. *Phonetics* is generally defined as the science of speech sounds, while *phonics* is defined as that portion of phonetics which is applicable in teaching children to read. For the purpose of teaching reading, it is neither feasible nor desirable to try to teach all that is known about phonetics.

One of the basic reasons for including any phonetic knowledge in a reading program is to improve the efficiency of the teaching process. To accomplish this good, programs should concentrate on content which occurs frequently in reading, is easy to teach, and is relatively regular in its application.

Studies by Clymer (6), Fry (10), Bailey (2), and Emans (9) have investigated the question of "what content" by making use of one or more of the preceding criteria in judging the value of selected phonic content. They have found that at least some of the phonic content that is usually included in reading programs is not adequately justified by these criteria. These studies need to be expanded and amplified into other pertinent areas, but they do provide some substantial data which should prove extremely helpful as teachers concern themselves with problems of what phonic content *should* and *should not* be included in the reading program.

Some basic considerations

In determining the proper role of phonics in a reading program one needs to consider underlying factors which relate to this role. Some of the basic considerations follow.

Children differ in their ability to Following one of the synthetic ap-

to the teaching of reading. It seems plausible to assume that some children learn better from a method which emphasizes a whole-word approach to word recognition while others probably learn better from a method which emphasizes sound-symbol correspondence. To put it another way, some children probably learn better through visual means while others learn better through auditory means. Generally speaking, teaching materials are designed with the underlying assumption that all children learn equally well with all modalities. This assumption may or may not be correct. Thus it seems logical to advise that whenever a child is experiencing difficulty with learning to read, the teacher should investigate the possibility that he may be emphasizing the least effective modality for the child in question.

Research studies that arrive at generalizations about which method works best for *large* groups of children miss a very basic point; i.e., methods which produce significantly higher mean scores for the total group do not necessarily work best for each individual student in the group. Certain individuals may profit more from a method which has been shown to produce significantly lower mean scores than another. Teachers should recognize this possibility and adjust their teaching accordingly.

It seems likely that some words are more easily learned by a phonic method than by a sight method, while others are more easily learned by the sight method. High frequency, but irregularly sounded, words probably are more efficiently taught by a sight method while phonetically regular words and words which contain easily learned sounds probably are better taught by a phonic method. Learning the word recognition skills is a step in a developmental process, one of the goals of which is to know a large number of words by sight. Accomplishing this goal by the most efficient method is important. Sometimes the most efficient method is determined by the nature of the word itself.

A given child may be able to utilize a sound-oriented approach better at one age than another. The concept of reading readiness suggests that there is an optimum time in the developmental process for a child to learn any given skill. Presumably, attempts to teach a skill prior to this optimum time will prove unsuccessful and may even cause emotional or psychological problems which seriously retard normal growth. Also, it is assumed that if instruction is postponed until later than this optimum time, the skill involved is not as readily learned as it would have been at the optimum time.

In a like manner, each child may have an optimum time in his total development for learning phonics content. For some, phonic readiness may be achieved relatively early in school while others may take considerably longer. In presenting phonics content, teachers should consider the natural growth patterns of the pupils.

How the teacher feels about the teaching procedure which he is following seems to make a difference in the effectiveness of the teaching method. If children can learn to read by any of several approaches, which apparently they can, then how the teacher feels about the method may well be one of the most important factors in determining its success. If the teacher is philosophically committed to the method he is using, then he is likely to do a good job of teaching reading regardless of how good or how bad the method might be. When selecting a particular phonics program or determining degree of emphasis on content or methodology, one of the key factors to be considered should be what the teachers think about it.

Interest may not be directly related to method. It is doubtful that one method is inherently more interesting than another. Enthusiastic teachers can take very dull content and make an interesting lesson out of it. Others can take what seems to be very interesting material and create pure drudgery for children. Whether a method is interesting is probably less related to method than it is to other factors related to the teaching-learning situation.

Two factors which influence pupil interest are variety of presentation and appropriateness of teaching level. If presentations are varied within a method, interest is not likely to be lacking. Likewise, if a child is given a learning challenge, but at a level where he has a relatively good chance for success, he will seldom lose interest. The important point related to phonics is that approaches probably should not be accepted or rejected because of interest or lack of it. Rather, *effective* approaches should be selected for use and then adjustments made in the teaching situation to maintain a high interest level.

Guidelines for the reading teacher

In teaching phonics, the major task which confronts today's reading teacher is how to maintain a proper balance between attention to phonics and attention to other important reading goals. The myriad of research results and the verbal wranglings of reading "experts" are likely to confuse the average teacher about the proper course of action as he performs the daily tasks of teaching reading. The following are suggested as broad guidelines to follow as teachers attempt to determine the role of phonics in the teaching of reading.

Phonics content is taught so that children have a tool to identify words which are known in the spoken form but not in the printed form. All decisions concerning the use of phonics should reflect this purpose. Teachers should regularly ask themselves whether the phonic content being taught and the methods being employed in teaching it contribute to the accomplishment of this major purpose. If not, the teacher should adjust accordingly.

Phonics is but one aspect of word recognition; word recognition is but one goal of the reading program. Phonics is best used in conjunction with other word recognition skills. As a child learns to read, he gradually learns several ways to identify words. Ideally, he learns them in such a manner so that he can coordinate and combine their use as he attacks unknown words. The ability to use sound-symbol relationships is one of the more important reading skills, but it is just one and should be so considered.

The second aspect of this guideline has to do with the relationship of word recognition skills to the total reading program. Word identification techniques should be taught in a manner that facilitates, not hampers, the attainment of other important reading goals. Intensive attention to phonics can seriously impair progress toward goals of speed, interest, and meaning; teachers need to recognize this possibility so

that emphasis can be adjusted to best serve the total reading program.

The teacher is the key person in determining the success of a reading program. Whether children learn better by one method than another is largely determined by the skill and enthusiasm of the teacher. In recent years, research has consistently shown that the quality of the teacher in the classroom is the most important variable relating to how well the pupils in a class learn to read. Effective functioning in such a key role requires that a teacher know as much as possible about 1) phonics and research related to phonics, 2) the total reading process, and 3) the pupils' reading abilities and needs.

Acting in terms of the preceding guidelines leads one directly to the next. *Teachers should take an active part in determining the role of phonics in the reading program.* On the whole, modern-day teachers are well-trained, competent people who are capable of determining the reading needs of pupils and adjusting the program to meet these needs. Caring for individual differences is a constant job, and only teachers are in a position to know these needs well enough to adjust instructional procedures to meet them; teachers should be encouraged to do so.

This guideline means, for example, that teachers should adjust content and method for children who are slow learners or fast learners; for children who have speech and hearing problems; and for those who learn better through visual means than through auditory means. It means that teachers need to recognize and adjust for the fact that some phonic content is learned by all pupils without any direct teaching.

It is recognized that adjusting for individual differences is an age-old problem that has no easy solutions. Nevertheless, with the wide variety of high quality materials available to today's teachers, intensive efforts toward recognizing differences and providing for them can produce rich benefits for the pupils.

Relatively speaking, phonics should be taught fairly early in the reading program. Basically, the two major goals of a reading program are *word recognition* and *comprehension.* These goals can hardly be separated, but for instructional purposes it is probably better to place the heavy emphasis on one and then the other. Early in the process of learning to read, word recognition (including phonics) should receive major attention; and as progress is made, the emphasis should be shifted to comprehension.

Summary

Phonics has an extremely important role to play in the teaching of reading. In this paper it is assumed that phonic analysis is best used in conjunction with other word-identification techniques for the purpose of unlocking words which are known in their spoken form but unknown in their written form. It is known that the pupils can learn to read by any of a number of methods. Thus teachers, rather than method, are the most important variable in the teaching process. Teachers are encouraged to know research relating to methods and materials and to utilize their knowledge in adjusting their procedures to the individual needs in their own classrooms. Guidelines for making these adjustments are provided.

REFERENCES

1. Bagford, Jack. *Phonics: Its Role in Teaching Reading.* Iowa City: Sernoll, 1967.
2. Bailey, Mildred Hart. "The Utility of Phonic Generalizations in Grades One Through Six," *Reading Teacher,* 20 (February 1967), 413-418.
3. Bear, David. "Phonics For First Grade: A Comparison of Two Methods," *Elementary School Journal,* 59 (April 1959), 394-402.
4. Bliesmer, Emery P., and Betty H. Yarborough. "A Comparison of Ten Different Beginning Reading Programs in First Grade," *Phi Delta Kappan,* 46 (June 1965), 500-504.
5. Chall, Jeanne. *Learning to Read: The Great Debate.* New York: McGraw-Hill, 1967.
6. Clymer, Theodore. "The Utility of Phonics Generalizations in the Primary Grades," *Reading Teacher,* 16 (February 1963), 252-258.
7. Durrell, Donald D., (Ed.). "Success in First Grade Reading," *Journal of Education,* Boston University, (February 1958), 1-48.
8. Dykstra, Robert. *Continuation of the Coordinating Center for First-Grade Reading Instruction Programs.* USOE. Project Number 6-1651. Minneapolis: University of Minnesota, 1967.
9. Emans, Robert. "The Usefulness of Phonic Generalizations Above the Primary Level," *Reading Teacher,* 20 (February 1967), 419-425.
10. Fry, Edward. "A Frequency Approach to Phonics," *Elementary English,* 41 (November 1964), 759-765.
11. Sparks, Paul E., and Leo C. Fay. "An Evaluation of Two Methods of Teaching Reading," *Elementary School Journal,* 57 (April 1957), 386-390.

A Critical Look at Instruction in Word Recognition at the Elementary Level

JUANITA LEWIS*

WORD RECOGNITION, the same as any other term in the field of reading, can become ambiguous when one examines it in the many different pieces of literature of a reading program. For the purpose of this paper *word recognition* refers to the child's ability to recognize a word and its meaning in context. Before a child can recognize a word, he must first have the opportunity and skills necessary to identify that word, or someone must tell it to him. Actually, one could hardly talk about word recognition without getting into word identification skills. Therein lies the ambiguity of *word recognition;* it is a result of word identification.

Instruction in word recognition

Consider the ways a child learns to recognize or identify a word. There are four major areas to be considered as far as instruction in word recognition is concerned. They are 1) Context, 2) Phonetic Analysis, 3) Structural Analysis, and 4) Comprehension.

Context

Anyone who has examined one or more of the available reading programs being used by children today is aware of the fact that attention is given to helping children through three different kinds of context.

Oral Context. The purpose of oral context is to give the child practice in using verbal clues to identify words. Frequently, it is supplemented with picture and/or printed context, structural and/or phonetic analysis, or in some cases any miracle that comes to the teacher's mind.

Picture Context. The purpose of this activity is the give the child practice in using picture clues to identify words. Most readiness programs and preprimers offer opportunities for the child to develop this skill. It, too, is frequently supplemented with oral and printed context.

Printed Context. The purpose of printed context is two-fold:

1. To give the child practice in using printed context to identify new words, and
2. To give the child practice in comprehension.

Oral and picture context used along with printed context seems to be a means to an end—what end? Reading!

Phonetic Analysis

Varying degrees of phonetic analysis appear in reading programs. A consensus seems to be that children need help with at least three skills:

Identifying likenesses and differences in beginning sounds. Attention is devoted here to giving children skill in sounding out the beginning of a word to enable them to identify words.

Identifying likenesses and differences in sounds in the medial position. Attention is devoted here to giving children skill in sounding out the "middle" of a word of syllable to help them identify words.

Identifying likenesses and differences in ending sounds. Attention is devoted here to giving children skill in sounding out the ending of a word to help them identify words.

Structural analysis

Again, almost any method of teaching reading that could be mentioned

Forging Ahead in Reading, IRA Proceedings, Vol. 12, Part 1, 1968, 55-59.

gives attention to structural analysis. This skill enables the child to take a word apart and sound out the parts to help him identify it. Children are helped with five different kinds of structural analysis:

Root words. It is believed that to find a root word in a strange word will help a child identify the strange word.

Prefixes. After the child has learned to identify the root word, he, identifies the prefix to further aid him in identifying the strange word.

Suffixes. Again the child is encouraged to find the root word plus the suffix to help him identify the strange word.

Compound words. Children are also given practice in discovering that the strange word may consist of two words that they already know.

Syllabication. Attention is devoted to helping children develop skill in dividing words into syllables as a means of identifying strange words.

Comprehension

The advocates of any method of teaching reading would strongly agree that their approach to reading leads to comprehension; otherwise, what is the purpose of context, phonetic analysis, or structural analysis? Some are happy if the child understands a word. Others are not happy unless the child understands the whole sentence. Many are not satisfied until the child comprehends a whole paragraph, a whole story, or the main idea of a selection. Literature shows that authorities expect the child to understand what he reads. Most authorities agree that it is from the printed context that comprehension comes.

Picture Context. Programs devote a sizable amount of time to helping children develop comprehension with picture symbols.

Oral Context. Programs devote time to helping children develop comprehension through listening to oral context.

Printed Context. No method ignores printed context and the role it plays in comprehension. The most common use made of printed context is.

1. Silent Reading. The child is given a purpose; he examines the printed context silently and through comprehension fulfills his purpose.

2. Oral Reading. Again the child is given a purpose for reading; he reads orally and fulfills his purpose.

3. Skimming. Sometimes the child is given a purpose and is called upon to skim the material with comprehension to fulfill his purpose.

4. Drill. The many different types of drill employed in helping children with comprehension would be too numerous to list at this time. Suffice it to say, the end result should be comprehension of the material which the children have handled.

A critical look at instruction in word recognition

Now for a critical look at instruction in word recognition. As was pointed out earlier in this paper, word recognition is the ability to recognize a word and its meaning in a particular context. It was also pointed out that there are four major areas in instruction in word recognition: 1) Context, 2) Phonetic Analysis, 3) Structural Analysis, and 4) Comprehension. Take a critical look at these four areas which have become sacred to people in the field of reading.

Context.

Picture Context. Let's look first at picture context. Couldn't we devote more time to printed context rather than picture context? When I examine a basal series, I never fail to ask myself this question. I will agree that in the beginning children do enjoy SOME picture reading, but through observing children during my classroom teaching experiences I found time after time that children became bored and restless when asked to read a picture to death. Agreed, some method needs to be used to "put words into the mouths of poor readers," but even they rebel after a while. I have nothing but sympathy for the six-year-old child who has to go through a reading readiness program where he is asked to read pictures and more pictures and more pictures.

Those who are first grade teachers have probably had the same experience I had in first grade reading: The child who can go through the whole story reading every detail in the picture plus adding numerous ones of his own, when asked to read the selection, looks at you with a question in his mind and asks, "What selection?"

Solution? Publishing companies and teachers must concentrate less on picture context.

Oral Context. How about oral context? Does it help the child or not? Have you ever sat in the back of the room and listened to a first grade teacher teach reading? If you have, I believe you will agree with me that much of the oral context given by the teacher is not what we are after at all. For example: when a child is reading a sentence and stops in the middle of the sentence because he can't identify a word, it would seem to me that he needs to know that word immediately for comprehension, otherwise, he loses his train of thought and begins to word call. In my opinion, teachers don't help by such oral context as "It begins with the same sound as ball, bird" or "We had that word yesterday, remember?" or "That's one of our new words." I'm concerned, too, when the teacher gives the child oral context that he will not have access to later

when he is reading independently. In summary, I suppose my major criticism is the fact that teachers using detailed oral context during a silent or oral reading lesson can be interfering with comprehension rather than helping the child.

Solution? Tell the child the word now; help him later with his problem!

Printed Context. Couldn't we have more words in beginning reading, and couldn't we include more than just one-syllable words?

Sometimes I wonder what children think of our schools when we take them to a reading circle, build up their interest in reading, and then hand them a story with such limited vocabulary that it couldn't possibly compete with library books they are reading or are having read to them or with their conversations during recess. Please don't misunderstand me. I am not advocating a recording of the conversation at recess time followed by a printed chart from which the child reads and rereads and rereads what a group had to say during a particular recess in a particular situation. I am not advocating this approach at all. I have tried that approach and it didn't work for me.

Solution? I would like to see more reading readiness programs devote attention to the skills basic to beginning reading and less attention to picture reading of everyday situations or nursery rhymes.

As for two-or more-syllable words, I recall from my own classroom experience that *Washington* was a word that all of my first grade children could recognize when they saw it in printed form—yes, even the children in the low group.

Solution? Put more words in primary reading material, and let's not be afraid to try the big ones.

Phonetic Analysis

I have several questions concerning

phonetic analysis:

Beginning Sounds. The r e a d i n g readiness program?

Why spend time in our reading readiness books with activities completely unrelated to beginning reading?

It seems to me that by the time a child completes his reading readiness program he should be on the road to reading. If this is true, it would seem to me that our reading readiness should get him ready!

How about teaching beginning sounds?

This makes sense to me, and since I have worked with kindergarten and first grade children, I know that many of them can successfully work with beginning sounds. Not only from observation do I know this, but I also know it from examining and conducting research. I have already heard the argument that all children cannot do this work at kindergarten level. Is this any reason for not letting those who can move forward? If we hold back for this reason, we can't have reading at first grade level or geometry at high school, can we?

Solution? Give the child more work with letter forms and sounds.

Medial Sounds. Why can't children be exposed to them earlier?

At first grade level it bothers me that we can't start working earlier with certain phonetic analysis skills—to be specific, with vowels. I don't recall too many words the child meets in his recreational reading where he wouldn't be confronted with vowels. I believe that if we would work with the vowels soon enough at early first grade level, we could help children become more independent in their reading habits. After all, aren't we supposed to give the child what he can put to use immediately? And surely one can't deny that even in the first word in the preprimer the child meets a vowel. I remember hearing a saying one time "get what you need but need what you get." "Needing what you get" brings me to my next comment. I am a little disturbed when I go into classrooms and see teachers using phonetic programs that are not in any way tied to the immediate needs of the child. I'm sure that teachers are using these highly advertised, colorful, phonetic programs with good intentions. I would just like to mention that according to the laws of learning, children tend to forget what they don't use and, secondly, that what they learn should be used immediately in a meaningful situation.

I would be happy to see a structural program in phonics *if* it is a program that goes along with the reading program the teacher is using at that time and *if* it concentrates on the high frequency needs of the children. Why should a child have to drill on a specific sound if he is not having trouble with it?

Solution? Give children practice in hearing likenesses and differences in words they are using now. Don't wait until that magic period, the second grade.

Structural analysis

I have three criticisms concerning structural analysis:

Why have children find little words in big words? I am concerned about programs that encourage children to find little words in big words. This procedure forms a BAD habit that children must break sooner than one expects. I can see no advantage in this activity whatsoever because the English language is not that consistent. The minute the child starts having two-syllable words he is going to run into trouble.

What about configuration? I am equally concerned about the series that wastes the child's time by having him look at a printed word and visualize a picture of that word that, probably, is completely unrelated to that word. When you have a child look at the word *been*, think of it with an outline around it, add wheels to it, and make smoke come out of the top, you're taking his mind off the word. Again, very rarely have I seen childrens books where, first of all the word was framed; and I never recall seeing one where the word's had wheels on them.

Why do we ask children to divide words in syllables? It is well and good to have children divide words into syllables, but many programs never go beyond this step. Children should then be taught to look at each syllable as an independent word that would be identified the same as any small word.

Solution? Have the child take the word apart in a logical manner and use these parts to identify the word.

Comprehension

Some of our programs make little, if any, provision for comprehension. Some of our teacher's manuals ask such regurgitative-type questions that the only thing a child has to do is to repeat a sentence whether it makes sense. Some of the drills provided by publishing companies and by teachers ask for such specific details that children lose the meaning of the whole story. Some teachers fail to help children see that the material they are reading silently or orally must make sense. Some of our teachers have resigned themselves to the fact that children simply can't use expression— therefore, "I'm not going to push the issue." Some teachers have become obsessed with *rate* at the expense of *comprehension*. And some teachers have not themselves fully understood what reading actually is.

Solution? Provide practice for children that will help them critically think and critically read so they will learn to demand meaning from printed material.

Summary

As I stated at the beginning of this paper, *word recognition* refers to the child's ability to recognize a word and its meaning in a particular context. We must realize that recognizing a word is only part of the job. Unless a child understands what he reads, we are not preparing him to cope with the printed material he will be meeting as he continues his education. Let's not be so involved in instruction in word recognition that we ourselves forget to take a critical look at it and the role it plays in helping children learn to read!

Word Recognition for the Junior High School

KATHLEEN CLAYTON*

WHEN considering the topic of word recognition skills for the junior high school, one has to think about what word recognition techniques these students have been taught in the elementary grades. Next, some type of evaluation or diagnosis, should be planned to determine if these junior high students have these skills. After administering a group or an individual instrument, the teacher has to plan the program around the needs of the students. Some groups of students may have little need for extensive work in word recognition techniques at the junior high level because their skills are already well developed. Some groups will need the kind of program that involves a heavy concentration on word recognition techniques.

What is word recognition? It has been defined as the "identification of a word by means of a context clue or skill in analysis of the word form" (2). Word recognition involves a number of techniques: the use of sight words, the use of phonetic analysis, the use of structural analysis, the use of context, and the use of the dictionary. Word recognition skills are those methods or techniques used by readers to identify, to pronounce, or to recall words. Before the reader can attach meaning to a word, he must be able to identify it. Learning to read and being able to read requires word recognition skills. Johnson has said:

> The ultimate aim of the reading program in relation to word recognition ability, should be the spontaneous recognition of virtually every word. Accompanying this ability to react effortlessly to the majority of words should be a reservoir of word analysis skills to unlock the few unfamiliar words which are met from time to time (5).

Let us consider the various word recognition techniques already mentioned that have been taught in the elementary school and that may need reviewing or reteaching in the junior high school.

Sight Words. Most professional books on reading and basal reader manuals have descriptive material on sight words in the discussion of teaching word recognition. Sight words are those words that are recognized as a whole. The sight word is the word that is told to the child and is the basis for teaching phonetic and structural analysis. The child becomes familiar with words already in his listening and speaking vocabularies by having the printed forms of the words presented to him as wholes in meaningful context. The sight word is used in a meaningful situation and discussed. Then there is the need for this word to be used frequently in different settings so that the word is recognized instantly and spontaneously.

Phonetic analysis. Phonetic analysis is a term that is a source of confusion in discussions on the teaching of reading. We talk about phonetics, phonics, and phonetic analysis. Phonetics is the science of speech sounds. Phonics is the science of speech sounds as applied to reading. Phonetic analysis is the analysis of a word into its phonetic elements for pronunciation purposes (2). Bamman says, "The recognition of symbols and the sounds which they represent is known as phonetic analysis (1)."

What we are to present or teach at a grade level will be dependent upon what the student already knows about phonics. Phonics is part of every sound reading program. The junior

*Forging Ahead in Reading, IRA Proceedings, Vol. 12, Part 1, 1968, 59-62.

high school program needs to be concerned with phonics and phonetic analysis to the extent that the student should be able to use phonics as a word recognition technique.

The teaching of phonetic analysis proceeds from the known to the unknown or from the simple to the complex. Teach those phonetic principles that are more generally and universally applied before moving to less frequently used analytic skills. The development of skills in phonetic analysis is based on phonetic understandings. The student must have a knowledge of the sounds that are used in our English language and of the symbols that stand for those sounds. It is generally accepted that we have about forty-three separate sound units or phonemes in our language. Each of these phonemes is either a vowel or a consonant sound. We have only twenty-six written symbols in traditional orthography to represent these sounds. We have more sounds than symbols, and some symbols must be used to represent more than one sound. This situation naturally makes it difficult to teach phonetic analysis.

The student should have learned to associate sounds with various types of consonant and vowel symbols. He should know the single consonant letters that are used to represent a single consonant sound. He should know or be taught consonant blends. Where two or three consonant letters are blended so closely that they are produced almost as one sound; e.g., *br, st, scr*. The special two-letter consonant symbols that are used to represent a single consonant sound should be known. The letters *sh* as in *shirt* or *shape*, for example, represent one sound that is different from that of either of the single letters in the symbol *sh*.

There are three general types of vowel symbols with which the student should be acquainted. These are single-vowel letters as *a* as in *cat* or *o* as in *go*. The student needs to understand that these single-vowel symbols can be used to represent variant single vowel sounds. He needs to know that two-vowel letters may be used to represent variant single vowel sounds; e.g., *oo* as in *book* or *food*; *ea* as in *tea, tear,* or *read*. The third general type is the knowledge of the dipthongs or two-vowel letters that are used to represent two-vowel sounds blended to form one speech sound; e.g., *ou* in *mouse*.

The understandings of silentness and variability of consonants and vowels are basic (4). Double consonants at the end of a word represent one sound; e.g., *sell, tall*. Words with double consonants followed by a vowel are likely to have two syllables, e.g., *middle, happen*. Silent consonant symbols in a word may have a meaning function. The student should know or be taught the hard and soft sounds of *c* and *g* and how he can determine these for pronunciation and meaning purposes.

He should know that vowel letters are sometimes silent and that they have a function. One should also know that each vowel letter represents several vowel sounds. Final *e* on a word is usually silent and usually prolongs the sound of the preceding vowel. If there are two vowels together in a word or a syllable, the first vowel is usually long and the second vowel is usually silent. If there is only one vowel in the syllable or word, the vowel is usually short unless it is at the end of the word. If the only vowel letter in a word or syllable is followed by *r*, the sound of the vowel is usually affected by the *r*. The teacher must be careful in teaching these principles as rules that are always true. They must be taught as principles that generally apply to word analysis, but there are exceptions to the rules or principles. The student needs practice and opportunities for applying these principles in his daily reading.

Many good sources list the phonetic principles that students should know and be able to use. Materials by Gray, Betts, Bamman, Karlin, Spache, and others are most helpful in the teaching of phonetic analysis.

Structural analysis. Structural analysis involves knowledge of compound words; inflected forms; derived forms including prefixes, suffixes, and roots; syllabication; and contractions. A compound word is a combination of two distinct known words that are joined to form one word. Students who do not recognize compounds are weak in word attack skills and have not learned to look at words for familiar parts. Students who are troubled by compound words need specific instruction if they are to learn to work with compounds which are a part of our everyday reading materials in the classroom.

Inflected forms of words have to do with person, case, gender, number, tense, and comparison. Common inflectional endings are -s, -es, -er, -est, -ed, and -ing. Uusually, the basic meaning of an inflected form is contained within the root word. Derived forms are those words which have prefixes or suffixes. These are both referred to as affixes. This form differs from the inflected form in that the affixes have meanings of their own. Then these affixes are added to a root form the meaning of the total word or form may be entirely different. The meaning of the root form does not change. The addition of the affix is what changes the meaning of the total word or form. Developing skill in the recognition of derived forms serves two purposes: expanding meaning vocabulary and gaining an understanding of the origin, or history, of words (1).

Syllabication. Syllabication is dividing words into syllables for the purpose of identifying unknown words. It functions as an aid in word recognition by helping the student break words into smaller units, pronounce these, blend, and thus recognize words in his speaking and listening vocabularies. Syllabication helps students in their spelling and writing. As most students mature in reading in the upper elementary grades, they become increasingly dependent upon their knowledge of syllables and less upon letter phonics. The student needs to understand that every syllable must contain a vowel sound. With this knowledge, he has a method of breaking words into divisions for pronunciation purposes.

Principles of syllabication can be found in the professional books of Spache, Bamman, Karlin, Gray, and Betts. Be careful of having students memorize syllabication principles. Generalizations which are formulated by the students will be more meaningful than memorized principles. These generalizations should be kept as few and as simple as possible. Emphasize those generalizations which clearly help in pronouncing a word.

Context clues. Contextual analysis or the use of context clues is identifying a new word by anticipation of the meaning or through the words and ideas adjacent to the new word (2). Readers frequently rely upon the context to help them with unknown or new reading words. Students should be encouraged to use context clues as an identification technique. We do need to teach students how to use contextual clues. Contextual clues should not be used alone to identify unknown words. Phonics and structural clues need to be combined with the contextual clues where possible. Spache states that most context clues demand some degree of inferential thinking. Such inferential thinking is an essential part of the reading process at all maturity levels and should be strongly encouraged (7).

Jan-Tausch has indicated that words are learned best when introduced in conjunction with meaningful context. This remark applies to the teaching of all word recognition skills.

The dictionary. The dictionary is used as an aid in identifying unknown words met in reading and as a check on a pronunciation or a meaning tentatively arrived at by the reader through the use of context clues, word-form clues, and systematic analysis (4). The dictionary is a storehouse of the meanings of words but is a word recognition helper.

Skills needed in using the dictionary as a word recognition technique are 1) being able to locate the word by opening the dictionary to the section in which the word is contained and being able to apply alphabetical knowledge to find the word; 2) being able to use guide words as aids in the location of words; 3) being able to identify the root form from alternate forms of the word; and 4) being able to pronounce the word (6).

Evaluation of needs. As stated earlier, in order to plan a program the teacher must know what are the student's needs. Different types of testing or evaluative instruments can be used to determine these needs. Standardized tests can be administered and compared with national norms. Individual informal reading inventories can be administered where word recognition skills of the student are carefully studied. Johnson has suggested pertinent questions on word recognition skills as listed below:

Does he see base words in affixed forms?

Does he apply the final- e principle?

Does he use the dictionary spontaneously to get the pronunciation of a word he cannot analyze on his own?

Does he use his oral language background as checkpoint for his analysis of a printed form?

Does he skip over unfamiliar words or use a slurred pronunciation rather than attempt to analyze them?

Does he drop word endings (5)?

Reading is a series of many skills intermeshed with one another. It is a thinking process and not subject matter to be taught. Word recognition techniques must be taught, evaluated, and retaught where needed for effective use and reading skill development.

REFERENCES

1. Bamman, Henry A., Ursala Hogan, and C. E. Greene. *Reading Instruction in the Secondary School.* New York: Longmans, Green, 1961.
2. Betts, Emmett A. *Foundations of Reading Instruction.* New York: American Book Co., 1957.
3. Caroline, Sister M., IHM. "Word Recognition and Vocabulary Development," in J. Allen Figurel (Ed.), *Reading and Inquiry,* Proceedings of the International Reading Association, 10 (1965), 227-229.
4. Gray, William S. *On Their Own in Reading.* Chicago: Scott, Foresman & Co., 1960.
5. Johnson, Marjorie S. "Evaluating the Secondary School Reading Program," *Reading Instruction in Secondary Schools,* Perspectives in Reading No. 2. Newark, Delaware: International Reading Association, 1964, 117-128.
6. Karlin, Robert. *Teaching Reading in High School.* Boston: Allyn & Bacon, Inc., 1964.
7. Spache, George D. *Reading in the Elementary School.* Boston: Allyn & Bacon, Inc., 1964.

Word Attack Skills for the Retarded Reader in College

MILDRED B. FORD*

GOOD READERS not only must be able to recognize quickly and accurately the words they have met before but they must also have at hand tools with which they can determine the meanings of new words. One of the most important of these tools is the ability to pronounce the words because sometimes one knows a word when he hears it spoken and yet does not recognize it when he sees it in print.

Principles of word recognition

The terms *word recognition* and *word attack* are used somewhat interchangeably as applied to reading skills *(5)*. Word recognition is an important basic reading skill. It is in word recognition skills that retarded readers most commonly are deficient. Even though comprehension is the primary goal of reading instruction, word recognition is prerequisite.

We are primarily concerned with finding the method of teaching that best advances the retarded pupil in auditory and visual discrimination.

Bond and Tinker (*1*) identify word recognition with the following basic skills:

1. Associating the approrpriate meanings with the printed symbol;

2. Using the context clues and other meaning aids to anticipate the words to be recognized and then checking the accuracy of the recognition;

3. Becoming flexible and efficient in visually analyzing the word into usable recognition elements;

4. Developing knowledges of visual, structural and phonetic elements, knowledge of consonant and vowel sounds, blends and diagraphs, prefixes and suffixes, etc.;

5. Learning skills in auditory blending and visually synthesizing word parts to rapidly pronounce or recognize the word as a whole; and

6. Forming the habit of using the more analytical and the pronunciation techniques when and only when needed.

Word recognition problems are often found to be at the root of the difficulty of disabled readers who fall into the descriptive categories of limiting disability and complex disability. College readers (retarded) fall into these areas; some can be helped with individualized instruction and some have problems that are too difficult to cope with in a classroom situation.

Effective teaching techniques of word attack skills

To determine the degree of difficulty the college reader has in being able to attack words, systematic evaluation should be administered. The evaluation techniques must be informal or standardized. *Reader's Digest* self-testing section is suggested as an eclectic procedure. Teacher observations should be used to determine what methods are used by the reader to attack new words. Does the student use context clues? Or phonetics? Or structural analysis? Does he know and use the rules syllabication?

Knowledge of word attack skills is important, but skill in using them while reading makes the knowledge of value (*6*).

Scholastic Scope (Scholastic Magazine), a weekly periodical for high school students, is one reading media which has been used successfully in teaching the use of word meaning and context clues to retarded college read-

*Forging Ahead in Reading, IRA Proceedings, Vol. 12, Part 1, 1968, 66-70.

ers.

Training in the utilization of context clues should be stressed in teaching word attack skills. The student at this level should be encouraged to employ shrewd guesses in an attempt to determine the meaning of a word from the way it is used in the text (3). A student proficient in utilizing context clues can usually derive enough sense from a word to satisfy his need at the moment. One method of increasing his ability is to present the student with a list of sentences in which the critical word is omitted and have the students fill in the blanks or have them read short interesting articles with words they should know, may not, but can determine the meaning of because of the context.

The problem a college student faces when he meets a new word is likely to be different from that of a child seeing a word for the first time. When a child first starts to read, the words that he encounters are, for the most part, strange to him in form only. That is, most of the words that a child finds in his beginning reading assignments are already in his speaking vocabulary. The words that are new to a college student, however, are usually strange in both meaning and form (6). When the college freshman enters his history class, the vocabulary is as foreign as German. He has had no previous experience which would give him familiarity to the concept or the abstraction for which the word stands. His success in the course is partially dependent upon his ability to understand the technical terminology.

In attempting to develop word recognition for college students, the requisite is to stimulate interest in learning new words and to make the student aware of the words he does not know.

The inherent factors which the student possesses when he enters college have not prepared him for college reading. More than one half of the students entering the small colleges are taking remedial courses. High school preparation has not been efficient; therefore, the student is in "trouble" with reading.

In structural analysis, words should be taught in terms of their components, prefixes, suffixes, and roots so that students can see the effects of prefixes and suffixes upon the meaning of the root, learn the meaning of common Latin and Greek roots and affixes, and get the meaning and pronunication of a word when the surrounding context is not enough (2). The students can build their own derivations, place them in original context, and exchange them with one another to try out their skills.

In order to use roots, prefixes, and suffixes most effectively the student must be proficient in syllabication. If he possesses scanty knowledge in this area, syllabication as means of word attack should be demonstrated and the rules for dividing words into syllables should be presented.

Roberts (4) has outlined the principles of syllabication with examples and e x e r c i s e s on the college level. Sometimes the student is so deficient that an individual approach should be adopted. He also suggests exercises using Greek and Latin roots so that students who have problems unlocking new words may review the rules.

If the college student cannot recognize words quickly and accurately and cannot begin the attack of new words by dividing them into syllables and pronouncing them, it is very probable he has never become a mature reader, with reading skills developed beyond those of the elementary school child. The student will not gain much from training in vocabulary, rate, and comphrehension unless he can recognize a key word by its context, by structural or phonetic analysis, or by syllabication, the next thing to do is look it up in the dictionary and learn how to pronounce the u n f a m i l i a r word. Independent use of the dictionary requires skills in the use of guide words, use of the pronunciation key, and the use of several definitions given for aid in word recognition. These four techniques should be stressed with the retarded reader if the techniques have been forgotten.

In the reading laboratory several levels of dictionaries should be available so that students may refer to them as they are needed.

The retarded reader should have at his disposal many kinds of reading materials of low levels but of high interest. The Globe Book Company (New York) has all of the classics on these levels. Careful selection of reading material is important so that the student will not feel that he is reading "child stuff."

One step of correcting a disability in word recognition is to make the student sound conscious (3). He must learn to hear sounds and to think of letters in terms of sounds, and his lessons may vary with a series of exercises that teach him the various sounds attached to the vowel and the consonants. After he has learned to hear the sounds and to associate them with the proper letters, he must be taught to blend them in combination. All this activity can be achieved through the use of simple words whose pronunciation he already knows; he simply learns to break their sounds down into their component parts until he can hear the value of each letter and combination of letters.

Next, the student should be given the basic rules for building these into words, that is, the rules of syllabication, accent, and pronunciation. These rules should be simple and general as possible, taking account of only the most common exceptions. "The student is not to be made a specialist in phonetics," states Triggs (6).

Once the basic facts have been mastered, the lessons become a matter of practicing their application in forms as varied as the instructor's ingenuity can supply and for as long as the student's disability requires. This application should include drill in discriminating among words of similar configuration and in retaining the visual image of the word once it is learned. This work must be done first with words in isolation, but it should be applied immediately in sentences so as to approximate the reading situation. Workbooks are recommended for this practice, along with teacher made exercises.

Materials for the retarded reader

Word Attack (Harcourt, Brace and World, 1956) is acceptable to college students because of its hard cover and format. It contains lists of words and permits the student to develop clues—an aid to word identification. The idea of becoming a word detective appeals to students and helps them develop the important concept that figuring out words is a responsibility each person must accept if he is to read independently.

Mentioned earlier, *Scholastic Scope* (Scholastic Magazine, Inc., 1966-67) is desirable because context clues and word meaning skills are presented in such a way that students are enthusiastic about performing those tasks.

Basic Reading Skills for Junior High School Use (Scott, Foresman, 1957) contains exercises which may be used in reviewing and developing word attack skills with older pupils.

Oral reading is necessary to assure the application of word attacks skills. Preparing a newspaper report, short book review, excerpts from magazine articles to read before a group helps to give the student the confidence he needs to read aloud in his regular classroom situation.

Reading Laboratory IIIb (Science Research Associates) has been accepted by retarded college readers as an aid to word attack skills because of its multilevel activities. The exercises are designed for culturally deficient readers. After completion of Laboratory IIIb the student is moved to Laboratory IVa, a more difficult reading aid, to promote learning of higher levels of prefixes, suffixes, context clues, and word meaning skills.

The use of *Flash X's and a Tachistoscope* (Educational Developmental Laboratories) with some of the college students for improving concentration and quickness in perceiving words and associating them with meaning has been used. Students like the feel of a machine; they think that this device is something new and scientific that will help them to learn to read better. Students at this age need motivation if results are to be expected.

Phonics We Use—Book F (Lyons and Carnaham—1964) is an excellent refresher course for students who are in need of independent attack on words. Analytical inspection of words plus context clues are used in attacking new words in a modern program of phonics.

The college retarded reader is often culturally inefficient because he has been carelessly taught by teachers who are not proficient in the teaching of reading.

Evaluation of progress

The appraisal procedures are as broad as the concept of reading and the program planned to achieve the broad objectives. Standardized text should not be used alone. Observation is of greatest importance; informal tests, practice exercizes, and interest inventories would give evidence of progress in word attack skills.

Concluding statement

Developing word attack skills for the retarded college reader is a slow and difficult process. Rapport should be established among the teachers and student to acquire the best results. The physical condition of the classroom should be conducive to learning. A soundproof room is recommended. Instruction should include the utilization of context clues, structural and phonetic analysis and the teachings of suffixes, roots, prefixes, and dictionary skills; and the devising of supplementary exercises by the instructor. Reliable measurement of growth should be provided for at intervals of nine-week periods.

REFERENCES

1. Bond, Guy L., and Miles A. Tinker, *Reading Difficulties: Their Diagnosis and Correction.* New York: Appleton-Century, Croft, Inc., 1957.
2. Fitzgerald, Frances. "In Corrective and Remedial Classes," *Reading Instruction in Various Patterns of Grouping,* Supplementary Educational Monographs, Vol. XXI, No. 89, The University of Chicago Press, 1959, 134-137.
3. Reed, James C. "In College," *Corrective Reading in Classroom and Clinic,* Supplementary Educational Monographs, Vol. IV, No. 79, The University of Chicago Press, 1953, 140-144.
4. Roberts, Clyde. *Word Attack: A Way To Better Reading.* New York: Harcourt, Brace and World, Inc., 1956.
5. Smith, Henry P., and Emerald V. Dechant. *Psychology in Teaching Reading.* Englewood Cliffs, New Jersey: Prentice-Hall, Inc., 1961.
6. Triggs, Frances Oralind. *Remedial Reading: The Diagnosis and Correction of Reading Difficulties at the College Level.* The University of Minnesota Press, Minneapolis, 1943.

Applying Research Findings in Word Perception to Classroom Practice

Mildred Wittick*

RESEARCH IN the area of word recognition generally uses subjects from the primary grades. Where older pupils are involved in word recognition investigations, the research tends to be concerned with methods and/or materials for use with remedial readers.

How one teaches reading depends upon how one defines reading. Word recognition is the process of producing the sounds represented by the printed symbols and putting them together into words. Sometimes it is called "identification," "decoding," or "breaking the code." However, word recognition is only the initial step if one considers reading to be the process of getting meaning and understanding from printed symbols. In completing the reading act the individual reacts to the material and integrates what he has read with what he already knows. In this way, his ideas and attitudes change and his intellectual growth continues.

Preschool reading experiences related to word perception

A few years ago, a popular women's magazine published an article on teaching one's baby to read and suggested this procedure might be started with two-year-olds; educators were alternately annoyed, appalled, and amused. This "system" began with teaching recognition of large letters in isolation. The idea was not really new as many generations of children have played with blocks that had letters, words, and pictures on their sides. Others have had cutout letters of wood or plastic with which to experiment and perhaps build words.

Montessori's methods, popular about 1915 and now enjoying a revival of interest, included teaching the young child to recognize, name, sound, and even write the letters of the alphabet.

O. K. Moore of Harvard has been interested in the past ten years in teaching three- and four-year-olds to read by the use of automated typewriters. His hypothesis is that early reading experiences are beneficial for children's general intellectual development. In what Moore calls a "Responsive Environment," the child first explores the typewriter and learns letters. When he strikes a typewriter key, the automated machine calls out the name of the letter or the symbol that was struck. In this way, he learns the names of the letters and what they look like. Later a teacher guides him in learning to reproduce on the electric typewriter individual letters that appear on a television-like screen before him. Finally, he types words and sentences. The idea of using typewriters with young children is not new, as experiments using regular typewriters in first grade classes were conducted at the University of Missouri in the early 1930's.

A study initiated in the Denver Public Schools was designed to show parents how to provide reading readiness activities for preschool children. *Preparing Your Child for Reading* was the guidebook used in conjunction with sixteen TV programs which elaborated on specific techniques that parents might use. These children were studied over a five-year period; the early reading experience appeared to have a positive and continuing effect.

*Perception and Reading, IRA Proceedings, Vol. 12, Part 4, 1968, 125-130.

Developing word perception skills
in the kindergarten

Since about 1955 there have been several studies concerned with the reading of kindergarten children. Investigators found that, compared with the preceding generation, five-year-olds today 1) have larger vocabularies; 2) do more reading of signs and labels; 3) use longer sentences; 4) use more complex sentence structures; 5) have traveled more; 6) have had more experience with books and records; 7) have more often had nursery school experience; 8) have substituted TV viewing for the radio listening of their parents as children; and 9) have vocabularies that are different in content.

Durkin (6) studied the progress of 49 Oakland, California, children who learned to read at home before entering the first grade of a public school. At the end of five years she reported that the majority of these preschool readers continued to be superior readers as they advanced in school. However, these pupils were described as 1) children who wanted to learn to read; 2) children who had many opportunities to do so; and 3) children who had favorable attitudes toward reading. Durkin pointed out that her findings do not necessarily support the proposal for earlier school instruction in reading.

Since 1960 the Denver Public Schools have been conducting a pilot study involving about 4,000 kindergarteners. The subjects received systematic instruction in beginning reading. Reading tests administered at the end of first grade showed that there was a significant difference in favor of the experimental group over the control group of children who had participated in the regular kindergarten program. Optimum reading achievement occurred when the first grade program was altered to take advantage of gains

the child had made in kindergarten (3). The study also showed that the early reading instruction created no special problems related to vision, hearing, or social or academic adjustment.

How do such pre-first grade reading experiences affect classroom practice in Grade One? The teacher finds a wider range of individual differences; some children do not need the conventional readiness program; grouping may be more difficult, requiring special flexibility; and placing each child in the most appropriate reading material may create problems because the teacher must evaluate the child's reading background with great accuracy and locate the appropriate reading materials. These changes must be reflected in the reading curriculum of all of the primary and even the later grades.

Word perception in grade one

The Chall Research. The most thorough recent study of the research on beginning reading instruction was reported by Chall (4) as an outgrowth of the City College-Carnegie Reading Study (1962-1965). She considered much of the research from 1910 to 1965 from several sources: the experimental research from classroom and laboratory; the findings from correlational studies; and the evidence from several well-known clinical studies of children who have failed to learn to read. Space here does not permit a discussion of her methods, but her point of view should be noted. She suggested that the first step in learning to read one's native language is learning the printed code for speech. This method agrees with Bloomfield's conclusion which may be said to represent the linguist's approach to initial reading instruction. However, Chall reported her analysis did not prove or disprove that any one method of code emphasis, i.e., linguistic approach, modified alphabets, or systematic phonics, was significantly superior to another. She commented that there is some experimental evidence that children of below-average and average intelligence and children of lower socioeconomic background do better with an early code emphasis. Brighter children and those with better socioeconomic backgrounds appear able to "break" much of the code independently, regardless of the methods used in the school reading program.

The U. S. Office of Education First Grade Reading Studies. In the school year 1964-65, 27 first grade reading studies were begun, all sponsored by the U. S. Office of Education. All used some of the same pretests and post-tests. All continued for approximately 140 school days. Bond, general coordinator, met three times during the year with all directors at the Coordinating Center for the Cooperative Research Program in First Grade Reading Instruction at the University of Minnesota. The center served two functions: to maintain communication among project directors and to collect, organize, analyze, and interpret the common data from the projects.

The studies were made in 16 different states: five were done in Pennsylvania; three, in California; and three, in New York. Except for Florida and North Carolina, no studies were done in the South.

Twenty of the studies explored the effectiveness of different methods of teaching reading or developing readiness. Two of these used Spanish-speaking children as subjects; one used the disadvantaged in a large city, and one used the low reading group. Other research examined problems related to an analysis of the interactions of professed methods, teacher implementation, and child background; a longitudinal readiness program; a comparison of two methods of reading supervision; the effects of an intensive in-service program on teacher classroom behavior and pupil reading achievement; the reading achievement of first grade boys versus first grade girls; and a comparison of beginning reading in three classroom organizational patterns.

Stauffer (*10*) commented on the studies in the May 1966, issue of *The Reading Teacher* that "No one method can be compared with another because the methods were not sharply and clearly different. For example: all taught the alphabet; all used writing experiences; and so on. Methods that were given the same label were often not the same. . . . Reading instruction time could not be defined so as to be acceptable to all twenty-seven studies. Much effort was devoted to an attempt to define reading instruction time at the Coordinating Center meeting, but to no avail."

Bond (*1*) made four tentative observations at the end of the first year of these studies:

1. There is no one method that is so outstanding that it should be used to the exclusion of the others.

2. The effectiveness of any one approach appears to be increased when it is broadened by the addition of other instructional components. For example, a basic program's effectiveness is increased when writing experiences are added, or a phonetic approach appears to profit from the addition of audio and visual instructional aids.

3. Specific approaches to first grade reading instruction appeared to increase children's achievement in certain instructional outcomes but are weak in other outcomes. Another method may develop different patterns of growth. This observation gives hope to the possibility that combinations of approaches that will encourage overall balanced reading growth will be found.

4. There was greater variation between the teachers within the methods

than there was between the methods. This finding again points up the importance of the teacher's role in learning. This latter point raises the important issue as to whether the methods debate is not an artifact and that the teacher should receive major consideration.

The U. S. Office of Education extended fourteen of the studies through the second and third grades. Such continued investigations should be especially valuable since one of the great weaknesses of general research in reading has been that too often it was characterized by a proliferation of bits and pieces looked at in isolation rather than as a part of the sequential development of the individual's reading pattern.

Phonics. Over the past thirty years probably more research in reading has attacked the problem of phonics—when? and how much?—than any other phase of the reading process. It is almost impossible to isolate completely the teaching of phonics from other parts of the first grade program.

Even where the program begins with formal phonics materials, the child comes in contact with many books and oral language experiences, so phonics can hardly be considered in isolation. Teachers also know more about the various programs in phonics than they do about any other area.

In the past four years, two basal reading programs with heavy phonics emphasis have been published. Children begin with letters and sounds, and one series presents stories only after a wealth of phonics materials has been mastered. One of the results of strong interest in phonics has been the strengthening of this material in all of the well-known basal readers.

The Modified Alphabets. There has been much interest in the past seven years in the use of modified alphabets to teach word recognition skills. The best known of these are the Initial Teaching Alphabet (i.t.a.), Unifon, and the Diacritical Marking System (DMS). All of these "systems" are too new to have conclusive research about them. A special problem has been created by school systems that have rushed to use them without developing a thoughtful, careful experimental design which will make the results meaningful to other educators.

In four of the U. S. Office of Education Studies which evaluate the i.t.a. medium, conclusions ranged from a) no difference from other methods tested; b) results not always consistent; c) inconclusive at the end of grade one; and d) to use in combination with other materials.

Other studies of i.t.a., those of Bosma and Farrow (2), Mazurkiewicz (9), and Downing and Jones (5), generally favored the i.t.a. group.

Experiments using Unifon have been carried on in the Chicago city schools, some of the Chicago suburban schools, in the St. Louis area, and in Detroit.

Word Perception and Linguistic Approach to Teaching Reading. The linguists believe that children should be taught the "decoding system" by first learning those words that are spelled regularly as *fat, pat, mat, sat.* Oral reading should be stressed in the initial stages, and often materials at this level have no illustrations. When a child does not recognize a word, he is usually taught to spell it rather than to "sound it out."

There are several linguistic series now published, and research is just beginning on the effectiveness of this approach.

Other Methods of Teaching Word Perception. New materials for teaching word perception are appearing with great rapidity at the moment. Little or no research related to their classroom use now exists. Programed learning has been developed for beginning readers; computer-assisted instruction in initial reading is being experimented with in California; a great variety of new teaching machines are on the market; audiovisual materials are abundant and are specifically designed into several of the experimental programs.

Comparison of Methods of Teaching Reading. In 1961 Van Allen (*12*) reported a three-year study, "Three Approaches to the Teaching of Reading," that had been carried on in the San Diego area. The hypothesis was as follows: There are numerous effective ways of teaching reading in our schools. Three methods were compared: the basic reading, the individualized, and the language-experience approach. Each teacher who participated selected the approach he understood—one for which he had materials to carry it out—and received a supportive in-service program. The hypothesis, as judged by observations and test results, was confirmed. The other findings included the following: 1) language-experience teachers who ruled out all other approaches found that their children made as much or more progress in the skills (measured on standardized reading tests) as did the children who had direct teaching skills; 2) there is a closer relationship between phonics and writing than between phonics and reading; 3) many teachers are now dealing with basic sight vocabulary on an individual basis —from oral language to written language to recall of written language (this practice usually results in recognition of high frequency words as a result of repetition); and 4) each child gradually gains a personally tailored sight vocabulary which is functional and which is in excess of words introduced in the controlled programs. Control becomes an individual matter. Ceilings are lifted for all children at all grade levels.

An elaborate study of reading methods is being carried on in the Detroit public schools in which five widely different methods are being compared. These include McGraw-Hills' *Programmed Reading,* the *Ginn Basic Readers,* Lippincott's *Basic Reading Program,* Unifon, i.t.a., and Harper and Row's *Linguistic Readers.* One criticism of this study is that Unifon was developed as a permanent spelling reform, not as an alphabet for teaching beginning reading. For this reason it is not especially designed, as is i.t.a., for making the transition to the conventional English alphabet. The findings of the Detroit study, which was begun in 1965 and will extend until 1968, should be especially useful.

Fry's (*7*) study compared his Diacritical Marking System (DMS) with the Initial Teaching Alphabet and the Sheldon readers (Allyn and Bacon) in traditional orthography. Among Fry's findings were the following: 1) there was no statistically significant difference between the mean scores of any of the subtests of the post-test (Stanford Achievement) for any of the three groups; 2) there were no significant differences on the Gilmore Oral Reading Test scores; 3) no method was better for boys or girls or better for younger first graders or for older first graders; 4) the variation between classrooms was much greater than the variation between methods; and 5) the best predictor for reading achievement was IQ raw score (M.A.). Fry also concluded that reading readiness materials are not necessary in the first grade. This opinion was based on the finding that four traditional orthography project classes that did not use reading readiness materials but began reading instruction immediately after entering first grade did significantly better at December testing on the Instant Word Recognition Test than four nonproject T.O. classes that had some formal readiness instruction. The value of readiness instruction cannot be based on the results from such a small sample; however, some of the linguists agree that readiness materials are not essential.

Summary and conclusions

As a classroom teacher, how does one translate research findings into classroom practice? 1) Check the relationship of the research findings to one's own school and/or classroom objectives in the area of word perception. 2) Be slow to abandon present methods if *objective* evidence exists that the program is successful in one's particular situation with particular pupils. 3) Be slow to move into a word perception program on which little or no research has been reported unless engaged in evaluating the program oneself. 4) Reevaluate the readiness program in terms of its content and its flexibility in providing for individual differences. 5) Reconsider the phonics program. (Decide how to handle the alphabet. Decide on the appropriateness of the order of teaching decoding skills. Check methods of integrating phonics skills with the rest of the word perception program.) 6) Reevaluate the materials in use. (Are these the best available for reaching objectives? Are newer publications superior? Would certain audiovisual equipment be more efficient?) and 7) If a new program is to be instigated, carefully study the theory upon which it is based as well as the materials to be used.

The conscientious teacher of reading may find comfort in Woodring's comments (*13*) on the proliferation of methods for teaching reading.

There is no one correct or sound method of learning to read. Successful teachers have always employed a variety of methods, children have learned to read in many different ways, and many bright children can read before they enter school. Enthusiasts for any one of the many systems which they themselves invented can demonstrate remarkable results with their own children in their own classrooms because any of several methods will yield good results when used by a brilliant teacher devoted to her work. It does not follow that the same system should be universally adopted because it is far from certain that it will be equally effective with the average teacher.

REFERENCES

1. Bond, Guy L. "First-Grade Reading Studies: An Overview," *Elementary English*, 43, 5 (May 1966), 468-469.

2. Bosma, Ruth L., and V. L. Farrow. "Teaching Reading with i.t.a.: a Research Report," *Reading Horizons*, 6 (1965), 6-19.

3. Brzeinski, Joseph E. "Beginning Reading in Denver," *The Reading Teacher*, 18 (October 1964), 16-21.

4. Chall, Jeanne S. *Learning to Read: The Great Debate*. New York: McGraw-Hill Book Company, 1967.

5. Downing, J., and Barbara Jones. "Some Problems of Evaluating i.t.a.: a Second Experiment," *Educational Research*, 8 (1966), 100-114.

6. Durkin, Dolores. "A Fifth-Year Report on the Achievement of Early Readers," *Elementary School Journal*, 65 (November 1964), 76-80.

7. Fry, Edward B. "Comparing the Diacritical Marking System, ITA, and a Basal Reading Series," *Elementary English*, 43, 6 (October 1966), 607-611.

8. Loban, Walter D. *The Language of Elementary School Children*. Research Report No. 1. Champaign, Illinois: National Council of Teachers of English, 1963.

9. Mazurkiewicz, A. J. "The Lehigh University-Bethlehem Schools ITA Study: Interim Report Nine," *Journal of the Reading Specialist*, 5 (1965), 9-11.

10. Stauffer, Russell G. "The Verdict: Speculative Controversy," *The Reading Teacher*, 19 (May 1966), 563-564.

11. Strickland, Ruth G. *The Language of Elementary School Children: Its Relationship to the Language of Reading Textbooks and the Quality of Reading of Selected Children*. Bulletin of the School of Education, Vol. 38, No. 4, Bloomington, Indiana: Indiana University, 1962.

12. Van Allen, R. "More Ways Than One," *Childhood Education*, 38, No. 3 (November 1961), 108-111.

13. Woodring, Paul. "Can Johnny Read?" *Saturday Review*, 45 (January 20, 1962), 40.

Translating Research into Practice: Reading Readiness, Visual Perception, and Auditory Perception

IRA E. AARON*

TRANSLATING RESEARCH into practice is the final and often neglected phase of research in reading. Although numerous research studies dealing with various aspects of reading are published yearly, very few of these make a real difference in reading instruction. The influence of most of these studies is restricted to the classrooms involved in the investigations.

How are teachers' practices in the teaching of reading influenced by research findings? What are the hazards of interpreting accurately the results of research in reading? What are some of the recommended practices growing from previous research on reading readiness, visual perception, and auditory perception? Before drawing implications from the studies reported each of these three questions will be discussed briefly.

Research findings and teacher change

Change in practice as a result of research occurs only if teachers in some way become aware of the findings of pertinent investigations. Four ways in which teachers may learn about research results are discussed.

Teachers read research reports in professional journals and translate findings into practice. This avenue is one that might be used to bring about changes as a result of research. Despite this possibility, very little change occurs through this medium. Most teachers are not well informed in the interpretation of research results, and persons who prepare research reports are not always helpful in the way they present the results. If a teacher sees a practical application from some published research reports, he does it in spite of the researcher. The studies from which generalizations can be drawn usually are so statistically oriented that a second course in statistics is a necessity for unraveling them; most teachers do not have a first course. Teachers are much more likely to be influenced by a noncontrolled study in which some teacher tries out something in her own classroom, finds it successful with her children, and writes about it. Teachers can read these studies with understanding; whereas researchers seem to write for other researchers.

Someone reviews the literature, draws conclusions, and suggests practical implications; teachers read these and put recommendations into practice. Research reviews are published in a number of periodicals that are readily available to teachers. Most of these reviews, however, do not include implications for practice, and many of them review studies uncritically. The teacher is more likely to be influenced by this type of article than by the original research article itself. Still, the amount of influence from such reviews is likely to be small.

Writers of professional textbooks review the literature and incorporate findings in their recommendations for practice. Those preservice and in-service teachers who enroll in courses using textbooks on reading methodology may be brought into contact with translations of research findings in the way of assigned or voluntary reading. The quality of these reviews varies greatly.

Authors and editors of elementary and secondary school textbooks in-

*Perception and Reading, IRA Proceedings, Vol. 12, Part 4, 1968, 130-135.

corporate findings in their materials.
Basal reading textbooks and their accompanying guidebooks are the major
influences on elementary reading programs in America. Some, but not all,
of the recommendations in guidebooks
are based upon research.

The dozen or more series of basal
readers now being used are not in
exact agreement on the elements of a
good reading program. If one were to
ask those who prepare materials if
their texts and instructional suggestions are based upon research, he
would get an affirmative answer.
That answer would be correct, to a degree. Some aspects of these programs
are based upon research; some, on intelligent hunches. It becomes difficult
to unravel the parts based on solid research and those based on opinions.

Those who prepare textbooks have a
responsibility to study available research carefully and to incorporate
sound research-based ideas in their
materials. The rush with which they
are faced in today's fast-moving world
forces them to act before all the evidence is obtained. They may, from
economic necessity, be forced into an
area *before* evidence to support the
move is on hand. Some of the more
recent popular movements which have
pressed publishers to take action before they were researched carefully are
the linguistic approach, programed
materials, and programs for the culturally disadvantaged.

At this point the reader probably is
disturbed over the futility of getting
action from the findings of reading research. Improvement in dissemination
is certainly needed. Persons in reading must find effective ways of dissem-
inating research findings to teachers.
If research does not influence practice,
then it serves no real purpose.

The hazards of research

The disseminator of research reports
must be concerned with accuracy in
reporting. A heavy burden of responsibility is placed upon persons who attempt to draw practical implications
from research investigations. If the
interpreter, either in speaking or in
writing, attempts to draw implications
for groups of people, then he is obli-
gated to view the limitations as well as
the strengths of the studies. He must
act with a full knowledge of the general limitations of educational research
in a school setting or in laboratory-
type situations.

An educational researcher in the
area of reading must face these problems:

*Many perception studies are per-
formed in laboratory-type situations
that differ considerably from the classroom setting.* It is relatively easy to
set up a one-time teaching situation
that may involve one teacher and one
pupil in an isolated setting outside the
classroom. Within the classroom an
unreal learning task may be assigned
and monitored for a short period of
time. Such studies may provide clues
which explain some parts of what happens in the larger setting. In interpretation, the fact that the setting was an
unnatural one should be kept in mind.
These are still useful studies if they
are continued long enough so that the
little pieces can be put together into a
larger explanation of how learning occurs.

In the regular classroom, the
learner, though he is unique in any
characteristic one may want to consider, is usually surrounded by 25 to
30 other unique beings, all of whom at
one time or another will influence his
learning. His teacher is an extremely
influential factor in his learning. Because of what he means to the child in
an emotionally positive or negative
way, the teacher can accomplish more,
sometimes less, than the researcher
who makes an infrequent or one-stop

appearance in the classroom. Even the routine interruptions or interferences in the school day influence learning. If these are removed in a research setting, the situation is unlike the regular classroom. Interpretations must be made with the foregoing in mind.

Research cannot always be in a natural setting. The interpretation should recognize that other influencing factors were ruled out in the study and that the combination of the eliminated factors with whatever was tested might have led to different results because the global setting was changed.

Broad generalizations may be drawn from a very limited study. Often when a writer or a speaker states, "Research says . . . ," he presents a small study performed with a limited number of subjects in a particular type of setting. Sometimes he generalizes to the universe. Summaries of research that one finds in college textbooks and in professional periodicals often fall victim to this hazard.

Because of necessity and sometimes because of convenience, the researcher uses a small sample when a large sample may be needed for what he is attempting to do. His subjects may represent a very limited segment of the total population of school children. This procedure is certainly acceptable if the researcher defines his population clearly. The interpreter should keep the subjects in mind as he generalizes. What applies to culturally and economically deprived children in one place may or may not apply to those in another section. The populations may be different.

Such studies are not useless. As particular studies are replicated, the findings are put together. In almost all situations the findings may be the same or may apply only for certain categories or types of children, as the intellectually superior or the culturally advantaged.

The interpreter of research must refrain from indulging in overgeneralization. Often he may have to settle for a partial answer before action must be taken. When the foregoing happens, he should not attempt to support his action by research; he should admit that he does not know nor does anyone else at this stage.

The researcher may clothe an insignificant or poorly designed study in an elaborate statistical dress. The interpreter of research often encounters studies that attempt to answer questions which are not very important, and yet the elaborateness of the statistical treatment makes the study appear to be a vital one. The commonness of the highspeed electronic computer influences the number of such studies today. An assistant in a computer center, who has a good grasp of his own field but little knowledge of the field in which the study was undertaken, can lend to a statistically overdressed study.

The interpreter of research may draw implications for practice when such implications are of doubtful value. If a study is presented orally or in writing, the unsuspecting consumer may falsely assume that it has practical implications. This conclusion is not necessarily so.

This hazard of expecting implications when they are not there is fostered by some professional journals and by some college people who must "publish or perish." The interpreter of research can at least refrain from being tripped by this hazard. Publishing exploratory studies is important. However, they should be published as *exploratory* research and not as *definitive* studies. It is too easy to mislead, even when seemingly adequate precautions are taken.

The foregoing are just a few of the hazards of research interpretation and research implementation. Among the others that could have been included are the following:

The subjects may consciously or unconsciously respond in a certain way and thus negate the study.

The attrition rate may be exceedingly heavy in a longitudinal study.

Statistical techniques inappropriate for the purpose may be used.

Assumptions underlying the use of the statistical technique may not be met.

The level of significance may be inappropriately selected.

The researcher himself may be so dependent upon the computer that he does not know the techniques being used or how to interpret them.

An usually large sample may lead to a statistical difference when the difference is so small that it is of no practical significance.

Generalizations from research studies on auditory and visual perception

Many studies have been undertaken to investigate auditory and visual perception and their relation to reading, especially beginning reading. A few of the generally accepted findings that are research-supported are presented here.

Children show individual differences in perception. Any given group of children will vary in their perceptual development. The speed with which they can respond to varied auditory or visual stimuli will differ, and their levels of development will vary. For example, some first graders will come into school knowing how to discriminate auditorially between similar words and to recognize identical words when spoken. Others will need much practice. This generalization is a part of what the teacher means when she says, "Some children are ready to read when they enter school; some children are not."

The implication for practice is that perceptual skill teaching must be geared to the child's particular level of achievement in so far as this can be done. Further, the teacher must expect some children to increase their perceptual skills at a more rapid rate than others.

The generalization just stated is widely accepted. However, hidden beneath the generalization are some unanswered questions. To what extent are these individual differences the result of the child's preschool environment? To what extent can a modified environment help to overcome what some persons think are the results of a deprived environment? What role does the central nervous system play in individual differences in perceptual abilities? What programs are best for children who are weak in a given perceptual ability? We have partial answers to some of these questions, but much remains to be learned.

Auditory and visual perception are related to success in beginning reading. This generalization is universally accepted. All beginning reading and kindergarten programs are concerned with assessing and developing auditory and visual perception. Reading readiness tests attempt to assess the level of development of these two perceptual abilities.

The evidence from the studies which have explored the differential learning modalities of pupils is somewhat conflicting. Still other studies have investigated the effect of simultaneous audio and visual presentations of stimuli.

Some of the materials in typical reading readiness materials are not needed by most six-year-olds. Gross visual discrimination exercises are useless for many children. By the time they get into kindergarten or first grade they can make these gross discriminations. In fact, some studies have indicated that most children entering the first grade can discriminate between and match letters.

One of the best predictors of begin-

ning reading success is the extent to which the child can name the letters. Several studies have come to this conclusion. Hidden beneath this generalization are some possible influencing factors that need investigation. Knowledge of letter names may not be the major factor in success; it may reflect the level of intelligence of the child and the attention he has received at home, both of which will influence his learning to read.

The foregoing are a few of the generalizations from research on perception in the area of reading. They have not been associated here with specific studies since they are generally accepted conclusions that have been supported by many investigations.

Research studies reported and their implications

The studies presented, though they fall within a general area, actually are separate studies and must be handled as such. Some of them deal with kindergarten and first grade children while the remainder range from second grade through junior high school.

The reader may refer to certain individual research reports in this monograph for the details of the studies. Following the name of the researcher and the title of the study will be given the study strengths and limitations and then the implications for practice. The latter will include replication of the study where applicable.

Bateman, Barbara. *The Comparative Efficacy of an Auditory and a Visual Method of First-Grade Reading Instruction with Auditory Learners and Visual Learners.* Among the strengths of this study were the careful handling of the placement of children into research groups, the in-service sessions held for participating teachers, and the very adequate discussion of study limitations.

Results must be interpreted with the following limitations in mind: the two sets of materials used in the study are not on opposite ends of the visual-auditory continuum; children in the study were considerably above average in intelligence, and the findings may not apply to other intellectual levels: no information was given about how the teachers were selected for each class; except for the extremes in the placement children, the pupils were not clearly shown to prefer one learning mode to another; and, on the section of the study dealing with "good" and "poor" readers, the poor readers were well above grade level in some instances.

The following implications for practice may be drawn from the study:

1. An approach similar to that followed by the teachers who used the "auditory" materials may have promise for teaching intellectually superior children.

2. Further studies should be undertaken to assess the extent to which the different modes of learning are important in selecting instructional techniques for use both in developmental and remedial reading.

3. Another study needs to be conducted in which a program designed to be primarily visual and another to be primarily auditory are used with visually and auditorially inclined first graders.

Faustman, Marion Neal. *Effects of Perception Training in Kindergarten on First Grade Success in Reading.* Strengths of this study include the careful selection of members of the control and experimental groups, the random assignment of teachers to the two groups, and the in-service training given to all participating teachers.

As interpretations are made, the following limitations should be kept in mind: the reader has no information on how the original 32 kindergarten classes were selected; the factors accompanying perceptual training (individualization of instruction, diagnosis of learning needs, and better opportunities for teachers to gain knowledge of child growth and development) might have favored the experimental group, aside from the actual training itself.

The following implications about practice can be drawn:

1. Visual perception can be improved through training programs, and improvement probably operates favorably on learning to read.

2. The techniques used by experimental teachers may be considered for incorporation into other kindergarten programs.

3. For well-organized kindergarten programs, a half-day program is not sufficient.

Rosen, Carl L., and Ohnmacht, Fred. *Sex Differences in the Factor Structure of Selected Readiness Measures and First Grade Reading Achievement.* Among the strengths of the study are the fact that the sample was selected with care and was of adequate size, and the related literature was interwoven at appropriate points in the discussion.

A limitation of the study is that the instructional program used was not described.

The following implications for practice can be drawn:

1. First grade teachers using standardized reading tests similar to that used in this study can obtain little information of predictive value from subtests of the Frostig and Metropolitan tests.

2. Teachers should be sensitive to perceptual disabilities in first grade children.

3. Teachers need to give attention to the development of skills like those measured by the Metropolitan subsections on word meaning, sentences, and information.

Wheelock, Warren H. *An Investigation of Visual Discrimination Training for Beginning Readers.* The sample was selected carefully, and the study was presented in a clear manner.

Interpretation must consider the following limitations: the teacher variable was not discussed; the class organizational patterns were not discussed; and degree of "highness" and "lowness" of the socioeconomic extremes was not given.

The following implications for practice may be drawn:

1. The study supports the contention that children can be taught visual discrimination in the form of letter recognition during the readiness phase of reading instruction.

2. The fact that low socioeconomic level children profit more from training suggests that these children should be helped early.

3. The children should be followed to see what happens in initial reading instruction.

4. The study needs replication as a basis for broader generalizations.

Gredler, G. R. *Performance on a Perceptual Test with Children from a Culturally Disadvantaged Background* The study was exploratory in nature.

The following limitations were noted: sample size was small; a more precise intelligence test was needed; and the discussion of results was longer than the results justified.

The study needs replication with a larger sample being used.

Otto, Wayne. *Color Cues as an Aid to Good and Poor Readers' Paired-Associate Learning.* This study was neatly designed and clearly presented. The researcher was especially cautious in drawing conclusions and generalizations.

The study was of necessity limited in scope.

The following implications can be drawn for further research:

1. The same study should be under-

taken, this time with color cues being pointed out to the subjects.

2. The study should be replicated to determine if the results reflect a chance happening.

3. A similar study involving a more realistic reading task, more like those encountered in reading instruction, should be undertaken.

Phonics Instruction—When? What? For Whom?

H. ALAN ROBINSON*

A complexity involved in determining "When should phonics instruction begin?" is in determining "What is phonics instruction?" Most of the studies do not describe programs of instruction in detail. They are vague about specific teaching procedures and content. Terms are used without suitable definition. Formal phonics, analytical phonics, synthetic phonics, incidental phonics, and phonic readiness are often used with the apparent expectation that the reader will understand without explanation. Hence, phonics instruction has become a term that often means different things to different people.

Phonics instruction, in this writer's opinion, is direct, planned teaching aimed at helping a pupil analyze printed or written words to determine their pronunciations. As Gray has indicated, the child uses visual clues ". . . as aids in determining consonant and vowel sounds, syllabic divisions, and accented syllables." Pupils must be helped to refine visual and auditory discrimination, ". . . to associate consonant and vowel sounds with letters of the alphabet, and to blend these sounds into syllables and the syllables into words with appropriate accent."[1] Phonics instruction, then, concentrates on helping pupils synthesize what they see with what they hear in order to achieve accuracy in pronunciation.

If this definition of phonics instruction is valid, *phonic readiness* must be considered much more than the "ear training" a number of investigators suggest it may be. From the investigations of people in the speech field (2, 8), it is obvious that articulation of sounds is an important concept in phonic readiness. By the chronological age of four and a half the aver-age child can articulate as many as twelve consonant sounds. On entrance into first grade he can articulate all vowel sounds and sixteen to twenty-one consonant sounds. However, it isn't until the end of grade three that most children are able to discriminate among most sounds (12). It appears that a great deal can be done with very young children in getting them to articulate sounds although more time seems needed in the development of auditory discrimination.

It also seems that much work needs to be accomplished in helping children discriminate visually—not for the so-called, nonexistent look and say program—but for the phonics program. Success in phonic analysis depends upon the achievement of skill in each modality—visual and auditory. In addition, it would seem imperative that much emphasis be placed upon training in synthesis. Visual and auditory discrimination must be synthesized if a pupil is to achieve ultimate success in phonic analysis.

When to Begin?

"When should phonics instruction begin?" is an ancient, confusing, and still essentially unanswered question. Only seven reports spanning the years from 1925 through 1958 (1, 3, 4, 5, 7, 10, 14) represent the total range of "answers" contributed by research. In these studies suggestions for when to begin phonics instruction are given in terms of mental age or grade placement.

Reporting in terms of mental age, Arthur (1) concluded that a mental age of six and a half was the optimum time for introducing phonics instruction al-

[1]William S. Gray, *On Their Own in Reading.* Chicago: Scott, Foresman and Co., 1960.

Reading as an Intellectual Activity, IRA Proceedings, Vol. 8, 1963, 224-228.

though some gains in phonic ability were made beginning at a mental age of five and a half. She based her conclusion on the results of a study of 171 first graders grouped according to mental age. Arthur's research design was well conceived, but the teaching variable was not controlled. Dolch and Bloomster (3) also conducted a study of mental age and phonic achievement. They found, on the basis of scattergrams made from 115 scores, that children of high mental age might *sometimes* fail in acquiring phonic skills but children of low mental age were certain to fail. A mental age of seven seemed to be the lowest at which a pupil could be expected to use phonics. Dolch and Bloomster's study, although it had a number of limitations recognized by the investigators, was carefully designed and replicated. The word-attack tests used, however, were experimental and no information was furnished about their validity and reliability.

Durrell's recent report (4) based on four doctoral studies challenged the importance of mental age. Three of the investigators found that mental age had a low relationship with the ability to use phonics and with reading achievement in general. Durrell recommended teaching phonics, at varying rates, to all pupils at the very beginning of the first grade. Helen Robinson, in a detailed critique of the Durrell report, concluded that it did ". . . not supply dependable evidence to determine . . . whether or not teaching letter names and letter sounds before teaching a sight vocabulary is essential."[2]

Reporting in terms of grade placement, Garrison and Heard (5) concluded that most of the training in phonics should be deferred until grades two and three. McDowell (7) and Sexton and Herron (10) found that the teaching of phonics was of little or no value during the first half of first grade. Sexton and Herron added that instruction in phonics was of greater value in grade two. Winch (14), in a study of teaching beginners to read in

England, also suggested delaying phonics instruction until grade two. The children in grade two of the English infants' school, however, were a year younger than American children in grade two; hence, Winch really concluded that phonics instruction succeeds with most school children who have reached the chronological age of five and a half. The studies concerned with beginning phonics instruction and grade placement, although interesting in terms of group trends, suffered from hazy control of significant variables.

These few studies, with their flaws and limitations, appear to represent the only available evidence of any substance relating mental age or grade placement to beginning phonics instruction. Numerous professional writers, apparently basing their conclusions on some of the available evidence, have generalized about the inadvisability of beginning phonics instruction before the mental age of six and a half or seven, or prior to a given time in the chronology of instruction. Perhaps such generalizations are necessary since no other conclusive proof is available and teachers need the guidance in order to develop an instructional program. On the other hand, such generalizations, repeated over the years, eventually seem to become accepted as factual information. Authors build them into reading series, curricula are based on them, and teachers accept them. After a while, especially in instructional situations, no one is sure of where a given generalization comes from, but its very existence gives it some magical importance. The doubter, the person with another concept, will find it difficult indeed to overcome the bias growing out of the "now-established-as-conclusive research evidence."

The professional literature does not contain, by any standards, adequate reports by teachers discussing classroom experimentation in detail or reflecting about possible changes in phonics instruction viewed by the teacher who has taught first graders for five or ten years. Since there is a paucity of controlled research

---

[2]Helen M. Robinson, "News and Comment: Methods of Teaching Beginning Readers." *Elementary School Journal*, LIX (May, 1959), p. 426.

concerned with when to start phonics instruction, and since it is most difficult to design research so that all variables are controlled, an accumulation of accurate reports by teachers would be of great value. Every effort must be made, however, to report evidence based on logical approaches tested and retested in many situations.

Even then questions about "Which came first, the chicken or the egg?" may be raised, and with reason. For example, the results of Russell's study (9) of teachers' views on phonics indicated that the teachers favored emphasis on phonics in grades two and three or in different grades dependent on need. What certainty is there that this opinion is based on years of experimental and creative teaching? Weren't these teachers probably taught how to teach reading through the use of professional materials and with the help of instructors dedicated to delayed phonics instruction? Weren't they probably teaching reading with the help of manuals and instructional materials based on the concept of delayed phonics instruction? Could they report without built-in bias?

Begin with Whom?

If phonics instruction incorporates the steps of visual discrimination, auditory discrimination, and synthesis of the two, the research on *when to teach phonics* is indeed inconclusive. Even those reading programs labeled "traditional" or "look and say oriented" introduce this kind of phonics instruction in the kindergarten or very early in the first grade. Perhaps research directed toward when the *various steps* of phonics instruction should take place is needed.

There is no reliable evidence that points to the latter part of kindergarten or to a mental age of five or to the first month of first grade as the best time for concentration on auditory or visual discrimination. There is no reliable evidence that proves 50, 100, or three sight words learned by pupils make them then ready for phase one of phonics instruction.

Can such evidence be obtained? Would such research not be subject to the same basic flaws obvious in almost all of the research concerned with phonics instruction—lack of attention to the individual abilities and needs of pupils. Certainly the research directed toward the appropriate time for instruction in phonics, reported here, has dealt with group behavior, medians, and averages.

A small body of research has been directed toward certain kinds of individual needs. Investigators (11, 12, 13) interested in the auditory learning modality, have indicated that all children may not profit from an auditory-approach to reading. Wepman (12) suggested that instruction, at least in the beginning stages, be individualized in terms of auditory and visual learners. He indicated that children ". . . who show inadequate discrimination of the discrete units of speech sounds usually have poor articulation in speech and equally poor ability to learn to read by phonic approaches." He suggested that ". . . the teaching of reading as well as therapy for the articulatory inaccuracy in speech production should first approach both tasks from other modalities, e.g., visual or kinesthetic."[3] If the question of when phonics instruction should begin were now posed, the tentative answer would have to be related to ability or needs in auditory discrimination.

In the Garrison and Heard and Dolch and Bloomster studies, there appeared to be some evidence to support the conclusion that bright children in the first and perhaps the second grades received more help from phonics instruction than the dull. One can assume, therefore, that another answer might be to start teaching phonics to the bright and delay instruction for the dull. Grimes and Allinsmith (6) on the basis of a study of third graders in two city schools, concluded that pupils who are highly compulsive,

[3]Joseph M. Wepman, "The Interrelationships of Hearing, Speech and Reading," *The Reading Teacher*, XIV (March, 1961), p. 246.

highly anxious, or both, will achieve better under a phonics program than under the "look and say" approach. In this case the question of *when* seems related to personality traits.

It seems essential that thought and research related to phonics focus on the individual needs of pupils. A great deal has been written and said about individuals and their needs, but research and instruction still seem pretty far removed from practical utilization of the concept. A number of questions related to the time for beginning phonics instruction must be answered. Do individual pupils learn to attack words in very different ways and at very different times? Are there enough similarities about the way some children learn so they can be grouped for instruction in terms of certain modes of learning? Would instruction based on specific learning needs accomplished in kindergarten or the beginning of grade one permit some children to use phonics earlier? Should some pupils never be given instruction in phonics? If phonics instruction is begun very early, can there be an adverse effect on pupils' school progress in later years?

In a recent address concerned with the future of beginning reading instruction, Gates stated that "whatever age is adopted as the 'normal' one for beginning reading, some children can start earlier and others should start later for optimum results. The one certain outcome of research on the age of beginning reading is that an educational-psychological case or clinical study should be made of each child to determine the best time and method of introducing him to reading."[4]

---

[4]Arthur I. Gates, *A Look Ahead*. Comments made at a Conference on Possibilities of Improving the Teaching of Reading in the Primary Grades, under the auspices of the Department of Health, Education, and Welfare, Office of Education, Washington, D. C., November 16, 1962, p. 2.

REFERENCES

1. Arthur, G., "A Quantitative Study of the Results of Grouping First-Grade Classes According to Mental Age," *Journal of Educational Research*, XII (October, 1925), pp. 173-185.
2. Davis, I. P., "The Speech Aspects of Reading Readiness," *National Elementary Principal*, 17th Yearbook, XVII (July, 1938), pp. 282-289.
3. Dolch, E. W., and Bloomster, M., "Phonic Readiness," *Elementary School Journal*, XXXVIII (November, 1937), pp. 201-205.
4. Durrell, D. D. (ed.), "Success in First Grade Reading," *Journal of Education*, CXL (February, 1958), pp 1-48.
5. Garrison, S. C., and Heard, M. T., "An Experimental Study of the Value of Phonetics," *Peabody Journal of Education*, IX (July, 1931), pp. 9-14.
6. Grimes, J. W., and Allinsmith, W., "Compulsivity, Anxiety, and School Achievement," *Merrill-Palmer Quarterly of Behavior and Development*, VII (October 1961), pp. 247-269.
7. McDowell, J. B., "A Report on the Phonetic Method of Teaching Children to Read," *Catholic Educational Review*, L (October, 1953), pp. 506-519.
8. Poole, I., "Genetic Development of Articulation of Consonant Sounds in Speech," *Elementary English Review*, XI (June, 1934), pp. 159-161.
9. Russell, D. H., "Teachers' Views on Phonics," *Elementary English*, XXXII (October, 1955), pp. 371-375.
10. Sexton, E. K., and Herron, J. S., The Newark Phonics Experiment," *Elementary School Journal*, XXVIII (May, 1928), pp. 691-701.
11. Schmidt, B. G., "Teaching the Auditory Learner to Read," *Chicago Schools Journal*, XIX (May-June, 1938), pp. 208-211.
12. Wepman, J. M., "Auditory Discrimination, Speech, and Reading," *Elementary School Journal*, LX (March, 1960), pp 325-333.
13. Wepman, J. M., "The Interrelationship of Hearing, Speech, and Reading," *The Reading Teacher*, XIV (March, 1961), pp. 245-247.
14. Winch, W. H., *Teaching Beginners to Read in England: Its Methods, Results, and Psychological Bases*, Journal of Educational Research Monographs No. 8. Bloomington, Illinois: Publishing School Publishing Co., 1925, pp. 185.

When Should Phonics Instruction Begin?

Joseph Brzeinski*

It is said, that in other times, a favorite topic for discussion and debate was the number of angels who could stand on the head of a pin. Currently, in its ability to engender discussion, the subject of reading perhaps occupies a similar position. Whenever topics such as the teaching of phonics or of beginning reading are mentioned, quite strong views are expressed by parents and teachers alike. Professional journals, books, newspapers, and magazines have had numerous articles on these subjects. Many of the stories contain conflicting and quite contradictory claims and counterclaims.

Research evidence is inconclusive. As Russell recently wrote concerning phonics, "Unfortunately, no investigation in this area can be labeled definitive. At least thirty experimental or applied researches have been carefully done but they all have some limitations in score or technique."[1] That no definitive answer has been found is also reflected by the question under discussion, "When should phonics instruction begin?"

To remove this problem from the realm of fruitless discussion, the Denver Public Schools decided to obtain objective data concerning the subject. Some national publicity has been given to this effort. The purpose of this report is to provide information concerning this research project which may be of some help in answering the above question.

A great deal of time during the first year was spent in reviewing pertinent research. It soon became apparent that studies concerning beginning reading and phonics abound. However, because this is such a complex subject, most studies tended to investigate a fragment of the

problem. This needs to be kept in mind when these research findings are cited. Then, too, the context of each research study needs to be remembered. In deciding when beginning reading and phonics should be taught, it is necessary to consider the individual learner, the kind and quality of the materials and processes to be taught. Obviously, the time at which a highly complex system of phonics dependent upon memorization of rules and their application could be taught would vary considerably from other less rigidly structured methods.

In summary, available research evidence appeared to establish that:

1. The mental age at which beginning reading and phonics could be taught is quite dependent upon the methods and materials of instruction.

2. Auditory perception and visual discrimination are essential for successful teaching of beginning reading and phonics. Some evidence also indicates skill in these areas can be developed by specific training.

3. Success in beginning phonics and reading achievement is highly correlated to the child's opportunities for reading prior to entry into first grade. Recent evidence supports the position that early knowledge of letter names and sounds correlates substantially with reading success in first grade.

4. Children have been taught beginning reading and phonics at ages earlier than at which they presently are being taught in most public school systems. More detailed and comprehensive investigations concerning introductory reading and phonics techniques in relation to

---

[1] David H. Russell, "Reading Research That Makes a Difference," *Elementary English*, XXXVIII, No. 2 (February, 1961), pp. 74-78.

*Reading as an Intellectual Activity, IRA Proceedings, Vol. 8, 1963, 228-232.

individual differences remain to be carried out; for, in most kindergartens, quite a wide range of ability exists. Some kindergarten children may be capable of learning beginning phonic and reading skills.

Parenthetically, since the study began, there is a growing body of evidence to support the hypothesis that "The foundations of any subject may be taught to anybody at any age in some form."[2] Reports emanating from Yale University, the University of Pittsburgh School of Education, and Teachers College, Columbia University, suggest that many three- and four-year-olds, if intellectually challenged and stimulated, can begin the intellectual learning process.

Perhaps, as was stated at the 1959 Woods Hole Conference, "Readiness, that is, is a function not so much of maturation as it is of our intentions and our skill at translating ideas into the language and concepts of the age level we are teaching."[3] With guidelines similar to these in mind, a research design was carefully framed. Its main focus was an experimental comparison of beginning the teaching of reading through the use of phonics and meaning clues in kindergarten with beginning such teaching in the first grade. Six hypotheses were formulated dealing with the comparisons to be made among four treatment groups. The main variable distinguishing the groups was the time of beginning the teaching of reading—kindergarten versus first grade. Numerous other variables of importance were included. These were concerned with reading vocabulary, reading achievement, reading habits, the quantity of reading, the incidence of reading disability, and the like.

Because of the complexity of the research design and the need for carefully planned instructional materials, it seemed desirable to approach the project in a cooperative manner. Such an approach secured the competencies of each of the participants needed in a project of this scope. Serving in an advisory capacity in the initial formulation of the research design were Dr. Wilbur Schramm, Director of the Stanford Institute for Communication Research, Dr. Howard E. Gruber of the Behavioral Research Laboratory of the University of Colorado, and Mr. Theodore E. Albers, Director of Research and Statistics of the Colorado State Department of Education. Dr. John L. Hayman of the Stanford Institute for Communication Research is statistical consultant and analyst for the project. Working with the Denver Public Schools as reading consultants are Professors Paul McKee and M. Lucile Harrison of the Colorado State College. Reading materials produced by them comprised the trial reading program.

Reading Method

Seven groups of beginning reading activities were developed. Primarily, these activities provided practice in using beginning consonant sounds with contextual or meaning clues to identify a printed word. In the pilot method, phonics, i.e., the teaching of letter names and sounds, played an important role along with the use of context or meaning clues.

The rationale for the system used is based on the fact that kindergarten children can recognize many thousands of words when they hear them spoken. They know both the sounds and the meanings of these words. They do need to be taught that the sounds they know are represented by the particular letters and letter combinations in the printed words. This skill, united with contextual or meaning clues, provides early steps toward independent reading.

No workbooks were used in the kindergarten. The reading activities combined

[2]Jerome S. Bruner, *The Process of Education.* Cambridge: Harvard University Press, 1960, p. 12.
[3]Jerome S. Bruner, *On Knowing—Essays for the Left Hand.* Cambridge: Harvard University Press, 1962, p. 108.

an auditory-visual approach suitable to group instruction. It has been suggested that the activities used are a kind of pre-reading or reading readiness program. Since readiness is a complex term subject to many understandings and misunderstandings, the teaching procedure was designated either beginning reading activities or simply reading. The method was designed to capitalize upon individual differences innate in children. Teachers were encouraged to advance at a rate consonant with the interest and ability of the children.

Research Procedure

Preliminary Study

In the Spring of 1959 the reading method developed was tried in fifteen kindergartens. Suggestions for improvements and modifications based upon this experience were received. While the materials were being revised, planning continued and a preliminary study was inaugurated in approximately 30 kindergartens during the second semester of the 1959-1960 school year. Purpose of the preliminary study was to test the research design which had been developed and to discover what problems might arise.

Main Study

In the Fall of 1960 the Denver Public Schools, with the aid of a grant from the Cooperative Research Branch of the United States Office of Education, began a longitudinal research study to determine the effectiveness of beginning the teaching of reading in kindergarten. Progress of pupils in the project is to be studied through the fifth grade.

When the main study began, the Denver Public Schools had about 9,000 kindergarten children divided into about 300 classes. This study involved 122 classes randomly assigned by school to control and research groups. This resulted in 61 classes in the control group and 61 classes in the research group. Thus, approximately 4,000 pupils were divided equally into control and research groups.

The children in the control classes followed the regular kindergarten program. Children in the kindergarten research classes received instruction in the beginning reading activities every day. The remaining two hours and ten minutes of the kindergarten session was devoted to established kindergarten procedures. When the children in the study entered first grade, the research and control groups were in turn divided into two groups. This division provided four first grade groups.

Group I which had the regular program in kindergarten and the regular program in the first and later grades; Group II which had a regular program in kindergarten and the research program in the first grade; Group III which had the research program in kindergarten and the regular program in the first and later grades; and Group IV which had the research program in kindergarten and the adjusted program in the first and later grades.

Group I provided a necessary basis for comparison with the research groups. Group II permitted a comparison between groups who had received the same instruction introduced at different times. Group III made possible the assessment of the effect of early reading not followed up—a danger often encountered in a short-term study. Group IV was established to test the full effect of beginning reading in the kindergarten followed by a program accelerated to take advantage of any gains made.

The study is longitudinal and the pupils are to be tested periodically using standardized reading tests and other appropriate measures including specially devised tests and evaluative techniques. The primary variable considered was time of beginning reading. Other variables included mental age, chronological age, I.Q., and family characteristics. The principal statistical technique used has been analysis of covariance. This method of analysis, in effect, equates or matches the groups being analyzed. Because the design has large numbers of experimental subjects, the statistical work has been programmed for computers.

Results

Since the present study is of a longitudinal nature, any conclusions based upon the findings reported at this time must be considered tentative and applicable only to the trial procedures. Indeed, it would be well to view these conclusions as hypotheses subject to further testing, modification, or verification.

Kindergarten Findings

Analysis of data gathered in the kindergarten was made to determine the suitability of the trial method and materials for that age level. This analysis involved a pretest administered in October 1960 and a post-test in May 1961. A teacher questionnaire provided additional information. The results indicated that:

1. Kindergarten children could and did learn certain beginning reading phonic skills.
   * Kindergarten-age children were able to learn letter forms, letter names, and letter sounds.
2. A planned program of systematic instruction in beginning reading skills appeared to be more effective than a program which incidentally provided opportunity for the development of reading growth. Both groups made gains. The classes with the planned program gained an average of 21.8 points while the classes with an incidental program gained 12.9 points. This difference was statistically significant at the .001 level of confidence.
3. Children taught the beginning reading skills in kindergarten did not forget them during the summer intermission. The possibility existed that since the pilot classes seemed to learn more than did the control classes, they would also forget more during the summer months. To test this hypothesis 49 children in the pilot group and 49 children in the control group were tested in September 1961 when these children had just entered first grade. The children in the pilot group had an average loss of 1.45 points while the children in the control

group had an average loss of 3.47 points. The difference in these means is not statistically significant, seeming to indicate that the children in the pilot group maintained their advantage during the summer months.

That not all children progressed at the same rate is among other findings shown by an analysis of kindergarten data. Some children made little progress in learning the seven steps of the trial program. Some children were able to read preprimers and primers during the latter part of the kindergarten. Most children were able to recognize letters, to learn letter names and sounds, and with the help of context, to read words. Analysis of teacher questionnaires and interview data showed that growth in reading in the kindergarten could be achieved without greatly modifying existing kindergarten programs through better utilization of the time presently available.

First-Grade Findings

Tests used to gather data in the first grade were the Gates Primary Reading Test and the Gates Advanced Primary Reading Test. Analysis of adjusted test scores suggests that

1. The children who had the beginning reading activities in kindergarten scored significantly better at the end of first grade than did the children who had the regular kindergarten program.
   * The pilot group which began reading in the kindergarten had an adjusted mean score of 114.35, which was 18.45 higher than that of the control group which started reading in the first grade.
2. Optimum reading achievement was obtained when adjustments were made in the first grade program to take advantage of gains made in the kindergarten.
   * Pupils in this category had an adjusted test score mean of 118.06. This was 10.70 higher than the group which had the beginning reading activities in kindergarten and the regular program in the first grade.
3. The time of introduction of the beginning reading activities had a significant effect on achievement. Those children who were taught the pilot materials in kindergarten were significantly better

readers than those children who began
the same method in the first grade.
  • The children who had the begin-
    ning reading program in kinder-
    garten and continued with an ad-
    justed program in the first grade
    scored 13.92 higher than those
    who began the pilot method in
    the first grade.

These differences reported are significant
beyond the .001 level of confidence.

Conclusions

Results at the end of two years of study
appear to establish an advantage for children who had an opportunity to learn
elements of beginning phonics and reading in the kindergarten. Knowledge of
letter names, sounds, and forms, used in
combination with context, seemed to help
children progress successfully when they
later began to read in books. A practical
implication would be the provision of
appropriate possibilities for growth in
reading in the kindergarten. Growth in
reading is too important to be ignored
or left to chance incidental development.
Results of the present research study suggest planning must occur if kindergarten-
age children are to experience continuous
growth in reading concomitant with their
growth in other important areas. Experience has shown such growth need not be
at the expense of growth in other areas
vital to a sound, balanced program of
kindergarten instruction.

Common Sense about Phonics

JOSEPHINE PIEKARZ*

WRITERS ON THE subject of "phonics in reading" are divided into two widely opposing factions, which seem to be separated by a vast chasm of incommunication due largely to misinformation and missing information concerning the relationship between the spoken and written forms of our language. Few feuds in history have had the enduring quality demonstrated by the protagonists and antagonists of phonics. No other single subject or area has had as much written about it over as long a period of time. Scarcely a month passes that the professional and lay periodicals do not carry a number of articles on the subject. These articles reveal that the two factions are as widely separated as ever—despite the fact that written English has been in use for many centuries. The defenders of phonics seem to believe that a rigid set of rules governing the pronunciation of letters is the one true road to success in reading; the opposition seems to believe that there is no point in teaching phonic generalizations because there are so many exceptions. The fact is that one belief is as wrong as the other. Only people naïve about the relationship between the spoken and written forms of the English language believe in either view.

The two most frequent and serious errors or shortcomings suggested by the popular writings on the teaching of phonics are: (1) that phonics is taught and used apart from word structure and other word identification techniques, and (2) that phonic principles or generalizations apply to all syllables within written words. Many champions of phonics behave as if our language were a consistently spelled one and belittle all except phonic techniques for word identification, unaware that they themselves rely on a combination of techniques in identifying words. On the other hand, many antagonists of phonics deny the underlying relationship between speech and writing in our language, discredit the use of phonics by pointing out what appear to them to be exceptions to phonic rules, unaware of how heavily they themselves rely on phonics in identifying printed words. The place of phonics in the reading of our language can be understood only in the light of the relationship between the spoken and written forms of our language. Some of the relevant facts are:

1. Language is man-made, having been developed by man over eons of time. Oral forms of language always precede written forms of language. Each individual child in his turn recapitulates the development of the language of his species, progressing from a stage of gestures and random babbling sounds in orderly sequence through speech and oral reading to silent reading, the most advanced stage of language development.

2. Language is symbolic and has expressive and receptive aspects. Meaning exists in reality, for which spoken and written words are merely symbols. Reading is the recep-

*The Reading Teacher, 18 (November 1964), 114-117.

tive end of the written communicative process.

3. Various forms of graphic language have been attempted during the course of time, bearing different kinds of relationships to reality and speech. Alphabetic writing, the written form of our language, is based on the premise that spoken words consist of combinations of sounds. Alphabetic characters are graphic representations of sounds. In other words, writing is manually recorded speech.

4. And finally, since the number of different alphabetic characters in our written language does not equal the number of different sounds in our spoken language, we do not have a one-to-one relationship between sound and letter. The disparity between sounds (approximately forty-five) and letters (twenty-six, three of which do not have sounds of their own) means that some letters must represent more than one sound. Experience with our written language also indicates that a single sound may be represented or spelled by different letters and combinations of letters. This does not mean, however, that our language is not alphabetic and phonetic. It merely means that there isn't a one-to-one relationship between letter and sound, and that it probably takes longer and is more difficult to learn the correct associations between what is seen and what is heard than in many other more consistently spelled languages. Difficulties in learning to read our language are due to the large number of associations between letters and sounds which must be learned, as well as to the surface variability of these associations. The letters though, however arbitrarily they seem to be put together in written words, still represent sounds, so our language is phonetic.

Learning to read our language involves learning to associate spoken sounds and written symbols while at the same time mentally reconstructing the things and ideas represented by the language symbols. With enough practice, the process of associating sounds and symbols recedes to a subconscious level, while attention is directed toward the meaning represented by the words. However, in learning to read, the associations must be made on a conscious level. The correct associations depend primarily upon knowledge of the sounds of the spoken form of the language, knowledge of the letters of the written form of the language, as well as knowledge of the various circumstances and conditions under which particular letters and combinations of letters represent particular sounds. This constitutes what is usually called phonics and word structure. It is essentially a process of reconstructing speech from written symbols. Phonics cannot be used apart from word structure since they are inseparably interrelated. Letters and combinations of letters in our written language . (particularly those representing vowel sounds) represent given sounds *depending upon the structure of the word* in question. Therefore, it is impossible to apply phonic principles until the structure of the word is known. Attempting to teach phonics apart from word structure or structural analysis will inevitably lead to frustration, discouragement, failure, and loss of confidence in our written language. It will most certainly result in countless exceptions to rules.

Even one-syllable words have to be established as one-syllable words before any phonic principles or generalizations can be applied correctly. The syllable "can" is pronounced with a short *a* sound in the root word *can*. The same syllable is pronounced with a long *a* sound in the word *chicanery*, since *chicanery* is derived from the word *chicane*. The verb *be* is pronounced with a long *e* sound; the same combination of letters in *bedim*, *bemoan*, and *beset*, however, are pronounced differently because "be" serves as a prefix in these words and is not part of the root words themselves.

Furthermore, the phonic rules or generalizations that are frequently taught apply only to single-syllable root words and to the accented syllable, but not to the unaccented syllables, of polysyllabic words. For example, many teachers teach that "when two vowel letters such as *ai* appear together, the first vowel letter has a long sound and the second vowel letter is silent," and then complain bitterly about all the exceptions. Words like *certain, captain,* and *curtain* are not exceptions to the rule, if the rule has been taught correctly. A short *a* sound will not be found in *orphan, woman,* or *husband,* since the letter *a* appears in the unaccented second syllable of these words. Nor can a long *a* sound be expected in the unaccented suffix of words like *wreckage, portage,* and *spoilage,* nor a short *a* sound in *errant, servant,* or *occupant.* None of these words is an exception to the rules or generalizations governing the pronunciation of vowel sounds. Phonics cannot be separated from word structure and taught in isolation. Doing so simply will not work in our language; it will only result in disillusionment. Structural-phonetic analysis would be a more appropriate term for this process since both aspects have to be considered simultaneously.

There is a great deal more consistency and logic inherent in our written language than most people apparently see, but it is not at the level of a consecutive letter-by-letter association with sound. Large complex bodies of learnings cannot be learned unless there is underlying order. If teachers do not teach this order in reading—the logical and correct relationships between spoken and written words—pupils are left on their own to try to figure this out for themselves. It is amazing that as many children manage to do this as well as they do.

It is ordinarily neither desirable nor necessary to analyze phonetically complete words while reading. Doing so makes reading a laborious and time-consuming process. Pupils should be taught to use only as much phonetic analysis as necessary to identify printed words correctly. Once a word is identified, there is no further profit to be gained in continuing its analysis. In actual reading situations the tedious analysis of entire words is seldom necessary if pupils have been taught to use configuration, picture, and meaning clues in conjunction with structural-phonetic analysis. Fluency in word identification and reading results from the combined use of the various word recognition techniques, not from structural-phonetic analysis alone. Structural-phonetic analysis, however, correctly applied remains the most valuable single technique for identifying the written words of our language.

Valuable as it is, structural-phonetic analysis cannot always identify words correctly in our language. The correct pronunciation, for example, of words like *close, live, tear,* and *rebel* can be determined only in the light of context. For this reason, also, other word identification techniques besides structural-phonetic analysis must be taught. Pupils must be taught how to utilize the various word identification techniques separately and together. None of them alone will succeed in identifying all the words of our written language accurately. Any pupil who cannot use them all is handicapped to some degree or other.

Since writing is manually recorded speech, reading is the process of reconstructing speech from written symbols in addition to mentally reconstructing the things and ideas represented by the symbols. Learning to read our written language involves learning to make the correct associations between sounds and letters or groups of letters. When the associations can be made easily and efficiently, they recede to a subconscious level, leaving the reader free to attend to the meaning of the symbols. Structural-phonetic analysis accounts for the major portion of the fixed relationships between the sounds and written symbols of our language. Phonetic analysis must always be carried on in relation to the basic structure of words. If word structure is ignored, phonetic analysis fails. Efficient word identification and reading are possible only through the combined use of structural-phonetic analysis *and* other word recognition techniques.

Phonics Materials: A Big Seller

Dolores Durkin*

EVEN A QUICK STROLL up and down the aisles of a convention exhibit hall provides ample evidence that educational materials are "big business." In fact, corporations like IBM, RCA, and CBS can now be viewed as the latest alphabet to dot the educational marketplace (4).

Predictably, the involvement of large corporations has led to some changes. Clearly apparent are more sophisticated advertising, more colorful materials, more urbane sales personnel—in fact, more of everything; for quantity is the very essence of big and successful business. In spite of the new and more glamorous façade, however, one thing remains unchanged: the unique importance of reading to the entire educational enterprise continues, making materials connected with the teaching of reading skills one of the most lucrative pieces to be found in the whole of the market place display. It is probably equally accurate to add that, of all the various skills comprising reading, phonics is the juiciest from an economic point of view. Why?

A variety of factors account for the special market value of phonics. For one thing, phonics instruction often is equated with reading instruction. While such an equation confuses a part with the whole, the association has still resulted in assigning to phonics a rather special place of honor. For the market place the confusion has resulted in "a big seller."

But there is another characteristic of phonics that makes it especially enticing to the publisher: its content can be packaged. It can fill up workbooks. It provides material for charts, cards, pictures, and filmstrips. It can be pressed into phonograph. records. It can be put into the form of a "game." It can be used to take advantage of the current interest in programmed instruction. And, even more recently, it provides ideal material for the teaching kit. Could we expect such potential to be overlooked by the publisher? Hardly. But as a result the question of discriminate buying takes on paramount importance.

The Discriminate Buyer

Discriminate buying, whether of a workbench or a workbook, always requires a knowledge of the product —what it can and cannot do, for instance. And this will not change. But what *is* changing, even as the nature of the market place changes, is an ever increasing need for the buyer to possess what might simply be called the will to resist temptation.

To be sure, temptation has always been the goal of the merchant and, correspondingly, the downfall of the buyer. But today the temptation held out to the man with money in

*The Reading Teacher, 20 (April 1967), 610-614.

his pockets must be, and often is, uniquely enticing and even manipulative. Reflecting the technological and affluent society which surrounds it and which also has created it, the modern market place no longer is characterized by the classical supply-demand relationship. The "good old days" in which what was produced was what was needed are now part of past history. Replacing them is an economic era in which the traditional sequence has been reversed. Today the first step is production, and the second step is the deliberate creation of a need for what has been produced. Indeed, the wares of Madison Avenue have never been so important—nor so effective.

Although in the past the schools have sometimes been accused of remaining apart from the realities of life, nobody now could deny that they are very much immersed in the reality of this new market place. There is not only a larger number of children to educate and teachers to help; there is also that "man with money in his pockets." Thanks to the generosity of federal funds, the educator has become a wealthy man, and so a most welcome customer in the aisles of the market. Perhaps it goes without saying that, among the counters devoted to reading, phonics materials are richly and enticingly displayed.

Motives for Buying Phonics Materials

While the allurement of the modern market place is undeniably great, it would be erroneous to think it is the sole reason why phonics materials are a big seller. Certainly other factors are at work too. One, for example, is related to the kind of public criticism that has been leveled at the schools for about the last ten years. Starting with the publication of *Why Johnny Can't Read* in 1955, the focus of a surprisingly large amount of criticism has been the charge that the schools are not teaching phonics (2). This has been the case whether the complaint was about reading, as in the Flesch book, or something as broad as the possible inferiority of American schools as compared with those of Soviet Russia (5).

Within the past decade, too, phonics instruction has worked its way into public debates about manners and morals, and frequently into politically conservative publications. As recently as November 1966, for instance, Russell Kirk was writing in *National Review* statements like, "Among the educationists phonics is a dirty word," and, as he gave his description of elementary schools, ". . . actual teaching by phonics is taboo" (3).

That statements like these could never be documented has less effect on practice than ought to be the case. In fact, public accusation about too little phonics is one of the factors that has resulted in too much phonics, in certain schools. In their eagerness to have very visible phonics programs, for instance, some administrators have gone all-out in stressing phonics and in purchasing phonics materials. While these efforts to "prove a point" are psychologically understandable, they are not always professionally defensible. Just as some schools would profit from a little more and a little better phonics instruction, others could probably be improved simply by having less.

Related to the public indictment of too little phonics instruction is still another factor which sometimes enters into a school's decision to introduce more and more phonics and, as is generally the case, to buy more and more phonics materials. This source of influence is parents.

Typically, what a parent knows about reading comes from the newspaper or, perhaps, one of the monthly magazines written for women. When this popular press reporting deals with reading, it most often focuses on its beginnings and, in conjunction with this, the advantages of phonics instruction compared to what is called the "look-say" approach.

It is doubtful that the frequent selection of beginning reading as the topic of popular press articles is accidental: never is a parent so concerned about reading as when his child is just starting to learn. How well the child progresses at the beginning is viewed not only as an indicator of future progress in reading, but even as a forecast of how well the child will do in all areas of the curriculum. Such uncommon importance makes the parent eager to learn about beginning reading. And it also makes him somewhat gullible as popular press articles offer sure cures and even "guaranteed"

results, if the cures are followed. Most of these prescriptions, of course, call for immediate and frequent instruction in phonics.

To think that parents' beliefs about the best way to teach beginning reading have no effect on a school's reading program would be naïve. As a minimum they encourage the administration to take another look at the way reading is taught in the early grades. At the other extreme, however, parents' beliefs about the special advantages of much phonics instruction have been known to result in obviously increased amounts in the schools, sometimes as early as the kindergarten year.

While nobody would deny the right of a parent to be concerned about his child's education, and even to have definite ideas about the way it ought to be effected, the priority of professionalism needs to be recognized when decisions about education are to be made. In the case of phonics instruction, decisions about its timing and, for instance, about whether it ought to be taught inductively or deductively are professional matters. When these decisions are affected by such factors as the desire to "pacify" parents, the results are not always what is best for the children learning to read.

There is still another reason motivating the purchase of volumes of phonics materials. It is neither a "right" reason nor a "wrong" one; but when it exists it ought to be recognized. This is the fact that some teachers are not prepared to tcach phonics and, as a result, feel an unusual need for materials.

Citing the possibility of this source of motivation is not to be critical of teachers. Rather, it is to be aware that many were elementary school children when phonics was given scant attention. As a result, unless these teachers are lucky enough to have had a reading methodology course which actually taught them the content of phonics, they enter their own classrooms with feelings of inadequacy and insecurity. These feelings are natural, but they lead to overreliance on materials. And while this might be advantageous for the merchant, it is hardly good for the classroom. What the dependency creates is a situation in which the teacher is merely an assistant to materials—a role hardly worthy of a professional person, and hardly productive of the best kind of instruction.

Some Factors in Considering Materials

If a school should decide to buy materials to help its faculty learn more about phonics—and this surely is laudable—the reason for the purchase ought to be taken into account as particular materials are selected. This is important because what might be suitable for educating teachers is not necessarily best for teaching children. With them, different criteria have to be kept in mind. With both, however, the requirements of prudent choices begin even before the customer gets to the market place.

Certainly the first step—whether the intent is to help children or teachers or both—is clarification of the role phonics is to play in a total reading program. In the opinion of this writer, phonics instruction is very important. It is one way to help a child develop independence as a reader and as a learner. But to recognize its importance is not to lay aside the fact that phonics is just one kind of reading instruction and, therefore, only one part of the total reading program. Without this perspective, phonics all too easily becomes isolated as an end in itself, actually losing its very reason for being: a means toward identifying unfamiliar words.

Once clarity about the contribution of phonics is achieved, decisions have to be made about whether its content will be taught inductively or deductively, and also when the teaching will begin. It is not the intention of this article to take a stand on these questions; that has been done with considerable detail elsewhere (1). Rather, the purpose is to recognize the existence of the questions, and to point out the need for a faculty to arrive at some answers, hopefully for "right" reasons. Once this is accomplished, a school is ready to consider whether there are materials in the market place that might be helpful.

When materials are being considered for children, the first kind to look for are those that might actually instruct. Assuming, for instance, that a school has some children who are able to learn at least part of the content of phonics from a book rather than a teacher, it then makes sense to try to find materials which allow for independent learning, and also for a pace of learning that can be matched to the abilities of individual children.

More frequently, though, schools will be looking for materials which review instruction given by a teacher, or which provide practice in the use of what has been taught. When materials are being considered to serve these functions, the most important requirement—and the only one that will be discussed here—is that they facilitate a teacher's efforts to individualize instruction.

For example, materials providing practice in the use of short vowel sounds ought to have enough coverage for the child who will need a great deal of practice. But, in addition, the various kinds of practice ought to be assembled in a way that allows a teacher to make selections on the basis of what is needed by individual children, and at a time when the need is identified. As practice material is now generally put together by publishers—in the typical workbook, for instance—individualized instruction is not only *not* facilitated; it is often made more difficult. In fact, materials like the typical workbook are the most prolific reminder that what is needed by a teacher is not always what is produced by the publisher.

A Summary

This brief article has tried to enumerate a few of the reasons why phonics materials are an especially big seller in the educational market place. Its content has been developed on the assumption that an awareness of some of the factors that affect buying will make the buyer more perceptive and discriminating.

In no sense does the selected focus infer that educators must rely only on published materials to do their job. Certainly some of the best materials used by children are what they themselves make, or what a teacher makes out of her knowledge of what needs to be taught and practiced. However, it is unrealistic to think that all the materials required by classroom instruction can be "home made." This being the case, there is the need to look to the publisher for help. But, as this article has tried to show, there also is an ever increasing need to be wary of his products, knowing that the motivation of the educator and that of the publisher will not always be the same.

(Dolores Durkin is Professor of Education at the University of Illinois.)

References

1. Durkin, Dolores. *Phonics and the Teaching of Reading.* New York: Bureau of Publications, Teachers College, Columbia University, 1965.
2. Flesch, Rudolph. *Why Johnny Can't Read.* New York: Harper, 1955.
3. Kirk, Russell. "Why Don't They Teach Phonics?" *National Review,* 18 (Nov. 15, 1966), 1169.
4. Silberman, Charles E. "Technology Is Knocking at the Schoolhouse Door," *Fortune,* 74 (Aug. 1966), 120 ff.
5. Trace, Arthur S. *What Ivan Knows That Johnny Doesn't.* New York: Random House, 1961.

The Differences between Linguistics and Phonics

DOROTHY Z. SEYMOUR*

READING TEACHERS who have taken the time to examine articles on linguistics and reading have not always been convinced that a linguistic approach offers anything new. On first examination, linguistics seems merely to be returning certain advantages of old-time phonics to reading instruction. The similarities are inescapable. There is a renewed emphasis on sound, on association of sound with letter, and on the use of sound-letter associations in the analysis of new words. But a true linguistic approach offers much more than phonics. It contributes the discoveries of scholarship in the field of linguistics to the field of reading instruction. The most important contribution can be summed up in one word: *exactitude*.

The precepts of phonics suffered from terminology that revealed a basic misconception about reading—that "words" are basically *written* words, and that children must be taught to "pronounce" them, or "sound" them. To this end, children were first taught about letters and then were told to "pronounce" the letters or "make" their sounds. Teachers constantly referred to "the sounds of the letters," and even to "silent" letters. The letters were also endowed with the power of dictating sounds and changes in sounds: "the *e* makes the *a* long." It is this same preoccupation with the letters which made teachers say there are five vowels, when actually there are fourteen. The linguists have shown how confused this approach was.

MISCONCEPTIONS IN PHONICS

1. "Words" are written words

In giving phonics instruction, teachers constantly referred to words as though they did not exist outside of the world of print, whereas, of course, speech developed before a means of symbolizing that speech in print. The assumption that "words" meant "written words" gave children the impression that words were not first oral words, or mental words, before the author put them into symbols. But of course, printed words did not spring into existence from nothing. Another way of saying this is that words were words before they were printed words.

The Reading Teacher, 23 (November 1969), 99-102, 111.

2. "Pronounce" the word

In phonics instruction, children were often given a list of new printed words to analyze. The teacher's job was to teach the children to "pronounce" them. This approach did not recognize the fact that children already know how to pronounce words when they come to school. In fact, they usually need no instruction at all in how to pronounce their own language. What the teacher needs to do is to teach them to read it. Directing a six-year old to "pronounce" the printed word *Mother* is patently ridiculous.

3. "Sound" the word

Phonics instruction was based on sounds that were associated with letters. Children were thus instructed to "sound" a word—that is, make the sounds that each letter "had." Children would then produce a series of pre-taught sounds, and the resulting chain of sounds was supposedly "a word." The fact that the child did not always recognize the result as a word he had spoken countless times, and was often just mouthing a chain of sounds, made the conscientious phonics teacher frustrated and confused. It was this aspect of phonics which brought complaints that phonics-taught children were not readers, they were sound-makers.

The instructional process should have been reversed. Teachers were presenting children with letters, and then superimposing the instruction of sounds upon those letters. But children already know the sounds of their language; they have had five or six years of instruction in language sounds (phonetics) by the time they come to school. What they need is not to learn a series of sounds that "letters have," but which symbols (letters) go with the sounds they already know. It is the letters that are new to them, not the sounds.

If children can be *shown* that they are making certain sounds when they say words, then they can be shown which letters symbolize those sounds. Thus they proceed from the known (sounds) to the unknown (letters).

4. "Each letter has a sound"

The phonics teacher's confused procedure—starting with a letter instead of a language sound—compelled her to find a way of dragging in the sound after the letter was already introduced. So she used a phrase which implied that, somewhere inside or behind each letter, there lurked a sound, and that each time that letter appeared, the child should "make" that sound. The truth is that the sounds have been around a lot longer than the letters, and the letters merely stand for the sounds; they do not "have" the sounds somewhere inside them. If it is made clear, and *kept* clear to the

child (by presentation in a logical manner and by judicious wording) that the letters represent the sounds made in speech, the child
has a better chance of analyzing the printed word as a word he
already can speak, such as "Mother," instead of as a series of extraneous sounds.

5. *"A letter makes a sound"*

The relation between speech and writing was often explained
by the phonics teacher as a series of letters which "make" certain
language sounds, as though if you pinched the letter *i*, it would
squeak out the sound /i/ as in *pin*. Lists of phonics rules might
claim that *a* makes the sound ă in *man*, *a* makes the sound ā in
angel, *ai* makes the sound ā in *train*, *ay* makes the sound ā in *say*,
or the *e* in *bake* makes the letter *a* say its own name. The linguist
expresses the relation between speech and writing by pointing to
the different symbols which can be used to represent our language
sounds. He refers to the sound (a phoneme) before listing the
symbol that can be used to represent it (a grapheme): the sound
/ey/ may be represented by *a* in *angel*, *ay* in *say*, *a-e* in *bake*, and
ei in *vein*. In this presentation there is no attempt to claim that
it is the letter which "makes" the sound. It is people who make
sounds, which are then symbolized in alphabetic spellings for the
purpose of reading.

6. *"Silent letters"*

Letters do not "make" sounds; similarly, they do not "make"
silence. The existence of a letter like *k* in a word like *know*, which
no longer represents a sound we speak, does not mean that the
letter is "being silent." It means that the English word *know* was
once pronounced /knaw/, and that its spelling still reflects that
pronunciation. In the present day, the sound /n/ in the word *know*
is represented by the letters *kn*. Thus it is not the letter *k* which
is failing to "make a sound;" people have stopped using the sound
/k/ at the beginning of that word. English spellings simply do not
keep up with changes in English speech, and examples like *know*
provide the best opportunity the teacher will ever have to demonstrate this phenomenon for the children.

7. *The* "e *makes the* a *long in* take"

The phonics teacher often explained language sounds as being
controlled by letters. But letters do not have the power to control
a change in sound. People utter the sounds, and the letters represent and reflect their utterances. And it is not the length of the
vowel sound that **is distinctive** in the word *take*. What the phonics

teacher meant is that this word is said with the phoneme /ey/ rather than with the phoneme /æ/, as in *man*. One of the ways of symbolizing the phoneme /ey/ in English is with the vowel pattern *a-e*, as in *take*.

8. We have "five vowels"

It is the supposed pre-emption of print over speech which made the phonics teacher assume that English has five vowels. She' meant that the written version of our language utilizes only five vowel letters. This statement obscures the important reality that English has at least fourteen vowel sounds; seven of them move from one sound to another and are called glided vowel sounds. The approach of the phonics teacher to vowels was to explain the different vowel sounds as functions of letter combinations—as if a letter could dictate spech. Actually, the letter combinations are the result, at least in part, of the vowel sounds. Older word-pronunciations explain much of the rest of our spelling.

9. "Write the sound"

The phraseology of phonics instruction often assumed that a letter *was* a sound. Children were told to *look* at the sound, and teachers were directed to *write* the sound on the board or on a chart—as though a sound were something that could be seen or written. In fact, teachers even referred to a letter as if it actually were the sound. When teaching the sound /æ/ as in *apple*, teachers would point to the letter *a* and say, "This is the sound /æ/." This tactic caused further confusion when at another point, the teacher pointed to the same letter *a* and stated, "This is the letter /ey/."

The fact of the matter, of course, is that the sound /æ/ as in *apple* can be represented by different symbols, but is most regularly represented by the letter *a*, particularly when the vowel letter is between two consonant letters. The letter *a* can stand for other language sounds as well. Teachers must clearly differentiate between letters and the sounds they represent, in order to avoid confusion between the two.

CONCLUSION

The main difference between a linguistic and a phonic approach to reading instruction is that phonics gave primacy to letters, and seemed to place spoken language under their control, whereas linguistics points to the priority of speech, and demonstrates that writing is merely a way of recording that speech by the use of symbols. Proof of the antecedence of speech to writing

lies in the work of linguists with "primitive" tribes; they often discovered that these groups had very elaborate language systems
which were, however, as yet unrecorded in writing. The job of these
anthropological linguists was to devise a method of writing such
languages. But the fact remained that, before the linguists entered
the scene, those languages were already in existence, albeit in oral
form. A linguist, in devising a method of writing the language, was
not creating the language itself; he was merely recording it. Thus
the language was not controlled by the symbols: the symbols were
dependent upon the language.

Similarly, the child who is taught reading from a linguistic
point of view is led to understand that a person who can speak can
also learn to read and write. He knows that he will be in control
of the symbols he uses to represent his language; the symbols will
not control him.

PART III: The Curriculum in Word Recognition

The twelve articles in Part III present data that will determine which elements in phonics are important enough to justify inclusion in the curriculum, and which elements are rarely used or may actually be misleading and harmful. The pioneer study by Clymer in January 1963 is included. His study covered the primary grades only. In more recent years, follow-up research by Bailey, Emans, and Burmeister includes only grades above the primary or the entire range of the elementary school years. All the articles deal with sounding out the letters in words except for the lone article by Winkley which evaluates generalizations for syllables.

To date, recent publications of the International Reading Association have not included the following aspects of the word recognition curriculum: structural analysis and contextual clues.

Fundamental Principles Underlying Phonics Instruction

DOLORES DURKIN*

VOLUMES have been written about the fundamental principles underlying phonics instruction. Not all writers, of course, agree on what is "fundamental." Some, for instance, insist that "good" instruction begins with the teaching of letter sounds which, later on, are blended into syllables and then into words. Other authors, to the contrary, maintain that "good" instruction starts with whole words, from which letter-sounds can be identified. Thus, the debate about deductive *vs.* inductive phonics continues.

I will not enter into this debate here; I have done that elsewhere.[1] Instead, I have selected one principle concerning phonics which would be considered fundamental by anyone gifted only with common sense. In general, the principle is: One cannot teach what one does not know. Applied to the theme of this meeting, the principle can be rephrased to suggest that one cannot teach phonics unless one knows phonics.

Teachers' Knowledge of Phonics

What *do* teachers know about the content of phonics? Are they adequately prepared to teach phonics, whether a deductive or an inductive approach is chosen? These are the questions to which I address my comments.

Actually, the questions have been of special concern to me since the fall of 1957. That was the beginning of my college teaching, and of my responsibility for reading methods courses. Having been educated in schools which, evidently, by-passed the popular thinking of the 1930's and the 1940's, I myself was taught phonics, beginning in first grade. Consequently, it probably was natural for me to assume that students in my methods courses needed help with how to teach phonics, but not with its content. And so, during that first year of college teaching, I discussed how I thought phonics should be taught and why I took this position. It happened though—and I suppose this is experienced by most new teachers—that for a class which was concerned with phonics, I ran out of material before I ran out of time. I recall how, with a kind of desperation, I suggested to the students that the remaining time would be used to review their knowledge about the content of phonics. I remember, too, that I wrote the word *ice* on the board, and began to ask questions: "What is there about this word that might help a child identify the sound which the letter *i* probably records?" "What is the likely sound of *c*, and what in the word suggests that sound?"

What took me completely by surprise was that such simple questions as these had absolutely no meaning for the 30 college seniors who sat before me. The surprise was followed by embarrassment—embarrassment because I had failed even to wonder whether the students knew what they were expected to teach.

Because, in 1957, phonics instruction still was not sufficiently fashionable to be given detailed coverage in reading methods textbooks, feelings of surprise, and then of embarrassment, were followed by efforts to put into writing some of the more basic content of phonics. I recall that in preparing the material I assumed its use would be unnecessary for the summer session classes because, in these, most students would be experienced teachers, not inexperienced college seniors.

But, that summer session led to the next surprise, for the experienced teachers did not know the content of phonics either.

---

[1] Dolores Durkin. *Phonics and the Teaching of Reading* (Second Edition). New York: Teachers College Bureau of Publications, 1965.

Reading and Inquiry, IRA Proceedings, Vol. 10, 1965, 427-430.

In fact, I still remember one teacher from that first summer class. I remember her because, following a class session concerned with phonics, she came to me and said, "I'm so glad you're helping us with phonics because, to tell you the truth, I only know second-grade phonics." What she meant, of course, was that she knew the phonics material included in the second-grade basal reader.

Since 1957, I have taught other students at other universities. In all of these places, and with most of the students, I have continued to find it necessary to teach, first, the content of phonics; and then, secondly, how the content might be taught to others. This need to teach the content, of course, is no longer surprising. What I have learned is that while I, as a child, was being taught phonics, many of the people now in reading methods courses were attending other elementary schools in which phonics instruction was "unfashionable."

The Teaching of Phonics

While helping teachers with the content of phonics I also have tried, over the past seven years, to discourage what might be labeled a "grade-level approach" to teaching phonics. That is, I have tried to help teachers see that it does not make good educational sense to think of the content of phonics as being divided into sections, each to be taught at a prescribed grade level. Rather, I have stressed that—as with all phases of reading instruction—we should first find out what children already know about phonics, and then move on to teach what they do not know.

To facilitate more individualized instruction, I recently constructed a diagnostic test in phonics, for children; this was done with the help of the principal and staff of an elementary school. I mention the test now because reactions to it convinced me again that much still needs to be done to help teachers learn at least the most basic of the phonics content.

Before this diagnostic test for children

was published, preliminary copies were sent to elementary schools in various sections of the country. The intent, of course, was to use the reactions of teachers to improve the test. Reactions that were returned can be summarized by quoting from part of one letter sent by a principal:

> We found these tests useful, especially for the teachers. It turned out that they found it difficult to administer the test because they themselves know so little about phonics. . . . This problem has been discussed at a staff meeting, and we have decided to use the test in a kind of in-service course for the teachers.

Reactions, typified by this one letter, indicated that my initial efforts in constructing tests had begun at the wrong place. I should have started with the teachers. Very briefly, this explains how the test called a "Phonics Test for Teachers" came into being.[2]

Phonics Survey

I bring this test into the discussion because I want to spend the remaining time reporting briefly on the results of a kind of national survey, just completed. For this survey, the "Phonics Test for Teachers" was given to 603 students enrolled in reading methods courses. The test was administered by 13 professors from five state and city colleges, and from six state universities. To make the survey somewhat national in scope, these schools were located in the East, the Midwest, and on the West Coast. At some future date, a detailed report of the survey will be prepared. For now, I will just mention a few findings. In fact, for the sake of brevity, I will mention only findings regarding the 204 participants who were experienced teachers. Here it is important to point out that of these 204 teachers, only 57 were taking their first course in reading at the time the phonics test was administered.

Results of Survey

In this very brief report of what these

[2]Dolores Durkin. *Phonics Test for Teachers*. New York: Teachers College Bureau of Publications, 1964.

204 people did and did not know about phonics, I am confining my comments to those aspects of the content of phonics which, I think, most educators would consider basic and elementary. For instance, what did the 204 teachers know about vowel sounds? Using averages, 89 per cent could identify long vowel sounds, but only 81 per cent recognized short vowel sounds. When asked how vowels in a syllable can offer help in arriving at a correct pronunciation of that syllable, the teachers' performance dropped considerably. For example, when asked to explain why, in a combination of such letters as *ek,* the *e* would probably record its short sound, only 29 per cent of the 204 teachers were able to give any explanation.

When the phonics test moved to questions about matters like the "hard" and "soft" sounds of the consonants *c* and *g,* this was what was found. Again based on averages, 90 per cent of the 204 teachers identified the "hard" and "soft" sounds. However, only 9 per cent could describe when *c* and *g* generally record the "soft" sounds, while a small group of 2 per cent seemed to know when the "hard" sounds predominate.

Test questions about diphthongs and consonant digraphs resulted in very low percentages of correct responses, and definitions of these terms sometimes were sadly humorous. For instance, one teacher wrote that a consonant digraph is "two consonants of different sizes."

Concluding Statements

Perhaps these few test findings are sufficient grounds for me to move, now, to some concluding statements about my own feelings regarding this matter of phonics instruction. Let me say, immediately, that I do not believe that phonics is the very

core of the reading program. I emphasize this because I have come to learn that when one writes about a particular topic —and I have written about phonics—a common conclusion is that the writing was done on that topic because the author thought it to be the most important of all possible topics. Let me say that I chose to write about phonics because I consider it to be one of the many important components of a good reading program; and, secondly, because the students in my courses seemed to know so little about its content.

I do not assume that the "Phonics Test for Teachers" is flawless. In fact, what I learned from putting the test together is the very real difficulty of constructing a really good test. Nonetheless, I still feel there is evidence to indicate that much more must be done, in reading methods courses and in-service workshops, to help teachers and teachers-in-preparation learn both what to teach, and how to teach, in this area of phonics.

Finally, I would like to make a prediction. It is simply to suggest that when teachers really know the content of phonics, there will be far less of the deadly phonics drill now going on in classrooms all over the country—even, I am sorry to say, at the kindergarten level. I am convinced, you see, that teachers who are secure in their own knowledge of phonics do not need to depend on high piles of phonics workbooks, or on long, tiresome miles of rote drill. It seems even common sense would suggest that it is the teacher who really knows phonics who also is the one who will never teach too little, or too much.

And this brings us back to the one principle underlying phonics instruction which I have focused on; namely, that one cannot teach what one does not know.

The Utility of Phonic Generalizations in the Primary Grades

THEODORE CLYMER*

THE ORIGINS of this study go back to Kenneth, an extraordinary elementary pupil. Prior to my encounter with Kenneth I had completed a reading methods course in a small teachers college which provided a background in the principles of teaching reading as well as a good introduction to techniques. Among these techniques were procedures to develop phonic generalizations and also *the* list (not *a* list) of the most valuable generalizations to develop. (To those of you who might like copies of the list, I am sad to report that somehow through the years it has been lost.)

Difficulties with Kenneth began as the class reviewed phonic generalizations at the start of the school year. Our procedures were like those used in many classrooms: Groups of words were presented, and the class analyzed their likenesses and differences with a view toward deriving a generalization about relationships between certain letters and sounds or the position and pronunciation of vowels.

Throughout these exercises, following the dictum of my reading methods teacher, we were careful not to call the generalizations "rules," for all our statements had a number of exceptions. As the class finally formulated a generalization regarding the relationships of letters, letter position, and sounds, such defensive phrasing as "most of the time," "usually," and "often" appeared as protective measures. We also spent time listing some of the exceptions to our generalizations.

At this point Kenneth entered the discussion. While the class was busily engaged in developing the generalization, Kenneth had skimmed his dictionary, locating long lists of exceptions to the generalization. In fact, he often located more exceptions than I could list applications. When I protested—somewhat weakly —that the dictionary contained many unusual words, Kenneth continued his role as an educational scientist. He turned to the basic reader word list in the back of his text and produced nearly similar results. Today, of course, Kenneth's behavior would be rated as "gifted," "talented," or "creative"—although I remember discussing him in other terms as I sat in the teachers' lounge.

As Kenneth had provided a memorable and even a "rich" learning experience for me, he furnished the impetus for a series of studies which will attempt to answer three ques-

*This paper is an extension of a report given at a joint meeting of the International Reading Association and the National Conference of Research in English, May 1961. Thomas Barrett, Harriette Anderson, Joan Hanson, and David Palmer provided invaluable assistance in various phases of the study.

*The Reading Teacher, 16 (January 1963), 252-258.

tions: (1) What phonic generalizations are being taught in basic reading programs for the primary grades? (2) To what extent are these generalizations useful in having a "reasonable" degree of application to words commonly met in primary grade material? (3) Which of the generalizations that stand the test of question 2 can be learned and successfully applied to unknown words by primary children?

What Generalizations Are Taught?

Four widely used sets of readers were selected to determine the phonic generalizations being taught in the primary grades. After a preliminary study of the manuals, workbooks, and readers, the manuals were selected as the source of the generalizations. The manuals presented the generalizations in three ways: (1) statements to be taught to the pupils, (2) statements to be derived by the pupils after inductive teaching, and (3) statements with no clear indication as to what was to be done. Generalizations presented by all three means were included in the analysis.

Five general types of generalizations emerged from the study of the teachers manuals. These types dealt with (1) vowels, (2) consonants, (3) endings, (4) syllabication, and (5) miscellaneous relationships. Arbitrary decisions were made in assigning some generalizations to one or another of the five types since certain statements might easily be classified under two or more headings.

If we eliminate from our consider-

ation the miscellaneous type of generalization, a total of 121 different statements were located. There were 50 vowel generalizations, 15 consonant generalizations, and 28 generalizations in each of the ending and syllabication groups. In evaluating these figures it should be kept in mind that any statement was considered a separate generalization when its phrasing excluded or included different sets of words than another statement. For example, the generalization, "When there are two vowels side by side, the long sound of the first is heard and the second one is usually silent" and "When *ea* come together in a word, the first letter is long and the second is silent" were counted as two separate generalizations, although the second statement is a special application of the first.

While not directly related to our discussion here, note should be made of the wide variation of grade level of introduction, emphasis, and phrasing of the generalizations. Of the 50 different vowel generalizations, only 11 were common to all four series. None of these 11 was presented initially at the same half-year grade level in all four series. Some series gave a much greater emphasis to the generalizations than did other series. One publisher introduced only 33 of the 121 generalizations, while another presented 68. These comments are not meant to detract from the usefulness of basic materials, but simply to point out some of their differences. These differences do call for careful adjustments in the classroom when pupils are moved from one set of materials to another. The teacher who changes from series X to series Y may need to make some important revisions in his word recognition program. These findings may indicate also the need for further experimentation on emphasis and the developmental aspects of our word recognition program.

Which Generalizations Are Useful?

Forty-five of the generalizations given in the manuals were selected for further study. The selection of these was somewhat arbitrary. The main criterion was to ask, "Is the generalization stated specifically enough so that it can be said to aid or hinder in the pronunciation of a particular word?" An example or two will make our criterion clear. The generalization, "Long *o* makes a sound like its name," is undoubtedly a valuable generalization, but it was not specific enough to meet our criterion. On the other hand, the statement, "When a vowel is in the middle of a one syllable word, the vowel is short," was included because we could judge by reference to a word list how often one syllable words with a vowel in the middle do in fact have a short vowel sound.

Our next problem was to develop a word list on which we could test the generalizations. A reasonable approach seemed to be that of making up a composite list of all the words introduced in the four basic series from which the generalizations were drawn, plus the words from the Gates Reading Vocabulary for the Primary Grades. Once this list of some twenty-six hundred words was prepared, the following steps were taken:

1. The phonetic respelling and the syllabic division of all words were recorded. Webster's *New Collegiate Dictionary* was used as the authority for this information.

2. Each phonic generalization was checked against the words in the composite list to determine (a) the words which were pronounced as the generalization claimed and (b) the words which were exceptions to the generalization.

3. A "per cent of utility" was computed for each generalization by dividing the number of words pronounced as the generalization claimed by the total number of words to which the generalization could be expected to apply. For example, if the generalization claimed that "When the letters *oa* are together in a word, *o* always gives its long sound and the *a* is silent," all words containing *oa* were located in the list. The number of these words was the total number of words to which the generalization should apply. Then the phonetic spellings of these words were examined to see how many words containing *oa* actually did have the long *o* followed by the silent *a*. In this case thirty words were located which contained *oa*. Twenty-nine of these were pronounced as the generalization claimed; one was not. The per cent of utility became 29/30 or 97. This procedure was followed for all generalizations.

When the per cent of utility was computed for each generalization, we set two criteria as to what constituted a "reasonable" degree of application. We have no scientific evidence to demonstrate that these criteria are valid; it can only be said that they seem reasonable to us.

The first criterion was that the composite word list must contain a minimum of twenty words to which the generalization might apply. Generalizations with lower frequencies of application do not seem to merit instructional time.

The second criterion was a per cent of utility of at least 75. To state the matter another way, if the pupil applied the generalization to twenty words, it should aid him in getting the correct pronunciation in fifteen of the twenty words.

The table gives the results of our analysis of the forty-five phonic generalizations. An inspection of the data leaves me somewhat confused as to the value of generalizations. Some time-honored customs in the teaching of reading may be in need of revision.

Certain generalizations apply to large numbers of words and are rather constant in providing the correct pronunciation of words. (See, for example, generalizations 19, 35, and 36.)

A group of generalizations seem to be useful only after the pupil can pronounce the word. Generalizations which specify vowel pronunciation in stressed syllables require that the pupil know the pronunciation of the word before he can apply the generalization. (See, for example, general-

ization 33.) This criticism assumes, of course, that the purpose of a generalization is to help the child unlock the pronunciation of *unknown* words.

The usefulness of certain generalizations depends upon regional pronunciations. While following Webster's markings, generalization 34 is rejected. Midwestern pronunciation makes this generalization rather useful, although we reject it because we used Webster as the authority. Such problems are natural, and we should not hold it against Mr. Webster that he came from New England.

If we adhere to the criteria set up at the beginning of the study, of the forty-five generalizations only eighteen, numbers 5, 8, 10, 16, 20, 21, 22, 23, 25, 28, 29, 30, 31, 32, 40, 41, 44, and 45 are useful. Some of the generalizations which failed to meet our criteria might be useful if stated in different terms or if restricted to certain types of words. We are studying these problems at the present time. We are also examining other generalizations which we did not test in this study.

Conclusion

In evaluating this initial venture in testing the utility of phonic generalizations, it seems quite clear that many generalizations which are commonly taught are of limited value. Certainly the study indicates that we should give careful attention to pointing out the many exceptions to most of the generalizations that we teach. Current "extrinsic" phonics programs which present large numbers

The Utility of Forty-Five Phonic Generalizations

*Generalization	No. of Words Conforming	No. of Exceptions	Per Cent of Utility
1. When there are two vowels side by side, the long sound of the first one is heard and the second is usually silent.	309 (bead) †	377 (chief) †	45
2. When a vowel is in the middle of a one-syllable word, the vowel is short.	408	249	62
middle letter	191 (dress)	84 (scold)	69
one of the middle two letters in a word of four letters	191 (rest)	135 (told)	59
one vowel *within* a word of more than four letters	26 (splash)	30 (fight)	46
3. If the only vowel letter is at the end of a word, the letter usually stands for a long sound.	23 (he)	8 (to)	74
4. When there are two vowels, one of which is final *e*, the first vowel is long and the *e* is silent.	180 (bone)	108 (done)	63
*5. The *r* gives the preceding vowel a sound that is neither long nor short.	484 (horn)	134 (wire)	78
6. The first vowel is usually long and the second silent in the digraphs *ai, ea, oa,* and *ui*.	179	92	66
ai	43 (nail)	24 (said)	64
ea	101 (bead)	51 (head)	66
oa	34 (boat)	1 (cupboard)	97
ui	1 (suit)	16 (build)	6
7. In the phonogram *ie*, the *i* is silent and the *e* has a long sound.	8 (field)	39 (friend)	17
*8. Words having double *e* usually have the long *e* sound.	85 (seem)	2 (been)	98
9. When words end with silent *e*, the preceding *a* or *i* is long.	164 (cake)	108 (have)	60
*10. In *ay* the *y* is silent and gives *a* its long sound.	36 (play)	10 (always)	78
11. When the letter *i* is followed by the letters *gh,* the *i* usually stands for its long sound and the *gh* is silent.	22 (high)	9 (neighbor)	71
12. When *a* follows *w* in a word, it usually has the sound *a* as in *was*.	15 (watch)	32 (swam)	32
13. When *e* is followed by *w*, the vowel sound is the same as represented by *oo*.	9 (blew)	17 (sew)	35
14. The two letters *ow* make the long *o* sound.	50 (own)	35 (down)	59
15. *W* is sometimes a vowel and follows the vowel digraph rule.	50 (crow)	75 (threw)	40
*16. When *y* is the final letter in a word, it usually has a vowel sound.	169 (dry)	32 (tray)	84
17. When *y* is used as a vowel in words, it sometimes has the sound of long *i*.	29 (fly)	170 (funny)	15
18. The letter *a* has the same sound (ô) when followed by *l, w,* and *u*.	61 (all)	65 (canal)	48

†Words in parentheses are examples — either of words which conform or of exceptions, depending on the column.

*Generalizations marked with an asterisk were found "useful" according to the criteria.

*Generalization	No. of Words Conforming	No. of Exceptions	Per Cent of Utility
19. When *a* is followed by *r* and final *e*, we expect to hear the sound heard in *care*.	9 (dare)	1 (are)	90
*20. When *c* and *h* are next to each other, they make only one sound.	103 (peach)	0	100
*21. *Ch* is usually pronounced as it is in *kitchen, catch,* and *chair*, not like *sh*.	99 (catch)	5 (machine)	95
*22. When *c* is followed by *e* or *i*, the sound of *s* is likely to be heard.	66 (cent)	3 (ocean)	96
*23. When the letter *c* is followed by *o* or *a* the sound of *k* is likely to be heard.	143 (camp)	0	100
24. The letter *g* often has a sound similar to that of *j* in *jump* when it precedes the letter *i* or *e*.	49 (engine)	28 (give)	64
*25. When *ght* is seen in a word, *gh* is silent.	30 (fight)	0	100
26. When a word begins *kn*, the *k* is silent.	10 (knife)	0	100
27. When a word begins with *wr*, the *w* is silent.	8 (write)	0	100
*28. When two of the same consonants are side by side only one is heard.	334 (carry)	3 (suggest)	99
*29. When a word ends in *ck*, it has the same last sound as in *look*.	46 (brick)	0	100
*30. In most two-syllable words, the first syllable is accented.	828 (famous)	143 (polite)	85
*31. If *a, in, re, ex, de*, or *be* is the first syllable in a word, it is usually unaccented.	86 (belong)	13 (insect)	87
*32. In most two-syllable words that end in a consonant followed by *y*, the first syllable is accented and the last is unaccented.	101 (baby)	4 (supply)	96
33. One vowel letter in an accented syllable has its short sound.	547 (city)	356 (lady)	61
34. When *y* or *ey* is seen in the last syllable that is not accented, the long sound of *e* is heard.	0	157 (baby)	0
35. When *ture* is the final syllable in a word, it is unaccented.	4 (picture)	0	100
36. When *tion* is the final syllable in a word, it is unaccented.	5 (station)	0	100
37. In many two- and three-syllable words, the final *e* lengthens the vowel in the last syllable.	52 (invite)	62 (gasoline)	46
38. If the first vowel sound in a word is followed by two consonants, the first syllable usually ends with the first of the two consonants.	404 (bullet)	159 (singer)	72
39. If the first vowel sound in a word is followed by a single consonant, that consonant usually begins the second syllable.	190 (over)	237 (oven)	44

†Words in parentheses are examples — either of words which conform or of exceptions, depending on the column.

*Generalizations marked with an asterisk were found "useful" according to the criteria.

*Generalization	No. of Words Conforming	No. of Exceptions	Per Cent of Utility
*40. If the last syllable of a word ends in *le,* the consonant preceding the *le* usually begins the last syllable.	62 (tumble)	2 (buckle)	97
*41. When the first vowel element in a word is followed by *th, ch,* or *sh,* these symbols are not broken when the word is divided into syllables and may go with either the first or second syllable.	30 (dishes)	0	100
42. In a word of more than one syllable, the letter *v* usually goes with the preceding vowel to form a syllable.	53 (cover)	20 (clover)	73
43. When a word has only one vowel letter, the vowel sound is likely to be short.	433 (hid)	322 (kind)	57
*44. When there is one *e* in a word that ends in a consonant, the *e* usually has a short sound.	85 (leg)	27 (blew)	76
*45. When the last syllable is the sound *r,* it is unaccented.	188 (butter)	9 (appear)	95

†Words in parentheses are examples — either of words which conform or of exceptions, depending on the column.

*Generalizations marked with an asterisk were found "useful" according to the criteria.

of generalizations are open to question on the basis of this study.

This study does not, of course, answer the question of which generalizations primary children can apply in working out the pronunciation of unknown words. The answer to the question of the primary child's ability to apply these and other generalizations will come only through classroom experimentation. Also, this study does not establish the per cent of utility required for a generalization to be useful. The percentage suggested here (75) may be too high. Classroom research might reveal that generalizations with lower percent-

ages of utility should be taught because they encourage children to examine words for sound and letter relationships.

The most disturbing fact to come from the study may be the rather dismal failure of generalization 1 to provide the correct pronunciation even 50 per cent of the time. As one teacher remarked when this study was presented to a reading methods class, "Mr. Clymer, for years I've been teaching 'When two vowels go walking, the first one does the talking.' You're ruining the romance in the teaching of reading!"

The Utility of Phonic Generalizations in Grades One through Six

MILDRED HART BAILEY*

PHONIC GENERALIZATIONS have long constituted a significant part of instruction in phonics. Many authors of textbooks in the teaching of reading recommend phonic generalizations as an important facet of the reading program, and basal reading series include phonic generalizations in the program of instruction. Despite such wide acceptance, little research on the utility of phonic generalizations had been reported until Theodore Clymer, in the January 1963 issue of *The Reading Teacher*,* reported the results of an investigation of the utility of forty-five phonic generalizations in the primary grades.

Clymer examined basal reading materials for the primary grades and selected the teachers' manuals of four basal series as the source of phonic generalizations to be investigated. Forty - five generalizations recommended in the manuals were identified for study. A list of some twenty-six hundred words was then assembled by Clymer through inclusion of all words introduced in the primary-level reading textbooks of the four previously identified basic reading series, plus the words from the Gates Reading Vocabulary for the Primary Grades. Webster's *New Collegiate Dictionary* was used as the authority in recording the phonetic respelling and syllabic division of the words. Clymer then checked the forty-five phonic generalizations against the composite word list to identify all words that conformed or were exceptions to each of the generalizations. A percentage of utility was computed for each generalization, and criteria were formulated by Clymer to determine a " 'reasonable' degree of application" for the generalizations. Only eighteen of the forty-five phonic generalizations met the criteria as set forth in the Clymer study.

The results of the above-described investigation proved disturbing to many people concerned with reading instruction. One question frequently posed was, "Would the results differ greatly if the forty-five phonic generalizations were applied to a vocabulary list for grades one through six, rather than just the primary grades?" In the belief that the answer to this question might possibly contribute toward an improved program of instruction in phonics, the following investigation was undertaken by the present writer. The purpose of the study was to investigate the utility of phonic generalizations in reading instruction through application of recommended generalizations to a list of words represen-

*Theodore Clymer, "The Utility of Phonic Generalizations in the Primary Grades," *Reading Teacher*, 16 (Jan. 1963), 252-258.

*The Reading Teacher, 20 (February 1967), 413-418.

tative of words encountered in reading in grades one through six.

Procedure

Forty-five phonic generalizations, previously identified by Theodore Clymer in the above-described investigation, were selected for study. A list of words was collected from the entire vocabularies of all textbooks, grades one through six, of the following eight basal reading series:

Emmett A. Betts and Carolyn M. Welch, The Betts Basic Readers (New York: American Book Company, 1963).

Guy L. Bond and others, The Developmental Reading Series (Chicago: Lyons and Carnahan, 1962).

William S. Gray and others, The New Basic Readers (Chicago: Scott, Foresman, 1962).

Paul McKee and others, The Reading for Meaning Series (Boston: Houghton-Mifflin, 1963).

Mabel O'Donnel, The Alice and Jerry Basic Reading Program (Evanston, Illinois: Harper and Row, 1963).

David H. Russell and others, The Ginn Basic Reading Program (Boston: Ginn and Company, 1961).

William D. Sheldon and others, The Sheldon Basic Reading Series (Boston: Allyn and Bacon, 1963).

Russell G. Stauffer and others, The Winston Basic Readers (New York: Holt, Rinehart and Winston, 1960).

Certain limitations regarding inclusion of words were observed. For example, only words that appeared in two or more of the eight series were included, and place names, proper names, and foreign words were excluded. A composite list of 5,773 words resulted.

Computers were utilized for the identification of all words in the composite word list to which each of the forty-five phonic generalizations applied. Conformations and exceptions to each generalization were de-termined according to the 1961 edition of Webster's *New Collegiate Dictionary*, and percentage of utility was computed by dividing the total number of conformations identified by the total number of incidents investigated for each generalization. A summary of the findings pertaining to the utility of the forty-five phonic generalizations is presented in the table.

Conclusions

A review of the literature failed to reveal either scientifically-evolved or widely-accepted criteria for judging the results of this study. Nevertheless, the following conclusions were drawn upon the basis of the evidence gained in the investigation:

1. Inclusion in the reading program of generalizations 1, 7, 12, 13, 15, 17, 18, and 34, all found to possess low percentage of utility, should be thoughtfully reconsidered by all persons concerned with reading instruction.

2. Since certain generalizations were found difficult to interpret and to apply, it is believed by the writer that children in the elementary grades would experience the same uncertainty. For this reason, generalizations 13, 16, 30, and 45 should be attended with caution.

3. Only generalizations 20, 22, 23, 28, 32, and 40 were found to be simple to understand and apply, to be applicable to large numbers of words, and to have few exceptions.

Recommendations

The findings of this study empha-

THE UTILITY OF PHONIC GENERALIZATIONS IN GRADES ONE THROUGH SIX

*Generalization	No. of Incidents	No. of Words Conforming	No. of Exceptions	Percent. of Utility
1. When there are two vowels side by side, the long sound of the first vowel is heard, and the second vowel is usually silent.	1732	586 (leader) †	1146 (breath)	34
2. When a vowel is in the middle of a one-syllable word, the vowel is short.	1021	730	291	71
Middle letter	430	335 (flank)	95 (her)	78
One of the middle two letters in a word of four letters	478	325 (glen)	153 (long)	68
One vowel within a word of more than four letters	113	70 (depth)	43 (knight)	62
3. If the only vowel letter is at the end of a word, the letter usually stands for a long sound.	38	29 (go)	9 (do)	76
4. When there are two vowels, one of which is final e, the first vowel is long and the e is silent.	578	330 (cradle)	248 (judge)	57
5. The r gives the preceding vowel a sound that is neither long nor short.	1604	1378 (depart)	226 (merit)	86
6. The first vowel is usually long and the second silent in the digraphs ai, ea, oa, and ui.	497	298	199	60
ai	121	87 (acclaim)	34 (plaid)	72
ea	259	143 (bean)	116 (create)	55
oa	66	63 (roam)	3 (broad)	95
ui	51	5 (pursuit)	46 (biscuit)	10
7. In the phonogram ie, the i is silent, and the e has a long sound.	88	27 (grieve)	61 (brier)	31
8. Words having double e usually have the long e sound.	171	148 (exceed)	23 (deer)	87
9. When words end with silent e, the preceding a or i is long.	674	340 (amaze)	334 (give)	50
10. In ay, the y is silent and gives a its long sound.	50	44 (spray)	6 (prayer)	88
11. When the letter i is followed by the letters gh, the i usually stands for its long sound, and the gh is silent.	35	25 (flight)	10 (weight)	71
12. When a follows w in a word, it usually has the sound a as in was.	78	17 (wand)	61 (sway)	22
13. When e is followed by w, the vowel sound is the same as represented by oo.	35	14 (shrewd)	21 (stew)	40
14. The two letters ow make the long o sound.	111	61 (flow)	50 (scowl)	55
15. W is sometimes a vowel and follows the vowel digraph rule.	180	60 (arrow)	120 (drew)	33

*See Conclusions for a discussion of the usefulness of these generalizations.

†Words in parentheses are examples, either of words following the rule or of exceptions, depending on the column.

UTILITY OF PHONIC GENERALIZATIONS, GRADES ONE THROUGH SIX — *Continued*

Generalization	No. of Incidents	No. of Words Conforming	No. of Exceptions	Percent. of Utility
16. When *y* is the final letter in a word, it usually has a vowel sound.	518	462 (lady)	56 (key)	89
17. When *y* is used as a vowel in words, it sometimes has the sound of long *i*.	596	63 (ally)	533 (silly)	11
18. The letter *a* has the same sound (ô) when followed by *l*, *w*, and *u*.	346	119 (raw)	227 (laugh)	34
19. When *a* is followed by *r* and final *e*, we expect to hear the sound heard in *care*.	24	23 (flare)	1 (are)	96
20. When *c* and *h* are next to each other, they make only one sound.	225	225 (charge)	0	100
21. *Ch* is usually pronounced as it is in *kitchen, catch*, and *chair*, not like *sh*.	225	196 (pitch)	29 (chute)	87
22. When *c* is followed by *e* or *i*, the sound of *s* is likely to be heard.	284	260 (glance)	24 (ancient)	92
23. When the letter *c* is followed by *o* or *a*, the sound of *k* is likely to be heard.	428	428 (canal)	0	100
24. The letter *g* often has a sound similar to that of *j* in *jump* when it precedes the letter *i* or *e*.	216	168 (genius)	48 (eager)	78
25. When *ght* is seen in a word, *gh* is silent.	40	40 (tight)	0	100
26. When a word begins *kn*, the *k* is silent.	17	17 (knit)	0	100
27. When a word begins with *wr*, the *w* is silent.	17	17 (wrap)	0	100
28. When two of the same consonants are side by side, only one is heard.	826	809 (dollar)	17 (accept)	98
29. When a word ends in *ck*, it has the same last sound as in *look*.	80	80 (neck)	0	100
30. In most two-syllable words, the first syllable is accented.	2345	1906 (bottom)	439 (attire)	81
31. If *a, in, re, ex, de*, or *be* is the first syllable in a word, it is usually unaccented.	398	336 (reply)	62 (extra)	84
32. In most two-syllable words that end in a consonant followed by *y*, the first syllable is accented and the last is unaccented.	195	190 (pony)	5 (apply)	97
33. One vowel letter in an accented syllable has its short sound.	3031	1960 (banish)	1071 (fortune)	65

UTILITY OF PHONIC GENERALIZATIONS, GRADES ONE THROUGH SIX — *Continued*

Generalization	No. of Incidents	No. of Words Conforming	No. of Exceptions	Percent. of Utility
34. When *y* or *ey* is seen in the last syllable that is not accented, the long sound of *e* is heard.	449	0	449 (ferry)	0
35. When *ture* is the final syllable in a word, it is unaccented.	22	21 (future)	1 (mature)	95
36. When *tion* is the final syllable in a word, it is unaccented.	102	102 (notion)	0	100
37. In many two- and three-syllable words, the final *e* lengthens the vowel in the last syllable.	430	198 (costume)	232 (welcome)	46
38. If the first vowel sound in a word is followed by two consonants, the first syllable usually ends with the first of the two consonants.	1689	1311 (dinner)	378 (maple)	78
39. If the first vowel sound in a word is followed by a single consonant, that consonant usually begins the second syllable.	1283	638 (china)	645 (shadow)	50
40. If the last syllable of a word ends in *le*, the consonant preceding the *le* usually begins the last syllable.	211	196 (gable)	15 (crackle)	93
41. When the first vowel element in a word is followed by *th, ch,* or *sh*, these symbols are not broken when the word is divided into syllables and may go with either the first or second syllable.	74	74 (fashion)	0	100
42. In a word of more than one syllable, the letter *v* usually goes with the preceding vowel to form a syllable.	184	119 (river)	65 (navy)	65
43. When a word has only one vowel letter, the vowel sound is likely to be short.	1105	759 (crib)	346 (fall)	69
44. When there is one *e* in a word that ends in a consonant, the *e* usually has a short sound.	149	137 (held)	12 (clerk)	92
45. When the last syllable is the sound *r*, it is unaccented.	761	601 (ever)	160 (prefer)	79

size the need for the supplementation of future research to establish the value of phonic generalizations in reading in the elementary grades:

1. Research designed to establish scientifically - evolved criteria for judging the usefulness of phonic generalizations should be undertaken.

2. The ability of elementary school children to apply phonic generalizations in reading has not been considered in this or any previous investigation known to this writer. Future research, conducted through classroom experimentation, should contribute toward a better under-

standing of the usefulness of phonic generalizations to children.

3. In the present study, phonic generalizations were applied only to words collected from basal reading series. It is recommended that future research relative to the utility of phonic generalizations include vocabulary derived from the various subject-matter areas in the elementary school—such as science, social studies, and arithmetic. Vocabulary collected from children's trade books, magazines, and newspapers should also be included.

4. The necessity of utilizing the 1961 edition of Webster's *New Collegiate Dictionary,* rather than the more recent 1963 edition, is of significance to the present study. The schwa symbol, utilized in pronunciations of words in the 1963 edition of that dictionary, is incompatible with many phonic generalizations that are concerned with vowel sounds. Because the schwa symbol is also being employed in several widely-used children's dictionaries today, it is recommended that investigations be conducted to ascertain the possibilities of evolving new phonic generalizations that would utilize the schwa sound and symbol as presented by those dictionaries.

5. Regional pronunciations of words were not considered in the present study. Resulting utility of certain generalizations would have been considerably different had the pronunciation of words been considered upon the basis of pronunciations commonly used, for example in the Southern or Midwestern states. Therefore, it is recommended that future research be designed to consider the effect of regional pronunciations upon the usefulness of phonic generalizations.

Finally, this study does not conclusively establish the utility of phonic generalizations in reading for children in grades one through six. It is agreed with Burrows and Lourie[*] who, in reporting an investigation of the utility of the "when two vowels go walking" generalization, stated that "to know what not to teach when error is so apparent is one step forward, but only a short one."

(Mildred Hart Bailey is Associate Professor of Education and Director of the Reading Center at Northwestern State College of Louisiana at Natchitoches. This article reports the results of her doctoral dissertation completed in 1965 at the University of Mississippi.)

*Alvina Treut Burrows and Zyra Lourie, "When 'Two Vowels Go Walking,'" *Reading Teacher,* 17 (Nov. 1963), 79-82.

The Usefulness of Phonic Generalizations above the Primary Grades

Robert Emans*

MOST MODERN authorities of reading advocate the teaching of phonics in some form. The consensus is that children need visual and auditory clues in word recognition. Phonics is one of the helps in providing these clues. Nevertheless, the issue of phonics remains cloaked in an aura of controversy.

An article in *The Reading Teacher*, "The Utility of Phonics Generalizations in the Primary Grades," by Theodore Clymer (2), was received with interest by many people. In the article Clymer reported a study of the use of phonic generalizations in primary school reading. He concluded, "It seems quite clear that many generalizations which are commonly taught are of limited value."

Clymer analyzed 2600 words found in four widely used sets of primary grade readers. Such authorities as Dolch (3) believe that phonic generalizations are learned to help pupils recognize words independently, not only in the primary years, but in later years of schooling and throughout life. Many words in the primary years are learned by "sight" because authorities recognize that many of the common, basic words do not reflect phonic generalizations. Therefore, do the generalizations hold true for the words which the child later meets and for which the phonic generalizations may be more appropriately learned?

Procedures

The procedures of this study were the same as those used by Clymer in his study.* They included the selection of the vocabulary, the identification of the words which might apply to each generalization, and the testing of each word against the generalization.

In Clymer's study the sample included words found in four basal reading series. This study used a random sample of 10 per cent of the words (1,944 words) *beyond* the primary level (grade four) in *The Teacher's Word Book of 30,000 Words* by Thorndike and Lorge (4).

The spellings, phonetic respelling, and syllabic division of the words were recorded. As in Clymer's study, Webster's *New Collegiate Dictionary* (1) was used for this information. A list of the words which applied to each of the various generalizations was made. The phonetic generalizations were checked against the words to find which were pronounced as the generalizations claimed and which were exceptions. Those generalizations which met Clymer's criteria as to a reasonable degree of

*The present research was supported by the Cooperative Research Program of the Office of Education, U. S. Department of Health, Education, and Welfare.

application were recorded. Clymer's criteria were as follows:

1. The word list must contain a minimum of twenty words to which the generalization might apply.
2. The generalization must have a per cent of utility of at least 75.

This study went one step further than Clymer's study. Clymer made no differentiation between primary and secondary generalizations, although some generalizations are explanations for the exceptions to other generalizations. For example, Clymer's seventh generalization, "In the phonogram *ie*, the *i* is silent and the *e* has a long sound," is an exception to his first generalization, "When there are two vowels side by side, the long sound of the first one is heard and the second is usually silent." Since generalizations may be learned as aids, and not hard and fast rules, levels of generalizations may be established. If a high priority generalization fails to aid in the recognition of a word, a generalization which accounts for the exceptions may be attempted. Thus, the manner and the order in which generalizations are applied may be as important as the generalizations themselves. Therefore, the analysis was repeated, only this time both the primary generalization and the secondary generalization were applied to each of the words. In addition, other generalizations which appeared to be useful as the analysis proceeded were studied.

Results

Clymer found that eighteen of the forty-five generalizations met the established criteria; in this study sixteen met the criteria. (See Table 1.) There are important differences between the results of this study and the one Clymer conducted using primary grade words. Five generalizations (10, 21, 25, 29, and 44) were found by Clymer to be useful for words on the primary level, although in this study they were not found to be useful for words beyond the primary level. Generalization 21 had a utility of only 67 per cent in this study, as compared with 75 per cent in the previous study. In this study, generalizations 10, 15, 29, and 44 failed to meet the criterion, "The word list must contain a minimum of twenty words to which the generalization might apply." However, generalization 44 would have met the criterion if a proportionate number of words to the length of the word list had been used.

Three generalizations (24, 36, and 38) met the criteria on words *beyond* the primary level, although they failed to meet the criteria for words on the primary level. Generalization 24 had a percentage of utility in this study of 80, while in the previous study it had a percentage of only 64. Generalization 36 was found to apply to only five words in the study by Clymer but to 85 words in this study. Generalization 38 had a utility percentage of 80 in this study but only 72 in Clymer's study. Therefore, there was found to be a difference between the two studies in a total of seven, and perhaps eight, generalizations.

Some of the findings related to

TABLE 1

THE UTILITY OF PHONIC GENERALIZATIONS ON WORDS BEYOND THE PRIMARY LEVEL

Generalization	No. of Words Conforming	No. of Exceptions	Percent. of Utility
1. When there are two vowels side by side, the long sound of the first one is heard and the second one is usually silent.	87 (resourceful-ness) †	393 (devout)	18
2. When a vowel is in the middle of a one-syllable word, the vowel is short.	101	38	73
Middle letter.	44 (blink)	10 (hew)	81
One of the middle two letters in a word of four letters.	52 (grit)	21 (jolt)	71
One vowel *within* a word of more than four letters.	5 (strung)	7 (berth)	42
3. If the only vowel letter is at the end of a word, the letter usually stands for a long sound.	1 (thru)	2 (ma)	33
4. When there are two vowels, one of which is final *e*, the first vowel is long and the *e* is silent.	37 (baste)	22 (bronze)	63
*5. The *r* gives the preceding vowel a sound that is neither long nor short.	459 (certainly)	99 (insecure)	82
6. The first vowel is usually long and the second silent in the digraphs, *ai, ea, oa,* and *ui.*	54	39	58
ai	19 (container)	4 (moun-taineer)	83
ea	23 (leakage)	14 (deafness)	62
oa	12 (hoarsely)	2 (oasis)	86
ui	0	19 (builder)	0
7. In the phonogram *ie, i* is silent and the *e* has a long sound.	5 (siege)	17 (impatience)	23
*8. Words having double *e* usually have the long *e* sound.	24 (volunteer)	0	100
9. When words end with silent *e*, the preceding *a* or *i* is long.	96 (authorize)	102 (elective)	48
10. In *ay* the *y* is silent and gives *a* its long sound.	6 (rayon)	0	100
11. When the letter *i* is followed by the letters *gh*, the *i* usually stands for its long sound and the *gh* is silent.	3 (blight)	0	100
12. When *a* follows *w* in a word, it usually has the sound *a* as in *was.*	5 (swan)	13 (renewal)	28
13. When *e* is followed by *w*, the vowel sound is the same as represented by *oo.*	1 (shrew)	6 (stew)	14
14. The two letters of *ow* make the long *o* sound.	9 (minnow)	9 (trowel)	50
15. *W* is sometimes a vowel and follows the digraph rule.	11 (widower)	25 (renewal)	31
*16. When *y* is the final letter in a word, it usually has a vowel sound.	265 (currency)	5 (repay)	98
17. When *y* is used as a vowel, it sometimes has the sound of long *i.*	14 (personify)	312 (surgery)	4

*Generalizations marked with an asterisk were found useful according to the criteria.

†Words in parentheses are examples, either of words following the rule or of exceptions, depending on the column.

TABLE 1

UTILITY OF PHONIC GENERALIZATIONS ON WORDS BEYOND THE PRIMARY LEVEL — *Continued*

Generalization	No. of Words Conforming	No. of Exceptions	Percent. of Utility
18. The letter *a* has the same sound (ô) when followed by *l*, *w*, and *u*.	27 (awning)	86 (awakening)	24
19. When *a* is followed by *r* and final *e*, we expect to hear the sound heard in *care*.	2 (flare)	0	100
*20. When *c* and *h* are next to each other, they make only one sound.	53 (poacher)	0	100
21. *Ch* is usually pronounced as it is in *kitchen, catch,* and *chair,* not like *sh*.	35 (rancher)	17 (champagne)	67
*22. When *c* is followed by *e* or *i*, the sound of *s* is likely to be heard.	79 (excel)	9 (racial)	90
*23. When the letter *c* is followed by *o* or *a*, the sound of *k* is likely to be heard.	151 (sarcasm)	0	100
*24. The letter *g* often has a sound similar to that of *j* in *jump* when it precedes the letter *i* or *e*.	60 (drudgery)	15 (trigger)	80
25. When *ght* is seen in a word, *gh* is silent.	3 (blight)	0	100
26. When a word begins *kn,* the *k* is silent.	3 (knuckle)	0	100
27. When a word begins with *wr,* the *w* is silent.	4 (wreckage)	0	100
*28. When two of the same consonants are side by side only one is heard.	274 (alley)	26 (illegal)	91
29. When a word ends in *ck,* it has the same last sound as in *look*.	9 (barrack)	0	100
*30. In most two-syllable words, the first syllable is accented.	396 (haggard)	134 (annul)	75
*31. If *a, in, re, ex, de* or *be* is the first syllable in a word, it is usually unaccented.	179 (devout)	36 (intellect)	83
*32. In most two-syllable words that end in a consonant followed by *y*, the first syllable is accented and the last is unaccented.	57 (clumsy)	0	100
33. One vowel letter in an accented syllable has its short sound.	959 (possum)	531 (urban)	64
34. When *y* or *ey* is seen in the last syllable that is not accented, the long sound of *e* is heard.	3 (yanky)	266 (powdery)	1
35. When *ture* is the final syllable in a word, it is unaccented.	6 (fracture)	0	100
*36. When *tion* is the final syllable in a word, it is unaccented.	85 (estimation)	0	100
37. In many two- and three-syllable words, the final *e* lengthens the vowel in the last syllable.	95 (concentrate)	132 (elegance)	42
*38. If the first vowel sound in a word is followed by two consonants, the first syllable usually ends with the first of two consonants.	648 (pension)	163 (atheism)	80

*Generalizations marked with an asterisk were found useful according to the criteria.

UTILITY OF PHONIC GENERALIZATIONS ON WORDS BEYOND THE PRIMARY LEVEL — *Continued*

Generalization	No. of Words Conforming	No. of Exceptions	Percent. of Utility
39. If the first vowel sound in a word is followed by a single consonant, that consonant usually begins the second syllable.	313 (superb)	346 (tenor)	47
*40. If the last syllable of a word ends in *le,* the consonant preceding the *le* usually begins the last syllable.	53 (monocle)	15 (squabble)	78
*41. When the first vowel element in a word is followed by *th, ch,* or *sh,* these symbols are not broken when the word is divided into syllables and may go with either the first or second syllable.	44 (atheism)	0	100
42. In a word of more than one syllable, the letter *v* usually goes with the preceding vowel to form a syllable.	36 (avocado)	55 (elevator)	40
43. When a word has only one vowel letter, the vowel sound is likely to be short.	95 (grill)	41 (torch)	70
44. When there is one *e* in a word that ends in a consonant, the *e* usually has a short sound.	15 (clench)	3 (berth)	83
*45. When the last syllable is the sound *r,* it is unaccented.	165 (sinister)	7 (volunteer)	96

*Generalizations marked with an asterisk were found useful according to the criteria.

specific generalizations are of special interest. Clymer found, "When there are two vowels side by side, the long sound of the first one is heard and the second is usually silent" to have a utility of 49 per cent. This study found it to have 18 per cent. When the specific vowel combinations of generalizations 6, 7, and 8 are omitted, the percentage of utility dropped to 3. Therefore, the usefulness of this generalization must be questioned.

Generalization 5, dealing with *r* as a modifier of preceding vowel sounds, appears to be an important rule. The rule could be applied to more than one-fourth of the words in this study and had an 82 per cent utility. Clymer's results were similar.

However, this rule fails to indicate what the sound is likely to be, only what it is likely not to be. The generalization may best be applied in the modification of some of the other rules, inasmuch as it indicates possible exceptions to them.

Table 2 presents these and other modifications to the various original generalizations. Such modification would raise the percentage of utility and enable the generalization to meet the criteria established by Clymer.

Summary and Implications

Mr. Clymer found 18 generalizations meeting the criteria in his study of words within the primary level;

TABLE 2

MODIFICATIONS OF THE ORIGINAL FORTY-FIVE GENERALIZATIONS

Generalization	Percent. of Utility
1. The letters *io* usually represent a short *u* sound as in nation..............	86
2. The letters *oo* usually have the long double *o* sound as in *food* or the short double *o* sound as in *good*. They are more likely to have the double *o* sound as in *food*..	100
3. When a vowel is in the middle of a one-syllable word, the vowel is short except that it may be modified in words in which the vowel is followed by an *r*...	80
4. When the vowel is the middle letter of a one-syllable word, the vowel is short.	80
5. When the first vowel in a word is *a* and the second is *i*, the *a* is usually long and the *i* silent....................................	83
6. When the first vowel is *o* and the second is *a*, the *o* is usually long and the *a* is silent..	86
7. The vowel combination *ui* has a short *i* sound..........................	79
8. The two letters *ow* make the long *o* sound or the *ou* sound as in *out*......	100
9. When *y* is used as a vowel, it most often has the sound of long *e*..........	92
10. The letter *a* has the same sound (ô) when followed by *w* and *u*...........	84
11. One vowel letter in an accented syllable has its short sound if it comes before the end of the syllable and its long sound if it comes at the end of the syllable	78
12. One vowel letter in an accented syllable has its short sound if it comes before the end of the syllable and its long sound if it comes at the end of the syllable except when it is followed by an *r*..........................	92
13. When *y* or *ey* is seen in the last syllable that is not accented, the short sound of *i* is heard.....................................	97
14. A *-tion* at the end of a four-syllable word indicates a secondary accent on the first syllable with a primary accent on the syllable preceding the *-tion*......	95
15. Taking into account the original rules 5, 28, 29, 31, and 41, if the first vowel sound in a word is followed by two consonants, the first syllable usually ends with the first of the two consonants....................................	96
16. Except in some words with a prefix, if the first vowel sound in a word is followed by a single consonant, that consonant begins the second syllable and the vowel sound in the first syllable will be long, *or* if the consonant ends the first syllable the vowel sound will be short........................	84
17. A beginning syllable ending with a consonant and containing a short vowel sound is likely to be accented...	95
18. When a word has only one vowel letter, the vowel sound is likely to be short unless the vowel letter is followed by an *r*................................	78

this study found 16. Although 13 generalizations demonstrated their usefulness in both studies, four and possibly five of those which proved useful on the primary level failed in usefulness for words beyond the primary level; and conversely, three of those generalizations which were judged not useful at the primary level were judged useful for words beyond the primary level. Therefore, different generalizations may need to be learned at different levels of schooling.

This study has been limited to the 45 generalizations used by Clymer, although additional possible rules have been suggested. There may be other generalizations, including some particularly suitable for the intermediate grades, unstudied in this investigation, which would be more helpful than the ones included. Similarly, the generalizations might be reworded to correspond better with the immature understanding of children.

The percentage of utility used as a criterion may be too high. Possibly 50, 25, or an even lower percentage of utility would be better than no aid at all. A better criterion may be the total number of words in which a generalization functions, rather than the percentage of utility.

This investigation has left unstudied the problem of which generalizations should be taught. While some rules may be so complicated that children have difficulty in applying them, other rules may be so obvious that children learn them without explicit guidance. Future studies need to be conducted to develop procedures for teaching generalizations and to try the procedures under controlled experimental conditions.

Inasmuch as some generalizations are exceptions to others, children may profit from learning which generalizations should be tried first and which generalizations should be tried second if the first effort fails. Some of the generalizations may be applied best in conjunction with others, instead of in isolation. The selection of such generalizations, their wording, their placement into a systematic framework, and their study in empirical settings would make challenging and appropriate areas for further investigation.

References

1. Bethel, J. P., Ed. *Webster's New Collegiate Dictionary.* Springfield, Massachusetts: G. & C. Merriam Co., 1959.
2. Clymer, Theodore. "The Utility of Phonic Generalizations in the Primary Grades," *Reading Teacher,* 16 (Jan. 1963), 252-258.
3. Dolch, E. W. *Teaching Primary Reading.* Champaign, Illinois: Garrard Press, 1941.
4. Thorndike, E. L., and Lorge, I. *The Teacher's Word Book of 30,000 Words.* New York: Teachers College, 1944.

Usefulness of Phonic Generalizations

Lou E. Burmeister*

ALTHOUGH MOST EDUCATORS TODAY favor the teaching of phonic generalizations, very few of them are able to enumerate with any degree of certainty the generalizations which are worthy of being taught. Evidence is beginning to accrue which would make any interested observer question the value of many phonic generalizations which have appeared for years in the literature and teaching materials in the field of reading.

Purpose

The purpose of this paper is to report and compare findings of seven recent studies which were designed to investigate scientifically the value of many commonly found phonic, structural analysis, and accent generalizations and in some cases to inductively formulate new generalizations which may prove useful.

Studies used

The studies were reported by Oaks in 1952, Clymer in 1963, Fry in 1964, Bailey in 1965, Emans in 1966, Burmeister in 1966, and Winkley in 1966. All but Fry and Winkley utilized a "utility level" concept in determining the usefulness of generalizations. Fry used a "frequency approach," and Winkley selected useful generalizations "because of their applicability to multisyllabic words" (similar to the utility level concept) "*or* because of their demonstrated usefulness to children in the identification of unknown multisyllabic words" (1965).

Content of the studies

Variations in findings among the studies might be expected because of the following factors:
1. differences in the types of materials from which the sample words were taken
2. differences in the method of selecting the sample words from these materials when the materials are alike
3. differences in dictionaries, or phonemic systems, used as "authorities" for accepted pronunciation

*The Reading Teacher, 21 (January 1968), 349-356, 360.

4. differences in the author's definition of "short" and/or "long" vowel sounds (e.g., Is the unique sound of a vowel before an "r" considered in a separate category? Is a schwa sound considered to be a short vowel? etc.)
5. differences caused by various ways of determining usefulness.

So that the reader may better understand basic similarities and differences among the studies, the following brief explanation of each study is offered.

Oaks looked at "vowel and vowel combinations which appear in certain basal readers designed for use in the primary grades" (1952, p. 604). She used Webster's *New International Dictionary* (1936).

Fry's frequency count is based on his 300 "Instant Words" (1960) and on comparisons made with findings by Moore (1951), Cordts (1925), Black (1961), and Kottmeyer (1954). He looked at phonic rules which were formulated from his own experiences in a reading clinic situation. The phonemic system which he used "was taken from Moore, which was based on work by Bloomfield. However, the rules make several departures from their system, most notable of which is the Y rule which states that Y on the end of a word containing another vowel makes a long E sound as opposed to the short I sound as is contended by most dictionaries" (1964, p. 759).

Clymer (1963) reported the utility levels of forty-five phonic generalizations found in grades one to three in four basal series. He used the combined vocabularies of these three levels from the four series plus the words from the Gates Reading Vocabulary for the Primary Grades to determine the percent of utility of these generalizations. Webster's *New Collegiate Dictionary* was used.

Bailey's (1965) and Eman's (1966) studies were partial replications of Clymer's study. Both Bailey and Emans studied the same forty-five generalizations as Clymer. Bailey used as her source of words the entire vocabularies of all textbooks, grades one through six, of eight basal reading series: "only words that appeared in two or more of the eight series were included, and place names, proper names, and foreign words were excluded. A composite list of 5773 words resulted."

Emans (1966) focused on words beyond the primary level (grade 4). He took "a random sample of 10 per cent of the words (1,944 words) beyond the primary level in *The Teacher's Word Book of 30,000 Words* by Thorndike and Lorge." Such a sample would include a heavy loading of words which occur infrequently since there are, for example, almost twice as many (5200) words that occur only once per million running words (according to the Thorndike and Lorge source) than there are words (2780) which occur from twenty to forty-nine times per million running words. (A frequency of forty-nine per million running words is the beginning point for grade 4.0 according to Thorndike and Lorge [1944, p. x-xi]). In addition, Emans inductively formulated eighteen generalizations which he found to be useful. Both Bailey and Emans used Webster's *New Collegiate Dictionary* (1959).

Burmeister (1966), in an attempt to obtain an even spread of easy and difficult words, chose her sample words from *The Teachers' Word Book of 30,000 Words* by Thorndike and Lorge at fourteen different "frequency of occurrence" levels. She took a 5 per cent random sample at each of eleven levels for words which occur from six to over 100 times per million running words, and a somewhat smaller (percentage wise) sample at three levels for words which ranged in frequency from one to five occurrences per million running words. She looked at generalizations which are frequently found in materials at the fourth grade level and above and also at generalizations which she had formulated through her own teaching experience. She tripled the number of sample words for her analysis of adjacent (double and triple) vowels and inductively arrived at generalizations which describe the sounds of such vowels. She used *The American College Dictionary* (1961).

Winkley (1965) reported on the applicability of eighteen accent generalizations suggested by Gray (1960) as they apply to multisyllabic words. The findings of her original study lent support to the teaching of seven generalizations; however her second study, the one being examined herein, suggests that twelve of these generalizations are worth teaching. By combining and rewording these generalizations she reduced the twelve generalizations to seven.

Tabulation of findings

Each of the generalizations stated and examined by any one of the investigators was listed. For each, the results of each study which considered this generalization were tabulated. The percentage of utility was recorded from the data of the studies where such computations were made. From the others, the author's conclusion as to whether or not the generalization was useful was recorded. Two groups of generalizations were formed as a result of comparison of the findings: those generalizations which apparently are commonly included in instructional programs but, according to the studies, had limited utility value; and those which according to the results of the studies had reasonably broad application. Certain others, which seemed to be infrequently encountered in instructional programs and of little value in terms of application, were eliminated from consideration.

Conclusions and implications

Usefulness of generalizations

GENERALIZATIONS CONSIDERED OF LIMITED USEFULNESS. Certain generalizations appeared to be commonly taught but to have very limited usefulness according to the included studies. The following fell in this category:

> The vowel in an open syllable has a long sound.
> The letter "a" has the same sound (ô) when followed by "e," "w," and "u."
> When there are two vowels, one of which is a "final e," the vowel is long and the "e" is silent.
> In many two and three syllable words, the "final e" lengthens the vowel in the last syllable.
> When a word ends in "vowel-consonant-e," the vowel is long and the "e" is silent.
> When two vowels are together, the first is long and the second is silent.
> If the first vowel sound in a word is followed by a single consonant, that consonant usually begins the second syllable.
> When two sounds are separated by one consonant, divide before the consonant, but consider "ph," "ch," "sh," and "th" to be single consonants.

It is recommended that teachers be particularly cautious when instructing children in situations in which these generalizations might apply in two or more specific ways until oral recognition is achieved. For example, the following generalizations might be helpful:

> Single vowels are usually short, but a single vowel may have a long sound in an open syllable (approximately 30 percent of the time), especially in a one syllable word.
> If a word ends in "vowel-consonant-e" the vowel may be long or short. Try the long sound first.

GENERALIZATIONS OF HIGH UTILITY VALUE. Certain other generalizations appeared to be particularly useful. This in no way suggests that other statements (or generalizations) are not important. The author, for example, does not consider Fry's statement "Single consonants are quite consistent in making the same sound. They should be taught in the following order: t, n, r, m, d, s (sat), l, c (cat), p, s, f, v, g (got), h, w, k, j, z, y" to be unimportant. She recognizes the need for teaching single consonants but not necessarily in the order listed.

The generalizations listed here are the most inclusive of the group, or they are the ones with the highest utility level, or both. Thus "C followed by e, i, or y sounds soft; otherwise C is hard (omit ch)" was selected because it describes every situation in which a "C" might be found; the other generalizations are more limited.

ESPECIALLY USEFUL GENERALIZATIONS. The following generalizations are those from the studies which seemed most useful, except for the "final e" generalization and the phonic syllabication number 2 generalization. The latter two generalizations were formulated by the current author as a result of the findings of the utility level studies.

Consonant sounds
1. "C" followed by "e," "i," or "y" sounds soft; otherwise "c" is hard (omit "ch"). (certain, city, cycle; attic, cat, clip; success)
2. "G" followed by "e," "i," or "y" sounds soft; otherwise "g" is hard (omit "gh"). (gell, agile, gypsy; gone, flag, grope; suggest)
3. "Ch" is usually pronounced as it is in "kitchen," not like "sh" as in "machine."
4. When a word ends in "ck," it has the same last sound as in "look."
5. When "ght" is seen in a word, "gh" is silent. (thought, night, right)
6. When two of the same consonants are side-by-side, only one is heard. (dollar, paddle)

Vowel sounds—single vowels
1. If the only vowel letter is at the end of a word, the letter usually stands for a long sound (one syllable words only). (be, he, she, go)
2. When "consonant + y" are the final letters in a one

syllable word, the "y" has a "long i" sound; in a polysyllabic word the "y" has a "short i" (long e) sound. (my, by, cry; baby, dignity)

3. A single vowel in a closed syllable has a short sound, except that it may be modified in words in which the vowel is followed by an "r." (club, dress, at, car, pumpkin, virgin)

4. The "r" gives the preceding vowel a sound that is neither long nor short. (car, care, far, fair, fare) [single or double vowels]

Vowel sounds—final "vowel-consonant-e"

When a word ends in "vowel-consonant-e" the "e" is silent, and the vowel may be long or short. (cape, mile, contribute, accumulate, exile, line; have, prove, encourage, ultimate, armistice, come, intensive, futile, passage)

Vowel sounds—adjacent vowels

1. Digraphs: When the following double vowel combinations are seen together, the first is usually long and the second is silent: ai, ay, ea, ee, oa, ow (ea may also have a "short e" sound, and ow may have an "ou" sound) [main, pay; eat, bread; see, oat, sparrow, how]

2. Diphthongs (or blends): The following double vowel combinations usually blend: au, aw, ou, oi, oy, oo ("oo" has two common sounds). [auto, awful, house, coin, boy, book, rooster]

3. "io" and "ia": "io" and "ia" after "c," "t," or "s" help to make a consonant sound: vicious, partial, musician, vision, attention (even ocean).

Syllabication—determination of a syllable

Every single vowel or vowel combination means a syllable (except a "final e" in a "vowel-consonant-e" ending).

Syllabication—structural syllabication

These generalizations take precedence over phonic syllabication generalizations.

1. Divide between a prefix and a root.
2. Divide between two roots.
3. Usually divide between a root and a suffix.

Syllabication—phonic syllabication

1. When two vowel sounds are separated by two consonants, divide between the consonants but consider "ch," "sh," "ph," and "th" to be single consonants. (assist, convey, bunny, Houston, rustic)
2. When two vowel sounds are separated by one consonant, divide either before or after the consonant. Try dividing before the consonant first. (Consider "ch," "sh," "ph," and "th" to be single consonants). [alone, select, ashame, Japan, sober; comet, honest, ever, idiot, modest, agile, general]
3. When a word ends in a "consonant-l-e" divide before the consonant. (battle, treble, tangible, kindle).

Accent

1. In most two syllable words, the first syllable is accented.
   a. And, when there are two like consonant letters within a word the syllable before the double consonant is usually accented (beginner, letter)
   b. But, two vowel letters together in the last syllable of a word may be a clue to an accented final syllable (complain, conceal).
2. In inflected or derived forms of words, the primary accent usually falls on or within the root word (boxes, untie) [Therefore, if "a," "in," "re," "ex," "de," or "be" is the first syllable in a word, it is usually unaccented.]

Implications for further research

VOWEL PHONEME-GRAPHEME RELATIONSHIPS. It seems important when thinking of vowel sounds to differentiate between single vowels and double vowels. When two vowels are together, they ordinarily compose a phoneme. To lose sight of this causes a lack of clarity and a lessening of utility level of a possibly good generalization.

For generalizations to be especially useful and clear the grapheme must be clearly defined. For example, some generalizations listed under VOWEL SOUNDS—"Single *or* double vowels" tend to be ambiguous. Vowels should always be looked at as *single vowels* or as *double vowels*. This can be clarified if we look at the following generalization: "When y is the final letter in a word, it usually has a vowel sound." Exceptions are, for example, words such as pl*ay*, tr*ay*, rep*ay*, k*ey*, th*ey*, words which end with two vowels which often form a digraph. Notice the 99 percent utility level, instead of the following more clearly stated generalization: "When 'consonant + y' are the final letters in a monosyllabic word, the 'y' has a 'long i' sound; in a polysyllabic word the 'y' has a 'short i' (long e) sound."

Another example might be cited. Generalization: "When the letter 'i' is followed by the letters 'gh' the 'i' usually stands for its long sound and the 'gh' is silent." Most of the common words which follow the generalization have a single vowel 'i': high, night, fight, flight, blight, etc. Words which do not follow the generalization are words with double vowels: neighbor, straight, weight, etc. The generalization would have a higher utility level if it were stated thus: When the single vowel 'i' is followed by the letters 'gh' the 'i' usually stands for its long sound and the 'gh' is silent."

SAMPLE MATERIAL.   Apparently the variation in the sources from which sample words were selected usually makes very little difference in the findings. This becomes obvious when one compares the findings of Clymer, Bailey, and Emans in particular. When the size of the sample is large, the "utility levels" of almost all generalizations are fairly standard. An exception might be that of the "g" generalization. Clymer's primary materials yielded a lower utility level for this generalization than the other studies. This can be explained by noting that words of Anglo-Saxon origin supply the exceptions to this generalization and Anglo-Saxon words are our most common words—words likely to be found often at the primary level (give, get, girl, tiger, finger, etc.). Another exception involves the vowel digraph generalization. The primary materials used in Clymer's study yield a higher utility level for this generalization than do any of the other materials.

The observation that level of difficulty of words in general makes little difference in the utility level for a generalization can also be affirmed by examining·the findings in Burmeister's study of the utility levels of each of the fourteen frequency of occurrence stratifications (Burmeister, 1966).

References

Bailey, Mildred Hart. An analytical study of the utility of selected phonic generalizations for children in grades one through six. Unpublished doctoral dissertation, University of Mississippi, 1965.

Black, Sister Mary Carla, B.V.M. Phonics rules verification by a thirteen hundred word count. Unpublished master's project, Loyola University of Los Angeles, 1961.

Bloomfield, L. Language. New York: H. Holt, 1955.

Burmeister, Lou E. An analysis of the inductive and deductive group approaches to teaching selected word analysis generalizations to disabled readers in eighth and ninth grade. Unpublished doctoral dissertation, University of Wisconsin, 1966.

Clymer, T. L. The utility of phonic generalizations in the primary grades. *The Reading Teacher*, 1963, *16*, 252-58.

Cordts, Anna D. Analysis and classification of the sounds of English words in the primary reading vocabulary. Unpublished dissertation, University of Iowa, 1925.

Dale, E., and Eichholz, G. *Children's knowledge of words*. Columbus, Ohio: Bureau of Educational Research and Service, 1960.

Emans, R. The usefulness of phonic generalizations above the primary grades. A paper given at the annual convention of the American Educational Research Association, Chicago, 1966.

Fry, E. A frequency approach to Phonics. *Elementary English*, 1964, *41*, 759-765+.

————. Teaching a basic reading vocabulary. *Elementary English*, 1960, *39*, 37-42.

Gray, W. S. *On their own in reading*. Chicago: Scott, Foresman, 1960.

Horn, E. The child's early experience with the letter "a." *The Journal of Educational Psychology*, 1929, *20*, 161-68.

Kottmeyer, W. A. Phonetic and structural generalizations for the teaching of a primary grade spelling vocabulary. Reported in Webster Publishing Company Reserve File No. 528-S and 529-S, St. Louis, Mo., 1954.

Moore, J. T. Phonetic elements appearing in a 3,000 word spelling vocabulary. Unpublished dissertation, Stanford University, 1951.

Thorndike, E. L., and Lorge, I. *The teacher's word book of 30,000 words*. New York: Bureau of Publications, Teachers College, Columbia University, 1944.

Vogel, Mabel, Jaycox, Emma, and Washburne, C. W. A basic list of phonics for grades I and II. *Elementary School Journal*, 1923, *23*, 436-443.

Winkley, Carol K. Utilization of accent generalizations in identifying unknown multisyllable words. Unpublished doctoral dissertation, University of Chicago, 1965.

————. Which accent generalizations are worth teaching? *The Reading Teacher*, 1966, *20*, 219-224+.

Utility of Vowel Digraph Generalizations in Grades One through Six

MILDRED HART BAILEY*

PHONIC GENERALIZATIONS have long played an important role in reading instruction in the elementary school. Numerous authors of textbooks in the teaching of reading recommend that phonic generalizations be included in the reading program, and most basal reading series include phonic generalizations in the instructional program. Of all the recommended phonic generalizations, possibly the generalization which is most widely known and most often taught is the vowel digraph generalization—the generalization commonly stated, "When two vowels are side by side, usually the long sound of the first vowel is heard and the second vowel is silent," or, in many first and second grade classrooms, "When two vowels go walking, the first one does the talking."

Despite such wide and time-honored acceptance, little research on the usefulness of the vowel digraph generalization had been reported prior to 1963, when two studies, by Clymer (5), and Burrows and Lourie (4), were published. Clymer reported the results of an investigation of the utility of forty-five selected phonic generalizations in the primary grades, one of which was the vowel digraph generalization, and concluded that many generalizations were found to possess limited value. Special attention was directed by Clymer to the vowel digraph generalization, which was found to possess only forty-five percent utility in that study. Burrows and Lourie (4) explored the reliability of only one phonic generalization, the vowel digraph rule, and found that only thirty-nine percent of the words investigated in that study followed the rule.

Recent studies on phonic generalizations by Bailey (2), Emans (6), and Burmeister (3) have also reported, without exception, failure of the vowel digraph generalization to be useful. Bailey reported findings of thirty-four percent utility, Emans, eighteen percent utility, and Burmeister categorized the generalization as one found to possess only limited usefulness.

Purposes. The purposes of the present study were to 1) investigate the overall utility of the vowel digraph generalization when applied to a list of words representative of words met by children in reading instruction in grades one through six, 2) determine the utility of all possible subgroups of adjacent vowels (*aa, ae, ai, ao, au, ea, ee,* etc.), and 3) explore the possibilities of evolving new vowel digraph generalizations that would apply to large numbers of words and possess high percentages of utility.

Procedure. The vowel digraph generalization, ordinarily stated, "When two vowels are side by side, usually the long sound of the first vowel is heard and the second vowel is silent," was applied to a word list collected in a previous study by Bailey (1). The original word list consisted of the entire vocabularies of eight basal reading series, grades one through six, published in the United States during or since 1960, and was pronounced, for purposes of the present investigation, representative of words met by children in reading in grades one through six.

Reading and Realism, IRA Proceedings, Vol. 13, Part 1, 1969, 654-658.

Table 1

Utility of the Original Vowel Digraph Generalization*

Number of Incidents Investigated	Number of Conformations	Number of Exceptions	Percentage of Utility
1506	490 (paint)**	1016 (been)*	33

* When two vowels are side by side, usually the long sound of the first vowel is heard and the second vowel is silent.
** Examples of words that conformed or were exceptions to the generalization.

Table 2

Utility of the Vowel Digraph Generalization When Applied to Twenty-five Adjacent Vowel Combinations

Adjacent-Vowel Combinations	Number of Incidents Investigated	Number of Conformations	Number of Exceptions	Percentage of Utility
aa	1	0	1 (bazaar)*	0
ae	1	0	1 (phaeton)	0
ai	118	84 (bait)*	34 (air)	71
ao	0	0	0	0
au	45	0	45 (caught)	0
ea	252	141 (peach)	111 (pear)	56
ee	166	145 (cheek)	21 (been)	87
ei	30	9 (ceiling)	21 (freight)	30
eo	13	1 (people)	12 (geography)	8
eu	4	0	4 (museum)	0
ia	45	0	45 (giant)	0
ie	86	6 (lie)	80 (friend)	7
ii	1	0	1 (taxiing)	0
io	178	0	178 (union)*	0
iu	7	0	7 (aquarium)	0
oa	66	63 (road)*	3 (cupboard)	95
oe	12	5 (toe)	7 (shoe)	42
oi	43	0	43 (boil)	0
oo	124	2 (door)	122 (cool)	2
ou	185	17 (four)	168 (fought)	9
ua	38	0	38 (equal)	0
ue	38	12 (continue)	26 (fuel)	32
ui	50	5 (nuisance)	45 (ruin)	10
uo	2	0	2 (buoy)	0
uu	1	0	1 (vacuum)	0
Totals 25	1506	490	1016	33

* Examples of words that conformed or were exceptions to the generalization.

The vowel letters *a, e, i, o,* and *u* only were investigated, and *Webster's New Collegiate Dictionary* (7) was used as the dictionary of authority for the pronunciation and syllabic division of all words considered in the study. In every instance, only the first-listed pronunciation was recorded.

Percentage of utility for the original vowel digraph generalization was computed by dividing the total number of incidents which conformed to the generalization by the total number of incidents investigated. Likewise, percentages of utility for the twenty-five subgroups of adjacent vowel combinations were computed in the same manner.

Results. When the original vowel digraph generalization was applied to the list of 1506 words containing adjacent vowel incidents, 490 words conformed to the generalization and 1016 words were exceptions, resulting in an overall utility of only thirty-three percent. Table 1 presents the results.

Data obtained from the analysis of each of the twenty-five subgroups of adjacent vowel combinations are presented in Table 2. Only four subgroups were found to have a percentage of utility above fifty percent: *ai, ea, ee,* and *oa.* Frequency of occurrence in

each of these four subgroups was considered sufficiently high to warrant further investigation.

In an attempt to determine the possibility of formulating new vowel digraph generalizations that would prove useful to children in grades one through six, two new generalizations were formulated and investigated. Examination of Table 3 reveals that a generalization stated, "When two vowels are side by side, usually only one vowel sound is heard," was found to possess a high utility of ninety-two percent. The second newly formulated vowel digraph generalization, "When *ai, ea, ee,* or *oa* is found in a word, usually only the long sound of the first vowel is heard," was applicable to 602 words. Four hundred and thirty-three words conformed to the generalization

Table 3

New Vowel Digraph Generalizations

New Generalizations	Number of Incidents Investigated	Number of Conformations	Number of Exceptions	Percentage of Utility
1. When two vowels are side by side, usually only one vowel sound is heard.	1506	1381 (juice)*	125 (idea)*	92
2. When *ai, ea, ee,* or *oa* is found in a word, usually only the long sound of the first vowel is heard.	602	433 (pail) (bead) (feel) (goat)	169 (pair) (steak) (been) (cupboard)	72

*Examples of words that conformed or were exceptions to the generalization.

and 169 words were exceptions, yielding a percentage of utility of seventy-two percent.

Although no attempts were made in the present study to investigate the possibilities of rewording, restricting, or formulating new generalizations relative to adjacent vowel combinations that yielded low percentages of utility, it should be noted that Table 1 reveals the following adjacent vowel sub-

groups, with low percentages of utility and high frequencies of occurrence, that presented definite and consistent patterns in regard to exceptions: *au, ia, io, oi, oo, ou,* and *ua.* Hopefully, children should learn to recognize *oi* and *ou* as diphthongs and, thus, eliminate any need for applying vowel digraph generalizations when *oi* and *ou* are met in word analysis. Likewise, *oo* was found to usually have its own distinctive sounds, as in *foot* and *cool;* *au* nearly always had the sound of circumflex *o* (ô), as in *caught; io* was usually found in the phonograms *tion* and *sion* and then was pronounced as short *u*, as in *vacation* and *permission;* and when *ia* and *ua* were found within words, usually both vowel sounds were heard separately, as in *giant* and *actual.* Furthermore, results of the present study reveal that the value of vowel digraph generalizations would be greatly enhanced if elementary school children also learn that vowel sounds are altered when followed by the letter *r*, as in *heard* and *fair*.

Conclusions

Children in grades one through six should gain help in word analysis if they understand that when two vowels are together in a word, only one vowel sound is usually recorded. The following generalization might well be the first developed by children regarding vowel digraphs, for it is basic and underlies other, more specific phonic generalizations: "When two vowels are side by side, usually only one vowel sound is heard."

Results of the present investigation indicate that the following, more specific phonic generalization should also prove useful to children in word analysis: "When *ai, ea, ee,* or *oa* is found in a word, usually only the long sound of the first vowel is heard."

The value of the newly formulated vowel digraph generalizations should be enhanced by affording children in the elementary grades the opportunities to learn that 1) *oi* and *ou* are diphthongs, 2) *oo* usually has its own distinctive sounds, 3) *au* nearly always has the same sound as *a* in *call* and *raw,* 4) *io* is usually found in the phonograms *tion* and *sion* and then is pronounced as short *u*, and 5) when *ia* and *ua* are found in words, usually both vowel sounds are heard separately. Children should be aided also in word analysis by the knowledge that the sounds of vowel digraphs are usually affected by the consonants that follow, notably *r* following a vowel digraph.

Finally, care should be taken to assist children in the development of flexibility in the use of all phonic generalizations.

REFERENCES

1. Bailey, Mildred Hart. "An Analytical Study of the Utility of Selected Phonic Generalizations for Children in Grades One Through Six," unpublished doctoral dissertation, 1965.
2. Bailey, Mildred Hart. "Utility of Phonic Generalizations in Grades One Through Six," *Reading Teacher,* 20 (February 1967), 413-418.
3. Burmeister, Lou E. "Usefulness of Phonic Generalizations," *Reading Teacher,* 21 (January 1968), 349-356, 360.
4. Burrows, Alvina Treut, and Zyra Lourie. "When 'Two Vowels Go Walking,'" *Reading Teacher,* 17 (November 1963), 79-82.
5. Clymer, Theodore. "Utility of Phonic Generalizations in the Primary Grades," *Reading Teacher,* 16 (January 1963), 252-358.
6. Emans, Robert. "Usefulness of Phonic Generalizations Above the Primary Grades, *Reading Teacher,* 20 (February 1967), 419-425.
7. *Webster's New Collegiate Dictionary.* Springfield, Massachusetts: G. and C. Merriam Company, 1961.

When Two Vowels Go Walking

ALVINA TRUET BURROWS and ZYRA LOURIE*

GEORGE BERNARD SHAW claimed that we needed at least eighteen vowels in order to write English phonetically. Among the vagaries of our language he pointed to "tough" and "cough," "sawed" and "sword," "sweat" and "sweet," "wheat" and "what." To eliminate this "reckless inconsistency" he suggested a new alphabet with twenty-four consonants and eighteen vowels (*12*). In England a thousand children are taking part in an experiment in learning to read with an augmented Roman alphabet based on rather consistent relationships between letters and sounds (*7*). Other attempts to simplify English spelling continue as they have for decades. But changes in language arrive slowly, and we must induct our exploding primary reading classes *now* using our conventional alphabet. Surely, teachers of reading must seek those generalizations which will be helpful; but, when we offer rigid "rules" to children for word recognition, are we really *helping?*

In the case of vowel rules, we have the added difficulty that scholars are still debating classification of vowels. For example, several linguists, among them Dr. Donald J. Lloyd of Wayne State University, state that English has three semivowels and nine vowels, as in the words *pit, pet, pat, just, putt, pot, put,* the first sound in *obey,* and the first in *audacious* (*6*).

With these and similar basic ques-tions about vowels still claiming attention, an investigation seems overdue into the specific reliability of such a widely taught rule as the "two vowels together" rule in primary reading.

In the early elementary grades, teachers often use a jingle to teach what is considered by many a basic phonic principle to help children "unlock" new words. Often the "rule" goes like this:

> When two vowels go out walking
> The first one does the talking.

Sometimes it goes like this:

> Big brother speaks;
> Little brother is silent.

A recent book presents these adjacent vowels as "polite" and "impolite" digraphs. The "polite" digraph consists of "two vowels together (holding hands), the first one speaking and saying its own name" (*3*). An impolite digraph, according to the same author, is "two vowels together (holding hands), the second one speaking and saying either its long or short name." The writer goes on to explain that a diphthong holds hands, too, but in this case the vowels both speak, making a "common sound." A child must then memorize the "rules" and proceed to apply them, one by one, to the new words met in his reading. Such complicated learning must surely be based on solid language facts! Perhaps!

The Reading Teacher, 17 (November 1963), 79-82.

Analysis of High Frequency Words

We decided to test the validity of the "two-vowels-together rule" by analyzing the five thousand words of highest frequency on the Rinsland list (9). We checked pronunciation of all words containing adjacent vowels in *Webster's New Collegiate Dictionary* (11). A total of 1,728 words were found to have two adjacent vowels, including *a, e, i, o, u, y,* and *w*. Of this number only 668 words followed the "big brother" rule. Furthermore, it should be noted that these 668 words include the words in which two vowels form diphthongs. Since the diphthong is usually not taught in the first grade, the beginning reader who is taught the "easy" rule sees only the "two vowels together." If he applies the rule he's been taught, he has less than a fifty-fifty chance of being right as the following data reveal.

When we examine some of the subgroupings of words with adjacent vowels, we see that the largest group consists of words containing the *ea* combination. In this group, 157 follow the "rule"; 111 do not. Among the latter are such common words as: *great, break, ocean, weather, steak, head, meadow, heart, heard,* and *heavy.*

Another large group of adjacent vowels is represented by the combination *ai.* The rule applies to 103, but does not hold for 36 words. The rule covers more examples than there are exceptions, obviously; but among these 36 exceptions are such common words as: *fountain, captain, certain,*

certainly, aisle, curtain, airplane, pair, dairy, chair, hair, fairy.

Of the 122 words with the *ie* combination, 29 follow the "big brother" rule; 81 do not. The other 12 words comprise a category in which each vowel is pronounced separately as in *diet.* Among the 29 words that illustrate the rule are such common ones as: *dies, flies, pie, replied, tries, tie, lies, cried.* But the exceptions to the first vowel domination are also common: *friend, field, fierce, piece, niece, candies, movie, puppies, mischief, stories, worried, ladies, soldier, ancient, armies, apiece, believe, relief.*

Even in words containing the double *ee,* where a consistent long vowel sound seems inescapable, the effect of a following *r* produces an important difference: *cheerful, engineer, pioneer, deer, cheer, steer.* The most obvious exception in the *ee* group is, of course, the word *been.*

Another group of words in which both vowels were sounded indicated that the first vowel had its long sound only occasionally. The *ia* combination in particular showed little consistency: *trial, diary, aviator, immediately, giant, colonial, piano, Indian.* In addition there are *museum, geography, rodeo.*

A study of words containing *y* revealed the difficulties to be met in formulating a rule for this "semivowel."

The "vowel" *w* proved no easier! Is *w* a silent vowel or a silent consonant in *towards, jewel, power, tower, answer, view, now, Halloween?*

It must also be noted that 49

Y AS A VOWEL (SILENT)		Y AS A CONSONANT (SOUNDED)
Follows the Rule	Follows No Rule	
		canyon
rye	coyote	beyond
dye	crayons	lawyer
dyeing	mayor	
bye		

words were counted with three vowels together. Among these are such high frequency words as: *beautiful, eye, view, curious, delicious.* Would "three brothers" now be helpful in word recognition?

There comes a time, hopefully, when the young reader quite readily identifies many diphthongs at sight. When these words are cast out of the list of five thousand, how much help is the two-vowel rule? Using Betts' definition of a diphthong, we included the following list: *oy, ow, oi, ou, ew* (*1*). There are 389 words containing diphthongs in the five thousand words of highest frequency in the Rinsland list. Omitting these words, we have a list of 1,399 words containing adjacent vowels.

SUMMARY OF VOWEL COMBINATIONS

IN FIVE THOUSAND WORDS OF HIGHEST FREQUENCY FROM RINSLAND'S LIST

Number of words containing two adjacent vowels, *a, e, i, o, u*	1,414
Number of words containing two adjacent vowels, *a, e, i, o, u, w, y*	1,728
Number of words containing three adjacent vowels	49
Number of words containing two adjacent vowels as diphthongs	389
Number of words containing two adjacent vowels not diphthongs	1,339
Number of words in which first long sound dominates	668
Number of exceptions to the long vowel "rule"	1,060

The Vocabulary of Beginning Readers

The stout defender of the two-vowel rule, however, will claim that the primary school pupil does not encounter five thousand words in his early reading. Perhaps the rule is consistent for those words met most often in primers and first readers? An analysis of the vocabulary of the beginning readers of five publishers, listed by Botel in 1955 (*2*) presented findings which are given in the tabular analysis below.

After studying the accounting given here, or any other analysis of the sounds of adjacent vowels, one might rightly ask, "When two vowels go out walking, what does either of them say?" If the vowels "say" anything at all to beginning readers, they make a baffling "speech." A considerably larger number of words refute the "rule" than obey it. This conclusion is essentially the same as that reached by Oaks in 1952 after analyzing a representative group of readers dated 1932-1939 to discover which "vowel situations" illustrate principles of pronunciation (*8*).

Recently Clymer (*4*) reported a study (not yet published when we collected our data) in which he speaks of the "rather dismal failure" of the adjacent vowel rule in providing correct pronunciation even 50 per cent of the time.

Our analysis of the Gates Primary Word List (*5*) revealed essentially the same facts as Sister Mary Christine's classification of the vowel sounds in the same list (*10*).

ANALYSIS OF VOWEL SOUNDS IN THE BEGINNING READERS

Reader	No. Words	No. Words Two Adjacent Vowels	First Vowel Long Sound (*blue, play*)	Other Single Vowel Sound (*you, said*)	Vowels Pronounced Separately (*lion*)
Preprimer	41	8	3	5	0
Primer	67	20	9	11	0
First	124	36	13	23	0
Second					
1st level	152	47	21	26	0
2nd level	207	64	17	46	1
Third					
1st level	283	85	38	44	3
2nd level	311	106	44	61	1
Total	1,185	366	145	216	5

Total words with three adjacent vowels (*a, e, i, o, u, y, w*) : 10
(*beautiful, flower, quiet, queer, eye, queen, toward, delicious, squeal, tower*)

Applications for Teaching

What recommendation for teaching can be made from the above data? To know what not to teach when error is so apparent is one step forward, but only a short one. What kind of generalization can one teach? Perhaps the only solution that can be tentatively applied is to help the beginning reader from time to time to note what vowel sound is used in the common words he meets. In reading *again* or *could*, in *said* or *guess* or *brought* or *ready*, he may gain his greatest help from context and from consonants. As he gains a larger and larger reading vocabulary, hearing that the vowel sounds vary may be the most substantial help that he can take to the analysis of new words.

References

1. Betts, Emmett A. *Foundations of Reading Instruction*. New York: American Book Company, 1954.
2. Botel, Morton. *How To Teach Reading*. Chicago: Follett, 1962. (List made in 1955.)
3. Caroline, Sister Mary. *Teachers Manual for Breaking the Sound Barrier: A Phonics Handbook*, p. 42. New York: Macmillan, 1960.
4. Clymer, Theodore. "The Utility of Phonic Generalizations in the Primary Grades," *Reading Teacher*, 16 (Jan. 1963), 252-258.
5. Gates, Arthur J. *A Reading Vocabulary for the Primary Grades*. New York: Bureau of Publications, Teachers College, Columbia University, 1935.
6. Lloyd, Donald J. "Reading American English Sound Patterns." Paper read at spring meeting, May 13, 1961, of the Chicago Area Reading Association.
7. *New York Times*, July 18, 1961, p. 31.
8. Oaks, Ruth E. "A Study of the Vowel Situations in a Primary Vocabulary," *Education*, 82 (1952), 604-17.
9. Rinsland, Henry D. *A Basic Vocabulary of Elementary School Children*. New York: Macmillan, 1945.
10. Sullivan, Sister Mary Christine. "A Phonetic Analysis of the New Gates' Primary Reading Vocabulary." *Educational Research Monographs*. Washington, D. C., 1939.
11. *Webster's New Collegiate Dictionary*. Springfield, Massachusetts: G. & C. Merriam, 1959.
12. Wilson, Albert Richard. *The Miraculous Birth of Language*. Introduction by George Bernard Shaw. New York: Philosophical Library, 1948.

When Two Vowels Go Walking and Other Such Things

Robert Emans*

FROM TIME TO TIME, research reports will stimulate the thinking and actions of other investigators. Such was the research reported in an article, "The Utility of Phonic Generalizations in the Primary Grades," in *The Reading Teacher* by Theodore Clymer (1963). Clymer selected forty-five generalizations and developed a word test from four widely used sets of readers in the primary grades. Then he set two criteria, admittedly arbitrary, as to what was meant by a "reasonable" degree of application. The first criterion was that there must be at least twenty words to which the generalization might apply. The second criterion was a percent of utility of at least seventy-five.

Only eighteen of the forty-five generalizations met the criteria of usefulness in Clymer's study. A number of generalizations which had long been considered to have merit were among those which did not meet the criteria. For example, the "When two vowels go walking, the first does the talking" or "When there are two vowels side by side, the long sound of the first one is heard and the second is usually silent," generalization was one of these. Clymer concluded that "some time-honored customs in the teaching of reading may be in need of revision." The need for revision has been interpreted by some people to mean that many commonly taught phonic generalizations should be discarded.

In a study supported by the Cooperative Research Program of the Office of Education (Emans, 1965) and reported in *The Reading Teacher* (Emans, 1967), this investigator replicated Clymer's study, but used a random sampling of words beyond the primary level. The writer reasoned that, although some phonic generalizations may not be useful with words in the primary grades, these same generalizations might have utility for the words which the child is required to recognize later.

The results of the two studies showed that thirteen generalizations demonstrated their usefulness at both primary and upper grade levels; at least four generalizations which met the criteria of usefulness on the primary level failed to do so for words beyond the primary level; and three generalizations, which were found not to be useful at the primary level, were useful for words beyond the primary level. Hence, when the results of the two studies were combined, only twenty-one of the forty-five generalizations identified by Clymer were found to be useful.

As this investigator's study progressed, he became increasingly aware that if certain changes were made in Clymer's generalizations, their utility could be raised. In some cases a simple rewording of the generali-

*The Reading Teacher, 21 (December 1967), 262-269.

zation could increase the utility from a few percentage points to nearly a hundred. Also, since generalizations need not be applied in isolation, but can be applied in conjunction with each other, their usefulness could be increased greatly by combining them.

Therefore, this paper reports some possible modifications in Clymer's generalizations which may increase their utility. Its purpose is not to encourage keeping practices which are basically weak, but to avoid discarding practices which may require only modification and not abandonment. In some cases, the writer suggests the rewording of generalizations which already have a fairly high percent of utility. Sometimes, such rewording increases the utility even more.

Related literature

Various attempts have been made to find consistencies in the English language to serve as aids in word recognition. Ironically, probably more inconsistencies than consistencies have been discovered.

One of the first studies (Vogel, Jaycex, Washburne, 1923) was conducted by a group of teachers in the Winnetka Public Schools, Winnetka, Illinois. The study, which was later expanded (Washburne and Vogel, 1928), listed common phonograms to be taught in the primary grades. In a similar study, Atkins (1926) examined the relation between the phonetic and unphonetic occurrences of high frequency symbols. He found sounds which were most apt to accompany the various symbols and concluded that the then often-taught phonetic elements were frequently not the most common elements.

More recent studies of English have shown it to be complex and seemingly inconsistent. An examination of even a few common words such as bread, once, laugh, straight, and knife reveals silent letters, inconsistent spellings and exceptions to established rules.

Hildreth (1958, p. 153) states that there are no unvarying sounds and that vowel sounds depend on associations with the other letters within words. She states that only 200 of the 350 commonest words can be written as they sound (1958, p. 152). Armstrong (1949) found that the twenty-six letters in the alphabet give rise to at least 117 sounds. Anderson (1964) states that there are three hundred different combinations which express the seventeen vowel sounds; for example, *ow* has one sound in owl, cow and clown, but another sound in grow, flow, and snow. Horn (1954, pp. 129-132) points out that the short *i*, as in *hit*, is spelled twenty-two different ways. And of course, the classic example of *ough* has different sounds in ought, rough, though, and through. Furthermore, nearly all letters of the alphabet are silent at some time. Hildreth (1958, p. 153) notes that about two-thirds of the words in an unabridged dictionary contain silent letters, e.g. here, were, through, once, one, enough, doubt, and sleigh. Sartorious (1931) found more exceptions than examples of the silent *e* rule. Clymer (1961) reported that in 35 percent of the cases involving the most common 220 words, the first of two vowels was not long when the second was a silent *e*. Dolch (1951, p. 35) found that there are about as many exceptions to the two vowel rule as there are instances when it applies. However, the rule does often apply, he found, for specific vowel situations such as *ai, ee, ea, oa,* and *ay.*

Although many studies have shown inconsistencies in the English language, others have demonstrated consistent patterns. For example, Hanna and Moore (1953) found English to be 86.9 percent phonetic, as they defined it. They found that single consonants are represented by regular spellings about 90 percent of the time.

A number of other specific studies have been conducted. Dolch (1938) lists 200 common syllables after determining that 81 percent of words studied were of more than one syllable. Osburn (1954) found the most common syllables in children's written vocabulary to be *ing, ed, er, by, es, tion,* and *y.* A study by Hildreth (1958, p. 154) showed that 25 percent of the words in English are composed of base forms with varied prefixes or endings. Thorndike (1941, p. 115) lists the common suffixes as *ion, tion, ation, er, y, al, ent, ful, ity, ty, ure,* and *ous.* Stauffer (1942) found that fourteen prefixes make up 82 percent of the total number of prefixes. These are *ab, ad, be, com, de, dis, en, ex, in, pre, pro, re, sub,* and *un.*

In respect to phonograms, Dolch (1938) showed that the twenty-four most commonly taught phonograms make up only 28 percent of the syllables in words children are likely to find in their textbooks. He recommended that teachers should, therefore, teach syllabication. Gunderson (1939) listed the phonograms found in the ten reading manuals for teaching in grades 1 and 2. Spache's (1939) study revealed that the three and four letter phonograms such as *ake* and *ight* are more phonetically constant than the two letter combinations such as *in, on, at, an.*

Oaks (1952) computed the frequency of vowel sound combinations in basal readers. She concluded that one-third of vowel situations appear as early as the primer. Anderson (1964, p. 130) states that the *schwa* vowel sound is found in half of the multisyllabic words. In respect to consonants, Black (1952) reports that they are evenly distributed between initial and final positions in syllables with very few consonants appearing in the middle of a syllable.

In a fairly recent article, Fry (1964) summarizes the findings of studies by Black (1952) and others in respect to phonic rules. He also presents a study of his own on 300 words usually taught in the primary grades and suggests twenty-one rules which he found to be worth teaching.

Possible modifications

In the discussion that follows, Clymer's original rule will be stated and the possible modifications will be given. Practical use of the modifications would probably indicate still other ways of restating them to correspond better with the understandings of children.

1. *When there are two vowels side by side, the long sound of the first one is heard and the second is usually silent.*

A total of 480 words were identified in the author's study as being words to which this generalization could apply. Only eighty-seven words conformed; there were 393 exceptions. Therefore, for the words beyond the primary level, it exhibited a utility of only 18 percent. Clymer found a utility of 45 percent for words in the primary grades. When the specific vowel combinations of *ai, ea, oa, ui,* and *ee* were omitted, 318 words remained to which one might hope to apply the generalization. Of these 318 words, only eight, or 3 percent, followed the rule. Therefore, the usefulness of this generalization must be questioned.

Nevertheless, a number of specific vowel combinations had a high percent of utility. The vowel combination *ai* had a percent utility of 83; *oa* had a percent utility of 86; *ee* had a percent utility of 100. In addition, a detailed study of the exceptions to the two vowel generalization indicated other possible generalizations which might be useful. Out of a total of 131 words, the vowel combination *io* had a short *u* sound as in *nation* 113 times, or a utility of 86 percent. The vowel combination *ui* was found to have a short i sound 79 percent of the time. In addition, the *oo* combination had the sound as in *food* in 74 percent of the words and the sound as in *good* in the remaining 26 percent of the time. Hence, the following generalizations replace, to some extent, the "When two vowels go walking the first does the talking" generalization.

  a. When the first vowel in a word is *a* and the second is *i*, the *a* is usually long and the *i* silent.
  b. When the first vowel is *o* and the second is *a*, the *o* is usually long and the *a* is silent.
  c. Words having double *e* usually have the long *e* sound.
  d. The letters *io* usually represent a short *u* sound as in nation.
  e. The letters *oo* usually have the long double *o* sound as in *food* or the short double *o* sound as in *good*. They are more likely to have the double *o* sound as in *food*.
  f. The vowel combination *ui* has a short *i* sound.

2. *When a vowel is in the middle of a one-syllable word, the vowel is short.*

This clue had a 73 percent utility for words beyond the primary level, as determined by this study, and a 62 percent utility for words within the primary level, as found by Clymer. However, of the thirty-eight exceptions for words beyond the primary level, thirteen had an *r* following the vowel. An important generalization found in both Clymer's and this study was that the vowel sound may be modified if it precedes an *r*. Therefore, if the clue is changed to state, "When a vowel is in the middle of a one-syllable word, the vowel is short except that it may be modified in words in which the vowel is followed by an *r*," it has a utility of 80 percent, increasing its usefulness considerably.

3. *When words end with silent "e", the preceding "a" or "i" is long.*

As stated, this generalization was found to have a utility of only 48 percent in this study. If words ending in *le* were excluded, the utility could be raised to 67 percent; to 71 percent if words ending with *le* and words with *ive* were excluded. These exceptions warrant further investigation in that Clymer found that his generalization had a 60 percent utility for words on the primary level. If the proposed exceptions were applied, Clymer's generalization might become useful in the primary grades, measured against the criteria used.

4. *The two letters "ow" make the long "o" sound.*

The generalization as stated had a 50 percent utility. However, if it were changed to, "The two letters *ow* make the long *o* sound or the *ou* sound as in *out*," it would have 100 percent utility in the sample of this study.

5. *When "y" is the final letter in a word, it usually has a vowel sound.*

This generalization had an 84 percent utility using words in the primary grades and a 98 percent utility using words above the primary grades. In all exceptions in this study, the *y* was silent, following the generalization that in *ay* the *y* is silent and gives "a" its long sound which Clymer found to be a useful generalization. Therefore, the two generalizations together would have 100 percent utility for words above the primary level. Similar findings might have been noted had Clymer applied the two generalizations together in his study—perhaps increasing the rules' usefulness on the primary level.

6. *When "y" is used as a vowel, it sometimes has the sound of long "i".*

Stated this way, this generalization has a utility of only 4 percent. However, if it were changed to read, "When *y* is used as a vowel, it sometimes has the sound of long *e*," it would have a utility of 92 percent.

7. *The letter "a" has the same sound (ô) when followed by "l", "w", and "u."*

As stated, the percent of utility is 24. Only four of the *al* words follow this clue, all but twelve of them having either long or short *a* sounds. Therefore, the *l* does not seem to modify the long or short *a*. However, of the thirty-two *au* and *aw* words, all but five, or 84 percent, follow it. If the generalizations were changed to state, "The letter *a* has the same sound (ô) when followed by *w* and *u*," its usefulness would be greatly increased.

8. *When "c" is followed by "e" or "i", the sound of "s" is likely to be heard.*

Eighty-eight words of the sample were possible applications. The clue had a 90 percent utility, meeting the established criteria. In the nine exceptions, the sound of sh was heard rather than *s*. Therefore, if the generalization were to be restated as "When *c* is followed by *e* or *i*, the sound *s* or *sh* is likely to be heard" the utility in this study would be 100 percent.

9. *When two of the same consonants are side by side only one is heard.*

This generalization was applied to 300 words with a 91 percent utility and, therefore, deemed to be useful. Of the twenty-six exceptions, all but three were a result of a prefix or suffix being added, for example, illegal. Ten of the twenty exceptions had an *ly* added to a root word ending in *l*, and both *l*'s were sounded, as in dreadfully.

10. *In most two-syllable words, the first syllable is accented.*

This clue met the criteria for usefulness in both this study and the previous study by Clymer. Approximately a third of the exceptions can be accounted for through application of the generalization that "If *a*, *in*, *re*, *ex*, *de*, or *be* is the first syllable in a word, it is usually unaccented" which was found in both studies to be useful. Additional prefixes such as *con-* and *pre-* could explain still other exceptions.

11. *One vowel letter in an accented syllable has its short sound.*

This clue applied to 1,490 words analyzed for this study and had a utility of 64 percent. If it is reworded to read, "One vowel letter in an accented syllable has its short sound if it comes before the end of the syllable and its long sound if it comes at the end of the syllable," the utility would be raised to 78 percent. Addition of the phrase, "Except when it is followed by an *r*" raised the percent of utility to ninety-two.

12. *When "y" or "ey" is seen in the last syllable that is not accented, the long sound of "e" is heard.*

As the generalization is stated, only three (1 percent) of the 269 applicable words conformed to its claim. However, if it is read "short *i*" instead of "long *e*" 261 words (87 percent) would have conformed.

13. *When "-tion" is the final syllable in a word, it is unaccented.*

This clue supports the original thinking which prompted this study— that the usefulness of phonic generalizations may differ for words above and below the primary level. Clymer found only five words from his list to which this rule might apply, while eighty-five words from this study's shorter word list conformed. In both studies the utility was 100 percent. Apparently, it is useful for words beyond the primary level, but it may be of questionable value, as defined in this study, for words within the primary level.

A -*tion* at the end of a four syllable word seems to indicate a secondary accent on the first syllable with a primary accent on the syllable preceding the -tion. This held true in forty or forty-two words, indicating a 95 percent utility. The primary accent failed to fall on the second to last syllable only three times out of all the -*tion* words on the list. The primary accent was on the second to last syllable in all the three-syllable words, all but two of the four-syllable words, and all but one of the five-syllable words. Similar results were found with words ending with -*sion*. Therefore, the generalization "When -*tion* or -*sion* is the final syllable in a word, the primary accent is likely to fall on the second to last syllable," would indicate the location of the primary accent in many words to which it would apply.

14. *In many two- and three-syllable words, the final "e" lengthens the vowel in the last syllable.*

Of the total number of words in the sample, this clue would be applied to 227 with a 42 percent utility; ninety-five words conformed and there were 132 exceptions. Of the exceptions, fifty ended with *le* and eleven ended with *ive*. In that no *le* or *ive* words followed it, their omission would increase the utility to 64 percent. Other consistent exceptions might be found to make the generalization more usable.

15. *If the first vowel sound in a word is followed by two consonants, the first syllable usually ends with the first of two consonants.*

Clymer found that this generalization had only 72 percent utility with the words he studied. In this study, it could be applied to 811 words, meeting the criteria of usefulness with 80 percent utility. However, of the 163 exceptions, twenty-four words included vowels modified with an *r*, thirty-six words had a double consonant with one of them silent, twenty-one words had a *ck* with the *k* sound, twenty were found to have common prefixes, and twenty-two words had one of the sounds *th, ch,* or *sh*. All five of these generalizations were found by Clymer to be useful. If these generalizations were applied in conjunction with this generalization, it would have a utility of 96 percent.

16. *If the first vowel sound in a word is followed by a single consonant, that consonant usually begins the second syllable.*

This generalization could be applied to 659 words of the list with a 47 percent utility. Clymer noted like results. Of the 346 words which were exceptions, ninety-three were root words plus a prefix, and 240 had beginning syllables which ended with a consonant with a short vowel sound. Consequently, if it read, "Except in some words with a prefix and a root word, if the first vowel sound in a word is followed by a single consonant, that consonant begins the second syllable and the vowel sound in the first syllable will be long, *or* if the consonant ends the first syllable the vowel sound will be short," the percent of utility would be 84. Of the 240 beginning syllables ending with a consonant and containing a short vowel sound, 227 or 95 percent are accented. Of the 237 beginning syllables ending with a long vowel, 138 or 58 percent are unaccented.

17. *If the last syllable of a word ends in "le," the consonant preceding the "le" usually begins the last syllable.*

This clue met the criteria of usefulness in both studies. In this present study a total of sixty-eight words could be applied to it with a utility of 78 percent. Of the fifteen exceptions, ten had double consonants, as in squabble, before the *le*.

18. *When a word has only one vowel letter, the vowel sound is likely to be short.*

This generalization could be applied to 136 words in the sample with a 70 percent utility, as compared with 57 percent in the previous study. However, of the forty-one exceptions, fourteen words had vowels which were modified by an *r*. Omitting these exceptions would raise the percent of utility to seventy-eight.

This article has suggested modifications and substitutes for some of the commonly taught phonic generalizations. There are probably other modifications which would also be helpful. The belief underlying this effort has been that greater improvement will come about in helping children learn to read if we first attempt to eliminate the weaknesses in existing practices before deciding that they should be discarded.

References

Anderson, P. S. *Language skills in elementary education.* New York: Macmillan, 1964.

Armstrong, S. *How words get into the dictionary.* New York: Funk and Wagnalls, 1949.

Atkins, Ruth E. An analysis of the phonetic elements in a basal reading vocabulary. *Elementary School Journal,* 1926, *26,* 596-606.

Black, E. B. A study of the consonant situations in a primary reading vocabulary. *Education,* 1952, *72,* 618-623.

Clymer, T. The utility of phonic generalizations in the primary grades. *Changing Concepts of Reading Instruction.* New York: Scholastic Magazines, 1961. P. 156-159.

Clymer, T. The utility of phonic generalizations in the primary grades. *The Reading Teacher,* 1963, *16,* 252-258.

Dolch, E. W. Phonics and polysyllables. *Elementary English Review,* 1938, *15,* 120-124.

Dolch, E. W. *The teaching of sounding.* Champaign, Illinois: Garrard Press, 1951.

Emans, R. The usefulness of word pronounciation rules: cooperative research project, No. S-340. Uinpublished research report, Cooperative Research Program of the Office of Education, United States Department of Health, Education, and Welfare, 1965.

Emans, R. The usefulness of phonic generalizations above the primary level. *The Reading Teacher,* 1967, *20,* 419-425.

Fry, E. A frequency approach to phonics. *Elementary English,* 1964, *41,* 759-765.

Gunderson, Agnes G. Simplified phonics. *Elementary School Journal,* 1939, *39,* 593-606.

Hanna, R. R., and Moore, T., Jr. Spelling—from spoken word to written symbol. *Elementary School Journal,* 1953, *53,* 329-337.

Hildreth, Gertrude. *Teaching reading.* New York: Holt, Rinehart & Winston, 1958.

Horn, E. Phonics and spelling. *Journal of Education,* 1954, *136,* 233-235.

Oaks, Ruth E. A study of the vowel situations in primary vocabulary. *Education,* 1952, *72,* 604-617.

Osburn, W. J. Teaching spelling by teaching syllables and root words. *Elementary School Journal,* 1954, *55,* 32-41.

Sartorious, I. C. *Generalization in spelling.* New York: Teachers College, 1931.

Spache, G. D. A phonics manual for primary and remedial teachers. *Elementary English Review,* 1939, *16,* 191-198.

Stauffer, R. G. A study of prefixes in the Thorndike list to establish a list of prefixes that should be taught in the elementary school. *Journal of Educational Research,* 1942, *35,* 453-458.

Thorndike, E. L. *The teaching of English suffixes.* New York: Teachers College, 1941.

Vogel, Mabel, Jaycex, Emma, and Washburne, C. W. A basic list of phonics for grades I and II. *Elementary School Journal,* 1923, *23,* 436-443.

Washburne, C., and Vogel, Mabel. A revised list of phonics for grade II. *Elementary School Journal,* 1928, *28,* 771-777.

Vowel Pairs

Lou E. Burmeister*

ORDINARILY WHEN TWO VOWELS APPEAR TOGETHER they should be viewed as a grapheme; that is, together they ordinarily represent one sound, known as a phoneme. Burmeister (1966) examined the validity of this statement in 537 randomly selected instances from the Thorndike and Lorge (1944) *Teacher's Word Book of 30,000 Words* and found it to be true 84.5 per cent of the time; she found one-third of the exceptions to be instances of only one vowel pair: *ia* (e.g., g*ia*nt, l*ia*ble, p*ia*no).

The words were selected on fourteen levels, according to frequency of occurrence. "Every vowel combination means a syllable" was true 90.6 per cent of the time for words that occur from six to over 100 times per million running words; it was true 75.8 per cent of the time for words that occur from one to five times per million running words.

Several investigators have examined the applicability of the commonly taught phonic generalization: "When two vowels are together, the first is long and the second is silent." They found this "generalization" to be extremely limited in usefulness even in the controlled vocabularies of primary materials (Bailey, 1967; Clymer, 1963; Oaks, 1952) and much more so in uncontrolled vocabularies above the primary level in difficulty (Bailey, 1967; Burmeister, 1966; Emans, 1967).

An important question yet to be answered from a linguistic examination of a large stock of words is: What specific phoneme (or phonemes) does each "vowel-vowel" graphemes represent? That is, what are the most common sounds of each vowel-pair? Carrying the question a step further, one might ask whether it is possible to group several vowel pair graphemes according to similar patterns in their phoneme behavior (e.g., digraphs, diphthongs) and which vowel pairs fit in each group. The question is not a new one; however the manner of answering it as set forth in this article is modern.

Procedure

Hanna, Hanna, Hodges, and Rudorf in 1966 published a volume titled *Phoneme-Grapheme Correspondences as Cues to Spell-*

The Reading Teacher, 21 (February 1968), 445-452.

ing Improvement. In it they reported the results of their computerized examination of 17,310 words: 15,284 words selected from Part I of the Thorndike-Lorge *Teacher's Word Book of 30,000* plus 2,026 words selected from the *Merriam-Webster's New Collegiate Dictionary,* sixth edition, "which were considered to be relevant to a study of a 'common core' vocabulary but had not been available from Part I of the Thorndike-Lorge word list" (Hanna, *et al.,* 1966, pp. 12-13). The authors of the Hanna, *et al.* study were concerned with furthering knowledge about spelling by examining phoneme-grapheme relationships.

The purpose of the present study is to further knowledge about reading, specifically about the phonic situation. To do so, it is necessary to look at grapheme to phoneme relationships. The procedure is the reverse of that used by Hanna, *et al.* Using as source materials the findings of Hanna, *et al.,* and reversing them to "grapheme to phoneme" relationships, the author of the present study was able to classify the sounds of all "vowel-vowel" combinations *which form a single phoneme* for the 17,310 words examined.

Results

The grapheme-phoneme relationship for each possible vowel pair in the English language was examined. In Table 1 the findings are presented. Vowel-pairs not listed did not occur—at least as single graphemes—in the material.

To analyze the data the author grouped some of the vowel pairs according to each pair's most common sound. The vowel pairs which occurred fewer than fifty times in the sample material (which means that in the sample material they occurred less often than once in every 346 words) were not included in this analysis because it was felt that generalizations covering their sounds would be of little value. (It would probably be easier to learn words which contain these vowel pairs as sight words.)

There are at least two ways of viewing the vowel pairs which are included. One way is to look at single phoneme percentages for each grapheme. Another way is to simply look at the frequency of occurrence of each phoneme for each grapheme. Each of these methods has a value. Looking at percentages will show the proportional value of each phoneme for each grapheme. Looking at frequencies will demonstrate the actual number value of each phoneme, both in relationship to its grapheme and also in relationship to the total sample. Thus, for example, although "ei's" most common sound (ā) occurs 40 per cent of the time when "ei" occurs as a grapheme in the sample material and "ou's" most common sound (ə) occurs 41.2 per cent of the time when "ou"

Table 1 Frequency and per cent of occurrence of each single phoneme for each vowel-pair grapheme

Grapheme			Phonemic Behavior		
Name	Frequency	Pronun-ciation Key	Example	Frequency	Per Cent
ae	(6)	ē	algae	5	83.3
		ĕ	aesthetic	1	16.7
ai	(309)	ā	abstain	230	74.4
		â	air	49	15.6
		ɪ	mountain	15	4.9
		ə	villain	9	2.9
		ĕ	again	4	1.3
		ă	plaid	1	.3
		ī	aisle	1	.3
ao	(2)	ô	extraordinary	2	100
au	(178)	ô	auction	167	93.8
		ō	chauffeur	5	2.8
		ä	laugh	4	2.2
		ə	epaulet	1	.6
		ā	gauge	1	.6
ay	(137)	ā	gray	132	96.4
		ī	kayak	3	2.2
		ĕ	says	1	.7
		ɪ	yesterday	1	.7
aw	(77)	ô	lawn	77	100
ea	(545)	ē	east	275	50.5
		ĕ	weapon	140	25.7
		ę̄	ear	49	9.0
		û	earth	31	5.7
		â	bear	13	2.4
		ä	hearty	18	3.3
		ā	great	14	2.6
		ɪ	guinea	2	.4
		ə	sergeant	3	.5
ee	(290)	ē	sleet	248	85.5
		ę̄	peer	36	12.4
		ɪ	been	6	2.1
ei	(86)	ā	reign	34	40.0
		ē	deceit	22	25.6
		ɪ	foreign	11	12.8
		ī	seismic	9	10.5
		â	their	5	5.8
		ə	sovereignty	2	2.3
		ę̄	weird	2	2.3
		ĕ	heifer	1	1.2
eo	(15)	ə	pigeon	10	66.7
		ĕ	leopard	3	20.0
		ē	people	2	13.3
eu	(40)	ū	feud	29	72.5
		û	amateur	6	15.0
		ōo	sleuth	4	10.0
		ŏŏ	pleurisy	1	2.5

Table 1 (continued)

Grapheme			Phonemic Behavior		
Name	Frequency	Pronun- ciation Key	Example	Frequency	Per Cent
ey	(69)	ĭ	honey	40	58.0
		ā	convey	14	20.3
		ī	geyser	8	11.6
		ē	key	6	8.7
		â	eyrie	1	1.4
ew	(64)	ū	news	39	60.9
		o͞o	flew	22	34.4
		ō	sew	3	4.7
ia		ĭ	carriage	3	60
		ə	parliament	2	40
ie	(156)	ē	thief	56	35.9
		ĭ	lassie	30	19.2
		ī	die	26	16.7
		ə	patient	23	14.7
		ȩ̄	cashier	17	10.9
		e	friend	4	2.6
oa	(138)	ō	road	129	93.5
		ô	broad	9	6.5
oe	(22)	ō	foe	13	59.1
		ē	amoeba	5	22.7
		o͞o	shoe	4	18.2
oi	(102)	oi	moist	100	98.0
		ə	porpoise	2	2.0
oo	(315)	o͞o	lagoon	185	58.7
		o͝o	wood	114	36.2
		ō	floor	9	2.9
		ŭ	blood	7	2.2
ou	(815)	ə	rigorous	336	41.2
		ou	out	285	35.0
		o͞o	soup	54	6.6
		ō	four	47	5.8
		ŭ	touch	30	3.7
		o͝o	your	25	3.1
		û	journey	22	2.7
		ĕ	glamour	1	.1
oy	(50)	oi	convoy	49	98.0
		ī	coyote	1	2.0
ow	(250)	ō	own	125	50.0
		ou	town	121	48.4
		ŏ	knowledge	4	1.6
ue	(43)	ū	due, cue	27	62.8
		o͞o	clue	16	37.2
ui	(34)	ĭ	build	16	47.1
		o͞o	fruit	10	29.4
		ū	suit	8	23.5
uo	(2)	o͞o	buoyant	2	100
uy	(3)	ĭ	buy	3	100

occurs as a grapheme, a look at the frequency data shows that teaching the first sound of "ou" (which occurs 336 times) would be more valuable than teaching the first sound of "ei" (which occurs only 34 times). Such comparisons can also be made when deciding to teach, or not to teach, the second most common sound of graphemes. For example, it can be seen that "ou's" second most common sound (ou) occurs 35 per cent of the time when "ou" occurs as a grapheme, but the frequency of this sound is 285, a frequency greater than the total number of occurrences of all of the vowel pair graphemes except "ai," "ea," "ee," and "oo," and a frequency value greater than the first sound of any other vowel pair.

In Table 2 these graphemes are grouped according to their most common phoneme. Included for each grapheme are the three most common sounds, or the number of sounds needed to reach the 90 per cent utility level, which ever occurs first.

In Table 3 the data are presented in frequency of occurrence form. The same number of phonemes are included in Table 3 as in Table 2 but a shaded area is added to show the total number of occurrences of each grapheme.

Conclusions

Phonemes for vowel-pairs tend to fall into four categories:

1.   The first vowel may dominate, as is usually true with the following combinations: ai, ay, ea, ee, oa, ow. (That is, when the above vowels "go walking, the first one usually does the talking," and what it says is its own name; however, "ea" may be a *long e* or a *short e,* and "ow" may be a *long o* or an *ou.*)

2.   The two vowels may *cooperate* (blend), as is usually true with the following combinations: au, aw, oi, ly, and oo. "Oo" may sound as it does in lagoon or wood. (Note the high utility level for this generalization.)

3.   A new sound may be *created:* ei=ā, ou=e, ey=i, ew=u*. [It may be surprising to find that ou's most common sound is schwa (rigorous). "Ou's" second most common sound is a diphthong (out); this sound has a very high frequency.]

4.   Vowel-pairs may *separate.* (See Limitations of This Study.)

Also, except for the most common sound of "ei" (which is ā), "ei" and "ie" may have the same sounds. In order of frequency they are: e, i, i.

---

*Many will question that "ey" as in honey = i; to many it sounds like an e; to these "ey" would be a digraph. Some will also question that "ew" as in news = u, the letter we say when we say the alphabet. It is interesting to note that *Webster's Seventh New Collegiate Dictionary,* 1963, based on *Webster's Third New International Dictionary,* gives the following keys for these words: honey /'hen-e/ and news /'n(y)üz/.

Table 2   Per cent of occurrence of the three most common phonemes, or the number of phonemes needed to reach the ninety per cent utility level—whichever occurs first—for commonly found vowel-pair graphemes

Most Common Phoneme Behavior	Grapheme	Per Cent (0 — 20 — 40 — 60 — 80 — 100)
digraph	ai	ā (spanning to ~80%), â (~80–90%)
	ay	ā (spanning ~0–100%)
	ea	ē (~0–40%), ē (~55–70%), ē (~75–90%)
	ee	ē (~0–55%), ê (~70–90%)
	oa	ō (spanning ~0–100%)
	ow	ō (~0–45%), ou (~45–100%)
diphthong	au	ô (spanning ~0–100%)
	aw	ê (spanning ~0–100%)
	oi	oi (spanning ~0–100%)
	oy	oi (spanning ~0–100%)
	oo	ōō (~0–50%), oŏ (~50–100%)
other	ei	ā (~0–35%), ē (~35–65%), ĭ (~65–85%)
	ey	ĭ (~0–50%), ā (~50–70%), ī (~70–85%)
	ew	ū (~0–50%), ōō (~50–90%)
	ie	ē (~0–30%), ĭ (~30–50%), ī (~50–65%)
	ou	ə (~0–35%), ou (~35–65%), ōō (~65–80%)

Implications for teaching

This study furnishes proof that what *discriminating* educators have been teaching is not too far from being correct. It also furnishes additional proof that the vowel digraph generalization has limited usefulness. However, the generalization "When two vowels go walking the first one does the talking" is still turning up in the literature *with no qualifications* about the limited number of graphemes for which this generalization is appropriate. This study furnishes proof, also, that the second most common sounds of "ea"

Table 3 Total frequency of occurrence, including frequency of occurrence of the three most common phonemes, or the number of phonemes needed to reach the ninety per cent utility level—whichever occurs first—for commonly found vowel-pair graphemes

Most Common Phoneme Behavior	Grapheme	Frequency

and "ow" should be taught.

This study also reinforces the value of teaching "au," "aw," "oi," "oy" as diphthongs and the two sounds of "oo."

The finding that "ou's" most common sound is a schwa may surprise many, but the frequency of occurrence of "ou" as a diphthong has been demonstrated.

The study may throw light on the relative importance of the various sounds of "ei" and "ie." Teaching a generalization which covers this may have dubious value because of its cumbersomeness. However, children might be taught to try several specific sounds when first meeting a word with either an "ei" or an "ie" in it.

Limitations of the study

Only vowel-pairs which represent a single phoneme were analyzed in this study. The author found no way of examining situations in which vowel-pairs form two phonemes. Such an analysis would be possible by looking at the raw data which is supplied in the appendices of the Hanna, *et al.*, study.

However, Burmeister (1966) found that the generalization: "Every vowel combination means a syllable" was true 84.5 per cent of the time. The following cases are the exceptions:

		Per cent of total vowel-pair sample
1.	"A vowel combination means no syllable." (e.g.,—*que*)	0.7%
2.	"A vowel combination means two syllables."	
	a. "ia" means two syllables (67% of the times "ia" occurs)	5.2%
	b. "ie" means two syllables (16.7% of the times "ie" occurs	1.1%
	c. "ea" means two syllables (12% of the times "ea" occurs)	1.5%
	d. "eous" and "ious" mean two syllables (47% of the times "ious" occurs; sample too small to judge % for "eous")	1.9%
	e. Miscellaneous	5.0%

References

Bailey, Mildred Hart. The utility of phonic generalizations in grades one through six. *The Reading Teacher*, 1967, 20, 413-418.

Burmeister, Lou E. An evaluation of the inductive and deductive group approaches to teaching selected word analysis generalizations to disabled readers in eighth and ninth grade. Doctoral dissertation, University of Wisconsin, 1966.

Clymer, T. L. The utility of phonic generalizations in the primary grades. *The Reading Teacher*, 1963, 16, 252-258.

Emans, R. The usefulness of phonic generalizations above the primary grades. *The Reading Teacher*, 1967, 20, 419-425.

Hanna, P. R., Hanna, Jean S., Hodges, R. G., and Rudorf, E. H., Jr. *Phoneme-grapheme correspondences as cues to spelling improvement.* Washington, D .C.: Office of Education, U. S. Department of Health, Education, and Welfare, 1966.

Merriam-Webster's new collegiate dictionary, sixth edition, 1961.

Oaks, Ruth E. A study of the vowel situation in a primary vocabulary. *Education,* 1952, 72, 604-617.

Thorndike, E. L., and Lorge, I. *The teacher's word book of 30,000 words.* New York: Bureau of Publications, Teachers College, Columbia University, 1944.

A Sound-Symbol Frequency Count

DAVID R. STONE*

A REAL PROBLEM faced by a reader in attacking a new word is to associate correctly the printed symbol with the sound appropriate to its place in a word. In English there are many symbols for the same sound, and a particular symbol may have several sounds.

For example, a reader who has learned that *a* in *cat* is a short *a*, finds that *a* says short *e* in *any*, and short *u* in *about*.

Many authorities have pointed out this problem as basic for beginning readers. Three principal solutions have been suggested: (1) establish a sound-symbol relation such that there is a separate symbol for each sound, (2) use cueing devices, such as color, to indicate which sound the symbol is being used for, and (3) teach the present system in terms of relative frequency. The latter stresses the sound-symbol relations most often encountered. In view of the extensive effort needed to change or simplify, the third approach seems the most practical at this time.

This study presents basic frequency data for sound-symbol relations, which will allow a more efficient approach to teaching those most used at the beginning level.

The source of data was content research done on approximately 6,000 sounds in a list of words common to five basal reading series.

These were compiled for grades one, two, and three.*

Pronunciation of each one was checked, sound by sound, in the *Thorndike Barnhart Beginning Dictionary.*† For schwa problems, a jury of thirty graduate students was used to decide whether emphasis favored the short *u* sound. Reference to the examples in tables will give the reader a guide to any particular decision he wishes to check. Except for some Brooklyn and Southern pronunciation variations, the percentage of such problems is under 5 per cent. Such accented regional or colloquial pronunciation was avoided. In the case of *pretty, any,* and the like, the *y* was listed as long *e,* rather than soft *i* as in many dictionaries. Intermediate sounds are usually given as either long or short.

Long Vowels

The long vowel varieties are listed in Table 1. Short vowels, combinations, and consonants follow.

The long a. The long *a* sound appeared a total of 138 times. For this letter sound the *a-e* combination was the most frequent, accounting for 43 per cent of the total. The *ai*

---

*D. R. Stone and Vilda B. Tracy, "A Basic Word List from Basal Readers, *Elementary English,* April 1963, pp. 420-427.

†E. L. Thorndike and C. L. Barnhart, *Thorndike Barnhart Beginning Dictionary* (New York: Scott, Foresman, 1952).

The Reading Teacher, 19 (April 1966), 498-504.

TABLE 1

LONG VOWELS

Long *a* Total 138 (regular 85, irregular 53)			Long *o* Total 125 (regular 77, irregular 48)		
*a-e	cage	60	*o	colt, horse	40
ai	wait	27	*o-e	pole	37
a	baby	25	ow	arrow	22
ay	birthday	17	oa	railroad	15
eigh	freight	4	ou	course, four	6
ey	obey	2	oo	floor	2
*ea	great	2	oe	goes	2
aigh	straight	1	ough	though	1
Long *e* Total 203 (regular 82, irregular 121)					
y	badly	62			
ea	bead	44			
*ee	agree	43	Long *u* Total 5 (regular 2, irregular 3)		
*e	eleven	39	*u	usual	2
ey	money	7	iew	view, few	2
ie	thief	4	eau	beauty	1
ei	neither	3			
eo	people	1			
Long *i* Total 103 (regular 65, irregular 38)			*Those called regular are starred (a vowel plus e combination, vce, or the vowel alone).		
*i-e	fine	47			
*i	behind	18			
y	lying	13	Total Regular	311	
igh	light	12	Total Irregular	263	
ie	tied	11			
ey	eye	1		574	
ig	sign	1			

combination appeared 20 per cent of the time, and *a* was made the long sound alone about 18 per cent of the time. The only other important combination was the *ay*, about 11 per cent. Other variations occurred mainly in the advanced levels and formed less than 1 per cent of the lone *a* sounds. These are the *ey, ea, aigh,* and *eigh* combinations.

The long e. The long *e* sound appeared a total of 203 times. Surprisingly enough it was formed most frequently by a lone *y* (approximately 31 per cent). The *ea* and *ee* combinations were almost equal in number, each about 21 per cent. The single *e* accounted for 19 per cent of

the total. The other combinations together comprised about 1 per cent. These were the *ie, ey, i, eo,* and *ei* sets. They were mostly found in higher grade levels. Teachers reviewing this study have commented on the fact that the *y* in *pretty* is listed as a long *e* and not short *i*, as many dictionaries give it. In this report, *badly* and *pretty* are taken to have the same ending sound, a long *e*.

The long i. The long *i* sound appeared a total of 103 times. It was formed 46 per cent of the time by the *i-e* combination. The long *i* sound was made by *i* alone 17 per cent of the time. The *ie, y,* and *igh* combinations appeared almost equally often, each about 11 per cent of the total. The *ey* and *ig* combinations each appeared once.

The long o. The long *o* sound appeared 125 times. The *o* alone and the *o-e* combination were most important, the first accounting for 34 per cent of the total and the latter, 32 per cent. The *ow* symbol was next with a total of 22 times. It accounted for about 18 per cent of the total long *o* sounds. The *oa* combination became quite important in the third grade levels and produced 12 per cent of the total. The other combinations—*oo, ou, oe,* and *ough* —accounted for about 6 per cent of the total.

The long *o* sound in words like *horse, born,* and *corn* are difficult to classify since there is some tendency to use a short *o.* Since regional emphases have not been used, these were classified as long *o.*

The long u. The long *u* sound in an initial position is a difficult sound to catalog. Formally, the sound is lone *e* plus *oo.* Some give it as *y* plus *oo;* otherwise it is *oo,* as in *blue,* which is not a long *u* sound.

The problem appeared rather infrequently, a total of only 5 times in the study. Only the *y* plus *oo* and the long *e* plus *oo* sounds have been included here. The *oo* sounds of *u* are listed in *oo* (as in *duty*). Long vowels are more irregular than regular. Findings for short vowels are given in Table 2.

Short Vowels

The short a. The short *a* appeared

TABLE 2

SHORT VOWELS

	Short *a* Total 149 (regular 147, irregular 2)			Short *o* Total 171 (regular 103, irregular 68)	
*a	hat	147	*o	hopping	103
au	laugh	2	a	harvest	53
			au	because	4
	Short *e* Total 176 (regular 148, irregular 28)		aw	hawk	4
			ough	fought	3
*e	egg, let	148	augh	naughty	2
a	arrow	13	oa	broad	1
ai	airplane	9	ea	heart	1
ue	guess	1			
ie	friend	1		Short *u* Total 291 (regular 103, irregular 188)	
u	bury	1			
ea	ready	1	*u	but	103
ay	prayer	1	o	come	63
ei	their	1	e	broken	56
			a	elephant	46
	Short *i* Total 178 (regular 169, irregular 9)		ou	trouble	9
			i	office	7
*i	hit	169	o	station	4
ui	build	2	ai	curtain	3
ea	dear	1			
ee	been	1		*Regular, except *u*	567
u	busy	1		Irregular, except *u*	107
y	bicycle	1		Regular *u*	103
a	language	2		Irregular *u*	188
o	women	1			

149 times. Except for two *au*'s, the *a* alone was used.

The short e. The short *e* appeared a total of 176 times. It was generally formed by *e* alone (85 per cent). The *a* and *ai* combinations each appeared only once. These are the *ue, ie, u, ea, ay,* and *ei* groups.

While there is the possibility of hearing "leg" pronounced "laig," this kind of regional inflection is not used in this study. While the long *a* may be heard in "prayer" and "their," they are included here as short *e* on the basis of most common usage. A middle course between "prissy" overexactness and coarse regionalism has been used for the problem cases. Since examples are given for each, the reader may observe how it was done.

The short i. The short *i* sound appeared a total of 178 times. Of these, 97 per cent of the time it was formed by *i* alone. Some schwa problems appeared. The *i* in animal, for example, was counted as short *u* rather than short *i*. In *music,* there is no problem for the short *i*. While many variations were seen, no particular one occurred often.

The short o. The short *o* sound was produced in a variety of ways, but the most important was a lone *o*. This accounted for 60 per cent of the total of 171. The only important variation was the lone *a,* which accounted for about 30 per cent of the total. The other combinations accounted for about 10 per cent. The lone *o* is a simplification of the *ah* sound. Its utility may be easily tested by writing it in an *ar* word. The

"bossy" *r* has an effect, but does not destroy the soft *o* sound. "Because," for example, could just as easily be spelled "becoz," using the soft *o*.

The short u. Of the short vowels, the short *u* sound occurred most often. It was formed in a variety of ways. The vowels *u* (35 per cent), *e* (20 per cent), *a* (16 per cent), and *o* (22 per cent) were the most important variations. Other combinations formed the sound about 6 per cent of the time; these were the *i, ou,* and *ai* combinations.

The issue of "nicety versus utility" is a problem here. The schwa *o* is clear in *come,* but other schwa sounds, such as the *i* in *office,* represent language in motion, and are hard to catalog. The examples indicate the ways in which the decisions were made. The short *u* showed more irregularity than regularity; otherwise, short vowels are approximately five times more regular than irregular.

Combinations and Silent Letters

Combinations of letters and silent letters are seen in Table 3.

The short oo (look) sound. This sound occurred 30 times in the study. It was formed 70 per cent of the time by the *oo* combination. The lone *u* accounted for about 17 per cent of the sounds and the *ou* combination, 10 per cent.

The long oo (food) sound. The sound occurred 63 times in the study. It was produced 30 per cent of the time by an *oo* combination. Varieties of combinations with the single letter *o* accounted for 19 per cent and the

TABLE 3

COMBINATIONS AND SILENTS

Short *oo* Total 30 (regular 21, iregular 9)				*er* Total 124 (regular 92, irregular 32)		
*oo	look	21		*er	another	92
u	push	5		ar	collar	8
ou	should	3		or	color	6
o	woman	1		ear	early	6
				ir	birthday	5
				ur	picture	4
Long *oo* Total 63 (regular 25, irregular 38)				ere	where	2
				wer	answer	1
*oo	food	25				
o	to, move, two	12		*ch (55)	change	45
ew	knew	8		tch	watch	5
u-e	rule	5		ti	question	4
u	duty	2		*sh (55)	shut	43
eau	beauty	2		ti	notion	8
ui	suit, juice	3		s	sure	2
ou	soup	2		c	ocean	2
ough	through	1		*th (35)	thin	35
oe	shoe	1		*th (34)	though	34
ue	true	1		*wh (13)	when	13
				*ng (26)	going	26
ou Total 41 (regular 25, irregular 16)				*le* Total 29		
				le	little	29
*ou	ground	25				
ow	allow	16		Silents		
oi Total 12 (regular 8, irregular 4)				Semi-irregular silent *e*		
				e	come	52
*oi	noise	8		Irregular silent *e*		
oy	boy	4		e	house	51
				*Regular		

ew combination, 13 per cent. Other combinations observed were the *ough, u-e, oe, u, eau, ui, ue,* and *ou* combinations. (In a single symbol system, if *oo* is reserved for the look sound, then *ew* can be used here.)

The ou sound. The sound occurred a total of 41 times. The *ou* combination was most used, with *ow* a little more than half as often. What is "regular" is rather arbitrary here. Is *ouch* more regular than *cow?*

The oi sound. The *oi* sound occurred seldom, only 12 times in all. Of this total it was produced 67 per cent of the time by the *oi* combination and 33 per cent by *oy.*

The er sound. The *er* sound occurred a total of 124 times in the data. The *er* combination accounted for about 72 per cent of the total. The other combinations were the *or, ear, ir,* and *are* sets.

Silents. Silent *e* was classified as being either irregular or semiirregular. Classification was semiirregular if the *e* was in a position to influence the sound of a preceding vowel but did not make the vowel long. Some examples of this are: are, come, here, were, cabbage, careful, policeman, automobile, and given. They were classified as irregular if they had no influence on a preceding vowel. Two methods were used to determine this:

1. If there were two consonants between it and the preceding vowel; for example, horse, else, change, ache, and waste.

2. If there were already two vowels together which could produce the given sound; for example, house, noise, please, because, leaves, choose, and squirrel. Regular silent *e*'s (the ones which made a preceding vowel long) were classified with the vowel in the respective tables.

Silent letters have usually been given with the adjacent letters (as *dj* for *j* in adjacent), but some seem completely unrelated and are given separately here: tongue *u*, island *s*, listen *t*, chocolate *o*, two *w*, whistle *t*, fasten *t*. These occur usually once, and no more than twice.

Consonants

The varieties of sound-symbol combinations for consonants are given in Table 4.

Note that the greatest kind of variation appears in the double-letter problem. The function of double letters is to guide the reader to a short preceding vowel sound (the short *e* in *letter,* for example). This function has been obscured, however, and is

TABLE 4

CONSONANTS

*b (170)	basket	167		*p (211)	perfect	200
bb	rubber	3		pp|	appear	11
*d (224)	duck	219		*r (384)	ran	370
dd	buddy	4		rr	error	11
ld	would	1		wr	write	2
*f (243)	father	132		er	prayer	1
ff	effect	6		*s (324)	stop	272
gh	enough	2		c	cent	37
lf	half	2		ss	mess	14
ph	phone.	1		sc	scene	1
*g (94)	good	92		*2 (412)	terrible	392
gg	egg	2		tt	sitting	18
*h (76)	have	72		ed	watched	1
wh	whole	4		d	second	1
*j (31)	just	12		*v (63)	very	61
g	general	15		f	of	2
dg	wedge	3		*w (97)	worth	83
di	soldier	1		u	quick	11
*k (257)	keep	86		o	one	2
c	cream	119		ui	squirrel	1
ck	luck	29		*x (9)	exit	9
q	quit	14		*y (15)	yard	10
lk	walk	5		u	cure	3
ch	chord	4		i	onion	1
*l (328)	leave	278		*z (59)	zero	14
ll	will	49		s	flimsy	41
tl	whistle	1		es	watches	2
*m (163)	Mother	154		zz	buzz	2
mm	summer	2				
mb	limb	7				
*n (366)	nothing	355		*Regular	3526	
kn	know	6		Irregular	447	
nn	funny	4				
nd	handkerchief	1			3973	

rather unreliable. It is particularly defective when all short vowels are considered. The word "defective," for example, would under the above rule be spelled "defecctivve." The functional utility of double letters may be seriously questioned. There are two aspects of the problem, (1) the sound of preceding vowels when double letters are found, and (2) the kind of consonant doubles found after short vowels. For reactive consistency, both should be functional.

Summary

When over 6000 sounds from the vocabulary of five basal readers were classified, it was found that greater variability of sound-symbol relationships occurred for vowels as compared to consonants. There were 311 (54 per cent) regular long vowels as compared to 262 irregular. There were 567 regular short vowels as compared to 107 irregular without the short *u*. The short *u* had 103 regular, and 188 irregular. There were 3526 regular consonants as compared to 447 irregular. The practical application lies in making clear the emphasis needed in teaching the most frequent sound-symbol combinations.

Some implications for those interested in phonetic efficiency which would require no type changes would be:

1. Eliminate all double letters.
2. Indicate a long vowel with an *e* following it (time, tiem).
3. Use a single *u* for all schwa sounds.
4. Use a single *o* for almost all of the *ah, ar, au* variations and single *i, e,* and *a* for their respective short sounds.
5. Use *ou* for all the *ouch* words, eliminating the *ow* (cow, cou).
6. Use the usual *t* in the *th* combination for *thin* and a double-bar *t* in the *th* combination for *this*.
7. Use *z* for *buzz* (buz), and *zh* for *azure* (azhure).
8. Use *oo* for the short double-o sound in *good* and *ew* for the long double-o sound in *duty* (dewty).
9. Use *k* for *c,* eliminating the *c-s* confusion.

Variations like these could be introduced, where appropriate, without undue printing problems.

(David R. Stone is a Professor in the Department of Psychology, at Utah State University. His specialities are learning and reading.)

The Effect of Syllabic Position and Accent on the Phonemic Behavior of Single Vowel Graphemes

Lou E. Burmeister*

WHEN TWO VOWELS APPEAR side-by-side they usually form a single grapheme, which is a written representation of a single phoneme. The phoneme commonly will be a long vowel sound, a diphthong, a short vowel sound, or a schwa, depending upon the particular vowel-pair being examined. An analysis of the phonemic behavior of each single grapheme vowel-pair is already available (3). The section titled "Related Findings" in the present article, however, may be viewed by some as a supplement to this report.

The present article is an attempt to describe the phonemic behavior of *each* single-vowel grapheme (*i.e.,* of each vowel when it appears without another vowel at its side, and when it does not appear in a "final vowel-consonant-e" construction).

Several investigators have examined the usefulness of two "generalizations" which presumably were formulated to describe the phonemic behavior of single-vowels in two syllabic positions: open and closed. The open syllable, long vowel generalization, was found not to be generalizable to words of more than one syllable (2), and even to have a relatively low (75 percent) utility level for monosyllabic words (1, 4). The closed syllable, short vowel generalization, seems to be more valid for polysyllabic words than for monosyllabic words, perhaps because exceptions tend to fall into families of one syllable words (*e.g.,* mild, child, wild; cold, bold, hold; night, fight, right).

The findings of former studies are somewhat unclear because of the apparent differences in the authors' definitions of short vowel sounds (*e.g.,* Is the short vowel sound before an *r* categorized as a short vowel sound, or is it placed in another category? Is the schwa sound considered to be a short vowel sound?).

Questions asked

The present study is unique because it examines the phonemic behavior of individual single-vowel graphemes in an attempt to determine whether the commonly taught generalizations are more valid for some vowels than for others. Information about accent, or stress, as a possible cue to phonemic behavior is also available in this study.

The questions asked were:

1. What is the phonemic behavior of each single-vowel grapheme when it is found in an open syllable?
2. What is the phonemic behavior of each of these graphemes in an accented open syllable?—in an unaccented open syllable?
3. What is the phonemic behavior of each single-vowel grapheme when it is found in a closed syllable?
4. What is the phonemic behavior of each of these graphemes in an accented closed syllable? In an unaccented closed syllable?

*Reading and Realism, IRA Proceedings, Vol. 13, Part 1, 1969, 645-649.

Procedure

Hanna, Hanna, Hodges, and Rudorf, in 1966, published a volume titled *Phoneme-Grapheme Correspondences as Cues to Spelling Improvement.* In it, they reported the results of their computerized examination of 17,310 words: 15,284 words selected from Part 1 of the Thorndike-Lorge *Teacher's Word Book of 30,000 Words* (*8*), plus 2,026 words selected from the *Merriam-Webster's New Collegiate Dictionary,* sixth edition, "which were considered to be relevant to the study of a 'common core' vocabulary but had not been available from Part 1 of the Thorndike-Lorge word list" (*6*: 12-13). The *Merriam-Webster's New Collegiate Dictionary,* sixth edition (*7*), was the source for the analysis of phoneme-grapheme correspondences (See *6*: 13-14). The authors of the Hanna, et al, study were concerned with furthering knowledge about spelling by examining phoneme-grapheme relationships.

The purpose of the present study is to further knowledge about reading, specifically about the phonic situation. To do so, it is necessary to look at grapheme-to-phoneme relationships. The procedure is the reverse of that used by Hanna, et al.

Using as source materials the findings of Hanna, et al, and reversing them to "grapheme to phoneme" relationships, the author of the present study was able to classify the sounds of all single-vowel graphemes for the 17,310 words examined.

Results

The grapheme-phoneme relationships for each vowel were examined. In Table 1 the findings are presented according to syllabic position, and within this, according to accent pattern —accented syllable (primary or secondary) or unaccented syllable. Both frequency and percentage data are supplied.

When available, the following phonemes appear for each grapheme: long sound, long sound before an *r*, short sound, short sound before an *r*, and schwa. Also included is every other phoneme which reached the 5 percent level in at least one percentage column. Phonemes not listed did not reach that 5 percent level in any column.

Conclusions

To answer the questions posed, the author decided to use a minimum of an *80 percent utility level.* Therefore, in this section the number of phonemes for each grapheme are given, in order to reach at least the 80 percent level.

1. open syllables

a. The most common phonemes for single-vowel graphemes in open syllables are

e: ē - 90.4%	a: ə - 53.4%, ā - 32.4%
o: ō - 92.0%	i: ə - 47.8%, ĭ - 37.3%
u: ū - 82.6%	y: ĭ - 87.8%

If we wish to disregard accent as a cue, the following generalization seems appropriate: In an *open syllable, e, o,* and *u* will have their own long sounds; *a* will have a *schwa* or a *long a* sound; *i* will have a *schwa* or a *short i* sound.

The findings about *y* in an open syllable may be misleading here. Burmeister (*2*) looked at the following generalization and found it to be highly valid (99 percent): "When *consonant* + *y* are the final letters in a monosyllabic word, the *y* has a *long i* sound; in a polysyllabic word the *y* has a *short i* (long e) sound." An analy-

Table 1: Frequency and Percent of Occurrence of Each Phoneme for Each Single-Vowel Grapheme According to Syllabic Position and Accent Pattern

grapheme	phoneme	example	open syllable						closed syllable					
			Total f	%	Accented f	%	Unaccented f	%	Total f	%	Accented f	%	Unaccented f	%
a	ā	halo	860	32.4	849	93.0	11	.6	142	2.8	139	4.1	3	.2
a	ǎ	vary	0	0	0	0	0	0	64	1.3	64	1.9	0	0
a	ǎ	baboon	304	11.5	1	.1	303	17.4	3888	76.6	2485	73.4	1403	82.7
a	ä	arm	58	2.2	49	5.4	9	.5	460	9.1	383	11.3	77	4.5
a	ə	canal	1418	53.4	0	0	1418	81.5	19	.4	0	0	19	1.1
Σa			2654		913		1741		5078		3382		1696	
e	ē	senior	1740	90.4	345	97.7	1395	88.8	25	.4	18	.6	7	.2
e	ę	hero	0	0	0	0	0	0	64	1.0	63	2.2	1	.03
e	ě	bet	44	2.3	1	.3	43	2.7	3272	48.3	2419	85.2	853	21.7
e	ẽ	after	6	.3	1	.3	5	.3	1660	24.5	0	0	1660	42.2
e	ə	angel	115	6.0	0	0	115	7.3	648	9.6	1	.04	647	16.5
e	ũ	her	0	0	0	0	0	0	313	4.6	288	10.1	25	.6
le	'l	able	0	0	0	0	0	0	620	9.2	0	0	620	15.8
Σe			1924		353		1571		6772		2840		3932	
i	ī	china	395	14.2	294	94.8	101	4.1	159	3.4	158	5.7	1	.1
i	ĭ	in	1039	37.3	0	0	1039	41.9	4307	91.5	2417	86.9	1890	98.0
i	ə	pencil	1332	47.8	0	0	1332	53.7	15	.3	0	0	15	.8
i	ē	ski	23	.8	16	5.2	7	.3	15	.3	13	.5	2	.1
Σi			2789		310		2479		4709		2781		1928	
o	ō	so	1629	92.0	545	97.0	1084	89.7	247	5.8	208	9.5	39	1.9
o	ô	cord	0	0	0	0	0	0	312	7.4	262	12.0	50	2.4
o	ŏ	dot	0	0	0	0	0	0	1557	36.7	1425	65.0	132	6.4
o	ô	off	0	0	0	0	0	0	123	2.9	102	4.7	21	1.0
o	ə	carton	114	6.4	0	0	114	9.4	1497	35.3	0	0	1497	73.0
o	ə̃	humor	0	0	0	0	0	0	265	6.3	0	0	258	13.1
o	ŭ	son	0	0	0	0	0	0	112	2.6	110	5.0	2	.1
Σo			1770		562		1208		4243		2192		2051	
u	ū	union	770	82.6	320	82.3	450	82.9	44	2.3	29	2.3	15	2.3
u	ũ	burn	0	0	0	0	0	0	203	10.6	188	14.7	15	2.3
u	ŭ	cup	2	.2	0	0	2	.4	1210	62.9	996	77.8	214	33.3
u	ə	submit	42	4.5	0	0	42	7.7	255	13.3	0	0	255	39.7
u	ōō	truth	82	8.8	69	17.7	13	2.4	11	.6	11	.9	0	0
u	ōō	put	36	3.9	0	0	36	6.6	164	8.6	51	4.0	113	17.6
Σu			932		389		543		1923		1230		643	
y	ī	by	209	11.1	123	100.0	86	4.9	2	1.2	2	1.7	0	0
y	ĭ	myth, baby	1647	97.9	0	0	1647	94.0	154	93.3	117	96.7	37	84.1
y	ə	idyl	20	1.1	0	0	20	1.1	3	1.8	0	0	3	6.8
y	ə̃	martyr	0	0	0	0	0	0	4	2.4	0	0	4	9.1
Σy			1876		123		1753		165		121		44	

sis of the data in the present study affirms that the vowel sound for a *consonant* + *y* in an accented open syllable is *long i,* and in an unaccented open syllable is *short i.* This suggests a partial confirmation of the above generalization, since all one-syllable words are in the *accented* category.

b. The most common phonemes for single-vowel graphemes in *accented*

A single-vowel in a *closed syllable* has its own short sound, except as modified by *r* (in the case of *a, e,* and *u*), or a *schwa* sound (in the case of *e, o,* and *u*). *Y* has a *short i* sound in a closed syllable (*e.g.,* synonym).

b. The most common phonemes for single-vowel graphemes in *accented* closed syllables are as follows:

a: ă̄ - 73.4%, ä - 11.3%

short	before r	schwa and other
a: ă - 76.6%	ä - 9.1%	
e: ĕ - 48.3%	ē - 24.5%	ə - 9.6%
i: ĭ - 91.5%		
o: ŏ - 36.7%		ə - 35.3%, ô - 7.4%, ē - 6.3%
u: ŭ - 62.9%	û - 10.6%	ə - 13.3%
y: ĭ - 93.3%		

open syllables are as follows:

e: ē - 97.7%	a: ā - 93.0%
o: ō - 97.0%	i: ī - 94.8%
u: ū - 82.3%	y: ī - 100.0%

Generalization: In an accented open syllable, each vowel has its own long sound (y = ī).

This generalization has a high validity level, but low frequency value.

The most common phonemes for single-vowel graphemes in *unaccented* open syllables are as follows:

e: ē - 88.8%	a: ə - 81.5%
o: ō - 89.7%	i: ə - 53.7%, ĭ - 41.9%
u: ū - 82.9%	y: ĭ - 94.0%

In an *unaccented open syllable, e, o,* and *u* have their own long sounds; *a* has a *schwa* sound; *i* has a *schwa* or *short i* sound; and *y* has a *short i* sound.

2. closed syllables

a. The most common phonemes for single-vowel graphemes in closed syllables are

e: ĕ - 85.2%	
i: ĭ - 86.9%	
o: ŏ - 65.0%, ô - 12.0%, ō - 9.5%	
u: ŭ - 77.8%, û - 14.7%	
y: ĭ - 96.7%	

The most common phonemes for single-vowel graphemes in *unaccented* closed syllables are as follows:

a: ă - 82.7%
e: ē - 42.2%, ĕ - 21.7%, ə - 16.5%
i: ĭ - 98.0%
o: ə - 73.0%, ē - 13.1%
u: ə - 39.7%, ŭ - 33.3%, ŏŏ - 17.6%
y: ĭ - 84.1%

Accent may serve as a cue in closed syllables for *e, o,* and *u,* since *schwa* sounds are found only in unaccented syllables. Accent is not a strong cue for *a* or *i.*

3. schwa sound

It may be interesting to note that *a* and *i* commonly represent a schwa sound in an open syllable, but not in a closed syllable. An *o* often represents a schwa sound in a closed syllable, but not in an open syllable.

Related findings—consonantizing of y, i, and u

Y served as a grapheme 2,095 times in the Hanna, et al material. It served as a vowel 2,041 times, and as a consonant 53 times, or 2.53 percent of the time. When it was a consonant, it was always the first letter in the syllable. Forty times it was the first letter of the word (yacht, yes); five times it was the first letter of the second root of a compound (barnyard). It always directly preceded a single or double vowel (buoyant, canyon) and at times followed a vowel pair. *Y,* of course, also occurs as part of several vowel-pair graphemes (ay, ey, oy, uy). In these cases it *follows* a single vowel. (See *3.*)

I occurred as a single-vowel 7,498 times. But it also occurred 1,141 times in a consonant function. Sixty-six times it served as a single consonant grapheme, and 1,075 times as a part of a consonant grapheme, according to the Hanna, et al coding system. When it was coded as a consonant, it had a *y* sound and always preceded a vowel. It, therefore, might be considered by some to be part of a vowel-pair (al*i*en, opin*i*on, sen*i*or). The remaining times, when *i* was coded as part of a consonant grapheme, it also always directly preceded a vowel. In all but 16 of these cases it followed a *c, t,* or *s,* and usually (995 times) it helped to make the *sh* sound (fac*i*al, vic*i*ous, lus-c*i*ous, pens*i*on, mans*i*on, dic*t*ion, fic-*t*ion, lo*t*ion). It also helped to make the *zh* sound 51 times (ero*s*ion, vi*s*ion, fu*s*ion) and the *ch* sound 13 times (ques*t*ion).

U also served as a consonant (*w*— 47 times), or as part of a consonant grapheme (*qu* = k—27 times; *qu* = kw—191 times; *cqu* = kw—5 times), for a total of 270 times, or 8.6 percent of the time that *u* was found in the Hanna listings. In each case, the *u* directly preceded a vowel (*u* = w: s*u*ave, s*u*ite, jag*u*ar; *qu* = k: bou*qu*et, mos*qu*ito; *qu* = kw: *qu*ack, *qu*ail, *qu*een; *cqu* = kw: ac*qu*ire, ac*qu*it).

REFERENCES

1. Bailey, Mildred Hart. "The Utility of Phonic Generalizations in Grades One through Six," *Reading Teacher,* 20 (February 1967), 413-418.
2. Burmeister, Lou E. "An Evaluation of the Inductive and Deductive Group Approaches to Teaching Selected Word Analysis Generalizations to Disabled Readers in Eighth and Ninth Grade," doctoral dissertation, University of Wisconsin, 1966.
3. Burmeister, Lou E. "Vowel Pairs," *Reading Teacher,* 21 (February 1968), 445-452.
4. Clymer, T. L. "The Utility of Phonic Generalizations in the Primary Grades," *Reading Teacher,* 16 (January 1963), 252-258.
5. Emans, R. "The Usefulness of Phonic Generalizations above the Primary Grades," *Reading Teacher,* 20 (February 1967), 419-425.
6. Hanna, P. R., et al., *Phoneme-Grapheme Correspondences as Cues to Spelling Improvement.* Washington, D. C.: Office of Education, U. S. Department of Health, Education, and Welfare, 1966.
7. *Merriam-Webster's New Collegiate Dictionary* (6th ed.), 1961.
8. Thorndike, E. L., and I. Lorge. *The Teacher's Word Book of 30,000 Words.* New York: Bureau of Publications, Teachers College, Columbia University, 1944.

Which Accent Generalizations Are Worth Teaching?

Carol Winkley*

A S A TECHNIQUE of word identification, several reading specialists and authors of basal reader manuals have advocated teaching children to apply certain accent generalizations to locate the accented syllable in unfamiliar multi-syllabic words. Recommendations have been made although there has been no evidence providing justification for teaching the application of accent generalizations as a word-attack method. Two studies conducted by Clymer (1) and Groff (5) raised questions regarding the advisability of teaching principles of accentuation at either the primary or the intermediate grade levels. There has been no agreement among reading experts as to whether accent generalizations should be taught.

A recent study (7) has provided the first experimental evidence of the value of teaching accent generalizations as a word recognition technique. Two groups of pupils of average ability and above at the intermediate grade levels were compared. Pupils in one group received instruction in applying accent generalizations to unfamiliar words (the "accent-generalization group"). Children in another group in a neighboring community learned only the dictionary skill of pronouncing words in which the accented syllables were marked (the "marked-accent group"). Compared with pupils who had not been taught the accent principles, pupils in the "accent-generalization group" were found to have greater "power" in (a) ability to attack unknown words, (b) vocabulary development, and (c) comprehension. It was concluded, therefore, that the reading proficiency of intermediate grade pupils with average ability was improved by a word recognition program that included the teaching of accent generalizations.

The Problem

From the findings presented, indicating that accent generalizations were helpful in the identification of unknown words, it was inferred that such generalizations should be taught to pupils of average ability and above at the intermediate grade levels. The question then arose as to *which* generalizations should be taught.

Of the reading specialists, Gray has presented the most comprehensive plan for teaching "clues to accent." These are fully explained in his 1960 edition of *On Their Own in Reading* (4) and were incorporated in his basic reader series for Scott, Foresman. Although linguists have discussed a few of the "stress patterns" of isolated words, their chief interest has been in the stress patterns of connected speech and the effects of shifts of accent on intended

*The Reading Teacher, 20 (December 1966), 219-224, 253.

meaning. Because isolated words have been the main concern of reading specialists, these were investigated in this study. Eighteen accent generalizations proposed by Gray were tested. The generalizations appear in the accompanying table.

The relative merits of each generalization were assessed in two ways. First, a word count was used to determine the percentage of multisyllabic words complying with each generalization and the percentage of words which were exceptions to each principle. Second, an attempt was made to determine the relative usefulness of each generalization to children faced with the actual task of identifying unfamiliar words of more than one syllable.

The applicability of accent generalizations to multi-syllabic words, through the use of word counts, has been reported elsewhere (7).

Columns one and two of the table show which accent generalizations had the highest percentage of words complying with the clue and those having the highest percentage of exceptions.

The findings of this aspect of the study seem to lend support for the teaching of the accent generalization clues numbered 3, 4, 8, 13, 15, 16, and 18. Since Clues 1 and 10 had a relatively high percentage of exceptions, they were not considered to be of value.

As the second step in determining the advisability of teaching the principles of accentuation, the relative merits of the generalizations were assessed through the administration of a written Accent Test, constructed by the experimenter. This test required the pupils to perform three tasks in relation to each unknown word: (1) to underline the accented syllable, (2) to select the right vowel sound for the accented syllable, and (3) to choose the correct meaning for the word.

The unknown words for the test were secured from two word lists— Dale and Eichholz, *Children's Knowledge of Words* (2), and Diederich and Palmer, "Difficulty in Grades 11 and 13 of 4,800 Words from 6,000 Through 20,000 in Frequency" (3). A total of 10,896 multisyllabic words which could be considered unknown to an average fourth grader were classified according to the accent generalization that was applicable.

The Accent Test was constructed using a random selection of words from the lists obtained for each generalization. The number of test words exemplifying each accent generalization reflected the percentage of words of that type in the total sample at each particular grade level. The "foils" originally used by Dale and Eichholz in their testing were obtained and used as the multiple-choice items of the test. The administration of the test in pilot studies provided an additional check on the familiarity of the words and made it possible to improve the content of the test and refine the procedures of administration.

Face validity, supplemented by evidence obtained in individual interviews with selected subjects, and

ACCENT GENERALIZATIONS AND THEIR USEFULNESS

Clues to Accent Generalizations	Highest Percentage of Words Complying With Clues	Highest Percentage of Exceptions to Clues	Clues Most Useful to Accent-Generalization Group	Clues Considered Worth Teaching
1. Compound Word Clue — In compound words, a common pattern of accent is a primary accent on or within the first word and a secondary accent on or within the second word. (foot" hold')	X	X		
2. Noun-Verb Clue — In two-syllable words which may be used either as a noun or a verb, the accent is usually on the first syllable when the word is used as a noun and on the second syllable when the word is used as a verb. (con' test *vs.* con test')				
3. "Ion" Clue — In words ending with —ion, the primary accent falls on the next to the last syllable. (tu i' tion)	X			X
4. Varied Suffix Clue — The primary accent usually occurs on the syllable before the suffixes —ity, —ic, —ical, —ian, —ial, or —ious and on the second syllable before the suffix —ate. (vi tal' i ty, ty ran' ni cal)	X			X
5. Dropped Final "e" Clue — A single consonant letter following a single vowel letter before an ending or suffix (beginning with a vowel) may be a clue that a final "e" was dropped and the last syllable of the root word is accented. (pro cur' ing)				
6. Unaccented Syllable Before Ending Clue — A single consonant letter following a single vowel letter before an ending or suffix (beginning with a vowel) may be a clue to an unaccented final syllable in the root word. (cov' et ed)				
7. Two Consonants Before Ending Clue — Two like consonants before an ending or suffix are a clue to an accented final syllable in the root word. (con trol' ler)			X	X
8. Twin-Consonant Clue — Two like consonant letters following the first vowel letter are a clue to an accented first syllable. (ag' gra vate)	X			X
9. "ck" Clue — The letters "ck" following a single vowel letter are a clue to an accented first syllable. (flick' er)			X	X
10. Final "e" Clue — Two vowel letters, one of which is final "e" in the last syllable of a word, may be a clue to an accented final syllable. (con trive')	X	X	X	
11. Two Vowels Together Clue — Two vowel letters together in the last syllable of a word may be a clue to an accented final syllable. (im peach')			X	X
12. Final "y" Clue — In a two-syllable word that ends in a consonant followed by "y," the first syllable is usually accented. (pal' sy)			X	X

ACCENT GENERALIZATIONS AND THEIR USEFULNESS (Continued)

Clues to Accent Generalizations	Highest Percentage of Words Complying With Clues	Highest Percentage of Exceptions to Clues	Clues Most Useful to Accent-Generalization Group	Clues Considered Worth Teaching
13. Common Beginning Clue — If de—, re—, be—, ex—, in—, or a—, is the first syllable in a word, it is usually unaccented. (re sort', a dieu')	x		x	x
14. "ture" "le" Clue — If the final syllable in a word is —ture, or —le preceded by a consonant, that final syllable is usually unaccented. (nur' ture, am' ble)			x	x
15. Root-Word Clue — In inflected or derived forms of words, the primary accent usually falls on or within the root word. (list' less, un mixed')	x		x	x
16. Long Word Clue — In words of three or more syllables, one of the first two syllables is usually accented. (cat' a pult)	x			x
17. Two-Accent Clue — In longer words where there is a secondary as well as a primary accent, often the secondary accent falls on the first or second syllable, which is then followed by one unstressed syllable before the primary accent. (su' per sede")				
18. Two-Syllable Word Clue — In a word of two syllables the first syllable is usually accented unless it is a prefix. (mer' chant)	x			x

reliability coefficients of .92 and .95 (using the Spearman-Brown "split-half" technique) established the Accent Test as a dependable instrument of measurement.

The subjects of the study were 409 pupils at the fourth, sixth, and eighth grade levels. Approximately half of these pupils (207), using the Scott, Foresman basal readers, had been taught accent generalizations as a part of their word recognition program at the intermediate grade levels (the "accent-generalization group"). The remaining 202 students, using the Lyons and Carnahan basal readers, had received instruction in pronouncing words which had their accented syllables marked (the "marked - accent group"). Each subject had an IQ of 100 or more, had attended his present school system since the beginning of fourth grade, and had been taught by teachers in the intermediate grades who had had at least two years of experience in that school system. The reading consultant and the principals in each system encouraged the use of the basal reader manuals and believed that concepts concerning accent were taught as suggested.

Following the administration of the tests, all data were coded and punched on IBM cards. An item analysis of test responses related to each generalization was made. Proportions were then computed comparing the total responses that were correct with the total possible responses for all of the test items exemplifying each generalization. A statistical analysis of the differences between the resulting proportions revealed any differences that were significant. The relative merits of each accent clue were thus assessed.

Statistically significant superiority in proportions was shown for the "accent-generalization group" over the "marked-accent group" in many generalizations at the end of fourth and sixth grades. In the fourth grade at the beginning of the year and in the eighth grade at the end of the year differences were not consistently in favor of either the "accent-generalization group" or the "marked-accent group," and the differences did not reach the 5 per cent level of significance in any instance.

Since the differences found at the end of the fourth and sixth grades were frequently statistically significant and, for each generalization, proportions were higher in the "accent-generalization group" than in the "marked-accent group," the data for the two grade levels were combined and new proportions computed for the "accent-generalization group." The purpose of combining the data was to secure a single proportion for each generalization which would make it possible to compare one generalization with another. Thus, the accent clues which were most helpful to the pupils to

whom they had been taught could be determined.

Eight of the generalizations had proportions significantly higher than the remaining generalizations. These generalizations are indicated in the third column of the table. The principles that appeared to have the highest utility, listed in the order of their apparent usefulness, were: (9) "ck" Clue, (11) Two Vowels Together Clue, (10) Final "e" Clue, (12) Final "y" Clue, (13) Common Beginning Clue, (14) "ture," "le" Clue, (7) Two Consonants Before Ending Clue, and (15) Root-Word Clue. (Clue 18 was not tested since the children in the "accent-generalization group" had not been taught to apply it.)

Discussion

Comparing the whole list of generalizations with those identified as "useful" through word counts, one finds Clues 13 and 15 identified as useful by both techniques. Although the generalization clues numbered 3, 4, 8, and 16 were not as helpful to the subjects of the "accent-generalization group" as were the eight clues enumerated above, their applicability to a relatively high percentage of multisyllabic words warrants consideration in the final selection of accent generalizations worth teaching.

Because about one-third of the words to which Clues 1 and 10 were applicable were found to be exceptions, the advisability of teaching these clues was questioned. Omitting these clues, the possible "utility" of twelve of the generalizations was demonstrated.

Conclusions and Recommendations

Twelve generalizations (Clues 3, 4, 7, 8, 9, 11, 12, 13, 14, 15, 16, and 18) appeared to be worth teaching to children. With these findings in mind, the recommended list of accent generalizations to be taught was shortened and simplified by combining and rewording the twelve generalizations.

The following seven generalizations are proposed as those worth teaching to children because of their applicability to multisyllabic words or because of their demonstrated usefulness to children in the identification of unknown multisyllabic words. Examples of words to which the clues are applicable are provided.

1. When there is no other clue in a two syllable word, the accent is usually on the first syllable. (Eliminates need for teaching Clues 8, 9, 12, 14, and 18) Ex.: basic, program.

2. In inflected or derived forms of words, the primary accent usually falls on or within the root word. (Clue 15) Ex.: boxes, untie.

3. If de-, re-, be-, ex-, in-, or a- is the first syllable in a word, it is usually unaccented. (Clue 13) Ex.: delay, explore.

4. Two vowel letters together in the last syllable of a word may be a clue to an accented final syllable. (Clue 11) Ex.: complain, conceal.

5. When there are two like consonant letters within a word the syllable before the double consonants is usually accented. (Clues 7 and 8) Ex.: beginner, letter.

6. The primary accent usually occurs on the syllable before the suffixes -ion, -ity, -ic, -ical, -ian, -ial, or -ious, and on the second syllable before the suffix -ate. (Clues 3 and 4) Ex.: affectation, differentiate.

7. In words of three or more syllables, one of the first two syllables is usually accented. (Clue 16) Ex.: accident, determine.

Further research should be conducted to assess the usefulness of the generalizations, as restated above, in unlocking unknown words; to determine the advisability of teaching accent generalizations to pupils of below average ability; and to recheck the merits of teaching the generalizations eliminated in this study. In the meantime, the list of seven clues presented above can serve as a useful guide to the accent generalizations worth teaching.

(Dr. Winkley is now Assistant Professor of Education in the reading clinic at Northern Illinois University. She formerly served as a reading consultant in the Aurora public schools.)

References

1. Clymer, Theodore. "The Utility of Phonic Generalizations in the Primary Grades." *The Reading Teacher,* 16 (Jan. 1963) , 252-258.
2. Dale, Edgar, and Eichholz. Gerhard. *Children's Knowledge of Words.* Columbus, Ohio: Bureau of Educational Research and Service, 1960.
3. Diederich, Paul B., and Palmer, Osmond E. "Difficulty in Grades 11 and 13 of 4,800 Words from 6,000 Through 20,000 in Frequency." Princeton, N. J.:

Educational Testing Service, 1956.

4. Gray, William S. *On Their Own in Reading,* pp. 121-225. Chicago: Scott, Foresman, 1960.

5. Groff, Patrick. "To Teach or Not to Teach Accents?" *Elementary School Journal,* 62 (Jan. 1962), 218-221.

6. Winkley, Carol K. "The Applicability of Accent Generalizations," *Academic Therapy Quarterly,* 2 (Fall 1966), 2-10.

7. Winkley, Carol K. "Utilization of Accent Generalizations in Identifying Unknown Multisyllabic Words." Unpublished doctoral dissertation, University of Chicago, 1965.

COMMENT

This study provides teachers, publishers and authors of reading texts with valuable information hitherto unobtainable. It provides specific guidance for an instructional program in higher level word analysis skills. Studies of this type are important and welcome additions to our knowledge.—s.w.

PART IV: Instruction in Special Aspects of Word Recognition

The twelve articles in Part IV deal with particular aspects of the word recognition program. Chambers discusses the extension of the sight vocabulary; Emans tells how to use contextual clues; Schell deals with the teaching of structural analysis. What research has revealed about the more effective ways of attacking new words is reported by King in terms of sensory cues, Muehl in terms of visual discrimination, and Glass with directions for perceptual conditioning. Railsback discusses procedures for substituting consonants; Hanson shows how children work with variant word endings; the more effective strategies for teaching the sound-letter relationships are presented by Botel. The innovative phonetic and/or alphabetic approaches for teaching beginning reading are presented by Dietrich, Heilman, and Fry.

It is evident that speakers and writers in the past seven years have been more or less preoccupied with the sounding of words in the teaching of word-attack skills. Few whose articles have been published by the International Reading Association have concerned themselves with visual and structural analysis and the constantly important use of contextual clues. Analysis that deals with meaningful prefixes, suffixes and stems of words, and with the clues that context affords would seem to give more emphasis to comprehension in reading, and it is to be hoped that such elements of word attack will receive more attention in the future. Certainly teachers who do stress phonics should constantly give parallel emphasis to the meaning of the words that have been so analyzed and to the contextual clues given in the passages in which such words appear.

Extending the Sight Vocabulary

J. RICHARD CHAMBERS*

SIGHT vocabulary belongs under the broad category of word recognition regardless of the grade level span one considers. Disregarding grade level further, word recognition (and therefore, sight vocabulary) also implies word meaning since the necessity of understanding the meaning behind words read is without question. As everyone knows, there is no meaning on the printed page since only the symbols of meaning are there, stimulating the reader to make his own meanings. Therefore, word recognition becomes the ability of the reader to recognize the word as a form he readily knows (a "sight" word), to correctly pronounce the word, and to know the particular meaning of that word in its present context.

Importance of a Sight Vocabulary

Lacking an adequate sight vocabulary, the child is without word recognition skills and necessarily then, without word meanings. When meaning is not present neither are comprehension and/or recall. The effect of the absence of an adequate sight vocabulary is also reflected in incorrect, inadequate phrasing or word-by-word reading resulting, then, in poor oral reading. Though one might approach the development of word recognition skills through word analysis, without immediate recognition of words, speed of reading is too slow and results in an interruption of flow of thoughts and, consequently, a reduction in memory of the content read.

Traxler's study[1] of the relationship between vocabulary and general achievement points out that a child's word meaning score on the Stanford Achievement Test is a reasonably good predictor of his total score on the complete test. It has also been suggested that, "Some psychologists think that we never have any ideas until we have words to express them. Words seem to be necessary tools with which to think."[2]

It appears that to read with comprehension, the ultimate goal of all reading instruction, one must be able to recognize words immediately and to transfer these symbols into their proper meaning as determined by the particular setting in which the words occur. Children should be given the responsibility of *demanding* meaning from material read even though historically it is known that children are often not good judges of words needing clarification. The scale becomes one of reading with comprehension on one extreme to verbalism on the other.

At the intermediate grade level, the problems associated with vocabulary are multiplied a hundred-fold as compared with those in the primary grades. The number of words met by the child in the middle grades is almost without limit, yet his power to learn words is obviously limited to a small fraction of this total. The sheer number of new words is further complicated by the specialized nature of the vocabulary associated with the content subjects of social studies and science and, indeed, with any of the many subjects taught within this three-grade span.

Limitations of Sight Vocabulary

Stockpiling words in his sight vocabulary permits the child to develop his reading power and increases his reading horizons. Yet, as he reads more widely, he must inevitably meet new words which are not a part of his ready supply of words. Here his "go-power" is limited and the usefulness of his sight vocabulary diminishes. Unless he has been taught some independent method of analyzing words his only alternatives are to ask his teacher what the words say (assuming she is available), to guess at the words, or to

[1]Arthur Traxler, "The Relationship Between Vocabulary and General Achievement in the Elementary School," *Elementary School Journal*, XLV (February 1945), pp. 331-33.

[2]Mabel Vinson Cage. *Reading in High Gear*. New York: Harper and Brothers, 1938, p. 30.

Reading and Inquiry, IRA Proceedings, Vol. 10, 1965, 29-30.

forget about them and to try to go on without figuring out what the new words might be.

Simply relying on his ability to remember the configuration of a word limits his knowledge to words already presented. If he has learned to examine the context surrounding the word he has increased his "octane" but still has restricted his potential power. These perception and association abilities must be implemented by the addition of analytical abilities. Structural and phonetic analyses become particularly valuable and necessary at the intermediate grade level when the range and infrequency of new words met in the many different types of reading materials increases.

Techniques of Teaching

As one considers ways in which upper elementary level children may be helped to extend their sight vocabulary it becomes necessary to consider the element of quantity or the practical question of the number of words children may be expected to successfully learn per day. The number of words met by children at this level is apparently high. Yet *all* of these words will not be learned by all of the children. This suggests that establishment of the learning rate of students at this level is just as necessary as it is at the reading readiness and primary levels. Teaching in relation to the established learning rate is an acknowledged method of providing for individual differences since it recognizes the existence of varying progress rates and is a sound criterion to consider when attempting to set up reading groups.

Children in the upper elementary grades must be encouraged and, if necessary, re-taught to make use of context clues as an aid in word recognition. Evidence indicates that students at this level do not appear to use these clues as frequently as they should even though they have probably been given this instruction in the primary grades.

Evidence suggests that tachistoscopic drill not only produces gains in quick word perception ability but also results in increases in rapid word recognition with meaning, speed of oral reading, reduction in the number of errors in oral reading, and overall reading achievement.

When teaching vocabulary it is important to add the dimension of depth to the existing one of breadth. Depth in this context means two things: a level of learning going beyond simple recognition, and a knowledge of the multiple meanings which most words have.

Word analysis ability, a necessary extension of skill in word recognition for the development of independence in extending sight vocabulary, offers many opportunities for middle-grade teachers. Exercises combining structural analysis (especially prefixes, suffixes, root words) and word meaning are probably the most valuable kind of word analysis practice for developing the reading vocabulary of intermediate-grade children. The relationship of these sub-skills to reading vocabulary is higher than the relationship existing among any of the other commonly taught word analysis skills and vocabulary.

Since studies show a positive relationship between phonic ability and reading achievement it is necessary to suggest, too, that phonetic analysis be added to the elements that need emphasis when developing independent vocabulary power. The inductive approach to word analysis as reflected in the Word Analysis Practice Cards by Durrell and others[3] will help children develop a "phonic sense" without the necessity of relying on a multiple rules-exception program.

Summary

Procedures in word recognition must continually emphasize meaning and extend over into the area of word analysis with attention to the use of context clues and structural and phonetic analysis. The vocabulary demands placed upon children at these grade levels, because of the specialized nature of the content in the various subject areas and because of the lack of a rigidly controlled vocabulary, make it imperative that they become self-sufficient in their vocabulary needs.

Different Sensory Cues as Aids in Beginning Reading

ETHEL M. KING and SIEGMAR MUEHL*

SEVERAL METHODS of beginning reading instruction make use of the so-called "sight-word" approach as a basis for subsequent phonic teaching. The success of the sight-word approach depends on the ability of children to learn rapidly to associate a meaningful sound sequence with a specific graphic configuration. Many basal reading series have emphasized the value of using pictures to facilitate this sight-word learning. Russell (6) suggested that picture cards " . . . may be used many times until recognition of the word symbols is possible. . . . " Smith (7) rationalized this approach by saying that pictures " . . . offer the child valuable assistance in making the transition from recognizing an object and naming it to recognizing a symbol which stands for the object. . . . " In contrast, Dechant (2) questioned the emphasis on pictures in preprimer and primer materials: "Reading perhaps too often becomes an exercise in picture reading rather than in identification and understanding of the word." A sharp break in the tradition of using pictures to accompany beginning reading material is illustrated by the complete absence of pictures in Bloomfield and Barnhart's Let's Read series (1).

Out of these conflicting viewpoints a question can be framed, and the answer has practical implications for the classroom and relevance to learning theory. What sensory cues, or combination of cues, make for the most effective learning situation when children are being taught sight words? When a sight word (visual cue) is presented, the appropriate sound sequence can be indicated by the teacher's saying the word (auditory cue), by presenting a picture (visual cue), or by doing both (visual and auditory cues). In addition, the child may be asked to say the word aloud (self-produced auditory and kinesthetic cues). An increase in the number of cues accompanying presentation of the printed word can be hypothesized to act in two quite different ways on the learning process. The increase in cues may (1) interfere with learning by distracting attention from the printed word or (2) facilitate learning, particularly if the sight words are similar in appearance or sound. The second outcome would be in accord with the acquired distinctiveness of cues hypothesis offered by the psychologist Miller (5). The hypothesis states that if a subject learns to make distinctive responses to similar stimuli, these responses will become part of the respective stimulus patterns, making the original stimuli more distinctive. The use of pictures with similar sight words could elicit distinctive verbal responses or mneumonic devices

*The Reading Teacher, 19 (December 1965), 163-168.

which could aid in discrimination or mediate between the word and the appropriate sound sequence. Kinesthetic stimulation produced by the child's saying words would presumably confer additional distinctiveness to the words, particularly if the visual cues of the words were similar when the auditory cues were dissimilar.

The purpose of the present study was to compare systematically the relative effectiveness of different sensory cues and combinations of cues for kindergarten children as they learned to associate printed and spoken words varying in similarity.

Procedure

Different methods were used in training five groups of subjects to read a common list of four similar words. The same methods of training were repeated using five other groups learning to read a common list of four dissimilar words.

A kindergarten-sized table and two chairs were provided in a classroom apart from the regular classroom. A wooden stand with an inclined surface was placed on the table. Specially constructed books rested on the sloping surface of the stand. These books were of a loose-leaf type, 5½ by 8½ inches. The pages were of heavy white paper covered with acetate to protect them during frequent handling.

Each book had two alternating parts: training and testing. In the training part of the book each of four stimulus words was presented on a separate page. A test on each of the words presented in a different order

followed on the next four pages; these four presentations comprised one test trial. The training and testing pages were repeated in different orders until twelve test trials had been made.

To provide for the five methods of presentation, two different books containing the same set of words were needed for each word list. In one book the training pages contained the words with an appropriate picture above each word. In the other book the training pages contained only the words.

The training cue was centered on each page. All words were typed in lower case on a primary-style typewriter. When the method of training involved a picture, a simple black line drawing illustrating the word was presented above the word.

Words were selected according to the following criteria: (1) suitability for illustration (nouns), (2) evidence of their presence in the speaking vocabulary of most kindergarten children, and (3) similarity in the number of letters in each word so as to keep the length constant. For purposes of this study one list of words was chosen because they were approximately the same in configuration and contained some of the same sounds. These "similar" words were: doll, ball, bowl, and bell. By way of contrast, another list of words was selected because of their differences in configuration and in sounds. These "dissimilar" words were: gate, drum, nest, and fork.

Five different methods of training were used. In all methods the printed word appeared as a visual cue. The methods differed with respect to the additional cues appearing with the printed word. These included: picture, auditory, picture and auditory, auditory and echoic response, and picture and auditory and echoic response cues.

The picture groups were shown the word and corresponding picture. After about two seconds the experimenter held a white cardboard marker over the picture to focus attention on the word. The subject was instructed to "Look carefully at the word." Subjects trained by the picture and auditory method used the same book, but in addition to seeing the picture and the word they were also told the word. After the picture had been covered by the marker, instructions were given to the subject to "Look carefully at the word. The word is ———." A further dimension was added to the method for the picture and auditory and echoic response groups. After the picture had been covered by the marker each subject was asked to, "Look carefully at the word. The word is ———. What is the word?" An interval of about two seconds was allowed in which the subject was expected to respond by saying the word.

When the method of presentation did not involve a picture, as in the auditory groups and auditory and echoic response groups, a different book was used. The second loose-leaf book contained words only. The auditory group was presented with one word on a page. After about two seconds the experimenter placed the

marker above the word to focus attention on it and said, "Look carefully at the word. The word is ———." Subjects trained by the auditory and echoic response method were provided with the same materials as the auditory group but with the following modification in instructions. "Look carefully at the word. The word is ———. What is the word?" Again, an interval of about two seconds was allowed in which the subject was expected to respond by saying the word. Table 1 shows the ten training groups used in the study.

TABLE 1
TRAINING GROUPS

Training: Printed Word +	Kinds of Words	
	Dissimilar	Similar
Picture	Group 1	Group 2
Auditory	Group 3	Group 4
Picture + Auditory	Group 5	Group 6
Auditory + Echoic Response	Group 7	Group 8
Picture + Auditory + Echoic Response	Group 9	Group 10

Subjects

The subjects were 210 children from eight community kindergartens in Calgary, Canada.* Twenty-one subjects were assigned in rotating order to each of the ten groups. Two subjects were not included in the

*The authors wish to thank R. Warren, Superintendent of Schools in Calgary, and the following kindergarten teachers: Mrs. D. M. Arbuthnot, Mrs. R. Dean, Mrs. W. Frise, Mrs. E. J. Miller, and Mrs. A. Rutherford, whose cooperation made this research possible.

data because they could read the test words before training. Ages ranged from 61 to 77 months. The mean age was 70.9 months. There were no significant age differences among groups. The experiment was conducted between May 25 and June 10. The training and testing period for each subject lasted about fifteen minutes.

Results

In analyzing the data by learning trials, the 12 trials were divided into 6 blocks of 2 trials each. Table 2 summarizes the mean number of correct responses and the standard deviations for all groups, averaged over trial blocks.

A three-factor analysis of variance was used for analyzing the data (3). The between-factors included training methods and kinds of words; the within-factor included learning trials. The analysis of the data revealed a significant difference in the mean number of correct responses between the kinds of words ($p<.001$) with similar words being more difficult. The trials effect was significant in the expected direction ($p<.001$), as was

the trials by kinds-of-word interaction ($p<.001$). Examination of the data showed the trials by kinds-of-words interaction resulted from a faster learning rate for the dissimilar word groups. There was a significant interaction between training-methods and kinds-of-words ($p<.05$). Table 2 shows the nature of this interaction. It will be noted that the order of difficulty is completely reversed when similar and dissimilar words are compared. The picture method of training provided the most efficient learning with similar words, and the auditory method of training provided the most efficient learning with dissimilar words.

A two-factor analysis was conducted for both similar and dissimilar word groups. In each analysis training methods was the between-factor and trial blocks the within-factor. The two-factor analysis of variance on the number of correct responses for dissimilar word groups indicated significance ($p<.001$) for trials only. An identical analysis on the number of correct responses for similar word groups revealed a significant difference in the mean number of correct

TABLE 2
MEAN NUMBER OF CORRECT RESPONSES AND STANDARD DEVIATIONS FOR ALL GROUPS*

Training Method: Printed Word +	Similar Word Groups			Dissimilar Word Groups		
	Mean (rank)		SD	Mean (rank)		SD
Picture	2.10	(1)	1.03	3.15	(5)	1.00
Picture + Auditory	1.97	(2)	1.09	3.48	(4)	1.24
Picture + Auditory + Echoic Response	1.90	(3)	.68	3.52	(3)	1.63
Auditory + Echoic Response	1.86	(4)	.69	3.68	(2)	1.27
Auditory	1.27	(5)	.59	3.89	(1)	1.67

*Averaged over trial blocks.

responses among the training methods ($p<.05$). The trials effect was also significant ($p<.001$). When all pairs of group means for the similar word groups were compared, t-tests indicated that performance in the auditory method was significantly poorer when compared to each of the other methods. None of the other differences was reliable.

Prior to the experiment the Lorge-Thorndike Test of Intelligence was administered to small groups of the subjects. Subjects within the similar and dissimilar word groups were divided into high and low I.Q. groups. The analysis for methods showed no reliable differences associated with I.Q. Similar results were obtained when subjects were grouped by sex.

Discussion

The study showed that the most appropriate method for teaching sight words in beginning reading varied with the similarity of the words introduced. When the words were similar, faster learning resulted when the printed word was accompanied by a picture or by having the child say the word, as compared to hearing the word alone. This finding, when interpreted according to the acquired distinctiveness of cues hypothesis, indicates that the cues did elicit distinctive verbal or kinesthetic responses which served to make the similar words more distinctive, therefore facilitating discrimination among them. When the words introduced were dissimilar, however, the results indicated that the kind of sensory cue or combinations of cues accompanying the printed word made little difference in learning performance, although there was a tendency for hearing the word alone to be the most effective method.

Practically speaking, the findings do not support the view that pictures should be dispensed with in teaching sight words or in beginning reading material. For the beginning reader it is likely that many words look somewhat similar. Therefore, providing additional cues may aid the visual and auditory discrimination, which is necessary if a consistent spelling-to-sound association is to be made.

The present results agree with the findings of McNeil and Keislar (4). These authors investigated the value of an oral response in beginning reading. The program of words in their study was presented orally and visually. Pictures were used only occasionally for motivation. Kindergarten subjects were divided into "oral" and "non-oral" groups. The oral group was instructed to say the words; the "non-oral" group to look at the words. A follow-up silent reading test showed better performance by the "oral" group. Table 2 from the present study shows that the same combination of auditory and echoic cues produced significantly better learning than an auditory cue alone with similar words. In the McNeil and Keislar study some of the items required the subjects to identify the test word from among words similar in letter configuration.

The finding that words similar in shape and sound were more difficult to learn to read than dissimilar words is not surprising. However, it would be interesting to determine whether the visual or auditory dimension of similarity contributes most to the learning difficulty. Are *ball* and *bell* difficult to discriminate because they look alike, sound alike, or both?

(Ethel M. King is at the University of Alberta at Calgary and Siegmar Muehl is at the University of Iowa.)

References

1. Bloomfield, L., and Barnhart, C. L. *Let's Read,* Parts 1-3. Bronxville, N.Y.: C. L. Barnhart, 1963.
2. Dechant, E. V. *Improving the Teaching of Reading,* p. 205. Englewood Cliffs, N. J.: Prentice-Hall, 1964.
3. Lindquist, E. F. *Design and Analysis of Experiments in Psychology and Education.* Boston: Houghton-Mifflin, 1953.
4. McNeil, J. D., and Keislar, E. R. Value of the Oral Response in Beginning Reading: An Experimental Study Using Programmed Instruction, *British Journal of Educational Psychology,* 33 (1963), 162-168.
5. Miller, N. E. "Theory and Experiment Relating Psychoanalytic Displacement to Stimulus-Response Generalization, *Journal of Abnormal and Social Psychology,* 43 (1948), 153-178.
6. Russell, D. H. Children Learn to Read, p. 161. Boston: Ginn and Co., 1961.
7. Smith, Nila B. Reading Instruction for Today's Children, p. 168. 1963.

COMMENT

This investigation provides empirical insight into a question some linguists have raised about the value of pictures in beginning reading materials. Although the results cannot be viewed as unequivocal, they certainly should generate further study in this area. Moreover, the careful attention the authors have given to writing their research report, particularly the section on procedures, should permit others interested in the problem to replicate the present study.

Recent Research in Visual Discrimination: Significance for Beginning Reading

Siegmar Muehl and Ethel M. King*

MANY SYSTEMS of beginning reading instruction use the so-called "sight-word" approach to introduce children to their first reading material. The children are presented with a basic set of words which they learn to read. Later these words provide the basis for formal instruction in word analysis skills including structural and phonic analyses.

Learning sight words is an association process. As such, certain general factors are known to affect the ease with which the association is learned. First, the responses to be learned must be available and readily discriminated from one another. Secondly, the stimuli to be associated with the responses must be discriminated so that recognition is consistent for each appearance of the same stimulus.

In teaching reading, we have been well aware of the importance of making reading responses readily available. This has been done by selecting beginning reading words that are of high frequency in children's speech. Unless children have culturally disadvantaged or culturally different backgrounds these words are available; at most, we need to provide some auditory discrimination training to sharpen discriminations among similar sounding words.

The stimuli or printed words in beginning reading present an entirely different problem. In the beginning these graphic patterns are not readily discriminable or consistently recognized. Assuming the beginning reader has the spoken responses available, he is faced with two learning tasks with respect to these graphic patterns. First, he must learn to discriminate among the visual symbols; second, he must learn to associate each of the graphic patterns with an appropriate spoken word.

This paper is concerned with the kinds of training that are most effective in helping children learn to discriminate among graphic patterns. Our purposes are twofold: to present an overview of the research bearing on this question of discrimination learning and to suggest implications for teaching which seem warranted on the basis of this research. We say, "suggest implications" advisedly, since the majority of the research cited will be experimental in nature. This means that it was carried out in highly controlled and artificial circumstances. For this approach we make no apology. This step in educational research is imperative in order to assess, unambiguously, the operation of certain factors in the learning process. However, this type of research can only be a beginning. Experimental research needs to be followed up with classroom studies to determine whether or not the manipulations and variables which produce significant effects in experimental situations will also produce differences in the classroom that are *practically* as well as statistically significant.

Historical Development

Before we look at the recent research in discrimination learning, it would be useful to review briefly the history relating to the question of how children see words, particularly why whole words have been considered the child's "natural" unit of perception *(14)*. Several sources have contributed to this thinking. American educators writing in the 1850's opined that words are more easily remembered than letters because they are not such minute objects and because they are more meaningful. At the turn of the century, Huey *(6)* cited evidence from tachistoscopic research using adult subjects indi-

*Vistas in Reading, IRA Proceedings. Vol. 11, Part 1, 1967, 434-439.

cating that word "form" was the critical cue for perception. In 1922, Buswell's *(1)* studies of eye movements showed that the mature reader seemed to organize his reading perceptions by words and even phrases. Although the data from tachistoscopic and eye movement research could be used to support the "whole-word view," these same studies also showed that as the reading material became more difficult, or when young and inexperienced readers were used as subjects, discrimination of words proceeded mostly on a letter-by-letter basis. The historical clincher for the "whole word" approach, however, appears to be psychological theory, not experimental evidence. In 1924, Max Wertheimer, the Gestalt psychologist *(3),* stated that the whole is greater than the sum of its parts, and that the form or grouping that is most natural is the one which involves the smallest interval. Since words are letter groupings set apart spatially from other words, this theory seemed to provide the answer to word perception.

Recent Research

What does more recent research say about how children learn to discriminate visually among words? Our research with prereaders takes its beginning where Goins left off *(5)*. Goins' study was the first that made a systematic attempt to train first grade children in visual discrimination. The fact that the results of her tachistoscopic training with non-verbal type visual stimuli did not facilitate reading performance suggested the need for visual discrimination training with stimuli that are immediately relevant to learning to read; namely, printed words and letters themselves. Our first study *(11)* confirmed the specificity of transfer in the area of reading (Table 1). Three groups were given visual discrimination training or matching practice with three types of material: words that appeared on a subsequent reading task, words that did not appear on the subsequent reading task, and geometric forms. The results on the reading test favored the first group that had practiced discriminating among the same words that appeared on the reading task. Since there was no difference between the geometric and different word group, the results indicated that what is learned in discrimination is very specific and that this learning transfers only when the words in the reading task are highly similar to those in discrimination training. These results raised the question: What specifically are the children attending to as they learn to dis-

TABLE 1
TYPE OF TASK AND ORDER

First		Second
Visual Discrimination Training (Matching)		Reading Words
Groups	Materials	All groups
Same	boat, help, play, come	boat
		help
Different	make, jump, work, find	play
		come
Control		

criminate among words? Is it the "form" or shape of the word as a whole, or is it individual letters within the word? A study designed to assess these factors *(12)* showed two interesting findings (Table 2). First, word shape or form did not seem to be an important cue to kin-

words and the other groups. In this group, the children saw a picture of the word when the word was first presented and, in addition, the word was pronounced. The results showed two groups clearly superior in their word reading performance: the different meaningful

TABLE 2
TYPE OF TASK AND ORDER

First		Second
Visual Discrimination Training (Matching)		Reading Words
Groups	Materials	All groups
Same form	feu, geu, reu	feu - "blue"
Different form	fjd, gjd, rjd	geu - "red"
Letters only	f, g, r	reu - "white"

dergarten children in discriminating among words. Specific letter differences between the words seemed to be the significant cue. Second, although discriminating letters in isolation was much easier than discriminating letters embedded in words, the isolated letter group did just as well on the reading test as did the groups that had discriminated the letters in the words. A similar study by Staats, Staats, and Schutz *(15),* however, failed to confirm these findings. They found that visual discrimination training using the whole words was more effective than training with the letters in isolation. Professor King's doctoral dissertation *(7)* attempted to resolve these conflicting findings. Her study design is shown in Table 3. It is important to note the difference between the visual discrimination training group with different meaningful

word group and the relevant letter matching groups. In visual discrimination training, the letter matching task was the easiest of all; the different meaningful word most difficult. What skills transferred from these two different types of training? The different meaningful word group presumably learned that it is appropriate, to respond to printed stimuli with meaningful responses, which, after all, *is* reading. By contrast the letter group apparently learned to attend to the visual features that provided a basis for discriminating among the words. A subsequent study by the Cornell group *(9)* indicated that training with the letter at the beginning of a word is relatively more effective than with letters that occur in other positions. Another factor we attempted to assess was the relative effectiveness of presenting the materials in the matching tasks either simultaneously or successively *(7)*. Table 4 shows the difference in these two approaches. In the top example, the matching stimulus is presented at the same time as the re-

with a word in visual discrimination training led to the question: What is the most effective combination of cues for helping children learn sight words? The study designed to answer this question

TABLE 3
TYPE OF TASK AND ORDER

First		Second
Visual Discrimination Training (Matching)		Reading Words
Groups	Materials	All groups
Different word (meaningful)	nest, cake, ring, duck	hand
Different word	nest, cake, ring, duck	coat
Same letters	h,a,n,d,c,o,a,t, g,i,r,l,s,h,o,e.	girl
Same word	hand, coat, girl, shoe	shoe
Control		

sponse choices; in the bottom example, the matching stimulus is presented first and then removed before the response choices are presented. We found no reliable differences between these two methods of matching as measured in performance on the reading task.

TABLE 4
TYPES OF VISUAL DISCRIMINATION TASKS
Simultaneous (same page)

| hand | hand | coat | girl | shoe |

Successive (different page)

| hand | | | | |

| | | hand | coat | girl | shoe |

Positive transfer to reading resulting from associating a meaningful picture

(8) is shown in Table 5. Children were asked to learn to read two lists of words.

TABLE 5
TRAINING GROUPS

Training	Kinds of Words	
Printed word +	Dissimilar (gate, drum, nest, fork)	Similar (doll, ball, bowl, bell)
Picture	Group 1	Group 2
Auditory	Group 3	Group 4
Picture + Auditory	Group 5	Group 6
Auditory + Echoic Response	Group 7	Group 8
Picture + Auditory + Echoic Response	Group 9	Group 10

In one list, the words were highly similar in sound and appearance; in the other list, highly dissimilar in sound and appearance. The same table also shows the different combination of cues that were used in teaching the words to different groups of children. In each group the printed word was always presented. In addition, the words were accompanied by one or more additional cues. For example, in groups three and four, the printed word was accompanied by the teacher's saying it and the child repeating it. In groups nine and ten, the word was accompanied by cues provided by a picture, the teacher's saying the word, and the child's saying it. After each of the four words and accompanying cues were presented to the various groups, a test trial was given using the word alone, with the child trying to recall the correct response. The results at the end of the learning session are shown in Table 6.

TABLE 6

MEAN NUMBER OF CORRECT RESPONSES

Training Method:	Word Groups (gate, drum, nest, fork)		Word Groups (doll, ball, bowl, bell)	
Printed Word +	Mean	Rank	Mean	Rank
Picture	18.62	5	12.62	1
Picture + Auditory	20.94	4	11.86	2
Picture + Auditory + Echoic Response	21.14	3	11.43	3
Auditory + Echoic Response	22.10	2	11.19	4
Auditory	23.38	1	7.67	5

They indicate that when words were highly similar, additional cues helped the child discriminate and recall the printed word and sound association. Thus, groups 1-4 were reliably better in performance than the group that just heard the teacher say the word. For the dissimilar word groups, just the opposite order resulted. Hearing the word alone provided the best learning condition while the picture cue

provided the least effect method. Since it is likely that most printed words appear more similar than different to the beginning reader, it would seem safe to conclude that the use of pictures and other accompanying cues will be helpful in mastering sight vocabulary.

One final area of our research remains for summary. The question can be asked: If training in discriminating among letters facilitates word discrimination and reading, what effect does knowledge of the letter-names have on this process? The results of a study just completed are shown in Table 7 (13). The columns

TABLE 7

DISTRIBUTION OF HIGH AND LOW READERS
ON THE HARRISON-STROUD
LETTER-NAMING CONTEST

	Giving Names of Leters	
	Lowest 50%	Highest 50%
High readers	0	24
Low readers	13	12

represent above and below the median groups based on the Harrison-Stroud letter-naming subtest administered in September of first grade. The rows represent extreme reading groups (matched in IQ) based on end-of-first grade year Metropolitan reading test performance. Letter-naming ability appears to be markedly associated with later reading success. No child below the 50th percentile in letter-naming ability was in the high reading group. Twice as many children above the 50th percentile appeared in the high as compared to the low reading group. These results support Durrell's (2) earlier findings. We are not certain whether this relationship indicates that *training* in the knowledge of letter-names would facilitate word discrimination and reading, or whether knowledge of letter-names is an indication of a basic ability to form associations between abstract visual stimuli and auditory sequences. Durrell's methods study involving teaching letter-names and sounds supports the training notion.

Implications for Teaching

Keeping in mind that we are now moving from controlled experimental situations to the classroom, the results of this experimentation appear to have some practical implications for the classroom teacher.

1. Visual discrimination training from the very beginning should be with word and letter stimuli. Having the child match animal pictures, geometric forms, or any kind of non-verbal graphic stimuli does not appear to transfer to word discrimination. Our data confirms a point of view expressed by McKee (10) almost 20 years ago.

2. The simultaneous matching format which exists in most prereading books and charts at the present time seems adequate. To date we have found that simultaneous matching is easier than successive matching and that the transfer of discrimination learning appears to be about as effective.

3. Since matching letters is an easy task for kindergarten children, the earliest visual discrimination exercises should use letter stimuli. Although we do not as yet know how knowledge of letter-names works in the discrimination and reading process, the evidence strongly indicates that teaching the letter-names is probably highly useful. Letter discrimination and naming can be taught simultaneously.

4. Just prior to beginning reading instruction, visual discrimination exercises should include training in making the "three-way association" of the sound and the meaning with the visual form. If words are accompanied by a representative picture (when possible) and the pronunciation of the word, then a child gradually learns to attach a meaningful verbal label to the printed word each time it is encountered in a matching exercise. Such training provides not only for skill in visual discrimination but also skill in responding to graphic symbols in a manner similar to that required in learning to read.

5. Since the transfer of visual discrimination training seems to be very specific, the teacher would do well to give children practice in discriminating among the new words to be learned at the beginning of a reading lesson. At this point, a successive presentation could be used in the discrimination training. This type of presentation demands greater attention to the words in order to recall their letter characteristics since the word is not in view when the choices are presented.

6. When presenting new vocabulary words, particularly words that are easily confused with other words because of sound and letter similarities, providing additional cues in the form of pictures, when possible, and having the children pronounce the words will probably facilitate learning.

If the above research has answered a few questions, it has raised many more. Much investigation needs to be done. We hope to continue our efforts.

REFERENCES

1. Buswell, Guy T. *Fundamental Reading Habits:* A Study of Their Development (Supplementary Educational Monographs, No. 21.) Chicago: University of Chicago, 1922.
2. Durrell, Donald D. "First-Grade Reading Success Study: A Summary," *Journal of Education,* Boston University School of Education, 140:3 (February, 1958), 2-43.
3. Ellis, William Davis. *A Source Book of Gestalt Psychology.* New York: Humanities Press, Inc., 1955.
4. Fries, Charles C. *Linguistics and Reading.* New York: Holt, Rinehart and Winston, 1962.
5. Goins, Jean Turner. *Visual Perceptual Abilities and Early Reading Progress* (Supplementary Educational Monographs, No. 87). Chicago: University of Chicago Press, 1958.
6. Huey, Edmund B. *The Psychology and Pedagogy of Reading.* New York: Macmillan Company, 1908.
7. King, Ethel M. "Effects of Different Kinds of Visual Discrimination Training on Learning to Read Words," *Journal of Educational Psychology,* 55:6 (December, 1964), 325-333.
8. King, Ethel M. and Muehl, Siegmar. "Different Sensory Cues as Aids in Beginning Reading," *The Reading Teacher,*

19:3 (December, 1965), 163-168.

9. Marchbanks, Gabrielle and Levin, Harry. "Cues by Which Children Recognize Words," *Journal of Educational Psychology,* 56:2 (April, 1965), 57-61.

10. McKee, Paul. *The Teaching of Reading in the Elementary School.* Boston: Houghton Mifflin, 1948.

11. Muehl, Siegmar. "The Effects of Visual Discrimination Pretraining on Learning to Read a Vocabulary List in Kindergarten Children," *Journal of Educational Psychology,* 51:4 (August, 1960), 217-221.

12. Muehl, Siegmar. "The Effects of Visual Discrimination Pretraining With Word and Letter Stimuli on Learning to Read a Word List in Kindergarten Children,"

Journal of Educational Psychology, 52:4 (August, 1961), 215-221.

13. Muehl, Siegmar and Kremenak, Shirley. "The Ability to Match Information Within and Between Auditory and Visual Sense Modalities and Subsequent Reading Achievement," *Journal of Educational Psychology,* (in press).

14. Smith, Henry P. and Dechant, Emerald V. *Psychology in Teaching Reading.* Englewood Cliffs, New Jersey: Prentice-Hall, 1961.

15. Staats, Carolyn K., Staats, Arthur W., and Schutz, Richard E. "The Effects of Discrimination Pretraining on Textual Behavior," *Journal of Educational Psychology,* 53:1 (February, 1962), 32-37.

Consonant Substitution in Word Attack

CHARLES E. RAILSBACK*

THE TEACHING of consonant substitution is a prominent part of several of the basal reading programs currently being used throughout the United States. The procedure is taught, however, for different purposes in various reading programs. Some reading programs teach the use of consonant substitution in the skills portion of their program as a way of reinforcing knowledge of letter-sound associations. As children make new words based upon changing the letters that represent one consonant sound, the letter-sound associations are strengthened through practice. For most students such practice is an essential part of learning to quickly associate letters with the sounds that they represent. Consonant substitution exercises can, in addition to reinforcing the letter-sound associations, be valuable as a way for students to incidentally learn many new words. For example, as students make the word "dike" from "like," they not only reinforce the letter-sound associations for "i" and "d," but they may incidentally add words such as "dike" to their recognition vocabularies.

In addition to consonant substitution being taught for the purposes of reinforcing letter-sound associations and developing recognition vocabulary, some of the most widely used basal reading series teach yet another use for the procedure, consonant substitution as a method of word attack. The procedure, when taught for this purpose, is often referred to as a part of "phonetic-analysis." The teacher's guide of a primer that emphasizes this method of word attack states: *"Consonant substitution is a simple method of phonetic analysis that will enable children to attack new words while reading"* (Robinson, et al., 1962). The way in which such phonetic analysis is to be used by the pupil may be read in the teachers' manuals, an excerpt of a typical lesson being:

> *Conclude by having children identify new words formed by consonant substitution.* Place on the upper part of the holder the words *let, find, ride,* and *good.* Place on the bottom ledge, or hold in your hand, the letter cards for *s, w, m, h.* Read aloud the sentence *The fence around the ponies was made of* —————. Quickly place *w* over the *g* in the word *good* and let children complete the sentence with the word *wood* . . . . (Robinson, et al., 1962)

QUESTIONABLE POINTS

The question must be asked, "Is this an efficient method of

The Reading Teacher, 23 (February 1970), 432-435.

word attack that is actually used in independent reading?" To help determine an answer to this question, the author and a classroom teacher presented to an above average group of second graders a list of nonsense words and a list of words the students had not yet met in their basal readers. After the students had attacked each word, they were questioned by the teacher as to how they identified each of the unknown words. Words from their readers that were presented included: "truck," "cap," "dry," "best," "snow," and "chop." Nonsense words which were presented included: "nost," "ped," "doot," "plock," "zell," "cloy," "stot," and "pilt.'

For a few of the words one student reported using consonant substitution in the identification process. In all other instances, however, no students reported attacking the words by using a known base word from which a consonant sound was dropped and another added. Instead, students reported using their knowledge of letter-sound associations to attack the words directly. For instance, in attacking the word, "truck," they reported using their knowledge of the sounds that "tr" and "ck" stand for to identify the word. At a later time the teacher repeated this experiment with her slowest group of children. Although this group was by no means seriously handicapped in reading, no student was capable of attacking the words by use of consonant substitution, a procedure which had been taught them since the primer level of instruction.

The question about the practical value of the consonant substitution procedure as a method of word attack may also be answered by considering the way in which the adult attacks strange words. As the reader of this article meets such nonsense words as "clib," "ning," "zick," or "pelp," it may be predicted that very few, if any, would naturally attack such words by first thinking of "bib," "sing," "quick," or "help," dropping the first sound, and then adding the sounds represented by the first letters of the nonsense words.

The use of consonant substitution as a method of word attack seems extremely inefficient. The reader must look at the word and decide whether he knows a word from which he changes the beginning *or* the ending sound. He then must mentally "remove" the sound and substitute the one from the strange word. For no other reason than the excessive amount of time it takes to think of a word that is similar and then to make the substitution, the process cannot be recommended as a word attack procedure.

A far more serious weakness in this process, however, is the matter of determining the "known" word that is similar to the "unknown" word. To "know" the word from which the derivation is to be made means that the reader must have a mental image, i.e., the spelling, of the word. For instance, with the word "truck" how else will the student be able to utilize the procedure unless he can mentally picture "buck," "luck," or "duck?" Only after he has a mental image of the similar word can he remove a beginning letter and substitute "tr." It is tempting to say that the child does not have to mentally spell the similar word, that he can hear that "ruck" rhymes with "duck." It must be remembered that such a rhyming procedure will not work for the reader who has not yet identified the sound of "truck;" hence he does not know with what words it rhymes.

The students who most need efficient methods of word attack are the ones *least* capable of creating the necessary mental images to use consonant substitution to unlock strange words that they meet in print. Any person who has worked with below average students knows that while they usually have trouble remembering sight words, they seldom, if ever, can create the mental images in their minds with which to successfully use the substitution procedure.

Observation of first grade students in a related area, spelling, also verifies the point that students usually will not use the substitution procedure. Students seldom will independently learn the spelling of a word by substituting from a word that they *can* spell. For instance, seldom will a first grade student who knows how to spell a word such as "duck" drop the "d" and add "tr" to independently determine the spelling of "truck." If such a procedure is not used in spelling, there is little reason to think it would be used in reading.

In skills lessons, basal readers attempt to skirt the problem of creating the image of the known word by putting the word from which the substitution is to be made before the child. In independent reading, however, no such word sits on the chalk tray!

The publisher previously alluded to recognized the problem under discussion by mentioning it in the manual of the first reader: "Whenever you *help children use consonant substitution to attack unknown words*, they must call up mental images of known words that are similar in form to the unfamiliar printed words. The following exercise will reinforce this ability" (Robinson, *et al.*, 1962). An exercise typical of many in the program follows the quotation. A known word is placed before the children, and it is pronounced. This word then becomes the basis for substitution to form a new word. For example, the word "right" may be placed before the children. After it is identified, an unknown word, such as "night" is displayed. The student is to attack "night" by dropping the "r" from "right" and substituting the "n" of "night."

Such exercises are of questionable value for two reasons: 1] In independent reading no "known" word from which a substitution can be made is conveniently sitting on the chalk tray. 2] The exercise is inefficient in that it will generalize to only a very few words. To practice visualizing "right" so that "night" may be derived from it will help the reader identify but a few words—those that are spelled just like "right" except for the first sound—"sight," "blight," "fight," "light," "might," "night," and "tight." In many instances not even this many words could be derived from one word for which the mental image could be recalled.

Textbook authors apparently have great faith that such roundabout word attack procedures will actually work for it is suggested that the unknown words "keeping" and "snowing" be identified from the known words "sleep" and "show" or "slow" (Robinson, et al., 1963). With these words the child is expected to go through four mental steps: 1] dropping the suffix, 2] thinking of a word that is similar except for one sound, 3] dropping the sound, and 4] substituting the sound represented by the letter(s) of the unknown word that are different from the known word. Both personal observation of students and common sense would indicate that such procedures will seldom, if ever, be the actual way in which a student identifies an unknown word. For slower students, particularly, it is completely unrealistic to think that such word attack procedures will work in independent reading.

SUMMARY

The utilization of consonant substitution exercises within the reading program can serve to strengthen letter-sound associations as well as to provide a way in which some new words may be added to students' recognition vocabularies. However, to teach children to use consonant substitution as a primary word attack skill is to teach them a skill that is not only inefficient in terms of the time it takes, but also one that is of very limited usage. Few children can independently create the necessary mental image of a word that is spelled like the unknown word except for one consonant sound.

REFERENCES

Robinson, Helen M., et al. Fun with our friends—teacher's manual. Chicago: Scott, Foresman, 1962. Pp. 87, 134-135.

Robinson, Helen M., et al. More fun with our friends—teacher's manual. Chicago: Scott, Foresman, 1962. Pp. 62-63.

Robinson, Helen M., et al. Friends old and new—teacher's manual. Chicago: Scott, Foresman, 1963. P. 85.

First Grade Children Work with Variant Word Endings

IRENE W. HANSON*

ONE OF THE continuing concerns of primary grade teachers and authors of beginning reading materials is when and how instruction should be given in the use of variant word endings. That this concern is an important one is shown by a study by Edward Dolch (2), in which he reported that the three most common syllables in 8,409 samples of 14,000 running words in elementary school textbooks in arithmetic, history, and geography were *ing, ed,* and *er. Ing* occurred 240 times with 135 different words. *Ed* occurred 165 times with 90 different words. *Er* occurred 223 times with 72 different words. *Est* occurred 53 times with 17 different words. Since 14,000 running words represent about fifty pages of textbook material, this investigation pointed up the great frequency of occurrence of variant word endings and also their breadth of applicability to words in the English language.

Worth J. Osborn (3) investigated the frequency of occurrence of initial, medial, and final syllables in words in the Rinsland word list. He reported that the syllable *ing* occurred 881 times, *ed* occurred 338 times, *er* occurred 323 times, and *est* occurred 65 times. Osburn also made the following interesting comment:

We are told that the amount of transfer that takes place in learning is due, in a large measure, to the learner's ability to perceive identical elements in separate activities. Since this is true, one very useful approach to the teaching of the slow learner is to make him conscious of identical elements. . . .

The syllable that recurs most frequently is final "-ing," which is found in 881 of the 9,000 words. With perfect transfer, a child who has learned the "-ing" syllable in, say "going," will know that syllable in 880 more words.

These studies establish without doubt the frequency of occurrence and the importance of teaching the use of variant word endings. The following investigation conducted by the author attempted to answer the question of when such instruction could most profitably be given.

Twenty-six first grade classes from the St. Paul, Minnesota, public school system were used in the study. Thirteen of the classes were in the experimental group and thirteen in the control group. The classes in the groups were equated for socioeconomic level. Pretest data revealed no significant differences between the experimental and control groups with regard to reading ability, mental ability, chronological age, or knowledge of the use of variant word endings. The total number of children included in the analysis of the study was 554.

Over a period of four weeks the experimental classes received eighteen periods of special instruction in generalizations concerning variant

*The Reading Teacher, 19 (April 1966), 505-507, 511.

word endings and the application of them in contextual material. The endings taught were: *s* added to nouns and verbs, *ed, d,* and *ing* added to verbs with no change in the root word and also with dropping or doubling of a final consonant in the root word, *er* and *est* to form the comparative and superlative forms, and er as a noun agent. Each day's lesson required about twenty minutes and was given in addition to all regular reading and phonics instruction. The lessons were conducted with each class as a whole and consisted of a preliminary presentation of a variant ending generalization by the teacher, largely through the inductive method, and a period of pupil practice, both oral and written, including the use of a worksheet. Teachers' manuals and daily worksheets were supplied to the experimental classes. Vocabulary for instruction was chosen from the set of readers already in use in the classes, and the format of the worksheets was similar to that found in primary reading workbooks. Thus attention could be concentrated on the variant endings rather than on new vocabulary or new methods. The control classes used the same periods of time for independent reading.

The study was conducted during March and April of the first grade school year. The Bond-Balow-Hoyt New Developmental Reading Test (*1*) and a specially constructed Variant Ending Test were administered to all classes during the pretest and posttest periods. IQs and ages were obtained from school records.

Personal data and the differences among class means of the experimental and control groups on the tests were compared by means of the *F* ratio for analysis of variance. Then all the children in the experimental and control groups were divided into three mental ability groups, five reading ability groups, and three socioeconomic level groups. The means of these groups were then also analyzed by using the *F* ratio for analysis of variance.

Findings

1. There was a significant difference between pretest and posttest means of class means on the Variant Ending Test in favor of the experimental group over the control group. The difference was significant at the .01 level for the total number of children and for the boys, but was in the region of doubt (between the .01 and the .05 level) for the girls.

2. There was no significant difference between the experimental and control groups in reading scores before or after instruction in using variant word endings when the Bond-Balow-Hoyt New Developmental Reading Test was used as the measuring instrument. No response items on this test required a utilization of knowledge of variant word endings; hence, it can only be said that general reading ability as measured by this test was neither improved nor harmed by the special attention to the endings of words.

3. There were no significant differences among the gains on the Variant Ending Test of children in

high, average, or low mental ability groups. The three groups profited about equally from the instruction.

4. There was a significant difference among the gains on the Variant Ending Test of children in the five reading ability groups. The three lowest reading groups, which had measured average reading grade equivalents of 1.5, 1.8, and 2.0 on the pretest, profited somewhat more than the two highest reading groups, which had average reading grade equivalents of 2.4 and 2.9 on the pretest. The significantly higher scores of the two highest reading groups on the Variant Ending pretest showed, however, that these groups had already acquired much knowledge of variant word endings.

5. The differences among mean scores of children assigned to the three socioeconomic levels were in the region of doubt (significance between the .01 and the .05 levels) on the Variant Endings pretest. There were no significant differences among their means of posttest scores or mean gains. These data seem to suggest that socioeconomic status may have had some effect on pretest scores but that this effect was lessened by the instruction in variant word endings.

Educational Implications

1. The findings of this study clearly indicate that the teaching of generalizations concerning the use of variant word endings is possible and effective in the second half of first grade and that many of the children by that time have already acquired a considerable knowledge of such word endings independently.

2. Since the mean scores on the Variant Ending Test were significantly different for each reading ability group and increased regularly from the low group to the high one, the investigator suggests a planned sequence of teaching variant word endings, starting with noun plurals at the preprimer reading level, verbs adding *s, ed,* or *ing* with no change in the root word at primer level, verbs with changes in the root word and noun agents at first reader level, and comparative and superlative adjectives at the second reader level. This sequence differs from most presently used ones in beginning earlier with verb endings and completing instruction at the second reader level rather than at the third reader level.

3. The findings of this study indicate that the present practice of severely restricting the use of variant word endings in first grade reading materials is unnecessary since most first grade children are already familiar with their use in speech and are learning to use them independently in reading, even though they have not been specifically taught to do so. Authors of first grade reading textbooks should be able to make use of the *s, ed,* and *ing* verb endings throughout primer and first reader levels, provided a planned sequence of instruction in the generalizations concerning the use of variant word endings is maintained in the teachers' manuals and pupil workbooks. Hopefully, this increased use of com-

mon verb endings in first grade reading materials should permit authors to produce beginning reading materials which can conform more easily and naturally to English speech.

(Mrs. Hanson is Assistant Professor of Education at Augsburg College, Minneapolis, Minnesota. This material was taken from her dissertation for the Ph.D. degree, which she received from the University of Minnesota in June 1965.)

References

1. Bond, Guy L., Balow, Bruce, and Hoyt, Cyril J. *New Developmental Reading Tests*, Form L-I and L-II, Lower Primary Reading. Chicago: Lyons and Carnahan, 1963.
2. Dolch, Edward W. "Sight Syllables Versus Letter Phonics," *Elementary School Journal*, 41 (Sept. 1940), 38-42.
3. Hanson, Irene W. "An Investigation of the Effects of Teaching Variant Word Endings to First Grade Children." Unpublished doctoral dissertation, University of Minnesota, 1965.
4. Osburn, Worth J. "Teaching Spelling by Teaching Syllables and Root Words," *Elementary School Journal*, 55 (Sept. 1954), 32-41.

Use of Context Clues

ROBERT EMANS*

Mary had a little lamb,
Its fleece was white as_____.

FEW four-year-old children would be unable to complete the sentence with *snow.* Likewise, "Becky and her mother wanted to go shopping. They climbed into the _____ to go to the store." Few children, even before entering school, would have difficulty with supplying any one of several words which would make sense: *car, automobile, bus, streetcar.* Children use context in their oral language, easily and naturally. Children, and adults too, use context clues to aid them in their reading.

It is easy to find testimonials to the importance of context clues in reading. Open almost any textbook on the subject and there are such statements as

It would be difficult to overestimate the value of the context in children's word perception in reading (7:16).
Contextual clues provide one of the most important aids to word identification and interpretation (6:84).
Context clues are perhaps the most important single aid to word perception (11:25).
The person who has not developed skill in the use of verbal context has not become a mature reader (22:23).

It is important to know, however, that many children who are thought to be in difficulty in reading because of limited skill in analytical techniques or because they have insufficient knowledge of phonetic, structural, or visual elements are usually in difficulty because they are not using context clues well (4:321).

Obviously, statements praising the worth of context clues are easily found. Much has been written about how the use of context helps the reader develop the meaning of words. As important as it may be this topic is not the concern of this paper. Rather, the purpose is to attack the more elusive problem and explore what aid the use of context clues gives the reader in respect to word recognition.

There are at least four uses of context clues in word recognition. These can be summarized as follows:

1. Context clues can help children remember words they have identified earlier, but forgotten. Most teachers can cite examples of a child's having difficulty with a partially known word and then recognizing the word in a new setting after being told that the word is a familiar one and that it makes sense. For example, if a child reads "Bill was a cow" for "Bill saw a cow," asking him if what he reads makes sense will often enable him to correct himself.

2. Context clues may be combined with other word-analysis clues (phonic and structural analysis) to check on the accuracy of words tentatively identified by the use of other clues. Bond and Wagner state that context clues serve as "checks on the accuracy of all the other techniques that are used" (5:172).

3. Context clues help in the rapid recognition of words for all readers by helping one anticipate what a word might be. The ability to draw an ac-

*Reading and Realism, IRA Proceedings, Vol. 13, Part 1, 1969, 76-82.

curate inference to what a word is can serve as a time—saver. It is a faster technique than other word recognition aids such as phonics. It enables the reader to use only those phonic and other analytical techniques which are necessary to distinguish one word from another. For example, instead of having to sound out a word, the efficient reader uses only enough phonic clues to recognize the word quickly when combined with the meaning clues.

4. Context clues are required for the correct identification of some words. Gray states, "The pronunciation of many words (*permit*, for example) depends upon their meaning in a given context" (*11*:148). Other words which require the use of context clues are *lead* in a pencil or *lead* the way, *wind* a ball of string or the *wind* blew, *tear* a piece of paper or a *tear* flowed down her cheek, and piggy *bank* or a *bank* to fish from.

How do context clues work in word recognition?

Following the importance of context clues and some of the uses of context clues in word recognition, one should ask how context clues work? By answering this question, one can gain a better idea as to how to teach the use of context clues.

To understand how context clues work it must be recalled that the child brings to reading a background of experience and oral language. Likewise, the child must bring to the reading situation a habit of demanding meaning from his reading. A child must combine his experience, his oral language, and the meaning he gets from his reading if he is to use successfully context clues in recognizing words. When he meets a word which he cannot recognize, he uses his experiences, oral lan-

guage, and the meaning of the words, phrases, sentences, and paragraphs surrounding the word to anticipate what the word might be. Bond and Wagner state, "Instead of having to recognize the word from the total of words in the English language, the use of context clues limits the choice of words to the few that would fit the meaning of the passage being read" (*5*:172). By also using the other word recognition skills the child has at his disposal, he tentatively identifies the word and checks to see if the word makes sense. For example, if a child reads the sentence, "Jenny picked up her _____ to draw," he can, from his experience, limit the words to such possibilities as *pen, crayon, pencil,* or *chalk.* He would not have to select the word from the 800,000 or so possible words in the English language. By combining this information with various phonic clues, the child could recognize the exact word more quickly than by using only phonics.

With respect to the point that context clues may be used in conjunction with other word recognition techniques, Bond and Tinker state, "Meaning clues alone are not enough for good reading at any level. They must be accompanied by the use of a flexible set of word recognition skills. It is the interaction of all the word-study skills that forms the foundation on which a competent reader builds his reading structure" (*4*:322). DeBoer and Dallmann state, "Context clues are most effective when they are employed along with other methods of word attack" (*8*:111). In actual reading, the use of context clues is probably so closely tied in with other word recognition techniques that neither can be separated. Context clues alone are seldom adequate because they provide only one aid to word recognition. They may suggest one of several possible words but seldom point to the specific word. For example, in the sentence. "The mouse nibbled a piece of _____," any number of possible words could fit the meaning. However, by combining the sense of the sentence with the phonic clue that the word begins with a *ch* sound, the reader can readily supply the word *cheese*. Children should probably be discouraged from using context clues alone. By combining them with other word recognition techniques a child would be discouraged from wild guessing. Therefore, in relation to the discussion that follows, it should be remembered that whenever context clues are taught, they should probably be combined with other word recognition aids.

Some people might regard the use of context clues as untutored or guessing; and in a sense it is. However, it is probably more accurately described as inferential reasoning which must be developed, guided, and used in many areas of life. Nila Banton Smith states, "Surely this process of examining meanings, reasoning, and deducing an unrecognized word is not just a matter of chance guessing" (20: 186). Kolson and Kolinger state, "Guessing is the mainstay of the contextual clue skill and should be encouraged, but wild guessing is a symptom of a disability in contextual clue use" (14: 65). The sophisticated use of context clues, therefore, should probably be developed along with reasoning and the use of other word recognition skills.

The classification of context clues

Various attempts have been made to classify the wide variety of context clues. Although these classification schemes may be closely related to those for developing word meanings, they also have relevance for the use of context clues in word recognition. Artley (3) identified ten types of contextual aids the reader might find in printed matter: typographical (e.g., quotation marks, parenthesis), structural (e.g., appositives, nonrestrictive clauses), substitute words (synonyms, antonyms), word elements (roots, suffixes, prefixes), figures of speech (similes, metaphors), pictorial representation (e.g., pictures, diagrams, charts), inference, direct explanation, background of experience of the reader, and subjective clues (e.g., tone, mood, intent). Likewise, McCullough (15) identified two general classes of clues, idea and presentation. Idea clues included pictorial illustration, verbal, experience, comparison and contrast, synonym, summary, mood, definition, and familiar expression. The presentation clues included the position of words, the sequence of a sentence or paragraph, and the general organization of a selection. From a study of 500,000 running words Deighton (9) identified four *key words* classes (definition, examples, modifiers, and restatement) and *inferential clues* for which the reader has no direct clue except his ability to draw inferences. In his dissertation, for which he won the IRA research award, Ames (1) found fourteen clues from his case studies of mature readers using a variety of contextual situations:

1. Clues derived from language experience or familiar expressions
2. Clues utilizing modifying phrases or clauses
3. Clues utilizing definition or de-

scription
4. Clues provided through words connected or in series
5. Comparison or contrast clues
6. Synonym clues
7. Clues provided by the tone, setting, and mood of a selection
8. Referral clues
9. Association clues
10. Clues derived from the main idea and supporting details pattern of paragraph organization
11. Clues provided through the question-and-answer pattern of paragraph organization
12. Preposition clues
13. Clues utilizing nonrestrictive clauses or appositive phrases
14. Clues derived from cause and effect pattern of paragraph and sentence organization

Concerning the Artley and McCullough classifications, Russell states, "these are often too technical for systematic use in the elementary school. . . ." (19:300-301). Likewise, Ames states in respect to his own study that "It must be stressed that much more research is necessary and one would be ill-advised to try to develop elaborate instructional procedures based on the present classification scheme" (2:81). An appropriate task regarding the implementation of context clues in word recognition would appear to be the development of a simplified scheme for classifying the numerous kinds of context clues identified. The next few paragraphs will suggest such a possible scheme.

Most context clues for use in word recognition seem to fall into one of three main categories: meaning bearing clues, language bearing clues, and organization clues. The meaning bearing clues use the sense of the sentence or sentences surrounding the unrecognized word. The category includes such clues for recognizing unknown words as familiar expressions and idioms, definitions, descriptions, examples, synonyms, antonyms included in the text, as well as comparisons and contrasts, and the tone, mood, and setting of what is being read.

The language bearing clues use knowledge of syntax, the structure of sentences, as aids in word recognition. Hildreth states, "The use of context clues has its roots in linguistics" (13: 156). There are a number of examples of language bearing clues. One such aid is the noting of phrases which may serve as a clue in recognition of modified unknown words. Another such aid is the recognition of unknown words through referral signal words, such as *these* and *same*, which refer to what has been stated previously. The associating of known words of one part of speech with closely related unknown words of another part of speech (such as nouns and verbs or adjectives and nouns) may serve as another clue. For example, birds fly and fish swim; grass is green, and old ladies usually have gray hair. Finally the recognition of the relationship of nonrestrictive clauses, appositive phrases, or prepositional phrases to other parts of a sentence may serve as another language clue.

Another group of clues involve how sentences or paragraphs are organized. Within this group are such aids as the realization that an unknown word is part of a series of words and an appreciation of the relatedness of main idea to details, of questions to answers, and of cause to effect within sentences or paragraphs.

Therefore, it would appear that many context clues fall within one of these three classifications: meaning bearing, language bearing, and organization. The scheme is not all inclusive. For example, the scheme does not include contextual aids from pictures or the typography. However, it seems to simplify the complex classification schemes previously suggested.

Possibly to date, sufficient emphasis has not been placed on the role that context clues play in word recognition because the classification schemes have appeared to be too complex. The preceding simplified, yet comprehensive, scheme for the classification of context clues is proposed in the hope that it will foster further investigation in this area. Because of the simplification, teachers may feel encouraged to teach the use of context clues as knowledge of the structure and implications for teaching context clues is more attainable.

Teaching context clues

Although the teaching of context clues seems complex, there is evidence that teachers should attempt to do so. McCullough (15) concluded that adults fail to use context clues because they were never taught how to use them. In a study by McKee, children were found to use context clues effectively in only about one third of the opportunities presented (17:73), while Porter (21:316) found that third grade children could give an appropriate meaning of a word left out of context in about 80 percent of the cases. Since children may not develop the skill of using context clues without specific training, they should be given help in its development. Hester states, "Systematic guidance is necessary to help him learn this important technique for recognizing words" (12:138).

The goal of instruction for the use of context clues in word recognition is probably to develop such skill that context clues are used easily and automatically. If a child makes as many errors in contextual reading as he does in reading a list of words, he is probably failing to make extensive use of context clues. The problem becomes one of developing instructional procedures.

There is little evidence that children will use context clues more effectively if they have knowledge of sentence patterns. McKee states, such knowledge "contributes little if anything to the pupils' comprehension of the sentences" (18:185). However, children will probably benefit from knowing that 1) a word makes sense within a sentence; 2) readers can use sentence meaning to help recognize an unrecognized word; and 3) more than one word may fit the meaning of a sentence and, therefore, structure and phonic clues are often necessary.

In preparing to teach the use of context clues, materials should be carefully scrutinized to determine if the content gives adequate clues to words which children have not yet learned to recognize in their reading but possess in their speaking-listening vocabularies. Only a few such words should be presented at any one time, as too many unknown words make using the context difficult and might encourage wild guessing. The exact ratio of unknown words to known words probably depends on the children's intelligence, maturity, and background, although Bond and Tinker suggest that about one word in every forty running words should be unknown (4:321). Nevertheless, the materials used should be easy enough for children to recognize the unknown word without too much difficulty.

The materials should reflect the language patterns of the child whenever possible, be at a concept level appropriate to the children, and have the unknown words evenly distributed throughout the text.

After the materials have been selected, provisions need to be made, as in any reading activity, to assure that children have the background to read the materials through prior direct and vicarious experiences, including discussions, explanations, demonstrations, and field trips. The children need then to be given direct guidance in reading using context clues. Such guidance may include talking about the idea so that knowing the meaning of a sentence or paragraph will help in recognizing unknown words; encouraging children to read the entire sentence before deciding on an unknown word, showing how context clues can be combined with other word recognition techniques, such as phonics; reading the exercises orally to the children and having the children supply the unknown word; covering a few lines in a story and having the children anticipate what will come; asking which part of a sentence or paragraph gives a clue to an unknown word; and showing that some words must be recognized in context, such as, *wound* the clock and *wound* a deer.

Pictures may be used in the lower grades to develop an orientation toward the use of context clues. Hildreth states, "The use of picture clues is similar to the use of context clues for deriving the meaning of new or forgotten words" (*13*:156). In the lower grades much of the content is carried by pictures in the readers. However, Weintraub found that children do not make as much of illustrations as they might (*23*). Therefore, children may be taught to look at pictures to get clues for unknown words since pictures are a part of the total context and since they may be helpful in demonstrating to children the concept of· using context clues. Picture-word cards, picture dictionaries, and introducing new words in advance of reading with the aid of pictures can be helpful in getting children to use pictures as aids in word recognition.

As soon as children have developed enough sight words to read sentences, pictures become less and sentences become more important for developing the use of context clues. Sentences, paragraphs, riddles, and stories with parts of words omitted may be given to children. Emans (*10*) found the following hierarchy of exercises, easiest to most difficult, to be significant at the .001 level of confidence for children from grades three to ten:

1. No clue given other than context
2. Beginning letter given
3. Length of word given
4. **Beginning and ending letters given**
5. **Four word choice given**
6. **Consonants given**

Teachers can probably think of variations to the exercises. For example, in the multiple-choice type of exercise, words with the same sounds or words with similar configurations may be used.

In summary, this paper shows the importance of helping children develop skills in the use of context clues in word recognition and makes suggestions as to how to teach these skills.

REFERENCES

1. Ames, W. S. "A Study of the Process by which Readers Determine Word Meaning Through the Use of Verbal Context," unpublished doctoral dissertation, University of Missouri, 1965.
2. Ames, W. S. "The Development of a Classification Scheme of Contextual Aids," *Reading Research Quarterly, 2* (1966), 57-82.
3. Artley, A. S. "Teaching Word-Meaning through Context," *Elementary English Review, 20* (1943), 68-74.
4. Bond, G. L., and M. A. Tinker. *Reading Difficulties: Their Diagnosis and Correction.* New York: Appleton-Century-Crofts, 1967.
5. Bond, G. L., and Eva B. Wagner. *Teaching the Child to Read* (3rd ed.). New York: Macmillan, 1960.
6. Carter, H. L. J., and Dorothy J. McGinnis. *Teaching Individuals to Read.* Boston: D. C. Heath, 1962.
7. Cordts, Anna D. *Phonics for the Reading Teacher.* New York: Holt, Rinehart and Winston, 1965.
8. De Boer, John J., and Martha Dallmann. *The Teaching of Reading.* New York: Holt, Rinehart, and Winston, 1964.
9. Deighton, L. *Vocabulary Development in the Classroom.* New York: Teacher's College, Bureau of Publications, 1959.
10. Emans, R., and Gladys Mary Fisher. "Teaching the Use of Context Clues," *Elementary English,* 44 (1967), 243-246.
11. Gray, W. S. *On Their Own in Reading.* Glenview, Illinois: Scott, Foresman, 1960.
12. Hester, Kathleen B. *Teaching Every Child to Read.* New York: Harper and Row, 1964.
13. Hildreth, Gertrude. *Teaching Reading: A Guide to Basic Principles and Modern Practices.* New York: Holt, Rinehart and Winston, 1958.
14. Kolson, C. J., and G. Koluger. *Clinical Aspects of Remedial Reading.* Springfield, Illinois: Charles C. Thomas, 1963.
15. McCullough, Constance, M. "Learning to Use Context Clues," *Elementary English Review, 20* (1943), 140-143.
16. McCullough, Constance M. "The Recognition of Context Clues in Reading," *Elementary English Review, 22* (1945), 1-5.
17. McKee, P. *The Teaching of Reading.* Boston: Houghton Mifflin, 1948.
18. McKee, P. *Reading: A Program of Instruction for the Elementary School,* Boston: Houghton Mifflin, 1966.
19. Russell, D. H. *Children Learn to Read* (2nd ed.). Boston: Ginn, 1961.
20. Smith, Nila Banton. *Reading Instruction for Today's Children.* Englewood Cliffs, New Jersey: Prentice-Hall, 1963.
21. Spache, G. D. *Reading in the Elementary School.* Boston: Allyn and Bacon, 1964.
22. Tinker, M. A. *Bases for Effective Reading.* Minneapolis: University of Minnesota Press, 1965.
23. Weintraub, S. "The Effect of Pictures on the Comprehension of a Second-Grade Basal Reader," unpublished doctoral dissertation, University of Illinois, 1960.

New Approaches to Easing Word Attack at the Beginning Reader Levels

DOROTHY DIETRICH*

OVER THE YEARS, new methods of teaching reading have been proposed regularly. In the past ten years, the number of new ideas has appeared to be astounding. Because no one approach works for all pupils, teachers need to be aware of a variety of approaches which might be used. A brief description of some of these approaches follows.

NEW APPROACHES

i.t.a. The Initial Teaching Alphabet was designed by Sir James Pitman for the purpose of providing an easier alphabet to use in the beginning stages of reading. The alphabet has forty-four characters. Of these, twenty-four are the same as our known lower case characters (q and x have been omitted). Fourteen other symbols are combinations of known symbols and the rest are specialized symbols used to represent different sounds of the same letter. The alphabet is not a method but a medium that may be used with the teacher's usual teaching style.

i.t.a. was designed to permit easier decoding of printed symbols during the early stages of learning to read. It also enables children to spell and write more easily at first grade level.

Transition to traditional orthography usually takes place at the end of first grade or beginning second grade. Since twenty-four of the i.t.a. symbols are similar to t.o., transition is not seen as a problem for most pupils.

Basal readers using i.t.a. have been developed in England and in the United States. In addition, supplementary materials are available from several companies.

Before deciding to use i.t.a. it would be advisable to consider the following points:

1. Approval from the administration to insure the necessary follow-through from grade one to grade two.
2. Training of all teachers who are to use i.t.a.
3. Purchase of new i. t. a. readers and supplementary materials.
4. Rewrite all classroom dittos, charts, and labels in i.t.a.
5. Subject area materials written in t.o. could probably be

*The Reading Teacher, 23 (March 1970), 511-515.

used by the brighter students but unit material would need to be developed in i.t.a. for slow pupils or provision made to teach without the use of published texts.

Research studies seem to indicate that some children taught to read through the medium of i.t.a. become better readers, especially if they are the type who learn best by a phonic approach or a decoding method. Other children's preferred and most advantageous mode of learning puts emphasis on meaning, with skills of decoding taught as need arises. The greatest advantage of i.t.a. seems to be in the early learning to write independently and to spell well. While first graders who use i.t.a. often make quite rapid progress in learning to read, this advantage tends to disappear after transition to t.o. and there seems to be but little residual advantage by the time third grade is reached. More careful research is needed before one can say for sure whether there is much if any permanent advantage in using i.t.a.

Words in color As an aid in helping pupils identify similar sounds of our language, various colors have been utilized by Gattegno (1962) in his Words in Color. While color is the most obvious aspect of this approach, the method also places the responsibility for learning and developing principles upon the learner. It is expected that the child will use his own ability to draw generalizations concerning the sounds of our language, he will develop an attitude toward checking his work and he will become critical of his own work and that of his peers.

The method uses a number of different colored chalks, each representing a particular sound found in the language. Symbols used to represent the same sound use the same colored chalk.

Gattegno has developed his own materials embodying Words in Color which might be used by the teacher. These include word charts, phonic word charts, sets of word cards, books, plus work sheets.

Many opinions have been voiced on the effectiveness or ineffectiveness of this method, but there are seemingly no definitive research studies. Words in Color was one of the methods not included in the national first grade study done several years ago. Glowing testimonials do little to help one evaluate the strengths and weaknesses of this approach. Carefully controlled studies done with a substantial number of children are needed.

Linguistics In recent years, linguists (those who have made a scientific study of the language) have proposed a number of approaches in using their scientific knowledge of our language as it applies to the decoding process of reading. While linguistic methods vary, all begin with a study of the alphabet and the speech sounds. Regular phoneme-grapheme relationships are presented early, giving the child a mastery over a goodly number of words. Basic words following an irregular pattern are taught as sight words; for instance, *the* and *of*.

In addition to teaching the phoneme-grapheme relationship, attention is also given in some linguistic readers to syntax, pitch, and stress. Syntax relates to ways words are used in phrases, clauses and sentences, pitch relates to intonation, and stress has to do with accent given to the more important words within a sentence.

There are numerous series available which incorporate a linguistic approach. Many follow a very routine pattern with little stress being given to comprehension skills. A few of the newer linguistic series are stressing comprehension to a greater degree.

Many early linguistic readers were rather dull for both teachers and children. Newer reading series using linguistic approaches have turned from the rather dull, rote material to more realistic material. While there has been some research done on the effectiveness of a linguistic approach, there are no clear-cut indications that the method produces any better results than any other method using a strong decoding approach.

Programmed instruction　Both machines and materials have been developed to teach beginning reading skills. The basic principle of programmed instruction is to provide children with small bits of information or with piecemeal skills, with constant reinforcement, to enable them to build a larger body of information or a major skill.

One example of programmed books is the Buchanan Programmed Readers prepared by Sullivan Associates. The material is linguistically based. Each frame has its own answer in a column along the left side of the page. The child covers the answer with a marker while he is working and as he finishes each frame he uncovers the answer and checks his work. The material begins with regular letter sounds and progresses to the reading of a variety of literary forms.

The Aud-X machine by Educational Developmental Laboratories uses a visual, auditory, kinesthetic approach to beginning reading. Pupils hear the sound or word, see the written form on the screen and usually reinforce their learning in the earliest stages by tracing or writing the letter or word. As the difficulty of the material progresses, pupils begin to react to the material present and then are given the correct response by which they may evaluate their work.

As with the other approaches just mentioned, there are few research studies to indicate the effectiveness of programmed instruction. In a controlled study conducted in the Uniondale District several years ago, at the end of second grade there was no difference in performance of those pupils using Sullivan's Program Reading Series as compared with those pupils using a basal reading series. The major difference noted was the response from the teachers who felt that the time and energy spent in working with numerous groups and preparing supplementary material did not warrant the adoption of the program.

Phonics Phonic series in the form of workbooks, worksheets, charts, and books have been available for many years. A few basal reading series begin with a strong phonics program before story reading is introduced. Most basal readers include well developed phonics programs introduced in grade one and extending to grade three and included as one part of a total reading approach.

Each phonic program and phonetically based reader series uses its own progression of skills. Some methods begin by teaching consonants, others begin with vowels. Some teach through a family approach (*ake,* make, cake, lake); others a helper approach (*ba,* bad, bath, bat). For this reason it is wise for a teacher to restrict initial use to one series in order to form a core for the phonics program and to supplement when necessary by carefully selecting skills practice from other sources.

Recent research by Clymer (1963) indicates that many of the generalizations previously taught hold true less than 50 per cent of the time and thus should not be taught as hard and fast rules.

Other research studies indicate that pupils at the end of first grade who have been taught to read through phonics-supplemented basal programs usually do better than children using just a basal program which neglects word attack skills. By the end of third grade the differences appear to level off. Again this area needs more research.

Teachers need to recognize several factors before considering phonics programs to begin to teach reading or to supplement basal readers:

1. Each child differs in the amount of phonics needed to make him an independent reader.
2. Too much phonics can be as harmful as too little.
3. Supplemental programs must be dovetailed to the phonics program found in basal readers.
4. As much time and attention needs to be devoted to the pupils' application of isolated phonic elements to total word attack as to their learning the element initially.

SUMMARY

While there are many ways of teaching children to learn to read and many ways of helping children to decode at the beginning levels, teachers should not rely on one method or approach for all children within their classes. Little research has been done to show the superiority of one decoding method over another. In some instances there is little research that tells conclusively how effective any one particular method is. Teachers must become skillful enough in knowing children and approaches to reading that the best approach might be found for each child. Flexibility in teaching is still the byword.

REFERENCES

Buchanan, Cynthia Dee, and Sullivan Associates. *Programmed reading.* New York: Webster Division, McGraw-Hill.

Clymer, T. The utility of phonic generalizations in the primary grades. *The Reading Teacher,* 1963, *16,* 252-258.

Gattegno, C. *Words in color.* Chicago: Learning Materials, Inc., 1962.

Phonic Emphasis Approaches

Arthur W. Heilman*

Two objectives of this discussion are to identify salient features of a limited number of phonic approaches to beginning reading and to stress the educational issues which are related to the debate on phonics emphasis which has characterized the past decade.

Background

The problem of what is the proper role of phonics in reading instruction is not new. Undoubtedly the pressures on schools and teachers today, which are traceable to this issue are unprecedented. In general, the most vociferous critics of present day reading instruction start from a number of erroneous premises which suit their purposes. These premises include:

1. There is a sight word method of teaching reading which makes no provision for teaching phonic skills.
2. All words met at various instructional levels are taught exclusively as "sight words."
3. There is an educational conspiracy in American education which is opposed to the teaching of phonics.
4. Phonics instruction is "good" and children cannot get too much of a good thing.
5. If we go back to the phonics emphasis of the 1890's, present reading problems in our schools would disappear.

To illustrate the present state of affairs we will turn to the Council on Basic Education, a non-profit organization dedicated to the improvement of American education. In so far as the Council on Basic Education has been concerned with reading instruction, that concern has focused entirely on the issue of phonics. In the January 1964 *Bulletin* (p. 1) of the Council we read:

> Perhaps the most encouraging development of the year (1963), was the increasing understanding on the part of the public of what the phonics *versus* sight reading controversy is all about. The issue has often been confused in the public mind, especially when the advocates of the sight, or look-and-say method, insist that they also are believers in phonics instruction.

In the CBE *Bulletin*, February 1962 (p. 2), one finds:

> From our observation of good teachers in the fields of reading and language we discern a few guiding principles and methods of operations.

*First Grade Reading Programs, Perspectives in Reading No. 5, 1965, 56-71.

1. The good teacher of beginning reading, where she is not bound by an imposed methodology, operates on the theory that *beginning* reading is not a 'thought getting' process but is based on translating letters into sounds.

No evidence was cited as to source of this data.

In discussing an article by Paul Woodring, (*Saturday Review,* January 20, 1962) which made a plea for less heat and less name calling in the discussion of reading methodology, the editor of the Council's *Bulletin* stated, "It seems to us that anyone who suggests, even by indirection, that the present reading controversy does not involve fundamental issues but is merely a reflection of temperamental differences between reading theorists, misreads the true nature of the controversy. There is a real war on in reading, and for the future well-being of American education it is *important that the right side win.*" [Emphasis added.] CBE *Bulletin,* March 1962, pp. 8-9.

The individual who wants to make beginning reading a meaningful and enjoyable experience may have cause to feel threatened by the almost unlimited number of phonic systems which deal only with this limited facet of reading. This factor, coupled with the emergence of the philosophy that a "fast start" in beginning reading based on early stress of phonics is an unmitigated virtue, poses an educational issue of major importance.

The writer has long been of the opinion that phonics is second in importance to no other reading skill, and that "the reader must have the ability to pronounce or to approximate the pronunciation of words he does not know as sight words. This is ample reason for teaching phonics and sufficient justification for teaching it well" (*9*). Nevertheless, holding such a view does not preclude resistance to critics and materials which would push us into:

1. Teaching more phonics than is necessary for the child to learn to read.
2. Neglecting procedures for differentiation of phonics instruction.
3. Overemphasizing phonics in *beginning* reading.
4. Teaching phonics "steps" in illogical sequence.
5. Developing an over-reliance on phonics, (or context, or any other word analysis skill), as all such extremes are uneconomical and indefensible.
6. Behaving as if we believed that a child's memorizing phonic rules assures the ability to apply these rules in reading situations.

With these cautions in mind we move to a brief analysis of a limited number of phonic-emphasis approaches to first grade reading.

The Carden Method

The Carden Method is a set of materials and a methodology developed and published by Mae Carden (*4*). Although the method stresses composition and spelling, its chief aim is the teaching of phonics. Book I deals primarily with the two-vowel rule. Book II teaches the sound of single vowels, and Book III introduces combinations which include *r* and *w*. The author suggests that *after* pupils have completed the Carden readers they move on to basal readers. Thus, the initial stage of reading is saturated with letter sound analysis. This approach:

I. *Stresses Rules*

Initial teaching is limited to "regular spellings," or words which follow the given rule. The child is taught to "cross off" silent vowels and the famous two-vowel rule is modified to read: "When there are 2 vowels in a word the second vowel is crossed off and the first vowel keeps its name sound."

The following steps are utilized in teaching two-vowel patterns:

A. The term *vowel* is not used until after children have studied all vowels.

B. *a, e, i, o, u* = "The little letters that change their sounds."

C. Find the two letters that change their sounds.

    1. Think! Which one comes first in the word and which one comes second in the word?

    2. Cross off the one that comes second.

    3. Sound out the word letter by letter (*coat* = cuh' o tuh).

Later a goodly number of amendments or new rules are advanced or taught. Examples:

A. "There are *ea* words where the *a* drops out." (head, bread)

B. "There are words in which the *o* drops out in the *ou* combination and has the sound of *u*." (double, trouble, country)

II. *Stresses Synthetic Sounding*

Each consonant (or digraph) is given the weight of a syllable, (b—*buh;* j—*juh;* g—*guh;* th—*thuh;* ch—*chuh;* etc.). The word *the* is pronounced *thuh* and once the sound of a few letters have been introduced the child is ready to read a sentence:

suh' e	thuh	buh' o tuh
see	*the*	*boat*

(preprimary manual, p. 42)

Since an ordinary three- or four-letter word is sounded as though it consists of three syllables, the teacher is instructed to place the accent on the initial letter. (*boat* = buh' o tuh; *coat* = kuh' o tuh)

III. Stresses Writing and Spelling from the Beginning of Instruction

The letter *c* plays an important role in the teaching of letter forms. The child is taught that:

A. "Seven letters begin with *c*." These are: *c, a, d, g, q, o, e,* (The point is that there is a *c* imbedded somewhere in each of these letters.)

B. "Two letters make a *c* backwards." These are: *b, p.*

C. "The letter *s* is a *c* up in the air and a *c* backwards."

The following is from "A Note on Learning to Spell." The teacher constructs a word letter by letter applying the two-vowel rule. Example:

The word *dime* is given.

The teacher says, "Write *duh.*"

She adds, "What did you write?"

The pupils answer, "*D.*"

The teacher says, "Write *i* next to the *d.*"

Then she says, "*m,* write *m, m—m.*"

The pupils write *m.*

The teacher asks, "How do you make the *i* stay *i*?"

The pupils answer, "Add an *e.*" (*The Carden Method, A Brief on How To Get Started.*)

In the opinion of the writer, this approach is extremely mechanistic and ritualistic. However, it should not be concluded that children exposed to this type of instruction in grade one will not "learn" what is commonly measured at the end of grade one as "reading achievement." This is a tribute to children, but perhaps an unfortunate educational phenomena since the fact that "learning takes place" is often cited as a justification for the use of such procedures.

Words in Color

Words In Color (7) is a system developed by Caleb Gattegno who also developed *Numbers in Color* based on the Cuisenaire Rods for teaching arithmetic. These materials are discussed as a "phonics emphasis approach" because instruction begins and continues with the systematic teaching of letter sounds. The child is exposed to a dual visual stimuli: (1) the letter configuration, (2) in color. He hears hundreds of repetitions of each letter sound while his attention is focused on the *letter configuration* in color.

In this approach 39 colors are used, each of which represents a speech sound in English—regardless of what letters represent that sound. Initial teaching is done entirely at the blackboard using different colored chalks, and through the use of some 29 large wall charts done in color. On these charts the various letters and letter combinations in a given word are shown in different colors. Thus, the word *and* utilizes three colors; *sand,* four colors; and *impossible* calls for the use of seven colors. (The writer being color-blind could not verify this latter fact for himself, but accepted the word of a trusted colleague.)

The following are some pertinent facts about *Words In Color*:

1. Sounding, or the association of colored-letter *forms* with speech sounds, is taught in a most systematic, repetitive fashion. The term *drill* used in this setting would not be an overstatement. In the teaching of letter sounds the individual consonants are not taught in isolation but are blended with vowel sounds.

2. At this moment there is, to the best of the writer's knowledge, not a single piece of research which even hints that the addition of color to *letter forms* adds one iota to the learning of letter sounds or phonic principles.

3. The child actually never reads anything in color (except letters and words on the wall charts or in blackboard drill). All reading materials used are printed black on white!

4. Thirty-nine colors is a goodly number of colors. It is a tenable hypothesis that children might develop problems in discrimination of just noticeable differences in color in the absence of letter configurations. Examples of one series of colors include: cadmium green, yellow green No. 15, yellow green No. 47, dark green, olive green, light green, deep green, emerald green No. 45, emerald green No. 26, leaf green, gray green, yellow ochre, brown ochre.

5. Materials include: for teachers, *Background and Principles, Teacher's Guide,* 21 Wall Charts, 8 Phonic Code Charts; and children's materials (printed black on white), Books 1, 2, 3, *First Book of Stories,* set of worksheets.

Programmed Reading (2)

While there are a number of materials which might merit the designation *programmed reading* our discussion is limited to one set of materials which meets the criterion of being a phonics emphasis approach to beginning reading (*Programmed Reading,* Webster Division, McGraw-

Hill Book Co.). These materials are primarily a program for grades one and two, and for remedial instruction. The program begins with the teaching of word symbols which have "a constant sound value." Thus, we meet again the "word family" of previous eras or "regular spellings" of one linguistic approach.

However, before beginning to work with the programmed materials the child must have mastered a sizeable portion of word analysis or the phonic skills program which includes the following:

1. The names of the letters of the alphabet (capital and small).
2. How to print all the capital and small letters.
3. That letters stand for sounds and what sounds to associate with the letters *a, f, m, n, p, t, th,* and *i* which are used as the points of departure for the programmed readers.
4. That letters are read from left to right and that groups of letters form words.
5. The words *yes* and *no* by sight; how to discriminate the words *ant, man,* and *mat* from each other, and how to read the sentences, *I am an ant, I am a man, I am a mat, I am a pin, I am a pan, I am thin, I am tan, I am fat.*

These skills are taught in a stage called programmed pre-reading which, by the nature of what is taught, emphasizes the association of letter symbol with corresponding letter sound.

The programmed materials are workbook type exercises calling for the child to circle the correct word or write a letter or letters. For instance, a picture of an ant is followed by the sentence: *I am an* $\frac{ant}{man}$. A later frame will be *I am an -nt.* It should be noted that these materials rely heavily on visual discrimination and that there is considerable emphasis on "word parts" or individual letters.

Without doubt programmed materials hold some promise for teaching certain facets of beginning reading. A promotional brochure heralds these particular materials as "the most significant breakthrough in the teaching of reading in 50 years!" This might be an overstatement. One of the virtues of programmed learning is the fact that the child can instantly check his response to see if he is correct. As the child writes a vowel, a consonant blend, or a word in a blank space he can look to the left on the same frame and see if he wrote correctly. He can also look before he writes if he learns this approach.

One strength of programmed reading is that it could be called an individualized approach. However, in this case every child uses the same material or book, but each goes through it at his own rate. Programmed materials deal with mechanical aspects of the reading process. These are important, but they are not all there is to reading. There has been little, if any, programming of critical reading or thought processes.

The Phonovisual Method *(14)*

The Phonovisual Method is a supplementary phonic instruction program designed for use with existing basal and other approaches. The authors offer their materials as a "middle course" stating, "The Phonovisual Method is not intended to be used instead of sight reading, but as a parallel teaching" (*14*, p. 6). As is the case with many other phonics instructional materials there are no major differences in the "content" of the phonics program of phonovisual and basal materials. The major differences are:

1. The degree to which phonic teaching dominates beginning reading instruction.
2. The emphasis on *drill* in associating letter sounds and graphic letter symbols.

It should be noted that the teacher is cautioned to always use the material as a game, not as drill. Yet, it is obvious that the amount of emphasis on teaching letter sounds makes this a difficult goal to achieve. "For best results the teaching [of letter sounds] should begin the very first week of school if possible the very first day. At the demonstration school one half-hour daily is given to each of these two subjects, (a) sight reading and (b) phonetic instruction . . ." (*14*, p. 11).

Materials. The Phonovisual materials are described as a phonics program for kindergarten, primary, and remedial instruction, and include the following:

1. Two 26″ x 40″ wall charts—one for teaching consonant sounds, the other for vowel sounds.
2. Phonovisual method book (a teacher's guide).
3. Pupils' books: Readiness book, transition book (preprimer), separate consonant and vowel workbooks.
4. Miscellaneous items: Phonograph recording, "Sounds on the Phonovisual Charts," skill building flash cards, consonant and vowel filmstrips, magnetic boards, phonic rummy games, and the like.

Of all the numerous phonic approaches, phonovisual probably most closely parallels the philosophy of a majority of basal materials. Consonant sounds are taught first, auditory-visual training is coordinated, learning words as sight-recognition units is encouraged. One of the major potential drawbacks in the use of phonovisual is that the actual instruction can easily go beyond simply systematic teaching and become a ritual.

The matter of differentiation of amounts of phonic instruction for different pupils is not stressed. Despite the warnings of the authors, and particularly in light of the procedures outlined, the teaching of sounding can easily become an end in itself rather than the means to achieving a balanced program whose goal is fluent, critical reading. On the other hand, the materials provide a concrete step-by-step program which introduces practically all of the phonics teaching in grade one. Some teachers may profit from this systematic approach while at the same time modifying techniques so as to minimize rote teaching.

Phonetic Keys to Reading

Phonetic Keys to Reading (8) is a quite accurate description of the materials which bear this title. The "keys" are the multitude of "rules" that have accumulated over a number of decades as a result of attempting to deal with the vagaries of letter sounds in written English. *Phonetic Keys* provides for teaching children all of the known rules including some which have very limited application. The data reported by Clymer (5), Oaks (13), and Burrows/Lourie (3), relative to the per cent of time various phonic rules actually apply, should be kept in mind as prospective users attempt to evaluate the materials under discussion.

Phonetic Keys is not a method of teaching reading but a set of supplementary phonics materials. The first two months of beginning instruction are devoted to teaching approximately forty separate phonic skills including both long and short vowel sounds, all consonant sounds, and a number of blends and consonant digraphs. For the first several weeks children are taught to sound letters (vowels) which are invariably located in the middle of words. Following this unique experience they are taught initial consonant sounds.

A reasonable rationale for attacking the middle of words has never been advanced. Promotional materials point out, "Since each word contains one or more than one vowel, no words can be sounded independently by the pupil until he has a knowledge of the more common vowel sounds." It might be pointed out that all words except *I, a* and *eye* contain consonants which must be noted if the word is to be solved.

As a result of the emphasis on sounding in beginning reading the child is in essence taught, and many learn, to acquire a set to sound out words. The same word is sounded out time after time, long after it should have been mastered as a sight word. The teacher's manual in discussing the use of experience charts cautions teachers against teaching words as sight words, "At first these charts are to be read by sight, but as soon as the children have learned enough sounds and phonetic principles to analyze words with the help of the teacher, teaching experience charts and reading charts by sight should be entirely eliminated" (*Teacher's Manual for First Grade*, 1964, p. 18).

Materials. First grade materials consist of three paperback workbook-type books, *Tag, Dot and Jim, All Around with Dot and Jim,* and a teacher's manual. The materials were developed by Cornelia Sloop, an elementary teacher in Texas.

The major educational issues with which users and prospective users of these materials should be concerned include:

1. Should beginning reading instruction concentrate on sounding letters to the degree these materials advocate?
2. Should initial sounding begin in the middle of words?
3. Should children learn dozens of complicated phonic rules in the process of beginning reading?
4. Can sounding be "overemphasized" to the detriment of future reading facility?
5. Can beginning instruction result in pupils' developing a "set" to sound out each word met?
6. All facile readers recognize words as units and sound out only those few words they do not recognize as sight words. Should children be taught to sound out all words to the neglect of developing a sight vocabulary?

Linguistic Approach
(Emphasizing Speech Sounds in Words)

This discussion does not attempt to deal with all linguistic theory and suggested practices which relate to beginning reading instruction. Reference is made only to one approach, that of limiting initial teaching to words which enjoy "regular spellings" in English. While the term *phonics* might be offensive to the linguist-authors, the materials merit discussion here since their chief aim is the early association of speech sounds with written letter combinations.

The first such serious proposal by a linguist was presented publicly in 1942. The April and May issues of *The Elementary English Review* contained articles by Leonard Bloomfield in which he outlined what in essence was later published in 1961 under the title, *Let's Read—A Linguistic Approach* (*1*). Reduced to its essentials this approach simply advocates teaching beginning reading through the process of teaching words which follow "regular spellings" in English.

This approach relies on a very rigid vocabulary control. Each lesson introduces and stresses what in the past was called "word families," such as *cat, rat, fat, mat, bat, sat.* The child first learns words in isolation, then phrases and sentences: *a bat, a cat, a rat, a mat, a fat cat, a fat rat, a· fat cat ran at a fat cat* (*Let's Read,* Bloomfield and Barnhart, p. 61).

In 1963, Charles Fries' book *Linguistics and Reading* was published. There are minor differences between Bloomfield's and Fries' approaches. The former advocated that children learn letter names and learn to distinguish both capital and lower case letters, while Fries advocated teaching only capital letters in beginning reading. However, in regard to methodology Fries and Bloomfield advocate almost identical content. The same words, phrases, and sentences are found in both sources, for example in Fries, *"a cat, a rat, a fat rat, pat a fat rat, cats bat at rats"* (6, p. 203).

Both Bloomfield and Fries (in the materials referred to above) oppose the practice of making beginning reading instruction a meaning-making process for the reader. In the words of Clarence Barnhart, coauthor of *Let's Read,* we find: "Bloomfield's system of teaching reading is a linguistic system. Essentially, a linguistic system of teaching reading separates the problem of the study of word-form from the study of word-meaning" (p. 9).

In Fries we find: "Seeking an extraneous interest in a story as a story during the earliest steps of reading is more likely to hinder than to help the efforts put forth by the pupil himself" (6, p. 199)*.

When a person in reading raises questions as to the actual contributions made by linguists he is put in the position of a mere educational practitioner questioning the role of the scientist. When a linguist has reservations about the contributions of linguists to reading we might listen. Raven I. McDavid of the University of Chicago stated:

> I am diffident about how much the linguist can contribute to the complex operation of teaching reading, which may utilize everything from information theory to the doctrine of original sin. Like many of my colleagues, I am

---

*Certain other linguists do not reject meaning in reading. Lefevre stresses "that language is meaningful behavior and that reading is the reproduction of sound patterns which carry meanings." In addition there has been a considerable body of writing which stresses the various *signal systems.* Under this heading the linguist discusses *intonation patterns, pitch, stress, juncture, transitions, pauses,* and the like. Teachers of reading have used different terminology without neglecting these important facets. (Reading terms might be, "reading with expression," "read it like you would say it." Juncture — pause — stops would be taught as functions of punctuation and phrasing.

disturbed that linguistics is currently fashionable, often considered a panacea for all the woes of education and society. For with the supply of professional linguists low and the demand for their services high, we find a proliferation of store-front linguists clamoring to perform these services . . . And when the linguist attempts to produce readers, he can expect them to be criticized on both linguistic and other grounds (*10*).

The Augmented Roman Alphabet

The objective of the Augmented Roman Alphabet is to present an initial teaching medium which approximates a one-to-one relation between letter-symbol seen and speech-sound heard when a word is pronounced. To accomplish this, 19 new letter characters were added to the present English alphabet after dropping the letters *q* and *x*. (For ITA materials see Mazurkiewicz and Tanyzer, *12*.)

Some of the methodological features of this system are:

1. Phonics or letter sounds associated with graphic symbols are taught systematically and thoroughly.
2. Child learns symbol sound, not letter name.
3. Children write this new symbol system from the very beginning of instruction.
4. Separate capital letters are not used. Capitals are indicated by making the letter larger.
5. Children are expected to make a transition from this initial teaching alphabet to traditional orthography and spelling within a year; four to five months for the rapid learners; seven to eight months for the average pupils. In data reported from England, the transition was reportedly made without difficulty. However, pupils transferred from Augmented Roman to the same materials printed in regular or traditional orthography.

Some Issues:

1. *Teaching children to write the Augmented Alphabet.*

A very important question is, "If the child is to transfer from the initial teaching medium to traditional in from 4 to 8 months, why should he learn and reinforce the Augmented Alphabet in his own writing?" The ITA is much more difficult to write as one meets symbols such as:

ᚦh, æ, rg, œ, ʃh, ie, ʒ, ɛɛ, ω.

2. *The compatibility of ITA and Traditional Orthography.*

In the promotional materials for ITA it is claimed that there is a high degree of compatibility between spellings in ITA and traditional spellings. A fact that is often overlooked is that in addition to the changed alphabet in ITA a great number of words are changed to phonetic spellings, some of which do not involve any of the new letters. The re-spellings result in visual configurations which are radically different from those the child will meet once he transfers to traditional English. This is, in essence, not a system for "cracking the code" but rather the teaching of a substitute code. Do no children experience difficulty in transferring from phonetic spellings to the traditional irrational spellings? The following examples come from one small first-grade book of less than primer difficulty.

was – wos	watched – wotᴄht	walked – waukt
excited – eksieted	enough – enuf	also – aulsœ
wife – wief	sixth – siksʄh	right – riet
called – caulld	find – fiend	thought – ʄhaut
large – larj	crossed – crosst	next – nekst
pleased – pleᴇsd	climb – cliem	boxes – boksᴇs
busy – bisy	night – niet	George – jorj
quieter – kwieter	castles – casls	six – siks

(a seesied holidæ for jæn and tœby, ann ʄhwaite, cunstabl and cumpany limited, lundon.)

In the promotional material the question is asked, "Is the traditional alphabet and spelling of English an important cause of failure in beginning reading?" It might be stated that failures do not stem primarily from the traditional alphabet, but from spellings of words. As noted above, ITA does not rely solely on a new alphabet but actually utilizes a considerable number of re-spellings of English words.

ITA actually attempts to follow the traditional "rules" found in most phonic approaches, particularly with regard to the "two vowel" and "one vowel in medial position" rules. When words do not follow the rules they are spelled phonetically:

one—wun	half—hav	come—cum
some—sum	have—hav	money—muny
said—sed	head—hed	once—wunz
more—mor	were—wer	

3. Emphasis on teaching Phonics

A point that is seldom stressed on the popular writings about ITA is the fact that in this approach sounding or phonic analysis is taught both early and systematically. A large number of letters (consonants) are the same in structure and sound in both the augmented and traditional alphabets (b, d, f, h, j, k, m, n, p, r, t, y). The digraphs *ch, th, sh, wh* have the same sound and are very similar in visual pattern, although joining the two symbols in writing is more difficult.

The early stress on sounding or phonic analysis thus becomes a con-taminating factor in research which purports to demonstrate that use of the Augmented Alphabet is the primary independent variable in com-parative studies. The efficacy of the Augmented Alphabet could be tested only if the traditional alphabet approach with which it is compared included the same amount of early phonics emphasis.

4. *Results of instruction using ITA*

There have been many reports in the popular press which contain suggestions, intimations and projections which often result in a reader's inferring that initial instruction using ITA, followed by transfer to traditional print sometime in grade one, will lead to significantly higher reading achievement at the end of grade one. The data covering the Bethlehem, Pennsylvania study, 1963-64, reported by Mazurkiewicz does not bear out this assumption, although that writer's tentative conclusions continue to be optimistic.

There was no significant difference in reading achievement between groups taught by ITA and traditional basal instruction:

TABLE I (*11*)

Total Raw Scores	ITA		Traditional		T. Test
	Mean	*S.D.*	*Mean*	*S.D.*	
California Reading Test (Lower Primary)	59.60	17.42	61.15	16.15	0.433
California Reading Test (Upper Primary)	41.11	19.28	41.29	16.90	0.064

Summary: The above phonic emphasis approaches cannot justifiably be labeled "methods of teaching reading." Each deals primarily with one important reading skill, namely, phonic analysis. To qualify as a method a set of materials would have to embrace a broad teaching program which attempts to deal with all of the essential skills which need to be taught in the entire program. A second criterion of a method would be that learning to read would of necessity be treated as a developmental process, extending over a relatively long period of time.

Each of the above approaches, as is the case with other phonic materials not discussed, deals only with beginning reading and attempts to saturate this instructional period with analysis of letter sounds. This extensive and intensive drill on sounding letters often has a salutary effect on reading achievement scores during the early stages of formal instruction. Standardized reading tests for grade one deal primarily with word recognition, and thus tend to measure what phonics-emphasis approaches teach.

Reading vocabularies of pupils at this stage of development do not approximate their capacity for dealing with oral language. The point of view of this paper is that this fact of human development does not serve as a justification for the position that beginning reading need not be a meaning-making process. Language is a system of agreements as to the meaning ascribed to particular speech sounds *as found in words and words-in-combination.* Meaning is the only thing that *can* transfer from oral language usage to facile reading of the graphic representation of oral language.

This question, as to whether beginning reading should be a meaning-making process is one of the major educational issues in the present controversy over the proper role of phonics instruction. Starting from the premise that *students must acquire the ability to sound out words not recognized as sight words,* other questions teachers of reading should answer as they think of methology and materials are:

1. When initial reading instruction centers on letter-sound analysis is it not likely that a number of pupils will develop a "set" to sound out all words met?

2. Will some pupils continue to sound out the same words long after they should have been mastered as sight words?

3. Is it not true that smooth, facile reading is characterized by a minimum of recourse to "sounding out words"?

4. Do some phonic-instructional materials overemphasize what teaching letter sounds can actually accomplish in reading English?

5. Does the large number of irregular spellings in English mitigate against teaching over-reliance on sounding?

6. Do phonic instruction materials tend to under-emphasize the value of combining phonic analysis and context clues in solving unknown words?

7. If a set of materials and instructional procedures results in higher first-grade reading achievement, is this *prima facie* evidence that this approach is a better learning experience than any approach which achieves lesser results over this relatively short segment of the total educational continuum?

8. Specifically, is the "fast start" which may accrue from hours of drill on analyzing letter sounds inevitably the best *introduction* to the long-term developmental process called *learning to read?*

The point of view emphasized in this presentation is that the educational issues in phonics instruction center around (1) initial learning *set* which materials develop; (2) that letter-sound analysis is limited by the nature of written English; (3) over-reliance on phonics can be taught; (4) that not to use all word-analysis clues (context, structure, pictures) is uneconomical; (5) the sequence in which steps are taught should be based on a psychologically sound rationale.

If one concludes that numerous phonic approaches err in saturating initial reading instruction with letter-sound analysis, and over-emphasize what this can accomplish in learning to read English, the original premise still remains intact. Namely, that children must learn sounding techniques and that these should be taught effectively.

Simply because approaches A, B, C, etc. over-emphasize analysis in beginning reading does not establish that materials which present much less phonic analysis have hit upon the "right combination." To not systematically teach vowel sounds in grade one is a methodological decision which handicaps a majority of pupils in first grade.

All reading-instructional-materials are offsprings of the free enterprise system. Promotional materials which describe and sell reading materials are often much more imaginative than the materials themselves. "Let the buyer beware" applies as well to the adoption of teaching materials as it does to the purchase of a used car. Education will have nothing to fear from this philosophy and practice when teachers and administrators develop the professional competency to ask the right questions and evaluate materials in light of their questions.

REFERENCES

1. Bloomfield, Leonard, and Barnhart, Clarence L. *Let's Read—A Linguistic Approach,* Detroit: Wayne State University Press, 1961.
2. Buchanan, Cynthia Dee, *et. al. Programmed Reading.* St. Louis: Webster Division, McGraw-Hill Book Co., 1963.
3. Burrows, Alvina T., and Lourie, Zyra. "Two Vowels Go Walking," *The Reading Teacher,* XVII, (November 1963).
4. Carden, Mae. *The Carden Method.* Glen Rock, New Jersey.
5. Clymer, Theodore. "The Utility of Phonic Generalizations in the Primary Grades," *The Reading Teacher,* XVI, (January 1963).
6. Fries, Charles C. *Linguistics and Reading.* New York: Holt, Rinehart and Winston, Inc., 1963.
7. Gattegno, Caleb. *Words in Color.* Chicago: Learning Materials, Inc., 1962.

8. Harris, Theodore, Creekmore, Mildred, and Greenman, Margaret. *Phonetic Keys to Reading.* Oklahoma City: The Economy Company, 1964.
9. Heilman, Arthur W. *Phonics in Proper Perspective.* Columbus, Ohio: Charles E. Merrill Books, Inc., 1964.
10. McDavid, Raven I., Jr. "Linguistics and Reading," *Reading and the Language Arts,* Supplementary Educational Monograph No. 93, University of Chicago Press, 1963.
11. Mazurkiewicz, Albert J. "Lehigh-Bethlehem ITA Study Interim Report Six," *Journal of the Reading Specialist,* Vol. 4 (September 1964).
12. Mazurkiewicz, Albert J., and Tanyzer, Harold. *ITA Program.* New York: ITA Publications, Inc., 1963.
13. Oakes, Ruth E. "A Study of the Vowel Situations in a Primary Vocabulary," *Education,* LXXII (May 1952).
14. Schoolfield, Lucille D., and Timberlake, Josephine B. *Phonovisual Method.* Washington, D.C.: Phonovisual Products, Inc.

New Alphabet Approaches

EDWARD FRY*

PERHAPS the most provable thing about new alphabet approaches is that they are not new at all. One need only scratch the surface of a library, and a cornucopia of revised alphabets, spelling reforms, and diacritical marking plans for beginning reading pours forth.

The history of the development of written language is exceedingly voluminous. There is no time in recorded history when it was not under attack and change. Probably the invention of movable type and the printing press has done more to slow down the change in written language in the last few centuries than any other single factor. In these last few centuries we have attained a high degree of rigidity in written language. We now find ourselves in the somewhat strange position of having dictionaries largely agree on exactly what letters should be used to spell each word in our language; it has not always been thus.

We could start a discussion of the need and desirability of new alphabets with a look at Cuniform and Linear B, but let us jump ahead thirty centuries to the annual report of the National Education Association in 1910.

> Your committee is able to make a report of progress that is very encouraging to those interested in the simplification of the spelling of English, as the year has been notable in the things that have been done and in the cooperation that has been secured. . . . The ridicule and the contumely heaped upon the movement five years ago has almost entirely disappeared, and the opposition to a reasonable consideration of its demands and claims is gone.

Alas the bright hopes of the educators of 1910 have been dashed on the hard rocks of history. The whole problem of alphabet reform or spelling reform is largely a political one. Any scholar could singlehandedly improve English spelling or the alphabet. However, the problem is that people with power—presidents, senators, giant corporations who publish books, even adults who vote—do not want a change because they already know the established system. On the other hand, the people who really need the change, the first-graders and the adult illiterates, have virtually no power at all. Apparently the education profession has very little power in this grave matter either.

The Reader's Problem

Lest one feel that we have gotten off the track by discussing simplified

*First Grade Reading Programs, Perspectives in Reading No. 5, 1965, 72-85.

spelling in a new alphabet approaches article, let us put the whole area in "perspective." The basic problem of the first grade teacher is to train the child to decode a set of symbols which constitutes what we call written language. This set of symbols is rather closely based on spoken language. The average first grade child already possesses a good knowledge of spoken language. His vocabulary is something in excess of 5,000 words and his knowledge of the rules and structure of the English language is amazingly good. An interesting proof of the first-grader's facility with structure is to compare him with a newly arrived foreign university student who, even though well-educated, uses torturous and often erroneous sentence structures and intonations.

Since it is the problem of the first grade student to learn to decode the written symbols, quite obviously the manner in which the language is incoded will have a profound effect. If the symbols follow strange and highly irregular principles it stands to reason that the child will have greater difficulty learning to decode them. Hence, anything that will improve the coding system, even temporarily, for beginning readers has been a concern of educators and many other intelligent people for at least centuries and probably for as long as there has been inaccurate coding systems. Thus, new alphabets, spelling reforms, and devices which temporarily add regularity, such as diacritical marks, are all part of our problem. Spelling is simply the obverse of the same problem—that of incoding, or having to write the symbol, as opposed to decoding, or having to read the symbol.

The Alphabet Problem

A good bit of the problem of incoding English developed during the 15th century in what scholars call "the great vowel shift." In this period between Chaucer and Shakespeare spoken English went through a noticeable change while written English failed to keep abreast. It was towards the end of this period that the spelling of English became somewhat crystallized due to dictionary makers like Samuel Johnson and technical innovators like Gutenberg.

The situation was further compounded by the inadequacy of the sound symbols or alphabet that the English chose to use. The alphabet which we use is really designed for writing Latin, not English. Hence, we note that modern Latin or Spanish and Italian have far fewer problems in spelling than does English. There are something like 44 different phonemes or distinctive sound units used in speaking English; however, our alphabet has only 26 letters and at least three of these are no good at all as they overlap or duplicate the work of other letters (*C* sounds like an *S* or a *K*,

X sounds like *KS*, and *Q* is used only with *U* and sounds like *KW*).

We get around this problem of an inadequate number of letters several ways. In consonants the situation is not too bad as we tend to use digraphs, or a special combination of two letters, to make a different phoneme. For example *CH* does not make a blend of *C* and *H*, but almost always makes the sound heard at the beginning of *chair*. But in the vowel sounds the situation is much more unpleasant, in that one letter makes many sounds. For example note the *A* in *at, all, above, ate.*

A Backward Glance

It will perhaps help to put the modern systems in better perspective if we have a quick trip through some historical antecedents.

In 1551 John Hart wrote an essay entitled "The Opening of the Unreasonable Writing of our English Toung." He later followed this up by suggesting a new orthography, and by 1517 he had zeroed in on the first grade problem with "A Methode of Comfortable Beginning for All Unlearned, Whereby They May Bee Taught To Read English, In A Very Short Time, With Pleasure." In the next century Charles Butler (1634) developed a phonetic alphabet for overcoming "uncertain writing and difficulty in learning." Because he found that the Latin Alphabet was "troublesome to the novice reader and writer."

America's own Benjamin Franklin, that intelligent dabbler in many things, developed in 1786 his own reformed alphabet. While technically not very good, he did see the need for consistency and the addition of six new letters. Franklin's alphabet apparently never received any acceptance but he did manage to carry on a small correspondence using it.

Leaping ahead another century, we find that Benn Pitman was producing phonetic readers for the American school market using a greatly modified alphabet. Another 19th century innovation was Fonotypy, a phonetically regular alphabet developed by Isaac Pitman and A. J. Ellis in 1884.

We have already noted the interest in spelling reforms around the turn of the century. From that time until this very day there are a number of simplified spelling organizations which actively correspond with each other in simplified spelling and regularly induce some local congressman to put a bill before the United States Congress ordering that spelling in all government documents be simplified, or proposing to write into law some other scheme which will insure the modification of the American English written language.

HISTORICAL "NEW" ALPHABETS
AND
DIACRITICALLY MARKED READERS

ĭt   stănd   Ann'ş

ĭş   lămp   măt

     ĭ

a mat   the stand

The Eaſieſt and Speedieſt-way, both for the
true ſpelling and reading of Engliſh, as
alſo for the True-writing thereof :
that ever was publickly
known to this day.

See the lamp! It is on a mat.
The mat is on the stand.

MC GUFFEY 1881   HODGES 1644

Hwen Jərj Woſ-iŋ-ton woz
a-bʊt siks yerz old, hiz ſq-ðer
gav him a haꞔ-et, ov hwiꞔ he woz
ver-i fond, and woz kon-stant-li

*Diir Madam :—ħi abdſiekſiyn.iu meek to rektifyiiŋ
aur alfabet, "ħat it uil bi atended uiħ inkanviniensiz
and diſikyltiz," iz e natural uɥn ; far it aluaz akyrz
huen eni reſarmeſiyn is propozed ; hueħyr in rilidſiyn,*

BENN PITMAN 1855   BENJAMIN FRANKLIN 1768

WUNS UPON A TΛM LITƆL RCD
HCN LIVD IN A BARN WIΔ HƱR
FΛV ꞫIKS. A PIG, A KΛT ΛND

ISAAC PITMAN & A.V. ELLIS   FONOTYPY 1844

But the atţic window̸ was pănẟless.   In eamẟ the
weşt wind.   Down to the fīrẟ wĕnt the litţlẟ girls.
They did not want any sickness.

EDWARD WARD 1894

CURRENTLY USED NEW ALPHABET AND DIACRITICALLY MARKED FIRST GRADE MATERIALS

Sample of Primer
Printed in ITA

"dœn't run awæ," ben sed tω his cat.

"dœn't fiet," miek sed tω his cat.

"wæt heer," sed ben and miek.

"wee will bee at scωl."

Sample of Primer
Printed with DMS

"Lòøk, Bill," săĭd Lindă.

"Hērĕ cômĕs Riĕky.

Hē is âll reɑdy fôr schöøl.

Lòøk up and sēĕ funny Riĕky."

Sample of Primer
Printed in Unifon

⅃EN M⧺CT꜓R H⧺PQ TRⵧD.   HI

P⧺KT UP BⵧBI HⱮB꜓RT. HELD

H⧺M ⧺N H⧺Z B⧺G ORMZ AND CAⱮ

U LULUBⵧ.

Sample from first drill
book for use with
Words in Color

t

at	ta	ut	tu
it	ti	et	te
ot	to		

England too has had its full share of alphabet and spelling reformers. No less a celebrity than George Bernard Shaw was so seriously interested in spelling reform that he left a major proportion of his estate to a trust which now is working on the simplification of the alphabet.

In the late 1950's Sir James Pitman, the head of the publishing firm and a member of Parliament, introduced a bill for greatly modifying the English alphabet. This bill was defeated before it became law but, more or less as a direct consequence, Sir James did receive the blessing of the

Minister of Education to experiment with An Augmented Roman Alphabet in the British Schools.

Some British parents, being not too well versed in the history of their language, prefer not to have their children learning from a "Roman Alphabet." Hence, the name of this new alphabet was changed to Initial Teaching Alphabet, or as it is popularly called the ITA. The name also reflects the current usage of this alphabet, namely that it is to be used for beginning instruction in literacy and later a transition is made to the traditional alphabet which ITA people like to call TO for Traditional Orthography. Though it would be impolitic to say so publicly, there is probably at least a secret thought in the minds of some supporters that ITA could become *the* English alphabet to be used by everybody at all times. Needless to say, one clever way of gaining acceptance for this would be to raise a generation of children who had equal facility in TO and ITA. Some future decades from now there might be considerably less resistance to changing spelling or an alphabet if the Prime Minister, the cabinet members, the senators, the heads of corporations and a sizeable portion of the population all had equal reading and writing facility in ITA.

An interesting thing about ITA is the wide acceptance of it before adequate research results are reported. Most of the research results (see bibliography) are reported by investigators who are closely identified with the ITA movement and in many instances have authored or published materials in the ITA medium. These research results are almost uniformly glowing. Typical reports show that teachers using the ITA materials have results that are definitely superior to other teachers using the old basal reader or traditional system. While we cannot deny that high reading achievement is a good thing no matter how it is obtained, it is something else again to prove that the superior results were due to this particular alphabet rather than the fact that a new method was used.

United States educators have recently had a multitude of claims from super-phonics enthusiasts. There is little doubt that some teacher who has been graying along through her basal reading series and suddenly gets inspired by the new super-duper phonics system is going to get better results. In fact, she would probably get as good results if the situation were reversed and all the humdrum ordinary teachers were using phonics systems and she suddenly discovered a super-duper new hot-shot word reading method. In fact, it must be a little discouraging for the educational researcher to learn that in 1851 the Massachusetts Teachers Association appointed a committee to consider the subject of "Phonetics" and that this committee reported in 1852 that teachers should study the merits of the phonetic system by themselves by actual trial in their schools. When one sees such a basic problem in existence for well over a century and yet so completely unresolved, the problem of whether or not a new alphabet will really prove superior can hardly be expected to be solved in the next few years.

The Initial Teaching Alphabet is a 43 character alphabet. It uses 24 Roman or Latin characters that are used in traditional English (X and Q are missing) plus 19 augmented or additional letters. Most of the new letters are formed by a fusion of two lower case Roman letters. Five of these new letters, the long vowels, are made by placing a lower case E immediately adjacent to the preceding vowel. Dipthongs, other vowel sounds, and consonant digraphs are frequently similarly formed by placing two letters in close juxtaposition. Writing in the ITA is also constrained by a special set of spelling rules. Hence, some words using no new letters look different because of the spelling rules only. Both the new letters and the spelling rules add a further constraint in that so far as possible traditional word form is preserved so that in a later stage of training the students may transfer to the traditional orthography with a minimum of difficulty.

In an early paper Pitman estimated that 39.25 per cent of the words were radically changed when written in ITA, 10.50 per cent were moderately changed, 23.75 per cent had minor modifications, and 26.50 per cent were unchanged. The goal of ITA is to have a consistent phoneme-grapheme relationship so that one letter will always make the same sound, and vice versa. This goal is not always achieved, partially because of the concessions to word form, but it is a tremendous improvement over the traditional orthography.

Despite the lack of conclusive research results, the spread of the use of the Initial Teaching Alphabet has been extremely rapid. The first regular use of the ITA in the public school was in Britain in September of 1960. The experimental population consisted of approximately 600 four- and five-year-olds. The British begin reading instruction a year earlier than the Americans. In the school year 1964-65 Pitman Publishing Company, the main publishers of Initial Teaching Alphabet materials, estimates that there were approximately 60,000 British children using ITA. ITA use in the United States began in 1962 in the Bethlehem, Pennsylvania school system with a Ford Foundation grant to Dr. Albert Mazurkiewicz at Lehigh University. During the school year 1964-65 the author estimates that approximately 10,000 United States children were learning to read using the ITA. Most of these children were taking part in either continuing research in the Bethlehem schools or in research projects sponsored by the U. S. Office of Education. However, there are also many school systems "trying it out" without special foundation or government research grants. Despite these seemingly large numbers this is still far less than one per cent of the U. S. first grade population.

Words in Color

Another British import aimed at taking advantage of some phonetic regularity principles is the Words In Color system by Caleb Gattegno. This system which has been commercially available for the past five years is used by fewer schools than is the ITA. Proponents of the Gattegno system also make some interesting statements such as, "Words In Color makes the English language phonetic through the use of color, enabling the learner to master the mechanics of reading in eight weeks or less." Forty-seven different sounds of English are taught by using different colors for each sound. Since it is difficult for children, or even adults, to distinguish 47 different colors some of Gattegno's symbols are split in half so that they are really two-colored rather than a unique color. This system does not have the color printed in children's workbook material, but rather there are 21 drill charts containing 270 letters or letter groups that make a phoneme and some phonetically regular words. The teacher drills the student to make the sounds in isolation, then blended together. For example, the first page of the first book simply contains a number of *A*'s of various sizes. The second page consists of a number of *U*'s. The third page consists of groups of *A*'s and *U*'s together which the student would blend as a word. After the five vowels are introduced (short sounds), consonants are introduced and the student can now begin to blend vowels and consonants to form short meaningful and meaningless words. The teacher is also instructed to get a large selection of colored chalk so that she can write letters and words on the board for drill.

Spache points out that this idea for the use of color to identify the common sounds was introduced by Nellie Dale in 1899.

The memorization of the 47 different sounds with their corresponding colors, as well as the 270 letter combinations which commonly are used in writing these sounds, appears at least on the surface to be the heighth of a mechanical memorization approach to beginning reading. Demonstrations put on by the publisher, Encyclopaedia Britannica, managed to be interesting and lively but, as yet, research proof is lacking for the superiority of this method over any other.

Diacritical Marks

Diacritical marking plans to aid beginning readers are not exactly new. One of the oldest currently-used languages, Hebrew, has a system of marks used to indicate vowel sounds for beginning readers. After a certain degree of reading maturity is established, the marks vanish and the reader and writer use only consonants.

In 1644 an English schoolmaster Richard Hodges developed a set of diacritical marks to be used with beginning readers which the publisher put forth as, "The easiest and speediest way both for the true spelling and reading of English as also the true writing thereof that was ever publicly known to this day."

In the 1890's E. G. Ward authored a set of diacritically marked beginning reading texts published by the Silver Burdett Company for the American schools. In addition to diacritical marks that made the letters-sound relationship much more regular, Ward also underlined groups of letters that were "Phonograms."

A large number of readers in the 19th century, including the famous McGuffey series, used diacritical marks for the introduction of new words.

In 1964 Edward Fry published an article in *Elementary English* describing the Diacritical Marking System (DMS) to be used for beginning reading instruction. Later that year an experiment was begun, using the DMS marks on the Allyn & Bacon readers, in seven first grades. This Diacritical Marking System has over 99 per cent phoneme-grapheme regularity and aims to achieve essentially the same goals as the Initial Teaching Alphabet without distortion in word form or change in spelling.

The DMS is somewhat simpler than diacritical marking systems found in most dictionaries, since the intention is to aid beginning readers rather than give extreme accuracy. Regular consonants and short vowels are not marked since these are the most common usages of the letters. Long vowels have a bar over them. Regular two-letter combinations which make unique sounds such as the consonant digraphs and dipthongs, have a bar under both letters. Silent letters have a slash mark through them. These marks plus a few others, such as those used for the broad *A* and other sounds of *U*, constitute the bulk of the marks used. Nearly every word the child sees in the first grade reading books is marked and likewise all work that the teacher duplicates or puts on the board has the DMS marks. In writing children have the option of using the marks or not.

Uniphon

Another new phonetically-regular alphabet currently being used with some experiments in the Chicago area is Uniphon, developed by John Malone. This 40 letter alphabet, which the author calls "a single sound alphabet," uses block letters which have an additional interesting characteristic of being specially designed so that they can be read by computers for automatic translating purposes.

Simplified Use of Latin Alphabet

Though not really new alphabets, there are several systems of beginning reading instruction which achieve a high degree of initial phoneme-grapheme regularity by simply carefully selecting the words used in initial instruction. For example, under one type of "linguistic approach" that is put forth by Bloomfield and Barnhart, the child uses only regular consonants and short vowels. The introduction of new words is further graded so that only one short vowel is introduced per lesson. This method of controlled introduction of regular letters, while purported to be "new" in some circles, actually has as very close historical antecedent in the McGuffey Readers of the 1850's which used a similar introduction of sounds and words in its primers. While a number of other readers of the 1800's used a similar approach, one unique variation was used in the books written with words of *one syllable* published by McLoughlin Brothers in 1901. Whole books were written using only one syllable words.

Methodology

New alphabet approaches to beginning reading have some strong inferences for methodology but in and of themselves are only partially a method. For example, the most widely used set of ITA readers in the United States, written by Albert Mazurkiewicz and Harold Tanzer, have a relatively strong emphasis on the "language arts approach." These materials, which consist chiefly of a set of paperbound books with interesting stories not greatly different from a basal series, tend to have a relatively stronger *phonic* emphasis, but much of the uniqueness of method is due to the emphasis on children's writing activities in the teachers manual. While the authors would claim that it is the regularity of the ITA alphabet which facilitates children's ability to write, nonetheless the emphasis on the language arts approach is not unique to the type of alphabet used.

The DMS methods used in the current experimentation are largely overlays on the basal series. The actual pages from a basal series have been reproduced after marks have been added. The same basal series teachers manual is available, in fact required, for the teacher's use. The chief methodological feature of the DMS instructional program is the use of a number of phonic charts which accompany the basal series manual. Each time a new story is introduced in a preprimer or primer a small chart is introduced which explains one letter and its corresponding sound. The chart contains a key word (for example the word *cat* with a picture of a cat) plus several other common words which use the letter being discussed. Regular consonants and short vowels are thus introduced at the rate of one per reading lesson, and gradually digraphs, second sounds of consonants, and other vowel sounds are introduced with DMS marks. After a chart has been introduced, it is left hanging in the rooms so that the children may refer to the chart when coming across a new word. For example, if a child comes across a new word beginning with the letter *L* and he cannot remember the sound made by the letter, he needs only to look up on the board and find the *L* chart with its key picture; he may do the same with each of the letters in the word.

Conclusion

At the present time active experimentation is going on in the United States using the Initial Teaching Alphabet (ITA), the Diacritical Marking System (DMS), Uniphon, Words In Color, and the gradual introduction of phonetically regular letters—sometimes referred to as the linguistic approach. Of the new alphabets the only one which has published research reports is the Initial Teaching Alphabet. These published research reports, both from the United States and England, show that the ITA is definitely superior to the "old method." Whether or not this superiority is due to the special characteristics of ITA or the fact that it is a "new method" has yet to be established.

Three of these methods, ITA, DMS, and the linguistic approach, are being included in the large U. S. Office of Education Coordinated First Grade Reading Research Projects, a study now under way. The other two methods, Uniphon and Words In Color are being given field experimentation by their authors or publishers. Hence, all of these methods are being given classroom experimentation using method A classroom *vs.* method B classroom type of research design. While this type of research design may yield some interesting information, it is also quite possible for it to yield conflicting information such as we have seen coming from the phonics studies over the last hundred years. It is possible that for additional valuable information the reading researcher is going to have to team.up with the experimental psychologist or learning researcher who designs much smaller and much more carefully controlled studies. For example, is ITA superior to the basal reader method because it is new and because it uses a language experience approach or because it uses a phonetically regular alphabet? Current investigations will probably not satisfactorily answer this question.

A further important question might be, "If ITA or DMS or any of the other systems is superior to the traditional method, is the ITA or the DMS the best method of achieving these goals?" While each of the methods that we have discussed has gone through some developmental gesticulation, each of them is essentially the work of one man. Hence, if one of the new alphabets turns out to be definitely superior to the traditional alphabet the next question should be, "Is this the best possible alphabet to do this type of job?" American educators should seek the answer to this question before any large scale adoption of a beginning reading method utilizing a new alphabet is seriously contemplated. It is perhaps a necessary step in the evolution of new ideas that there be reasonably widespread interest in the current new alphabets and classroom experimentations of the type now under way. However, for the education profession to demonstrate itself to have achieved a reasonable degree of maturity, much more money should now be spent for research and development of new alphabets rather than wide scale adoption of them.

REFERENCES

1. Downing, J. A. *The ITA Reading Experiment*. London: Evan Brothers, Ltd., 1964.
2. Downing, J. A. *Experiments With An Augmented Alphabet for Beginning Readers in British Schools*. Pamphlet published on a talk to the 27th Educational Conference sponsored by the Educational Records Bureau, New York, November 1962.
3. Downing, J. A. "The Value of ITA," *NEA Journal*. Ivan Rose, Part 1; Warren Cutts, Part 2.
4. Downing, J. A. *The Augmented Roman Alphabet. A New Two-Stage Method to Help Children to Learn to Read*. Thirteen page pamphlet printed at Pitman Press, Bath, England, undated, circa 1962.
5. Downing, J. A. *Too Bee Or Not To Be, The Augmented Roman Alphabet*. London: Cassell and Company, Ltd., 1962.
6. Downing, J. A. The I.T.A. (Initial Teaching Alphabet) Reading Experiment. *The Reading Teacher,* November 1964.
7. Franklin, Benjamin. "A Scheme For A New Alphabet And Reformed Mode Of Spelling With Remarks And Examples Concerning The Same and An Inquiry Into Its Uses In A Correspondence Between Miss Stephenson and Dr. Franklin Written In The Characters Of The Alphabet," 1768, reprinted in *Complete Works of Benjamin Franklin,* John

Bigelow, Editor, G. P. Putnam's Sons, New York, 1887.

8. Fries, Charles C. *Linguistics and Reading.* New York: Holt, Rinehart & Winston, Inc., 1962.

9. Fry, Edward. "A Diacritical Marking System To Aid Beginning Reading Instruction," *Elementary English,* May 1964.

10. Gattegno, Caleb. "Words in Color" (mimeographed). Chicago: Learning Materials Inc., circa 1963.

11. Harrison, Maurice. *The Story of the Initial Teaching Alphabet.* London: Pitman Publishing Co., 1965.

12. Hodges, Richard. *The English Primrose.* London: Richard Cotes, 1644.

13. Keller, Linda. *Herbert The Hippo* (children's book in Uniphon). Chicago: Peppermint Press, Inc., 1962.

14. Mazurkiewicz, Albert J. "The Lehigh-Bethlehem ITA Study" (First Year), ITA Report, mimeographed, undated, circa 1964.

15. Mazurkiewicz, Albert J. "Teaching Reading in America Using the Initial Teaching Alphabet," *Elementary English,* November 1964.

16. National Education Association. *Journal of Procedures & Addresses.* Winona, Minnesota: 1910.

17. Pitman, Benn. *First Phonetic Reader.* Cincinnati: American Phonetic Publishing Association, 1855.

18. Pitman, Sir James. *The Ehrhardt Augmented (40 sound-42 character) lower-case Roman Alphabet.* The reasons and intentions underlying its design together with a specimen. Twenty-three page printed pamphlet. London: Pitman House, 1959.

19. Pitman, Sir James. "Learning to Read," *Journal of the Royal Society of Arts,* February 1961.

20. Pitman, Sir James. "Learning to Read. A Suggested Experiment," *The Times Educational Supplement,* May 29, 1959.

21. Pitman, Sir James. "Spelling With The Augmented Roman Alphabet." Ten-page mimeographed pamphlet circulated by Mr. Downing at teacher training meetings.

22. Pitman, Sir James. "The Future of the Teaching of Reading," *Keeping Abreast of the Revolution in Education,* edited by Arthur E. Traxler. Report of the 28th Educational Conference, American Council on Education, 1964.

23. Spache, George D. "Interesting Books for the Reading Teacher," *The Reading Teacher,* April 1964.

24. Ward, Edward R. *The Rational Method of Reading,* First Reader. Silver, Burdett & Co., Boston, 1894.

25. No author. *McGuffey's Eclectic Primer,* Revised Edition, copyright 1909, Henry H. Vail, American Book Company, New York.

Strategies for Teaching Sound-Letter Relationships

MORTON BOTEL*

TODAY'S TEACHER has a real problem in planning and teaching phonics or word attack. He has his choice of the use of simplified alphabets, color, linguistic programing, "programed learning" materials, new phonics programs in basal readers, spellers, language books, workbooks, filmstrip, tape and computer form. These alternatives have increased the problem of making judgments about what should be taught and how it is to be taught.

Not too many years ago, the matter was more simple. Word attack was taught as the fourth or fifth step in a reading lesson. The content was built into the design of the lesson by the authors of basal readers. With a minimum of supplementation, teachers felt that these guidebook and workbook activities, correlated as they were with the story in the basal reader, provided the material needed to do the job. But in the last decade or two, methods and materials for teaching pupils how sounds are represented by letters have proliferated. This has happened partly, of course, because of a pendulum swing back to "phonics." Much vital and productive activity, however, has come from new insights into linguistics, the perceptual process, inductive or discovery methods of teaching, and the overriding concern for intensifying instruction for every pupil at his own level and rate.

I would like to suggest five standards my colleagues and I have used as the basis for the development of a program for teaching sound-letter relationships. Perhaps these standards might serve as guidelines for teachers who are developing or evaluating the validity of programs in this aspect of reading and spelling.

Standards for Teaching Sound-Letter Relationships

1. The program must provide linguistically sound content and structure.

2. The program must provide for self-discovery by the pupil.

3. The program must provide multisensory experiences including touch and movement.

4. The program must provide pupils with opportunities for the application of skills in many settings.

5. The program must provide opportunities for each pupil to work at his own level and rate.

Obviously, the "strategies" referred to in the title of this paper have to do with a technology which provides strong affirmative answers to the questions suggested by the standards.

For each standard I will discuss elements of a program that contribute to better pupil understanding of sound-letter relationships.

1. *Is the program linguistically sound?* In the light of present day linguistic research, a program designed to teach sound-letter relationships should, I believe, have the following characteristics:

a. It should include strong emphasis from the beginning on the idea that vowel and consonant speech sounds are represented by letters.

b. It should develop this understanding by programing its beginning vocabulary in large measure on words in which there is a one-to-one correspondence between sounds and letters.

c. It should present these words in spelling patterns in which there is a minimal contrast in sound and letter representation from word to word in the pattern.

*Vistas in Reading, IRA Proceedings, Vol. 11, Part 1, 1967, 156-159.

d. It should lead pupils systematically and logically from such spelling patterns to those which are less regularly represented.

e. It should include the study of vowel sound-vowel letter relationships practically from the beginning.

f. It should immediately provide oral experience in which the words studied are used in phrases and sentences so that pupils become aware of the need for thinking of the way the words sound in the larger intonational setting.

g. It should be flexible enough to include words which are less regular or even irregular in the early stages if these words are needed to make language more interesting, more meaningful, or more like the sound of language.

In short, linguistic research supports two major ideas which must be wed in programing sound-letter relationships: (1) it must capitalize on the consistent sound-to-spelling correspondences and patterns or rules in American-English spellings, and (2) it must immediately provide contextual settings for words studied that cause them to be used in a more natural linguistic environment.

2. *Is the program structured to provide for self-discovery by the pupil?* All of us as teachers respect the importance of discovery. Discovery is one of the most rewarding experiences in teaching. It might be called the "Aha!" experience . . . a gasp, the light dawns! "I've got it!" These are events teachers strive to bring about. How is this done in teaching sound-letter relationships?

As we have noted already, pupils must understand that spelling patterns represent sounds. We want this understanding to grow by their involvement in and exploration of these patterns. In this way pupils will be led to discover significant sound-letter relationships. I should like to illustrate a way of programing for discovery through pattern studies. We sometimes call such exploration the game of "What's My Rule?".

Put the following patterns on the chalkboard:

Pattern 1	Pattern 2	Pattern 3
hat	*hat*	*hat*
mat	*hit*	*had*

We ask pupils (1) to read the words in the pattern aloud, (2) to sort such words as *has, cat, hut, ham* and *hot* into the pattern sets, (3) to extend the pattern sets with other words that belong, and (4) to formulate the rule. Actually pupils who can sort given words into the right patterns and who can find other words that belong to the patterns, have "found the rule" in the most essential sense. The ability to verbalize the pattern or formulate the rule should not be hurried. Indeed, it is questionable whether it is helpful at all to many young pupils or to slow pupils to focus on the abstract statement of the rule.

Here are further pattern contrasts programed into the *What's My Rule?* form. Notice that they provide minimal contrast between words not only within a pattern but also from pattern to pattern:

Pattern 4		Pattern 5
bat	→	bet
mat	→	met
sat	→	
↓		

Pattern 6		Pattern 7		Pattern 8
tan	→	tin	→	ten
pan	→	pin	→	
man				
↓				

Here are further examples of patterns designed for discovery activity. Patterns 9 to 12 maintain the one letter-one sound change in successive words and between patterns as a way of introducing the spelling patterns of long sounds.

Pattern 9		Pattern 10
pan	→	pane
man	→	mane
can	→	
↓		

Pattern 11   Pattern 12
  pan   →   pain
  ran   →   rain
  man   →
  ↓

The more complex aspects of sound-letter relationships in English are gradually presented in related patterns like these:

Pattern 13   Pattern 14   Pattern 15
  hope   snow   boat
  home   low   coat
  mole   yellow   soap
  ↓   ↓   ↓

in which pupils get to know the alternative ways a consonant or vowel sound (long o in above patterns) is represented in English.

3. *Does the program provide multisensory experiences including touch and movement?* Certainly our knowledge of the psychology of perception should suggest a strategy for improving the quality of perceptual response to words and to spelling patterns.

In the earliest experience with words and patterns, all pupils should have experience in tracing and writing as well as seeing and saying these elements. Further, for those pupils whose memory is poor as evidenced by lack of recall or weak recall from day to day, tracing and writing should be extended.

At one time it was widely believed that tactile-motor experiences in learning words should be restricted to the language disabled pupil. Today, we are more and more coming to the view that such perceptual training should be developmental and preventive.

4. *Does the program provide opportunities for application of skills in many settings?* It is quite common for teachers to say, "Johnny knows the rule when we work with it on the board, but he can't apply it when he meets a new word in his reading or spelling."

The reason for a pupil's inability to apply rules in part resides in the way in which rules are taught. Frequently, pupils are too strongly directed toward the verbalization of the rule rather than to the pattern of words which are the substance of the formulation of the rule.

But even when the primary emphasis is on the pattern itself and when a discovery technique is used, we still will not get transfer to reading and spelling unless we program for it. Application of what the pupil learns about spelling patterns should be provided for in several different settings—in context and in lists.

Let us use the silent *e* spelling pattern as an example: Here are some ways in which we can help pupils make this pattern a tool for independence in word attack:

a. *In independent wide reading.* Have pupils read in self-selected materials. In such books, the transfer occurs naturally in a highly motivated reading environment. Certainly many new and unfamiliar words will belong to the silent *e* pattern and with the help of the context and the high interest, such words will be attacked in their most natural setting. This medium for application is like going into the water to practice a new swimming stroke. Is there a better way?

b. *In contrived sentences.* Have pupils read sentences made up to give emphasis to the principle. In such sentences, all words except the new ones should be known.

> I *hope* to get a jump *rope* and *kite*
>   for my birthday.
> Please write your *name,* the *date,* and
>   *place* you *came* from.
> In the *dim* light, he saw a *dime* in
>   the street.
> He *made* us *mad* when he *spit* in
>   *spite* of the warning.

c. *By extending patterned lists.* We have already indicated under the discovery method how pupils may extend any patterned lists as far as they can by finding words that fit.

d. *By having pupils invent and read aloud nonsense words.* Perhaps pupils can give meaning to these words by relating them to naming some new discovery in medicine or interplanetary travel.

spane
clibe
dufe

e. *By having pupils read aloud patterned lists of words with clues built in.*

cap	cope
cape	cape
tape	tape
tap	take
tapping	bake
snapping	brake
snipping	broke
snipe	bloke
sniping	

f. *By having pupils spell dictated lists and sentences which include words that fit the silent e pattern.*

g. *By having pupils spell words in self-dictated tests.* In such phrases and sentences as those below, pupils spell the word called for. These words are cued by a sound-spelling representation of the word, by context, or both.

to /tayst/ the food

a pretty snow /seen/

to slip and /sl___/ on the ice

The Navahos are an Indian /tr___/.

5. *The program must provide opportunities for each pupil to work at his own level and rate.* The word attack program must be tailored to the individual differences in level and rate to be found in every group. Many ways should be compiled by the teacher or by a staff for accomplishing this task of intensifying the instructional process. Three very important techniques in this category include:

a. Placing pupils at their instructional level in basal readers and textbooks; i.e.,

materials in which pupils read with at least 95% oral fluency and with at least 75% comprehension.

b. Using discovery activities such as those described earlier in which open-ended activities provide automatically for different levels and rates.

c. Testing to determine which spelling patterns pupils have mastered and which need to be reviewed or introduced.

In summary, by considering such matters as linguistic validity, self-discovery, perception, transfer of learning, and individualization of instruction, the curriculum builder will be able to develop or adopt programs which deal efficiently and effectively with the problems of sound-letter relationships.

REFERENCES

1. Botel, Morton; Holsclaw, Cora; Brothers, Aileen. *Patterns in Spelling and Writing, Levels A through F; 3140 Important Words;* and *1620 Power Words.* Chicago: Follett Publishing Company, 1963.

2. Fries, Charles C. *Linguistics and Reading.* New York: Holt, Rinehart and Winston, Inc., 1963.

3. Hall, Robert. *Sound and Spelling in English.* Philadelphia: Chilton Co., 1961.

4. Hodges, Richard E. "The Case for Teaching Sound-to-Letter Correspondence in Spelling," *Elementary School Journal,* 327-336, March 1966.

5. Lefevre, Carl A. *Linguistics and the Teaching of Reading.* New York: McGraw-Hill, 1964.

6. Lloyd, Donald J., and Warfel, Harry A. *American English in its Cultural Setting.* New York: Alfred A. Knopf, 1956.

7. *The Reading Teacher.* "Linguistics and Reading." Newark, Delaware: International Reading Association, December 1964.

The Teaching of Word Analysis through Perceptual Conditioning

GERALD G. GLASS*

IT IS MOST important that we carefully and objectively examine what is involved in the teaching of word analysis. It is this writer's objective to demonstrate that many of our "approved" methods are either unreasonable or unwarranted in light of the tasks involved. Some of these may actually be detrimental to the development of proficiency in word analysis. The following points need to be made.

The teaching of word analysis should not be considered the teaching of reading. Reading, at even its simplest level, is responding to meaning. Just "calling" a word is not reading. (We took a pound of Flesch when someone said it was.) In a sense word analysis is a pre-reading ability. It could be considered that "reading" comes into play only after one knows the sound of a word. Actually, even if this were not accepted, the problem of meaning in word analysis work below the middle grades would rarely be a problem. This writer surveyed the new words introduced in major basals and (to no one's surprise) close to 99 per cent of the words were already within the average youngster's vocabulary. Because of this an efficient word analysis "method" need not include the teaching of basic meanings, for to do so may be superfluous.

Word analysis work may actually be hampered by having the word analysis skills taught utilizing words within a phrase or sentence context. Too often is the context (and not the early grader's ability to discover phonic and structural elements in words) a major factor in identifying the correct sound of a word. Words in context may undermine the need of a developing word analysis skill's coming to the fore and being practiced. Context (and pictures) frequently give both the student and the teacher a spurious idea of the actual ability of the student in word identification. It leads to apparent ability vs. actual ability. It is best that while the student has the helpful guidance of the teacher available he should not also have the contextual aids available. Most often if one can "sound out" out of context one will surely be able to identify the word with the added clues of context when the reading is for actual content learning and not word analysis training. Many of the word analysis difficulties which are "discovered" by middle grade and junior high teachers are the result of the context's becoming too difficult to shelter the previously concealed weakness in word analysis.

It is dishonest to say that words in our language can be sounded out phonetically, i.e., letter-by-letter sound. Other than that there are over 2,000 ways the twenty-six letters of our alphabet can be sounded. The sounds of the vowels (the most difficult problem in word analysis) are usually controlled by their place in the syllable. So, one cannot discover the sound of any vowel before first determining the syllable structure of the word (structural analysis). The *e* in pepper can only be known (if you are really using "approved" techniques) when you decide that the *e* is within a first syllable and is followed in the syllable by a consonant that is not part of a digraph. Only *after* this process of syllabication can phonetic analysis be used. However, it is also dishonest to advise the use of syllabication as a technique in word analysis. The narrowness of its rules, the contradictions, the complexity of its "ifs," the mental gymnastics necessary to store information in order to decipher a word of two or more syllables,

*Reading and Inquiry, IRA Proceedings, Vol. 10, 1965, 410-413.

makes it ludicrous to suggest that the technique be used in word analysis. (In fact, one set of rules actually requires that you know the sound of the word [*motor, rapid*] before you decide where the break occurs to discover the sound of the word!) Fortunately it is of little import. That people use syllabication to discover the sound of a word is a myth now too long in the literature (almost every methods book on the teaching of reading). Syllabication, in populations totaling over 500 adults and children, was applied *after* the word was identified, *never* (yes, not once) before the sound of the word was known. To this point the writer seriously questions the necessity of the teaching of meaning with word analysis, the use of context and contextual clues in the teaching of word analysis, and the use of syllabication and phonic principles. Remember, we are concerned with word analysis and not with the operationally defined problem of teaching reading.

Other factors that, because of space limitations, can only be mentioned here, should be taken into consideration when attempting to explore what is involved in learning and utilizing word analysis techniques.

The Gestaltists have long ago made us aware that the size of a configuration has little or nothing to do with the person's ability to "learn." It is the familiarity and the meaning one can bring to the object that will determine what one will do with it. The eleven letter word *grandmother* for obvious reasons is less difficult than the four letter word *here*.

We know that objects composed of discrete elements initially can be seen as wholes and then, if necessary, seen as composed of various parts. A child, by the nature of his being, first identifies a car, a house, and a toy before he needs to deal with the parts which make up the whole.

We can "learn" to see what we want to see and subordinate what we do not. Hold a pencil up to someone and say only "What do you see?" Everyone (yes, every-

one) will say "a pencil." Actually, the observer will see a great deal more. Your fingers, hand, arm, shoulder, head, torso, the area behind and around you, etc. are in his view. But he has "learned" to discriminate out of the field based upon his learned mental sets. These factors suggest that in word analysis it is possible, and maybe even natural, for a child to find a three- and four-letter combination such as *ing, ate,* and *ight* as easy to learn as single-letter phonic sounds; such phonograms may be seen as *one whole* rather than three or four separate wholes. In addition, as one learns to "see" only a certain part of a complete view depending upon one's mental set, one might be able to look at an unknown word like *distenationing* and see only what one has learned to see.

The reader is advised to say the unknown word aloud. Did you read the word at sight or did you sound the word out? You sounded it out. Did you use syllable and phonic rules such as vccv, vcv, open syllable and closed syllable, two vowels together, etc.? Of course not. Did you notice the little words in the big one and use the sound of these words in the analysis; e.g, *at, on, in, nation?* I hope not.

What then was used? The reader had no choice. He has been conditioned through his consistent and extended dealings with words used in American writing, uniquely to notice clusters of letters in an unknown word that seem naturally to come together. We see (and hear) within the whole word *dis/ten/a/tion/ing* or possibly *d/is/t/en/ation/ing,* but never the /ste/ or /ena/ or /tio/ or /nin/ (all of which are orthographically possible). Any activity, then, which fosters seeing the "correct" clusters would contribute a great deal toward developing word analysis proficiency.

The belief of this writer is that unknown words are correctly identified through a process which utilizes a conditioned perceptual set that scans a word for its structural sounding elements (letter clusters) as they have been historically consistent in the reader's experience. The reader of this article is asked to examine the unknown words *"blassment, trepulation, trom* and *deplistrationer."* It is most certain that you "read" the words letter-cluster by letter-cluster, as you have learned these letters arrange themselves in your experiences with the language. It is almost as if there were unique spacing between the common structures in the word. You probably used nothing more than your instant (conditioned) knowledge of these "phonograms." (For words which have structures that do not fit a consistent pattern [*police, great*] no word analysis method can apply). If we agreed upon how successful readers identify unknown words, it would be fruitful to backtrack and attempt to develop ways of learning word analysis which would be consistent with what we desire the end result to be.

An approach called "perceptual conditioning" has been developed to be consistent with the positive factors which seem to be valid in word analysis. The "method" requires youngsters to examine known words (out of context) both visually and auditorily in a way that would foster the correct visual clustering of letters. Mental sets to see "correctly" are controlled and fostered by the teacher's complete direction of how a youngster is to examine a word and identify the sounds within it. A note should be made here. In the word analysis process it is important not only to identify sounds in a word and the letters that make that sound, but it is crucial that a reader see letters and then come up with the sound that the letters make. One is from auditory to visual and the other from visual to auditory. Both skills are necessary for effective word analysis.

Perceptual Conditioning

Words to be used must be within the child's listening vocabulary and listed out of context. The child should either know the whole word or be told its name. Youngsters are learning to identify sounds in words correctly so that they will be able to transfer these learnings when they read unknown words.

The whole word must always be presented. Parts of words should not be covered up then exposed. Letters should not be added on to structural elements to form the whole word. The elements (phonograms) must be seen with the letters before and after as when seen during reading. The *ong* in isolation is not the same perceptual image as the *ong* in stronger. Readers must perceptually isolate the letter clusters *within* a word (as with *distenationing*).

The teacher directs how a pupil will examine a word. She *always* directs the examination with two crucial questions to develop mental set. These are: "What letters make what sounds?" "What sounds do what letters make?" For example, in the word *black,* what letters make the *buhll* sound; what letters make the *ack* sound? In the word *black* what sound does the *bl* make? What sound does the *ack* make? Here we have required the student to examine the word in a way that we know will be of benefit to him when he sees other words with the same phonograms. We required that he examine the letters (cluster fashion) and apply a sound. We did not allow him to examine the word in any way other than what we think would be consistent with the way he will examine words when he becomes proficient in word analysis. He did not, and never will be allowed to, insult the integrity of a digraph, phonogram, or any of the meaning or pronunciation units which are structurally consistent in our written language. If the youngster is consistently required to examine whole words in terms of these common internal structures (e.g., *team, dreaming, streamline*) utilizing the mental set questions, he theoretically must condition to the phonograms as they are visually isolated as a part *within* the whole word. This, as has been suggested, is just what we want.

The question that immediately comes

to mind is how many of these phonograms or letter clusters do we have in our language? Are they so numerous that it would be unreasonable to become conditioned to their existence in words. Or, in fact, do they really exist frequently enough for us to depend upon them in sounding out unknown words? This writer and his staff have intensively examined the words used in the basals of the first three grades. All new words were examined to determine structural sound make-up. It was discovered that less than 100 vowel phonograms are included five or more times in the new vocabulary of the first three grades. Only 42 vowel phonograms are used 10 times or more. If these vowel phonograms could be consistently identified in whole words the youngster will have the vowel sounds introduced in over 90 per cent of the new vocabulary. For example, it was discovered that *ing* was repeated at least 109 times in new words; *er* 105 times; *ar* 47 times; *ad* 17 times; *ear* 6 times; *ore* 5 times. (The complete set of approximately 100 vowel phonograms and their frequency is available through the writer.) The reader should recall that the writer feels that it is just as easy to learn that three or four letters make one sound as it is to learn that one letter makes a sound. Also, it should be noted that if clusters of letters are taught as producing a sound, rather than single letters, the problem of teaching vowel sounds and their variations is virtually eliminated. A vowel here makes a sound as part of a letter cluster not because it

has a place in a syllable or any other such "rule." Careful count was made of the consonant blends and the consonant digraphs. It was found that when teaching word analysis through perceptual conditioning, these sound elements are learned relatively easily compared to the vowel phonograms; that their random distribution throughout words which are controlled just for the vowel phonogram gives enough repetition to bring about the conditioned effect when the consonant elements are seen within a whole word.

To date the approach has been used by the writer, his colleagues, and graduate students. The results have been gratifying enough for us to do continued research. Lists of words have been developed which include the specific vowel phonograms that are to be worked with during the lesson. For a ten-minute period pupils are directed to examine selected words according to the rigid requirements discussed. If this is done *consistently* for two ten-minute periods a day, each of the five days in a school week, the writer predicts that within a three- or four-month period the average first-grader will be able to analyze unknown words with the proficiency of the average third-grader. The only words he will not be able to sound out would be those words which need to be learned at sight. There is evidence that this approach should be considered where early training in reading is desired. Because it minimizes factors of an emotional and intellectual nature it may be "easier" and therefore applicable.

Teaching Structural Analysis

Leo M. Schell*

TO TEACH CHILDREN how to figure out the pronunciation and/or meaning of an unrecognized word through the use of phonic and structural analysis is one important goal of reading instruction. Yet Clymer (1963) has shown that many phonic generalizations lack either validity or frequency of application and that consideration should be given to some possible revisions in the commonly taught content of phonic analysis. Recently, Winkley (1966) has raised some similar disturbing questions about the worth of certain generalizations about accenting. It therefore seems a propitious time to examine some of the problems concerning the content of structural analysis as found in both professional methods textbooks and basal reading series.

The meaning of affixes

Methods textbooks typically list prefixes and suffixes which the elementary school pupil should know. Usually, it is not clear whether it is the pronunciation or meaning or both which pupils should know. If it is the meaning which is intended, some problems arise.

Few prefixes are valuable for meaning. Four prefixes commonly recommended to be taught—and their meanings—are:

con- . . . together, with, very
ex- . . . out of, from, beyond, without
pre- . . . before in time
re- . . . backwards, again

Yet, consider the plight of the intermediate grade pupil trying to apply what he has been taught to any of these words commonly found in elementary school textbooks: conserve, exclaim, present, and resin.

The obvious problem is that these prefixes have meaning to an elementary school child only when there is a known base word. Even though in Latin these prefixes were attached to base words, over the years these bases have lost their independent standing and the prefixes have become known as "absorbed prefixes." In such words, knowledge of the meaning of the prefix is virtually worthless.

Suffixes present difficulties in two ways. Many suffixes have multiple meanings; e.g., -ment may mean act, condition, or concrete instance. To use the suffix to help derive the word's meaning, the reader must 1] recall these three meanings, 2] choose the appropriate one, and 3]

*The Reading Teacher, 21 (November 1967), 133-137.

apply this meaning to the base form—a prodigious task for most elementary school pupils. Surely, there must be a *more efficient* procedure.

Suffixes are most valuable to the reader when they are affixed to a known base word; e.g., development. But, in some cases it does the reader little good to detach the suffix in order to locate the base word because the base changes forms when a suffix is added, e.g., admission and deceptive. In such instances, recognition and knowledge of the meaning of the suffix seem of little value in determining the meaning of an unrecognized word.

Inaccurate instruction

Not only are there difficulties inherent in the construction and meaning of affixed words, but the accuracy of the content taught is sometimes questionable. Instructional techniques frequently fail to distinguish between reading and spelling. For example, one prominent reading specialist writes, "When a word ends in *y* following a consonant, *y* is usually changed to *i* when adding an ending as in *cried, ponies, tinier, happily*" (Smith, 1963). This rule goes from the base to the inflected form, a spelling sequence. The reading sequence should go from the inflected form to the base. Perhaps it isn't too confusing to children, but it seems to indicate some lack of understanding by those engaged in teaching teachers.

It appears that sometimes it is not clear whether pronunciation or syllabication comes first. The senior author of one of the best selling basal series writes in his professional text, "Lead pupils to note that the vowel sound (in *"paper"*) is long and therefore, the first syllable is probably *"pa"* (Gray, 1960). Similarly, another basal series author writes in her professional text, "When two vowels come together and each keeps its own sound, they form separate syllables, as *pi-o-neer"* (Hester, 1964).

Both of these principles imply that the pupil must pronounce the word before he can syllabicate it. But, if he can already pronounce the word, why should he need to syllabicate it? Furthermore, the latter generalization is a tautology: the dependent and independent clauses say the same thing, just in different words. The definition of a syllable is such that this statement does not really tell one anything; it only masquerades as information.

Unfortunately, most principles of syllabic division are based on the vocabulary entry in the dictionary rather than on the respelling, a procedure excellent for composition but questionable for reading. Troup outlines the historical process by which the present system evolved and points out that

The way a word is pronounced has nothing whatsoever to do with the way it is divided at the end of a line in writing. . . . Over the years, educators set up a kind of a phonics system based on a mechanical practice that was never intended to relate to speech. In any dictionary, for example, you will find the word *vision* divided *vi-sion* in the entry and re-spelled the only way it can be pronounced in English, the first syllable being *vizh*. (1961, p. 142).

Pupils are told that affixes form separate syllables and then asked to divide and pronounce words such as "building" which everyone pronounces in context as *bil-ding* rather than *bild-ing*. It is surprising there is not a complete generation of skeptics, unwilling to accept what is told them. Maybe teachers are lucky students do not take instruction too seriously!

Directions for how to use structural analysis to unlock an unrecognized word may be inefficient even if not inaccurate. One fourth grade basal workbook tells pupils to syllabicate the word and then look for affixes (Russell, 1961). Since affixes are predominantly monosyllabic, it seems easiest to locate known affixes first. This leaves only the base word to be syllabicated.

Practice exercises in workbooks, basal series, etc. leave much to be desired. One fifth grade workbook presents this principle, "If a word ends in *le* preceded by a consonant, the consonant is included in the last syllable," and then asks the pupil to apply it to the word "single" (Unknown, 1961). A widely used methods text uses "don-key" as appropriate practice for the rule about dividing syllables between medial consonants (Bond and Wagner, 1966). These words may follow the respective generalizations, but they would be of little help in pronouncing an unknown word.

Valuable principles?

It may be a waste of pupils' time to teach them certain structural principles. One methods text recommends teaching this accenting generalization: "In multisyllabic words, the first or second syllable has either a primary or secondary accent (su-per-vi′sor, re-spon′si-bil′i-ty)" (Harris, 1962). If the reader syllabicates correctly and then accents incorrectly, is he at much of a disadvantage? The purpose for learning accenting principles is to allow the reader to recreate the sound of a word he already knows, to activate its auditory memory. Should the reader give the first rather than the second syllable a primary accent, it hardly seems that this minor deviation will hinder the desired recreation. Having children learn this principle seems to be the educational equivalent of "overkill."

From here, where?

The foregoing discussion was not intended to be a comprehensive survey of all the problems associated with the content and methodology of structural analysis. It was meant only to highlight, to call attention to, certain facets of the topic which deserve critical scrutiny. Some suggestions for dealing with these problems seem warranted.

That pupils should be made aware of the limited applicability of the meaning of prefixes seems an obvious first step. But, if it has ever been previously suggested, it has never been practiced systematically. Intermediate grade pupils should have a realistic perception of what they can—and cannot—do with their learnings. To help them attain this goal, after introducing and practicing on prefix meanings, it would be wise to present and discuss some common exceptions, e.g., disaster, illusion, and uncouth.

In dealing with the meaning of suffixes, perhaps it would be more efficient to stress the grammatical function of the suffixed word in the sentence than to teach the meaning of individual suffixes. For example, rather than teach that -al means "pertaining to" and that therefore musical means "pertaining to music," have pupils examine the location of "musical" in the sentence and note its relation to other words. In "We went to a musical comedy," the grammatical function of the word is an obvious cue to the grammatically informed that music had a dominant role in the play.

To rectify inaccurate instruction, there must be more precise understanding of how structural analysis aids in unlocking unrecognized words. Possibly better than teaching a set of separate and independent rules (tactics), concentration should be on a general technique (strategy) applicable to various situations. The first three steps of such an approach could be:

1. Visually locate and isolate any recognized affixes.
2. If the base word is not recognized, syllabicate it.
3. Determine the vowel sound in each syllable.

This approach begins with the affixed form and goes to the base form, a realistic reading procedure. It also treats syllabication as an integral part of phonics, which is its correct role.

It seems probable that linguists with their emphasis on the subordination of writing to speaking may provide a more functional set of principles governing syllabic division than those now used. Teachers need to know how best to handle the syllabication of words such as connect and how to cope with the problem of neutral (schwa) sounds in unaccented syllables.

The most practical way to teach accenting generalizations would seem to be to coordinate them with dictionary work rather than to present and practice them in isolation. This approach not only gives pupils independence with unrecognized words in their listening vocabulary, but also helps them pronounce words not already in their listening vocabulary—the two functions of accenting. "Two birds with one stone."

There must be studies using the techniques of Clymer (1963) and Winkley (1966) to provide information about as yet uninvestigated areas of structural analysis and to extend their ideas to other material and grade levels. However, twiddling collective thumbs until someone produces this information hardly seems the proper attitude. Teachers need to be selective in what they teach and how they teach it. They should feel free to omit a principle that has little applicability or to revise suggested procedures so they are correct and accurate. A teacher is primarily a decision maker and should not be shackled to suggestions in teachers' manuals.

There seems to be sufficient evidence that some of the content of structural analysis is incorrect and seldom applicable and that some current methodology may be inefficient and questionable. All teachers must be aware of these shortcomings and must search for more accurate content and better methods of instruction.

References

Bond, G. L., and Wagner, Eva. *Teaching the child to read.* New York: Macmillan, 1966. p. 167.

Clymer, T. The utility of phonic generalizations in the primary grades. *The Reading Teacher,* 1963, *16,* 252-258.

Gray, W. S. *On their own in reading.* Chicago: Scott, Foresman, 1960. p. 128.

Harris, A. J. *Effective teaching of reading.* New York: McKay, 1962. p. 369.

Hester, Kathleen. *Teaching every child to read.* New York: Harper & Row, 1964. p. 149.

Russell, D. H., and McCullough, Constance M. *My do and learn book to accompany roads to everywhere.* Boston: Ginn, 1961. p. 23.

———. *My do and learn book to accompany trails to treasure.* Boston: Ginn, 1961. p. 13.

Smith, Nila Banton. *Reading instruction for today's children.* Englewood Cliffs, N. J.: Prentice-Hall, 1963. p. 225.

Troup, Mildred. Controversial issues related to published instructional materials. Controversial issues in reading and promising solutions. *Supplementary Educational Monographs,* No. 91, 1961, 135-144.

Winkley, Carol K. Which accent generalizations are worth teaching? *The Reading Teacher,* 1966, *20,* 219-224.

PART V: Articles Partially Related or Very General

Word Analysis and Comprehension

Donald A. Benz and Robert A. Rosemier*

BECAUSE OF THE IMPORTANCE placed on reading ability in typical classroom learning experiences, educators have been greatly concerned over the procedures by which reading ability is developed. While some investigators have considered the format of presentation and methods for teaching reading, others have been interested in the particular skills involved in reading development. The present study, as one of the latter type, employed two methods to determine the relationship between performance on tests designed to measure certain reading skills and their relationship to reading comprehension at the fourth grade level.

One method involved observations of the ways in which children of high comprehension levels differed from children at lower levels. This particular grouping was selected rather than one based on the factor of intelligence, such as those which might result in over-under achiever groupings or classification into those of high-average-low IQ. Although these latter types would seem appropriate for the study of effective teaching methods with various levels of student abilities, such as those performed by Dolan (1963) and Strand (1956), it was felt that a clear insight into the fundamental elements of reading comprehension could come only from study of children who were classified by their comprehension level alone and not by any other criteria.

If those at a low comprehension level were observed to perform significantly lower on a skill than those at a higher level, this skill would seemingly be related to reading comprehension ability. It might be inferred then, and could subsequently be studied experimentally, that additional work on this skill could aid the development of reading comprehension.

The second method of determining the relationship between performance on a skill and reading comprehension involved the computation of partial correlation coefficients. These partial correlations can be interpreted in essentially the same way as the more familiar simple correlation coefficients, except that these partials would indicate the relationship between two variables when the confounding effects of the other variables were removed. This technique is especially valuable when one realizes that much of an observed relationship between two variables may result from the mutual dependence upon a third variable. If the effects of the third

*The Reading Teacher, 21 (March 1968), 558-563.

variable were to be removed, the coefficient would give some measure of "pure" relationship between the first two. In the present
study, the partial correlations were computed between reading
comprehension scores over all levels and scores on each of six tests
of word analysis skills while removing the effects of performance
on the other five skills.

The subjects

The participants consisted of all fourth grade children in six
towns and cities in five northeastern states. These fifty-five classrooms of 1490 children included what the authors believed to be a
representative cross-section of school environments. Included were
a college town (n=273), a resort village (n=148), a state capital
(n=115), an industrial-professional community (n=274), an
agricultural center (n=248), and a so-called "bedroom" community
serving a nearby metropolitan center (n=432).

The specific cities were essentially selected by random procedures, with stratification according to geographic location, size, and
environment type. Although none of the communities was considered "culturally deprived", a wide range of socio-economical levels
did exist among and within the systems considered. Likewise, these
schools represented a wide variety of instructional methods for
teaching reading, with varying degrees of emphasis on word analysis skills. The wider sampling would allow more generalizing of
findings than would a more restricted sample which represented
only one method for teaching reading.

The number of classrooms in the systems ranged from five to
eighteen. The population appeared to be only slightly above normal
(mean IQ=107) on the basis of intelligence test scores which were
available for 94 per cent of the population.

The instruments

Each fourth-grade class was administered the Gates (1958),
Level of Comprehension Test, Type LC, to determine reading comprehension and the Bond, Clymer, Hoyt (1955), *Silent Reading
Diagnostic Tests*, Form D-A, to measure proficiency in syllabication,
locating root words, words in context, word elements, beginning
sounds, and rhyming sounds. The classroom teachers were trained
to administer the tests which were given in consecutive half-day
testing sessions. Children scoring between 6.0 and 9.2 on the Gates
test were considered high level readers (n=474); those between
4.6 and 5.9, middle level (n=450); and those from 2.0 to 4.5, low
level (n=478). Eighty-eight subjects were dropped from the

analysis either because of absence during testing or failure to achieve the minimum level reported on the comprehension test, thus leaving 1402 children available for analysis.

The analyses and results

The statistical test of analysis of variance was conducted to determine whether or not differences existed between these three comprehension levels of readers for each of the six word-analysis skills. When a skill showed a significant difference among the three levels, a t test was conducted between pairs of levels to determine which levels differed from one another on this skill.

The results of this first phase, presented in Table 1, indicate that on the basis of mean scores, the high readers tend to perform better than middle readers, and that middle readers tend to perform better than low readers on each of the six word-analysis skills.

Table 1   Mean-scores for high, middle, and low readers in fourth grade on six word-analysis tests

Skill	High	Middle	Low
1. Words in context	25.5	23.3	20.6
2. Syllabication	16.0	13.2	10.7
3. Root word	23.8	22.1	19.1
4. Word elements	26.7	24.9	22.6
5. Beginning sounds	27.6	26.2	23.9
6. Rhyming sounds	25.6	22.7	19.1

All comparisons between adjacent groups within a skill were statistically signficant at the .01 level. It might be concluded that performance on these word-analysis skills is related to reading comprehension level, assuming of course, that the opportunity to learn these skills did not favor a particular comprehension level. The validity of this assumption, which confounds every investigation within existing classrooms, is questionable, and could be the sole or major cause of skill differences among comprehension levels. However, until better measures of opportunity as reflected in the ability to learn are derived and can be tested for importance, this conclusion seems at least partially justified.

The previously-mentioned partial correlation coefficients between each of the six word-analysis skills and word comprehension were computed over all levels, with the effects of the other five word-analysis skills statistically removed. These values are shown in Table 2.

Table 2 Partial correlation
coefficients between tests of
each of six word-analysis skills
and reading comprehension

Skill	Coefficient
1. Words in context	.5548
2. Syllabication	.4300
3. Root word	.3230
4. Word elements	.2651
5. Beginning sounds	.0975
6. Rhyming sounds	.4793

For this group of fourth grade children, the skills of words in context, rhyming sounds, and syllabication attained the higher partial correlation coefficients with reading comprehension. The coefficient for the skill of beginning sounds appears much lower than the coefficients for the other five skills.

An equation of multiple regression (prediction) was also computed for the six analysis skills with reading comprehension as the criterion. The weights with which each skill entered into the regression equation also allowed a ranking of the skills (Ezekial, 1959). These weights appear in Table 3.

Table 3 Weights (beta)
assigned to each word-analysis
test in predicting reading
comprehension scores

Skill	Coefficient
1. Words in context	.3189
2. Syllabication	.1830
3. Root word	.1102
4. Word elements	.0673
5. Beginning sounds	.0101
6. Rhyming sounds	.2295

Again it is observed that the three skills of words in context, rhyming sounds, and syllabication have the larger values and that the other three skills (especially beginning sounds) have smaller values.

The multiple correlation coefficient (R) between the reading comprehension scores which could be predicted from this regression equation and the actual reading comprehension scores attained by the subjects provides a global picture of the importance of the selected variables as a group with respect to all the variables which might have been considered. This view is attained by squaring the multiple correlation coefficient (R^2), which indicates the proportion of fluctuation in reading comprehension scores which may be accounted for by fluctuation in the six word-analysis skill scores. For the six word-analysis skills, the multiple correlation coefficient was .734, indicating that approximately 54 per cent of the variation in reading comprehension could be accounted for by these variables.

By employing an extension of a formula by Tate (1955) this percentage can be subdivided into the component parts from the unique contributions of each of the six skills and from the joint effects of the skills. These percentages are shown in Table 4.

Table 4 Per cent of variation in reading comprehension contributed by the word-analysis skills

Skill	1	2	3	4	5	6
1. Words in context	10.2	6.4	3.5	2.2	*	8.3
2. Syllabication		3.4	1.9	1.3	*	4.5
3. Root word			1.2	*	*	2.1
4. Word elements				*	*	1.8
5. Beginning sounds					*	*
6. Rhyming sounds						5.3

Note: 1) diagonal values represent unique contributions, off-diagonal represent joint effects
Note: 2) *these variables contributed less than 1 per cent

Approximately 20 per cent of the variation in reading comprehension at this grade level (for this sample) can be accounted for by the unique contributions of the skills of words in context, syllabication, root word and rhyming sounds, while 33 per cent can be accounted for by joint contributions of the six skills. It is probably this joint influence that caused the skill of beginning sounds to be adequately discriminated by comprehension levels (analysis 1), while allowing it to appear virtually unimportant in explaining variation in reading comprehension (analysis 2).

Further investigations of the relative influence of these skills on reading comprehension should be conducted at other grade levels. These studies along with experimental verification, may suggest that some skills could be more fruitfully taught at certain grade levels than at others.

Of incidental interest, the preceding analyses were also conducted by statistically removing the effects of intelligence. Since intelligence scores were available for only 94 per cent of the subjects on a variety of intelligence tests, the results from this portion would, at best, be only grossly indicative of the effects of this variable. When intelligence was considered in the analysis, none of the six original determinations varied by more than .02. The variation in reading comprehension attributable to the seven variables was raised only to 57 per cent. Although the improvement resulting from the addition of the variable of intelligence was slight, this variable became the third highest in accounting for variation in reading comprehension.

Implications

Because both phonic and visual skills were among those relating most closely to reading comprehension, these results would further support the need for employing both kinds of skill instruction in primary grade reading. Since all word-analysis skills (except for, perhaps, beginning sounds) seemed important at this grade level (i.e. contributed to differential comprehension scores), it is recommended that each teacher make every attempt to identify the status of skill attainment among children in his classroom and make individual efforts to improve these skills, possibly by changing the order in which these skills are typically taught or the relative emphasis they receive. In general, it would seem that certain skills can be identified as "most influential" in affecting reading comprehension at this grade level and that good proficiency in these skills is highly desirable. Further research would seem vital in identifying causes why certain skills pose difficulty for certain children. Of particular challenge would be the derivation of an answer to the question of whether or not curricular or instructional practices could be altered to improve the word skill performances of "low" and "middle" level readers, thus significantly improving their reading comprehension performance.

References

Bond, G. L., Clymer, T., and Hoyt, C. *Silent reading diagnostic tests,* form D-A. Chicago: Lyons and Carnahan, 1955.

Dolan, Sister Mary Edward. A comparative study of reading achievement at the fourth grade level under two methods of instruction: modified linguistic and traditional basal. Unpublished doctoral dissertation, The University of Minnesota, 1963.

Ezekial, M., and Fox, K. A., *Methods of correlation and regression analysis— linear and curvilinear.* New York: John Wiley, 1959. Pp. 192-197.

Gates, A. I. *Level of comprehension test,* type LC. New York: Bureau of Publications, Teachers College, Columbia University, 1958.

Strand, Helen A. The differential contribution of specific word recognition techniques to reading ability at various levels of educational advancement. Unpublished doctoral dissertation, The University of Minnesota, 1956.

Tate, Merle W. *Statistics in Education,* New York: The Macmillan Company, 1955. Pp. 316-318.

Linguistics and the Teaching of Reading

DOLORES DURKIN*

THEMES and titles of recent articles (6, 8, 10), and even of some not so recent ones (1, 11), continue to call attention to a linguistic approach to the teaching of reading. Now, too, a few reading texts "based on a linguistics approach" are beginning to trickle from the presses. Before the reading field gets swamped by still another panacea, it is imperative that ample time and careful thought be given to the very basic question, "What, in fact, *is* a linguistic approach?"

Any effort to deal with such a question immediately suggests a still prior one; namely, "What is linquistics itself?" The quickest and the most general answer is to say that the field of linguistics is concerned with a scientific study of language. One major focus of this study is the structural features of the sound systems of language. Here, there is interest in the physical features of speech (phonetics). There would also be concern for the identification and study of the sounds of language (phonemics).

The second major focus of linguistics is the structure of language on a grammatical level. Here, attention is given to word order patterns, intonation, and inflection.

At times, both of these major foci also include a study of the evolution of particular languages (historical linguistics), and of comparisons among them (comparative linguistics).

The Linguist and Reading

Early concern shown by a linguist for the teaching of reading can be found in two articles by Professor Leonard Bloomfield, both published in 1942 in *Elementary English* (1). Subsequently, but especially throughout the fifties and into the sixties, the number of similar kinds of articles, each generally offering a proposal for teaching reading, has grown steadily. At the same time the interest of professional educators in these proposals has also grown. Now, in fact, the interest can be characterized as being wide and enthusiastic—but, generally speaking, not as probing and constructively critical as it might be.

What factors have encouraged this kind of reaction to the pedagogical proposals of linguists? Many factors, of course, but two seem particularly influential.

The first factor is the ever present one of too easy acceptance of cure-alls when the thing to be "cured" or improved is as basically important as reading ability. The second factor is more modern for it is rooted in the temper of the times in which we now live. This is a temper that continues to beget not only great respect for specialists but, sometimes, even a naive kind of homage toward them.

*The Reading Teacher, 16 (March 1963), 342-346.

And, when homage rather than critical respect predominates, two tendencies result. One is the tendency for pseudospecialists to talk and to write as if they were specialists. To a small extent this has happened in current attempts to bring together linguistics and the teaching of reading.

A second and equally undesirable tendency fostered in this climate of unquestioning adulation is for specialists to speak "authoritatively" about a field that is actually outside their own area of competence. And it is toward this tendency that many linguists have drifted as they now make proposals for school programs in reading. Such a tendency in any area of study is unfortunate, mostly because it is unfruitful. It too often leads to responses of rejection in which the authoritative as well as the nonauthoritative proposals are lost.

To avoid, therefore, the loss of help for reading that might come from the field of linguistics, it is essential to distinguish between valid proposals that are the direct outgrowth of this specialization, and those which are only the conjectures of individual linguists. Once the distinction is made, the first set of proposals will merit serious attention from reading specialists. The second set might serve to suggest new directions for research —or, perhaps, old paths that must be trudged again, this time more carefully.

Linguistic Publications

With the question "What help for reading?" as the focus, a careful survey of linguistic publications suggests there are (1) technical findings that

might be incorporated into the teaching of reading, and (2) pedagogical proposals that might be investigated. A third category suggested can be labeled as "hoped-for contributions that are yet to come."

Technical Findings

The technical findings having special relevance for reading are primarily concerned with the language of teaching reading, in particular, of teaching phonics. Here, the possible contribution of the linguists lies in correcting misconceptions.

For example, it is routine to hear in a classroom such pedagogical talk as "The letter b has this sound," or "The letters sh have that sound." In response to this, linguists correctly point out that letters do not have sounds; they are not "pronounced." Rather, they suggest, it is oral speech that is comprised of sounds, and these sounds are then represented or recorded by various letters of the alphabet.

Another illustration. References to the long sound of o or, for example, to the short sound of e are common occurrences in phonics instruction. In this instruction the terms are used to refer to a particular sound represented by o, and to another particular sound represented by e.

Not so, say the linguists. Instead, they explain, the terms "long vowel" and "short vowel" actually refer to the duration of a vowel sound as it is heard within a particular word. According to this linguistic classification, therefore, the letter e represents a long vowel sound in a word such as *be*, but a short sound in a word like *beet*. Or, to cite another example, the letter *o* would record a long sound in *road* but a shorter sound in *rote*.

With the help of linguistic publications other examples could be given of misconceptions about language, especially prevalent in the teaching of phonics. But, essentially, the question raised by all of the examples is whether it makes good pedagogical sense. to shift, at this point in time, from traditional but technically incorrect usage to more precisely accurate language. Regardless of the decision, of course, the linguist certainly has the right to suggest corrections that are directly concerned with the conceptions and the language of his specialization.

But, it might be asked at this point, does the linguist also have the right, *qua* linguist, to issue proclamations about how reading ought to be taught? For instance, is this particular linguist "out of his field" when he suggests that "The entire structure of English graphemics can easily be presented in ten elementary readers, which can be covered in not over two years. . . , after which a pupil of ordinary intelligence can start reading in the third grade what is normally read in the fifth" (5).

Is this next linguist also going beyond his specialization when he claims that "The ability to relate the melody of speech to the written page is the key to good reading" (9).

What about the following proposal from still another linguist: "I believe we should pay much greater attention to the larger structures of our language . . . and much less to 'phonics' and word methods. . . . Children who are taught reading with the main emphasis on larger patterns would be expected to develop their own generalizations of spelling-sound relationships. . . ."(8).

Role of the Linguist

The position taken by this writer assumes that the gap between linguistics and instructional methods for reading is wide, and that the gap will be bridged most effectively and securely not by proclamations like those cited above, but only by the findings of careful research. The position also assumes, and even includes, the hope that some of the foci of this research will come from pedagogical proposals now being made by linguists—many of which, it must be added, have been made over the years by reading specialists.

Pedagogical Proposals

What are some of these proposals? In addition to those already cited, the most frequent proposals of linguists are noted below, each followed by a listing of some of the questions that need to be asked about them.

1. *The vocabulary of beginning texts in reading ought to include only words that show a regular correspondence between their spelling and their sound.* (What, in fact, *is* a "regularly spelled" word? Are linguists ready to provide us with groupings of words that show gradual change from the most regular to the most highly irregular? Does the proposal amount to an over-

simplification of our spelling system? Will this kind of introduction to reading make children less flexible and, therefore, less ready to cope with the many words in our language that show an almost capricious kind of spelling?)

2. *In initial reading instruction, concentration should be on single, regularly spelled words, and even on nonsense syllables.* (Does not the calling off of lists of individual words, and even of lists of syllables, inevitably become monotonous and also meaningless? Does the proposal encourage a return to the rote drill that prevailed in the earlier years of this century? Will it lead to over-concentration on individual words and insufficient attention to meanings of groups of words, sentences, and paragraphs?)

3. *The style of textbook language ought to be like the style of children's spoken language.* (What, precisely, is meant by "style of language"? Might it not be that "style" varies greatly among children? For instance, wouldn't different family backgrounds make for major differences in speech styles? If certain styles were clearly identified and if, in turn, they became a part of reading texts, would this necessarily simplify the task of teaching reading? Would it, for example, improve reading comprehension? Would the material excite new interest in learning to read?)

4. *Pictures should be omitted from reading texts. Helpful cues for word identification should come from letter-sounds, not pictures.* (To what extent, and in what kinds of ways, do children use pictures as a source of help with word identification? Would the omission of pictures make for less interesting texts? Would the omission of pictures make a text unlike the materials children read outside the classroom? And, ideally, shouldn't the situation in which a skill is learned and practiced be typical of the one in which the skill is to function?)

The few proposals noted here, combined with a study of other proposals made by still other linguists, suggest two conclusions. First, there seems to be no such entity as "a linguistic approach to the teaching of reading" and, secondly, many of the individual proposals of linguists pose important questions which are still without an answer.

Hoped-for Contributions

Even a limited knowledge of linguistics also suggests, however, that it is still a kind of specialization which ought to hold much for the teaching of reading that has not yet been realized, but which is needed. For example, it is the linguist who can offer scholarly help with the important job of teaching reading to bilingual children—not so much by advocating particular methods as by identifying major similarities and differences in the alphabetical system, and in the grammatical structure of the child's two languages.

It is the linguist, again, who can help teachers gain competence in developing newer kinds of language study. Even in elementary school classrooms attention could be given to the history of American English, to the factors that have affected its development, to the histories of individual words, and to the ways in which pronunciation and meanings of words have changed over time. For too long, it seems, the most interesting aspects of language study have been unknown to teachers, and therefore unavailable to children. Linguists have the ability, and the opportunity, to bring this study into focus now.

In addition, the linguist can also offer much more guidance than he has thus far given in helping teachers organize and systematize, for themselves and ultimately for the children they teach, both the regularities and the irregularities found in our writing system. With this kind of systematization—and with a willingness on the part of teachers to *study* the results—phonics instruction, for example, could become much more productive because it would be so much more knowledgeable and secure.

In Summary

The hope expressed in this article is that the specialist in linguistics will be willing to share, with both preciseness and simplicity, findings that are the fruit of his special areas of study. It is also hoped that educators will study these findings, and then test those proposals that seem to have special relevance for the teaching of reading. Only with this combination of specialists, each working in his own area of competence, will the field of linguistics be given optimum opportunity to make genuinely productive contributions to the field of reading.

References

1. Bloomfield, Leonard. "Linguistics and Reading," *Elementary English Review,* 19 (Apr., May 1942), 125-130, 183-186.
2. Bloomfield, L., and Barnhart, C. L. *Let's Read: A Linguistic Approach.* Detroit: Wayne State University Press, 1961.
3. Carroll, John B. *The Study of Language.* Cambridge: Harvard University Press, 1953.
4. Dawkins, John. "Reading Theory — An Important Distinction," *Elementary English,* 38 (Oct. 1961), 389-92.
5. Hall, Robert A., Jr. *Sound and Spelling in English.* Philadelphia: Chilton Company, 1961. Page 30.
6. King, Harold V. "Linguistic Aspects of the Reading Program," *Language Learning,* 9, No. 1 (1959), 19-23.
7. Lefevre, Carl A. "Reading Instruction Related to Primary Language Learnings: A Linguistic View," *Journal of Developmental Reading* (Spring 1961), 147-158.
8. Lefevre, Carl A. "Language Patterns and Their Graphic Counterparts: A Linguistic View of Reading," *Changing Concepts of Reading Instruction,* IRA Proceedings, 1961. Pages 245-249.
9. Lloyd, Donald J. "Reading American English Sound Patterns," *A Monograph for Elementary Teachers — No. 104.* Evanston, Illinois: Row, Peterson, 1962. Page 2.
10. McDavid, R. I. "The Role of the Linguist in the Teaching of Reading," *Changing Concepts of Reading Instruction,* IRA Proceedings, 1961. Pages 253-256.
11. Soffietti, James B. "Why Children Fail to Read: A Linguistic Analysis," *Harvard Educational Review* (Spring 1955), 63-84.
12. Womack, Thurston, "Is English a Phonetic Language?" *Elementary English,* 34 (Oct. 1957), 386-88.

The Effectiveness of Code- and Meaning-Emphasis Beginning Reading Programs

Robert Dykstra*

IN her recent book, Chall (1967) concluded that code-emphasis reading programs tend to produce better overall reading achievement, at least in the initial stages of instruction, than do meaning-emphasis programs. She defined code-emphasis programs as those which aim at the beginning to teach the pupil mastery of the alphabetic code rather than expecting from him a mature reading performance. Meaning-emphasis programs, according to Chall, are those which emphasize from the very beginning the necessity of reading for meaning, undoubtedly a more mature skill than mere code-breaking. The typical basal reading series belongs to the meaning emphasis category. Many current programs, however, are characterized by an early concentrated emphasis on learning the alphabetic code which characterizes printed English. This is especially true of a number of recently-published "linguistic" programs.

The Cooperative Research Program in First-Grade Instruction provided considerable data with which to test Chall's conclusion. Many of the projects which participated in this research venture compared the relative effectiveness of basal programs and certain innovative instructional programs, a number of which belong to Chall's code-emphasis category. The Coordinating Center at the University of Minnesota reported, in two separate volumes, the results of the combined analysis of the data which compared basal and various other programs at the end of grades one and two (Bond and Dykstra, 1967; Dykstra, 1967). The present report draws together specific data from the Cooperative Research Program pertinent to the issue of the relative effectiveness of code-emphasis programs in initial reading instruction.

PROGRAMS

Information about three relevant types of reading programs evaluated in the first grade reading studies is presented in Table 1. Programs are categorized as conventional basal, linguistic, and phonics-first basal in accordance with Chall's classification scheme. The Programmed Reading Series was not labeled "linguistic" by Chall, but because of its claim to be linguistically based and its similarity in many respects to linguistic materials it has been placed in that category for purposes of this report.

*The Reading Teacher, 22 (October 1968) , 17-23.

Table 1   Classification of reading programs used in the cooperative research study according to publisher, common label, and certain instructional variables.

Variables	Conventional Basal			Linguistic Approaches				Phonics–First Basal
	1*	2	3	1**	2	3	4	1***
Goals of Beginning Instruction: Reading for *Meaning* (M) or Learning the *Code* (C)	M	M	M	C	C	C	C	C
Motiv. Appeal at Beginning: *Content* (C) or *Process* (P) of Learning to Read	C	C	C	P	P	P	P	P/C
Major Criterion For Selecting Words: *Meaning Freq.* (MF) or *Spelling Regularity* (SR)	MF	MF	MF	SR	SR	SR	SR	SR
Vocabulary Load: First Year	LOW	LOW	LOW	HIGH	HIGH	HIGH	HIGH	HIGH
Phonics Instruction: *Analytic* (A) or *Synthetic* (S)	A	A	A	A	A	S	S	S
Phonic Load: First Year	LOW	LOW	LOW	HIGH	HIGH	HIGH	HIGH	HIGH
Cues to Use: *Structural* (S) or *Meaning* (M)	M	M	M	S	S	S	S	S
"Set" For *Regularity* (R) or *Diversity* (D)	D	D	D	R	R	R	R	R
Structural Clues Employed: *Sounding* and *Blending* (SB), *Visual Analysis* and *Substitutions* (VAS), or *Spelling* (SP)	VAS	VAS	VAS	SP	SP	SB	SB	SB
Response Modes: *Whole Words* (WW) or *Letters First* (LET)	WW	WW	WW	LET	LET	LET	LET	LET

1*   Scott, Foresman—The New Basic Readers
2   Ginn—Ginn Basic Readers
3   Allyn and Bacon—Sheldon Basic Readers
1**   Barnhart—Let's Read

2   Merrill—Basic Reading Series Developed on Linguistic Principles
3   Singer—Structural Reading Series
4   McGraw-Hill—Programmed Reading
1***   J. B. Lippincott—Basic Reading

Certain of the instructional variables which differentiate the three types of programs are presented in Table 1. More complete descriptions of these variables are found in Appendix A of Chall's book. It is apparent that conventional basal, linguistic, and phonics first basal programs are differentiated by a number of instructional variables such as vocabulary load, type of vocabulary control, phonics load, and initial response modes. The first row of the table indicates that conventional basal programs are characterized by an early emphasis on meaning, while the various linguistic programs and the phonics-first basal program belong to the code-emphasis group. It was possible, therefore, to make certain comparisons of the relative effectiveness of meaning-emphasis and code-emphasis instructional materials in beginning reading.

The experimental design utilized by the Coordinating Center enabled comparisons between basal and linguistic materials and between conventional basal programs and phonics-first basal series. The rationale underlying the analysis is presented in detail in other reports of the Cooperative Research Program (Bond and Dykstra, 1967; Dykstra, 1967). The analysis conducted by the Coordinating Center utilized data collected from various projects participating in the research program, thereby giving information about the relative effectiveness of various types of materials across a number of projects.

Achievement was measured in the Cooperative Research Study by means of a number of instruments. Oral word pronunciation was measured by the word list from the *Gates-McKillop Reading Diagnostic Test* and the Fry Phonetically-Regular Word List which was developed specifically for the research program. Accuracy of connected oral reading and rate of reading were assessed by the *Gilmore Oral Reading Test*. The *Stanford Achievement Test* was used to evaluate spelling, silent reading, word recognition, and silent paragraph comprehension.

FINDINGS

The findings of the analysis comparing basal and linguistic programs are reported in Table 2. Relative performance of basal (meaning-emphasis) and linguistic (code-emphasis) pupils on the various measures is reported for both the end of grade one and the end of grade two. At the end of first grade, 1357 pupils were used to evaluate spelling and silent reading ability. This number dropped to 959 by the end of the second grade. Approximately 250 pupils were used at both testing points to analyze oral word pronunciation, accuracy of oral reading, and reading rate.

Linguistic pupils were better in oral word pronunciation and silent reading word recognition at the ends of both grades one and

Table 2   Reading and spelling achievement of pupils in code-emphasis and meaning-emphasis reading programs.

	Programs compared	
Achievement variables	*Conventional Basal (Meaning Emphasis) vs. Linguistic (Code Emphasis)*	*Conventional Basal (Meaning Emphasis) vs. Phonic/First Basal (Code Emphasis)*
Oral Word Pronunciation		
Grade 1	CODE	CODE
Grade 2	CODE	——
Accuracy of Oral Reading		
Grade 1	MEANING	CODE
Grade 2	MEANING	——
Spelling		
Grade 1	MEANING	CODE
Grade 2	CODE	CODE
Silent Reading Word Recognition		
Grade 1	CODE	CODE
Grade 2	CODE	CODE
Silent Reading Comprehension		
Grade 1	MEANING	CODE
Grade 2	MEANING	CODE
Rate of Reading		
Grade 1	MEANING	CODE
Grade 2	CODE	——

two. Pupils in the code-emphasis linguistic programs were also better spellers at the end of grade two, although the reverse was true at the end of the first grade. Therefore, it is apparant that early emphasis on learning the alphabetic code resulted in superior ability at decoding words in isolation as well as superior ability at encoding spoken words by the end of the second grade. It should be emphasized, however, that not all of the differences favoring either linguistic or basal pupils were statistically significant. The analysis was very complex because of the number of projects involved and in many cases it was impossible to come up with a simple straightforward comprehensive test of the relative effectiveness of the two treatments for this reason, the data presented in this article may best be used to illustrate trends. Details concerning the significance of observed differences are presented elsewhere (Bond and Dykstra, 1967; Dykstra, 1967).

Differences in accuracy of reading a connected passage orally and in understanding paragraphs read silently favored the basal pupils at both testing points. This finding lends some support to the view expressed by many reading authorities that concentrated early emphasis on learning the code to the virtual exclusion of reading for meaning may have a negative effect on comprehension. However, the differences favoring basal pupils on the second-grade comprehension test were negligible (Dykstra, 1967, P. 105). The evidence concerning reading rate is less clearcut. Basal pupils were faster readers at the end of grade one, but pupils whose initial instruction had been in linguistic materials were reading at a higher rate by the end of the second grade. Therefore, it does not appear that an early emphasis on learning the alphabetic code necessarily produces halting word-by-word reading at least through the second grade.

The Cooperative Research Study also evaluated the relative effectiveness of conventional basal materials and the phonics-first reading series. Chall's analysis of this series indicated that it differs from conventional basal materials primarily in its approach to teaching and practicing new words. In other aspects of the instructional program, however, Chall found that the phonics-first basal system did not differ greatly from conventional basal readers.

The comparative effectiveness of these programs in terms of first-grade and second-grade reading and spelling achievement was evaluated. All of the performance measures at either testing point favored the code-emphasis phonics-first program. Code-emphasis pupils were superior in the word recognition and comprehension skills involved in silent reading after one year and two years of instruction. They were also better spellers at both testing points. Information regarding reading rate, oral word pronounciation, and accuracy of oral reading is available only at the end of the first grade, where all differences favored the phonics-first code-emphasis group. Furthermore, practically all of the differences reported for this particular comparison of code-emphasis and meaning-emphasis programs were statistically significant (Bond and Dykstra; 1967; Dykstra, 1967). Pupils comprising the sample for the first-grade reading measures numbered 191, while the sample used for evaluating first and second grade silent reading and spelling totaled 1013 and 441 respectively.

DISCUSSION

Data from the Cooperative Research Program in First-Grade Reading Instruction tend to support Chall's conclusion that code-emphasis programs produce better over-all primary grade reading and spelling achievement than meaning-emphasis programs. This superiority is especially marked with respect to pronouncing words orally in isolation, spelling words from dictation, and identifying words in isolation on a silent reading test. It is apparent that concentrated teaching of the alphabetic code is associated with improved initial ability to encode and decode words. This evidence reinforces the view that pupils can be helped to learn sound-symbol relationships.

It is difficult to make conclusions about the relative effectiveness of analytic and synthetic phonics programs. The relatively successful code-emphasis programs utilized both types of instruction. Evidence is also inconclusive about the relative effectiveness of unlocking a new word by sounding out the word and blending it together versus spelling the word letter-by-letter as advocated by the Bloomfield-Barnhart and Fries materials. The code-emphasis programs differed on this point, yet were relatively successful as a group in producing pupils with above-average word recognition skills. For further information on this point it would be well to look at individual studies which evaluated separately each of the types of code-emphasis programs or which compared two or more code-emphasis programs (Schneyer, 1967; Sheldon, 1967; Ruddell, 1967; Tanyzer, 1966; Hayes, 1967).

The relative effectiveness of code-emphasis and meaning-emphasis programs in influencing ability in reading comprehension is still somewhat ambiguous. Taken as a group pupils who learned to read by means of conventional basal readers were slightly superior in silent reading comprehension to pupils whose initial instruction had been in linguistic materials. However, this finding was reversed in the comparison of conventional basals with phonics-first basal materials. In this latter comparison all differences favored the code-emphasis phonics-first basal program.

It should be noted that Chall in her analysis of various types of instructional programs found the phonics-first program to differ little from conventional basals in its emphasis on comprehension, follow-up activities for a lesson, teacher guidance in reading, and similar variables. Perhaps this indicates that it is essential to direct the beginners' attention to a variety of reading tasks and to stress understanding of what is read in addition to developing the ability to decode words. Evidence seems to indicate that some direct early instruction in the more mature aspects of reading behavior may be helpful.

Conclusions regarding the influence of code-emphasis and meaning-emphasis programs on rate of reading are likewise ambiguous. At the end of the first grade pupils in linguistic programs were slower oral readers than pupils in basal programs. By the end of grade two, however, this finding was reversed. Pupils in the phonics-first code-emphasis program read at a higher rate than conventional pupils at the end of grade one, but no evaluation of rate of pupils in these programs was reported at the end of grade two. On the basis of the limited information available, there appears to be little reason for concern that first-grade and second-grade pupils in code-emphasis programs become slow, halting readers. Longitudinal data are necessary to test the long-range consequences of the two types of programs.

Similar problems exist in drawing conclusions from the data on accuracy of connected oral reading. Basal pupils read more accurately than linguistic pupils at both testing points. However, phonics-first basal pupils read more accurately than conventional basal pupils at the end of grade one. Here again the evidence can best be termed conflicting. It is likely that other variables peculiar to certain code-emphasis programs account for the lack of unanimity in the findings.

NEEDED CLARIFICATION

Although this study supports, in general, Chall's conclusions concerning the superiority of code-emphasis programs in beginning reading, a note of caution is in order. There is no clear evidence that the early emphasis on code per se is the *only* or even the *primary* reason for the relative effectiveness of the code-emphasis programs. The major types of programs which were compared differed in a number of respects in addition to the varying emphases on code and meaning. The possibility exists that some other characteristic of these programs (higher expectations of pupil achievement, for example) may be a more crucial element in determining pupil achievement than the emphasis on code-breaking. It is also possible that some particular combination of factors within the code-emphasis programs accounted for their effectiveness. There is some evidence for this conjecture in that the various code-emphasis programs did not appear to be equally effective. Unfortunately, studies of the nature discussed in this report compare *one complex* of instructional factors with *another complex* of instructional factors, thereby making it impossible to isolate the single characteristic (if indeed there is one) which makes one program more effective than another. Researchers interested in this question will likely have to turn to laboratory investigations.

REFERENCES

Bond, G. L., and Dykstra, R. *Final report of the coordinating center for first-grade reading instruction.* (USOE Project X-001) Minneapolis: University of Minnesota, 1967.

Bond, G. L., and Dykstra, R. The cooperative research study in first-grade reading instruction. *Reading Research Quarterly,* 1967, 2 (4), 9-142.

Chall, Jeanne. *Learning to read.* New York: McGraw-Hill, 1967. P. 137.

Dykstra, R. *Final report of the continuation of the coordinating center for first-grade reading instruction programs.* (USOE Project 6-1651) Minneapolis: University of Minnesota, 1967.

Hayes, R. B., and Wuest, R. C. I.t.a. and three other approaches to reading in the first grade—extended into second grade. *The Reading Teacher,* 1967, *20,* (8), 694-697; 703.

Ruddell, R. Reading instruction in first grade with varying emphasis on the regularity of grapheme-phoneme correspondences and the relation of language structure to meaning—extended into second grade. *The Reading Teacher,* 1967, *20,* (8), 730-736.

Sheldon, W. D., Nichols, Nancy, and Lashinger, D. R. Effect of first grade instruction using basal readers, modified linguistic materials, and linguistic readers —extended into second grade. *The Reading Teacher,* 1967, *20,* (8), 720-725.

Schneyer, J. W. Reading achievement of first grade children taught by a linguistic approach and a basal readers approach—extended into second grade. *The Reading Teacher,* 1967, *20,* (8), 704-710.

Tanyzer, H. J., and Alpert, H. Three different basal reading systems and first grade reading achievement. *The Reading Teacher,* 1966, *19,* (8), 636-642.

Linguistics and Reading Problems at the Junior High School Level

CHARLES C. FRIES*

ABOUT THREE years ago the following headline appeared in *The New York Times,* attached to an article concerning the New York City School System.

10,000 in 7th Grade Found
4 Years Behind in Reading

In other words, a tremendous number of boys and girls of twelve years of age cannot read well enough to do the studying required beyond the third grade.

Two years later a new superintendent of that same school system insisted, "There is just no sense at all in pretending to teach world history and biology to a tenth grade student who reads at the fourth grade level." And he proposed, for "the child who slips behind in learning to read," to "put him in a class half as big, and double the time spent on reading . . . because *he has to learn to read.*"

These quotations seem to indicate first, a school situation that may be a more general and continuing problem, and, second, the belief that *more* teachers and *more* time to do *more* of what is *now* being done constitutes the only remedy.

It is true, I believe, that the child who has been in school for six years, enters, at the junior high school level, academically, as well as physically and emotionally, an especially critical period. Here, often for the first time, he is faced with the necessity of serious study-reading of a considerable range of subject-matter content. For this subject-matter content he must produce results of knowledge and understanding derived solely from his reading.

Inadequacies in his reading competence will inevitably show themselves at this time and make it impossible for him to meet the reading demands of this school level. One can, of course, blame the textbooks and demand that the books be brought to the level of the pupil's reading competence. If, however, such a realistic reading testing does not occur at the junior high school level it is simply postponed to a later time and a more difficult body of material—to the senior high school, to the college, or to the reading level required for a job other than that of unskilled labor. Potential "dropouts" often can be identified by such reading difficulties at the beginning of the junior high school level.

The remedy proposed in the quotations seems limited to setting up smaller classes for reading instruction and to doubling the time given to these classes. There seems to have been no questioning of the *materials* used as the content of the teaching for these smaller classes and doubled time.

It is of these two matters—the realistic testing situation at the junior high school level and the practical preparation of the pupils to meet it successfully that I would bring a consideration of the knowledge and understanding achieved in the field of linguistics.

The real test of whether the elementary school pupil has actually learned to read during grades 1 to 6 must ultimately be the efficiency with which he meets the challenge of the serious study-reading of the junior high school subject-matter content. His "readiness" for the kind of reading required at this level is the function of the reading teaching that precedes. In other words, the beginning steps of elementary reading and the whole of the reading activities of the "transfer" stage must be analyzed, planned, programed, and measured in terms of the competencies essential for the kind of reading required for full success at the junior high school level.

Some specific examples from our actual classroom materials "developed upon linguistic principles" for the teaching of beginning reading through the transfer stage may help to put more precise meaning content into these general statements. These examples should also show that the goals set and the series of small steps toward their attainment as set forth in these materials do not require any "forced feeding." The materials have been used with hundreds of "slow learners." These examples should also serve to contradict the many assertions that our "linguistic approach" is a "segmental method" with the "same basic aim as the phonic method of teaching reading;" the assertion that it is a "phonemic approach to reading" with "word lists as the basic learning material;" the assertion that it applies the "principle of matching letters with sounds;" and the assertion that it "ignores meaning" and centers the attention of the pupil on formal and mechanical features."

As a matter of fact the *primary objective* of our materials built upon linguistic understanding *is the ability to read for meanings.* Reading for meanings requires not only that the pupil must grasp the meanings of the words he reads and the meanings attached to the grammatical structures in which these words are placed, but also and especially that he must build up as he proceeds all the situational meanings that come from the succession of sentences in each story unit. Even from the very beginning of the first reading lesson with only three content words, *cat, fat, Nat,* (and the two structures words *is* and unstressed *a* as in *a cat*) there is some meaning added to the whole with each sentence. The pupil must grasp this cumulative meaning.

The very first reading unit is the following.

> Nat is a cat.
> Nat is fat.
> Nat is a fat cat.

The first sentence specifies the meaning of the word *Nat* by identifying it with the well-known animal, *cat.* For us this identification is that *Nat* is the cat's name.

> Nat is a cat.

The second sentence adds to the meaning by asserting that this particular cat, *Nat,* has a special physical feature to be described as *fat.*

> Nat is fat.

The third sentence adds more to the meaning by bringing the description and the identification together in one summary sentence.

> Nat is a fat cat.

The three sentences are tied together into a sequence by the repetition of the word *Nat.*

To be a "sequence" of sentences in our use of the term there must always be in the sentences some type of "sequence signals." Here the repetition of the name *Nat* serves the purpose. A discourse is a sequence of sentences tied together linguistically by "sequence signals."

Each of the two sentences after the first adds something to the "growing" meaning. The last sentence brings together what we have called the "cumulative" meaning of this unit. All sequences of sentences that belong to a unit as shown by sequence signals have not only individual sentence meaning but also this "growing accumulation of meanings."

Only through continued and consistant practice in the reading of "sequences of sentences" in units of growing size and complexity does the pupil build up responses to these cumulative meanings as they develop, and make maximum progress toward what we have called "productive" reading. Real reading is never a passive receptive process of recognizing written words and the grammatical structures in which these words occur. It is not even an active responding to all the signals of meaning actually represented in the writing. Real reading demands that the reader build up and carry along such a complete understanding of the cumulative meaning of the sequences of sentences that he habitually supplies, fills in, the patterns of tone (intonation), the special stresses, and the pauses of grouping that the live language of speech uses but which are either not indicated at all by our writing system or only crudely hinted at by our present system of punctuation. Real reading is thus "productive" reading.

Oral reading with "expression" is not only the avoiding of a monotone; nor are the variations of pitch in their sequences haphazard and lawless. They fit into certain major patterns characteristic of the English language. These patterns of intonation are not solely related to the separate sentences, but also and especially to the relations between sentences as they follow one another in a discourse.

Children do not need to be taught to use the intonation patterns of English. As a matter of fact, fitting into the tone patterns of the intonation sequences of English is perhaps the very first thing the child learns of the language. Most normal children of five speak their language using all the intonation patterns of their linguistic community. Usually, however, neither the pupils nor the teachers (if they have not had contact with the formal study of linguistics or of speech) are aware of what the major English intonation patterns are. Problems arise with pupils because, at the beginning of learning to read, in their struggle to recognize the written representations of the words, they often develop habits of pronouncing the words as separate items rather than as words in the sequences of utterances in real "talk."

Children will use the patterns of intonation naturally whenever they realize the meaning of what they are saying. Oral reading must become the telling of the meanings which they have received from the written sequences of sentences. To put it another way, their intonation will demonstrate whether they have really realized vividly the meanings or are simply pronouncing words which, as a succession of

groups, do not stimulate for them any recognition responses. The case for a considerable amount of properly directed and properly used oral reading from the very beginning rests primarily on the need to develop the habits of "productive" reading.

One other matter deserves attention in respect to developing in the pupils the ability to *read* for meanings. The most commonly used Pre-primers, Primers, and First Readers for teaching the first stages of learning to read have large pictures* on practically every page—pictures that show the situations of each "story." These pictures give meaning to the words and sentences in the reading text. In fact on many pages of the pre-primers the words and sentences have no real meaning without the pictures. From all the reading books of our linquistic series pictures have been excluded as a matter of principle in order to compel the pupils to build the habit of seeking the meaning, even the situational meaning, in the words and sentences of the written text alone. The usual use of pictures in the teaching of beginning reading builds the habit of looking first at the pictures and then guessing at the identification of the words used. We would emphasize the necessity of completely reversing the process—having the pupils *read* for the meanings, and then, as a means of strengthening their vivid imaginative realization of the situation, having them draw their own pictures to depict parts of the situation or some of the persons involved as they individually imagine them to be. Many of the very slow learners do very well with such exercises and certainly do not need to have ready made pictures as crutches.

At this point an objection will probably arise. With some justice one may insist that the immediate problem for the junior high school is the great number of seventh graders who can read at the

---

*The Scott, Foresman Series—The three Pre-primers, and the Primer—have a total of 351 pages with a picture on every page. The First Reader, out of a total of 187 pages, has 171 pages with pictures and 16 without pictures.

fourth, or fifth, or even sixth grade level but who cannot read well enough to meet the realistic test of the serious study-reading that the various subject-matter texts require. He will then point out that I have been concerned with the child at the beginning stage of reading and the materials and teaching practice that, for beginning readers has served to lead up to the mature reading habits and competancies required, and that normal "beginning readers" require at least five years of reading practice to reach this level.

I offer two comments and suggestions, based on a limited experience with small groups of these twelve and thirteen year olds.

First, these pupils cannot profitably break into this series of readers in the middle or near the end. The sequence of the significant contrasts embedded in the materials has been "programed" in small steps so that the responses at each level depend on the habits established earlier. To be effective the pupil must start at the beginning and proceed through the materials as organized. For seventh graders the amount of time necessary for each step will be greatly reduced and should progressively decrease as pupils realize more clearly the steps of their own growing skill. This realization must come from the *doing* itself, *not* from attempts of the teacher to *tell him* about what he is doing.

Second, as I have insisted elsewhere, a person can read insofar as he can "respond" to the language signals of his native language code when these signals are represented by patterns of graphic shapes *as fully* as he can to these same language signals represented by patterns of vocal sounds. Stress the words "respond as fully," for the most significant base from which to measure reading ability must be the receptive language control of the person being measured. Reading ability must be evaluated against a particular language ability. Any junior high school pupil's reading competence must be evaluated in terms of that pupil's receptive ability in the English language—his ability to respond to the "talk" addressed to him.

All reading at any level in the schools should be evaluated in terms of progress toward active "productive" reading and some type of vivid imaginative realization.

Vowel Sounds in VCC Words

PAULA FULD*

IN *The Reading Teacher* FOR APRIL 1966, David R. Stone states that "the function of double letters [consonants] is to guide the reader to a preceding vowel sound (the short *e* in *letter,* for example)." He says that "this function has been obscured, however, and is rather unreliable . . . particularly . . . when all short vowels are considered. The word 'defective . . . would under the above rule be spelled 'defecctive' " (pp. 503-504).

The present author has had considerable success teaching remedial reading pupils in junior high school to decipher long words by using a similar, but more general rule. The pupils were taught to attack words like "defective" in the following manner: 1] Look for any common word parts you can recognize (de . . . tive). 2] Look at the rest of the word. The chief question is how the vowel sound should be pronounced. 3] *The vowel is a single vowel. Since it is followed by two consonants, it is probably short.* Say the short sound of *e.* Try it in the word: de-fec-tive, defective.

This method by-passes the complicated rules of syllabication and makes use of whatever scattered information the remedial pupils have. Upon reading Dr. Stone's remarks, however, it occurred to this investigator that success with the vcc rule might have been a result of the fact that the procedure directed pupils' attention to the middles of words, the part that remedial pupils tend most to neglect in deciphering long words. The present study was therefore done to investigate the frequency with which single vowels that immediately precede pairs of consonants actually have short sounds. By "pairs of consonants" is meant either double consonants (-tt-) or dissimilar consonants (-st-).

The words selected for analysis are those "introduced in five of the most widely used basal reading series, together with the Dolch (1942) and Fry (1960) lists" (Stone and Tracy, 1963). There are 1450 words on this list, which extends from pre-primer to high third reader. The average number of words introduced in each series by the end of third grade is 1628. This leaves an average of only 178 words in each series unaccounted for, since according to Stone, all of the words in the list appear in every one of the series. The "Basic Word List from Basal Readers" may therefore be considered a reasonable sample of all the words a child is

The Reading Teacher, 21 (February 1968) , 442-444.

expected to be able to read by the end of third grade.

For this study, all the words that contain a single vowel followed by two consonants (vcc words) were checked off. This combination was found in 613 words (42 per cent of the words on the list). After the vcc words were identified, the investigator identified those which had a short vowel immediately preceding the two consonants and those which did not. Two criteria were used: 1] The sound was unquestionably short in the author's dialect; and   2] For a pupil to identify it as short before he knew the word would not, in the author's opinion, tend to prevent recognition of the word by distorting it excessively.

If a word had a short vowel before the two consonants, it was considered to be evidence in favor of the rule. If it had any other vowel sound, it was considered to be evidence against the rule. The rule would be considered useful if it held in a proportion of cases substantially exceeding the likelihood of a single vowel being short in any position at all. An estimate of the likelihood of a single vowel being short was obtained by counting the number of short vowel sounds in all the words on the list from pre-primer through the first half of second. There were 203 short vowel sounds in 531 syllables. The likelihood of getting a short vowel sound in any position is .38.

Results

Of the 613 vcc words, 431 contained a short vowel before two consonants. Thus, 70 per cent of the vcc words tended to favor the usefulness of the rule. When words of five or more letters were considered separately (in general, words of more than one syllable plus short words ending in -dge), the percentage of conformity was 75. For the rest of the words (three or four letters) the percentage was 67. Statistical tests showed that   1] the proportion of words that have a short vowel before two consonants is significantly greater than is expected by chance, and   2] that longer words are likely to be more consistent than shorter words in this respect. (Both findings were significant at the 1 per cent level.) These results seem generally consistent by grade level, particularly for the longer words. There appear to be more irregular short vcc words in readers at the primer level than regular words, but the proportion of regular vcc words approaches the proportion for the entire sample by first reader.

Of the long vcc words that did not have short vowel sounds where expected, 17 per cent contained -ar and 10 per cent contained -or. About 9 per cent contained -on, sounding like -un (wonderful). The only other exceptions to the rule that occurred more than twice involved -other (mother), -al (almost), and -u (bullet). The shorter words appeared to involve similar exceptions.

Table 1   Number of regular and irregular vcc words by grade levels

Reader Level	Regular vcc words	Irregular vcc words	Total number of words on list at each level	Total number of syllables
Preprimer	2*	1*	58	59
	2**	1**		
Primer	5	9	78	90
	4	0		
First	18	12	115	139
	12	3		
2¹	36	22	188	243
	19	7		
2²	45	21	206	256
	17	2		
3¹	58	23		
	42	13		
3²	87	35		
	84	33	801	1,076
TOTALS:	431	182	1,450	

*Top figure for each level is for words of four or fewer letters.
**Bottom figure for each level is for words of five or more letters.

Per cent of conformity to vcc rule

Long words: 75 per cent   Short words: 67 per cent   Composite: 70 per cent
Long words are significantly different from short words at the 1 per cent level, and all of the observed percentages are significantly different from the chance expectation of 38 per cent at the 1 per cent level.

Implications for teaching

It is interesting to note that the first words children are expected to learn do not seem to conform to the general pattern. This means that the vcc rule would not be useful at the very beginning of reading instruction. By the second half of first grade, however, 60 per cent of the short vcc words and 80 per cent of the long vcc words fit the rule. Therefore, it would probably prove helpful in deciphering about 30 per cent of all words. By the third grade, the vcc rule would be confirmed 73 per cent by long vcc words and 71 per cent by short vcc words.

Spelling rules and syllabication rules could be taught as special cases of the vcc rule; they conform to it, but they are more restricted.

Since the rule seems more consistent for long words than for short, it should be particularly helpful for remedial cases. Older pupils do not like to be confined to "baby" words. If they are encouraged to tackle long words with the help of this rule, they have a chance to make use of what "advanced" knowledge of common word parts they may have.

Reference

Stone, D. R., and Tracy, Vilda B. A basic word list from basal readers. *Elementary English*, 1963, 420-427.

Reading Achievement and Word Recognition Skills

BEN H. HACKNEY, JR.*

DESPITE CONSIDERABLE RESEARCH, one still knows relatively little about how individual children learn to read. The current literature is in agreement that reading is not composed of one skill, but a large number of interrelated skills which are developed over a period of years. Research indicates that children learn to recognize words by different methods and that no one method is best for all children. It cannot be assumed that all children develop equal facility with each skill. Individuals may be good readers and still be deficient in one or more of the basic word recognition skills. The purpose of this study was to determine which of the word recognition skills normally taught in a basal reading series program has been acquired by a random sample of fourth grade students in the public schools of North Carolina. The skills analyzed were the basic word recognition techniques taught in the basal reading series program in the primary grades of the public schools in North Carolina. The fourth grade level of students was chosen for study because all of the word recognition skills have been introduced in the primary reading program. The study identified the word recognition skills possessed by a random sample of fourth grade students and attempted to answer the following questions:

1. Is there a basic pattern of word recognition skills acquired by students in designated reading achievement levels?

2. Are there word recognition skills which are commonly taught in a basal reading series program that do not contribute to reading achievement?

In completing this study, the primary null-hypothesis was the following: A random sample of fourth grade students in the public schools of North Carolina who score differentially in achievement on the *California Reading Test* (Tiegs and Willis, 1957) do not differ significantly in their word recognition skills as determined by the *Doren Diagnostic Reading Test of Word Recognition Skills* (1956). The Doren Test which is a test designed specifically to measure, in a group situation, the word recognition skills presented in the basal reading series was used to measure the word recognition skills of the sample. The *California Reading Test* was used to determine the reading achievement level. Patterns of skills in relationship to achievement may indicate the need for adjusting priority in the instructional emphasis on certain word recognition skills.

The Reading Teacher, 21 (March 1968), 515-518.

Design

The study involved the selection of a random sample of 1,711 fourth grade students by utilizing a probability sampling technique developed by the NEA Research Division Staff (1960). The random sample was of sufficient size to give an accuracy of plus or minus five percentage points with a level of confidence of 98 per cent. This means the chances should be at least ninety-eight in 100 that the scores obtained on the standardized tests from the random sample of fourth grade students in the public schools of North Carolina do not vary more than five percentage points from the true test scores of all the fourth grade students in the public schools of North Carolina. The random sample of students was selected from a total population of 106,617 fourth grade students during the school year of 1963-1964.

The sample was divided into three differential reading achievement level groups. Percentile norms for the total reading score of the *California Reading Test* were used as reference points in defining the limitation of each. A student was assigned to a group on the basis of his total percentile score obtained from the *California Reading Test*. Percentile scores included in each group were the following:

Group One .... 99, 98, 95, 90, and 80
Group Two .... 70, 60, 50, 40, and 30
Group Three .... 20, 10, 5, 2, and 1

California Reading Test percentile norms are not inclusive of all possible percentile scores, but are limited to the major percentiles used in dividing the sample. For general interpretation, group one, consisting of 676 students was above average in reading achievement; group two, consisting of 809 students was average in reading achievement; and group three, consisting of 226 students was below average in reading achievement. A *t* test of difference between means verified the significant differences among the three groups on the total percentile scores of the *California Reading Test*. The level of significance was .01. Total reading percentile scores of the *California Reading Test* for group one had a mean of 89.142 with a standard deviation of 6.935; group two had a mean of 53.449 with a standard deviation of 13.670; and group three had a mean of 12.185 with a standard deviation of 7.123.

The Doren Diagnostic Reading Test of Word Recognition Skill was administered to all students. By utilizing scores obtained from this test, the three groups were compared. Eleven specific null-hypotheses were stated concerning each of the eleven measured word recognition skills: letter recognition, beginning sounds, whole words, words within words, speech consonants, ending sounds, blending, rhyming, vowels, sight words, and discriminate guessing.

Treatment of data

The primary null-hypotheses and each of the eleven specific null-hypotheses were accepted or rejected on the basis of the determination of the existence of significant differences between the means of the respective Doren Test scores of the groups when compared one group with another. The three possible group comparisons were: group one with group two; group one with group three; and group two with group three. The t test of difference between means was utilized to determine if there were significant differences at the .01 level of significance. Data obtained from the analysis were used to *reject* the primary and all eleven specific null-hypotheses.

Results

Groups composed of students high in reading achievement made better scores on each of the eleven word recognition skills tests than did groups composed of students who were considered average or below average in reading achievement. The average did better than the below average group. The pattern was consistent in that the lowest scores on the word recognition tests were made by the below average group in reading achievement. Good students in reading seemed to possess better word recognition skills than poor readers in each of the eleven word recognition skills measured.

Apparently, all of the eleven word recognition skills measured contributed to reading achievement. If there had been a comparison in which a low achievement group made high scores on one or more word recognition tests, or a high achievement group made low scores on one or more word recognition tests, there would have been doubt as to the contribution of this skill to reading achievement. In all group comparisons of scores obtained from the word recognition tests, the scores of the lower reading achievement level group never equaled or surpassed the word recognition scores of the group higher in reading achievement. The t tests for differences between means of the Doren Test scores for the three groups when compared one group with another revealed significant differences. The means of the test scores for each unit and total score of the Doren Test were significantly different when compared with the mean scores of the other groups. The level of confidence was .01 with 1,708 degrees of freedom.

A standard deviation was obtained for each unit score and total score of the Doren Test for each of the three groups. The standard deviations obtained from group one scores were lower than the standard deviations obtained from group two scores. With no exceptions, the standard deviations on the Doren Test scores for group two were lower than standard deviations obtained from group three scores. This meant that the lower a group was in reading achievement as measured by the *California Reading Test*, the greater was the spread of scores obtained from the Doren Test. The higher a group scored on reading achievement as measured by the *California Reading Test*, the less was the spread of scores of the Doren Test.

Conclusions

In answer to the two questions raised at the beginning, an interpretation of the data revealed a consistent pattern of word recognition skills for students in designated reading achievement level groups. The interpretation of the data collected in the study implied that each of the eleven word recognition skills measured by the Doren Test contributed to reading achievement. Because of the sampling technique, it is felt that the findings of this study would likely be found true for the total population of fourth grade students in the public schools of North Carolina. Additional research is needed for further study to determine the extent to which these eleven word recognition skills contribute to reading success.

References

Doren, Margaret. *Doren diagnostic reading test of word recognition skills.* Minneapolis, Minnesota: Educational Test Bureau, 1956.

————. Small sample techniques. *The N.E.A. Research Bulletin*, 1960, 38, 99-104.

Tiegs, E. W., and Clark, W. W. *California reading test, elementary grades 4-5-6, form x.* Del Monte, California: California Test Bureau, 1957.

Phoneme-Grapheme Correspondences in Monosyllabic Words

Richard E. Hodges*

IN THIS STUDY the spellings of all monosyllabic words in the core vocabulary of American English were analyzed in order to determine the degree to which the orthography approximates the alphabetic principle (i.e., a one-to-one correspondence between a phoneme and a single graphemic representation) in this set of words. Most beginning spelling and reading programs, for a number of reasons, typically use vocabularies comprised largely of monosyllabic words. With the proliferation of linguistically oriented spelling and reading programs in which pupils are guided toward gaining an understanding of the alphabetic structure of our writing system, it seems important to describe the orthography of those words which are the basis for the child's introduction to a structural analysis of American English orthography.

Monosyllabic words and the orthography

Monosyllabic words constitute a rich and functional part of our language. Indeed, 340 of the first five hundred most frequently used American English words have monosyllabic structures (5). Why is there a predilection to employ monosyllabic words with high frequency in our language? It seems likely that it is simply easier to remember and to pronounce monosyllabic words than other words having more complex structures. This "principle of least effort" (6), in fact, probably accounts for such highly functional monosyllabic words as *phone, zoo, ad, lab, math,* and *bus* that are clipped forms of polysyllabic words.

Monosyllabic words are therefore characterized by their *functionality* and their *structural simplicity,* and both of these characteristics cause monosyllabic words to be quite useful in beginning spelling and reading programs. Each characteristic, in fact, can be used as the most basic rationale for the selection of words for beginning spellers and readers.

In terms of functionality, it is generally assumed that the child's introduction to written language should begin with the study of words he will most likely be acquainted with and which are useful to him in verbal communication. Numerous studies, the Rinsland study for example (4), have attempted to determine children's uses of words and these studies have, in turn, been important sources for word selection. Because monosyllabic words tend to be among the most frequently used words of the American English core lexicon, it is easy to see why these types of words predominate in beginning spelling and reading programs.

Structural simplicity, on the other hand, refers to the idea that the words a child initially encounters in learning to spell and read should be controlled in terms of their structural complexities. Monosyllabic words, of course, do not necessitate that the child concern himself with such linguistic factors as syllabication and affixation. Monosyllabic words are, in short, the simplest structural forms of the lexicon and therefore are assumed to be the logical starting points for subsequent structural analysis of written language.

Structural simplicity, however, has a second important consequence, particularly in light of recent linguistic in-

*Forging Ahead in Reading, IRA Proceedings, Vol. 12, Part 1, 1968, 560-566.

sights into the nature of American English orthography. In order to understand this consequence, we should first examine briefly the notion of an *alphabetic orthography,* since this is the principle upon which American English orthography is based.

An alphabetic orthography is based upon the idea that the constituent speech sounds of oral language—the *phonemes* of a language—each have individual graphic representations in writing. The majority of the world's writing systems are of this type chiefly because alphabetic orthographies are more efficient than other types of orthographies. "Word" writing systems (technically, such systems are called *logographic* orthographies), for example, employ graphic symbols to represent the morphemes, or meaning elements, of a language. These writing systems do have the advantage of circumventing various language forces, such as sound change and dialect, that can interfere in the translation of speech into writing and vice versa. But logographic writing systems also require their users to master a prodigious number of graphic symbols if they are to use this type of writing system, for each word of oral language requires its own graphic symbol.

A second type of órthography is called a *syllabary.* In such writing systems, graphic symbols are devised to represent the syllables that, in combination, make up the words of a language. Syllabic writing is an improvement over logographic writing because there are fewer syllables than words in a language and therefore fewer graphic symbols that must be mastered in order to spell and read. Yet, syllabically-based orthographies still require substantial "memory loads."

An ideal alphabetic orthography, on the other hand, employs only as many graphic symbols as there are phonemes (speech sounds) in oral language. A thirty-phoneme language, for example, would use only thirty distinct graphic symbols to represent these phonemes in writing. Theoretically, at least, an individual should be able to spell and read correctly any written representation of a spoken word once he has mastered the ability to differentiate speech sounds and has mastered their graphic representations.

American English orthography is alphabetically *based.* It uses alphabet letters and their combinations to represent the phonemes of American English speech. We are all keenly aware, however, that our writing system does not attain the idealized state of a pure alphabetic orthography; but it is based upon this principle, and for this reason, linguists and others propose that a basic, indeed crucial, aspect of a child's understanding of written language involves his understanding the nature of the American English orthography. Most important, too, it is argued that a knowledge of the alphabetic structure of the orthography can be applied as important components of mastering written American English.

But, because American English orthography does not truly reflect the alphabetic principle, we cannot rely with complete assurance upon the knowledge that a given phoneme is spelled a certain way. In our orthography we are forced to play *odds;* we are obliged to determine which graphemic representation of a phoneme most often represents that phoneme in words, and we must also master those exceptional phoneme-grapheme correspondences which exist in the orthography. The basic reason underlying our orthograpy's disparity with the alphabetic principle lies not only in the fact that we have but twenty-six letters to represent some three dozen or so phonemes but that we use these letters in various combinations, with the consequence that we have far *more* graphic symbols than necessary.

In any case, the notion of structural simplicity, in linguistic terms, also refers to the need to *control* the selection of words for beginning spelling and reading such that the dominant sound-to-letter correspondences are mastered initially by children before they progress toward more complex and less productive orthographic characteristics. Such linguistically based reading programs at the Bloomfield-Barnhardt materials typify this condition.

Differences between spelling and reading processes

The discussion to this point has been directed toward an understanding of the nature of American English orthography. But, particularly in terms of the study reported here, it should also be noted that the processes of spelling and reading differ in an alphabetic orthography. At the risk of oversimplification, spelling is an *encoding* operation. The speller's task is to translate speech sounds into writing, a task that necessitates the development of an ability to select from a set of possible graphic representations of a phoneme that graphic symbol which correctly represents the phoneme in the word to be spelled. Reading processes, on the other hand, involve *decoding* operations. Reading an alphabetic orthography, in short, requires an individual to determine which of several possible phonemes is represented by a given graphic symbol in a word.

In sum, spelling involves sound-to-letter correspondences while reading involves letter-to-sound correspondences. In a pure alphabetic orthography these processes are reciprocal. But in an imperfect alphabetic orthography such as the American English writing system, spelling and reading have their own unique complexities.

The distinction, while useful for analytic purposes, also has important educational consequences.

Phoneme-grapheme correspondences in monosyllabic words

The study reported here involves the encoding process of *spelling*. Its purpose is not particularly to identify educational implications for beginning spelling and reading programs but to describe the orthographic structures of monosyllabic words that are or could be used in such programs and to demonstrate a technique that might be useful in examining the orthography for reading purposes.

A recently completed study of phoneme-grapheme correspondences in American English orthography (*1*) analyzed the spellings of over 17,000 different words to determine the degree to which this core vocabulary of American English approximates the alphabetic principle. The findings of this research have been reported elsewhere in the literature (*1, 2, 3*); but these findings may be summarized quickly by noting that the researchers found that most phonemes are typically represented at least 80 percent of the time by a particular graphic symbol either anywhere in a syllable or in particular positions in syllables. In other words, recalling that in our imperfect alphabetic orthography we must rely on odds that a graphic symbol will represent a phoneme, American English orthography is alphabetically based; but we must utilize cues in addition to simple sound-to-letter correspondence to spell correctly American English words, using alphabetic principles.

The Stanford Research Project did not isolate monosyllabic words for critical analysis; rather, all words in the core American English orthography were examined, each word being broken down into syllables, with the result that monosyllabic words were treated as syllables rather than as discrete words. The present study isolated the 3,428 monosyllabic words of the earlier study, and these words were subjected to an examination of their phoneme-grapheme characteristics.

A phonemic classification was devised, a system that employed forty-eight phonemes—twenty-eight consonants and twenty vowels. Conventional phonemic systems, of course, use fewer numbers of phonemes to classify American English phonology. But, it was felt appropriate *for spelling purposes* to include phonemic notations for the occurrence of vowel phonemes before /r/, as well as for the consonant clusters /kw/ and /ks/, which have unique orthographic characteristics.

The possible graphemic representations of phonemes used in American English orthography were then derived from the previous Stanford Research, with some reclassifying of those graphic symbols that include a final letter *e* as in *bake* or *spoke*.

Computer technology was then employed to analyze the phoneme-grapheme correspondences in monosyllabic words in two ways:

1. To examine them in terms of how a given phoneme is spelled *anyplace* in monosyllabic words. This examination was intended to describe the orthography of monosyllabic words as though the orthography were ideally alphabetic. No factors were considered, other than how is a sound spelled when it appears in a monosyllabic word. This classification was termed *simple phoneme-grapheme correspondence.*

2. To examine them in terms of how a given phoneme is spelled in *particular positions* in monosyllabic words; that is, initial, medial, and final position of monosyllabic words. This examination thus described the orthography of monosyllabic words using additional cues that are needed to as-

certain how some phonemes are spelled in our alphabetically *based* orthography. This classification was termed *positional constraints.*

By rank-ordering the spellings of each phoneme at each of these levels of analysis it was therefore possible to assess how nearly each phoneme in monosyllabic words *approximates* the alphabetic principle. In this way, a determination could be made of the odds that a given phoneme would be represented by a particular graphic symbol at least 80 percent of the time in monosyllabic words or in some position in them. The *80 percent criterion* is a useful measure of the degree to which the orthography approximates the alphabetic principle, since it means that any phoneme-grapheme correspondence achieving this criterion could be applied to the spelling of monosyllabic words and the resulting spelling would be correct at least four times out of five.

Findings

In terms of the phonological characteristics of monosyllabic words as compared to polysyllabic words, it was found that

1. All phonemes of the general lexicon are not present in monosyllabic words. The neutral vowel /ə/, occurring in unstressed syllables, for example, does not occur in monosyllabic words since, by definition, all monosyllabic words, when isolated from running speech, have primary stress.

2. More important for spelling purposes, however, is the apparent fact that the number of spellings of certain phonemes in the general lexicon as classified in the Stanford Research are considerably reduced in numbers when monosyllabic words are separately classified. In the general lexicon, consonant phonemes employ 141 graphic symbols, while in monosyllabic words

89 graphic symbols are employed. This is also true of vowel phonemes. In the general lexicon, 234 graphic symbols are employed to represent vowel phonemes, while in monosyllabic words 156 graphic symbols are used. In short, 130 fewer graphic symbols are used in monosyllabic words than in the general lexicon.

Such reductions in the number of graphemes used to represent phonemes in monosyllabic words as compared to the general lexicon would seem to infer that phoneme-grapheme correspondences in monosyllabic words more nearly approximate the alphabetic principle in these words than in all words of the general lexicon. But, is this the case?

3. At the level of simple phoneme-grapheme correspondence, American English phonemes in the general lexicon fail to achieve the 80 percent criterion (73.13 percent) while phonemes in monosyllabic words only exceed this criterion (81.36 percent). Mean percentage tabulations, however, obscure the important information concerning consonant and vowel phonemes, respectively, as well as individual phonemes. Consonant phonemes as a group increase in approximations to the alphabetic principle from 83.99 percent to 88.35 percent at the level of simple phoneme-grapheme correspondence. Vowel phonemes as a group also increase, but from 62.27 percent to 64 percent, well below the 80 percent criterion.

4. In terms of positional constraints, consonant phonemes further approximate the alphabetic principle in each position of monosyllabic words as compared to their occurrences in the total lexicon. Vowel phonemes, on the other hand, also approach this principle although in no position do vowel phonemes exceed the 80 percent criterion. Table I summarizes approxima-

tions to the alphabetic principle of the total phonemic system used in this study as well as the separate consonant and vowel classifications. This table also points out how position affects the numbers of phonemes that are used in respective positions in monosyllabic words.

Findings such as the foregoing provide us with general information about the orthography. But they do not help us determine the conditions that characterize American English orthography's departure from the alphabetic principle.

5. Twenty-four of the twenty-eight consonant phonemes classified in this study exceed the 80 percent criterion at the level of simple phoneme-grapheme correspondence. The four phonemes that do not are /j/, /k/, /ng/, and /z/. However, all consonant phonemes exceed this criterion when positional constraints are considered. That is, even the four errant phonemes which fail to exceed the 80 percent criterion at the level of simple correspondence do so in some position in monosyllabic words. Clearly, then, consonant phonemes as a group are not primarily responsible for American English orthography's departure from the alphabetic principle.

6. On the other hand, only seven of the twenty vowel phonemes classified in this study exceed the 80 percent criterion at the level of simple phoneme-grapheme correspondence, these phonemes being the so-called "short vowel" phonemes and two vowel phonemes occurring before /r/. Even when positional constraints are considered, vowel phonemes as a group do not appreciably increase in approximations to the alphabetic principle, although /oi/, /ou/, and /ɔh/ (the vowel sound in one pronunciation of law) exceed the 80 percent criterion in some position in monosyllabic words. In sum, this examination of the ortho-

TABLE I

SUMMARY TABLE OF PERCENTAGES OF APPROXIMATION TO ALPHABETIC
PRINCIPLE OF PHONEMES IN MONOSYLLABIC WORDS

Phonological Level:	48 Phoneme Classification		28 Consonant Classification		20 Vowel Classification	
	No. of Phonemes Used	%	No. of Phonemes Used	%	No. of Phonemes Used	%
Simple Phoneme-Grapheme Corres.	48	81.36	28	88.35	20	64.00
Position Factors						
Initial	43	95.17	24	96.00	19	73.77
Medial	39	80.37	19	98.08	20	68.48
Final	33	81.46	23	83.15	10	59.66
Mean %		84.92		91.71		68.05

graphy of monosyllabic words reveals that the phonemes largely responsible for the orthography's failure to approximate the alphabetic principle in monosyllabic words are the so-called "long vowel" phonemes and certain diphthongs.

Discussion

Such seeming disparities with the alphabetic principle should not require that we "throw the baby out with the bath water." For the fact of the matter is that American English orthography *is* alphabetically based and although *as a system* is more complicated than it might be, contains many sound-to-letter correspondences that, if learned, can ease the burden of mastering our writing system. The consonant and "short vowel" phonemes, for instance, are rich sources for helping children to understand the nature of the orthography and to apply this knowledge in correctly spelling words. In fact, it is precisely these phoneme classifications that are so heavily utilized in linguistically-based beginning spelling and reading programs and are often used to initiate traditional phonics-oriented reading programs.

American English words, however,

are obviously comprised of other phonemes having less consistent spellings. What might be done about them? One alternative is to present lists of words, selected for their functionality in writing, in which particular phoneme-grapheme correspondences, although failing to exceed the 80 percent criterion, occur in large numbers of words. This "spelling pattern" approach, for example, could be used to demonstrate one of the several spellings of the "long" vowel /ow/, the so-called "long o" sound spelled *oa*. Although this spelling of /ow/ occurs only 17 percent of the time in monosyllabic words, 45 of the 51 words in which it occurs are extremely functional words. A number of these words are *board, boat, cloak, coach, coal, coast, coat, croak, foam, goat, groan, load, loaf, loan, road, roam, roar, roast, soak, soap,* and *throat.*

In short, one possible solution is to present *individual* phoneme-grapheme correspondences in terms of the functional words in which they occur. Rare spellings of phonemes would, in this instance, be treated as exceptions and learned by whatever instructional methods appear to be appropriate.

A second alternative suggests itself, however, when we review the degree to which phonemes approximate the alphabetic principle in monosyllabic words as compared to their spellings in the general lexicon, particularly the spellings of those phonemes which depart farthest from the alphabetic principle in monosyllabic words. The vowel phoneme /ey/, for example, (the so-called "long a" sound) in monosyllabic words does not achieve the 80 percent criterion at the level of simple phoneme-grapheme correspondence nor in any position in these words. But, in the general lexicon, this phoneme is spelled *a* approximately 81 percent of the time in the final position of syllables that are not word final. Examples of this observation are *able, crater, lady, radio, acorn, flavor, major, table, baby, gravy, bacon, paper,* and *cable.*

In other words, should we wish to do so, an earlier introduction of the factor of syllabication and affixation into beginning spelling and reading programs would enable children better to understand the alphabetic principle underlying our orthography and to induce useful sound-to-letter correspondences that pertain to the total lexicon. Such an alternative, of course, necessitates that words be selected with precision and with a concern for their functionality. But, the concepts of functionality and structural simplicity which were discussed at the outset of this report are not either-or proposi-

tions. What is suggested here is that balanced spelling programs must contend with both criteria; that is, if we wish to provide pupils with spelling content that accurately describes the alphabetic structure of the orthography and has utility for them as well.

The purpose of this study, however, has not been to search for curriculum implications per se but to provide a description of the alphabetic nature of the orthography of American English words and to illustrate a research design and methodology that has potential usefulness for further studies of the orthography in terms of reading. Studies such as this, it is hoped, contribute to a better understanding of the structure of American English orthography; and with such understanding may well emerge more effective and accurate spelling and reading program.

REFERENCES

1. Hanna, Paul R., *et al. Phoneme-Grapheme Correspondences as Cues to Spelling Improvement.* Washington, D. C., U. S. Dept. of Health, Education and Welfare, Office of Education, 1966.
2. Hodges, Richard E. "The Case for Teaching Sound-to-Letter Correspondences in Spelling," *The Elementary School Journal* (Mar. 1966).
3. Hodges, Richard E., and E. Hugh Rudorf. "Searching Linguistics for Cues for the Teaching of Spelling," *Elementary English, 42* (May 1965), 527-533.
4. Rinsland, Henry D. *A Basic Vocabulary of Elementary School Children.* New York: Macmillan Co., 1945.
5. Thorndike, Edward L., and Irving Lorge. *The Teacher's Word Book of 30,000 Words.* New York: Bureau of Publications, Teachers College, Columbia University, 1944.
6. Zipf, George Kingsley. *Human Behavior and the Principle of Least Effort.* Cambridge, Mass.: Addison-Wesley Press, 1949.

Conference on Perceptual and Linguistic Aspects of Reading

Evan Keisler*

A CONFERENCE on Perceptual and Linguistic Aspects of Reading was held on October 31 and November 1-2, 1963 at the Center for Advanced Study in the Behavioral Sciences in Stanford, California, with twenty-seven participants representing specialties in linguistics, psychology, education, and sociology. The meeting was sponsored by the Committee on Learning and the Educational Process of the Social Science Research Council and was planned by Sub-Committee Chairman Eleanor J. Gibson of Cornell University. The meeting was made possible by funds granted by the Carnegie Corporation of New York. The conference focused upon the acquisition and transfer of beginning reading skills, and a central issue was the way in which the teaching of reading should be guided by the correspondences between written and spoken English. It was generally agreed that, if one considers the relation only of individual letters to their sounds in English speech, there is not one-to-one correspondence between graphemes and phonemes. Divergent views were expressed with respect to the significance of this fact for reading instruction.

Alphabet Revision Proposals and Field Studies

With an "ideal" writing system there would be a total of perhaps forty letter-to-sound relationships for the beginning reader to learn. In English, however, a single letter may represent many different sounds, and it is largely for this reason that alphabet revision is advanced as an aid in reading instruction. The proposals for alphabet revision presented at the conference were offered primarily as transitional orthography in reading; beginning readers would first encounter printed materials in the revised alphabet system, switching over to traditional orthography after some degree of reading fluency had been attained.

John Downing (2) reported on the Initial Teaching Alphabet (i.t.a., formerly the Augmented Roman Alphabet), which uses forty-three characters, of which twenty-four are traditional. The nineteen new characters have a marked resemblance to traditional forms to aid in transition.

In a study begun in 1961 in England, over 2,000 four- and five-year-old children have been learning to read from primers printed in i.t.a. Each child moves through a graded series of readers at his own pace and is transferred to books printed in traditional orthography (t.o.) whenever the teacher decides that he is ready to make the shift. A control group of children has been learning to read under similar teaching techniques

*The Reading Teacher, 18 (October 1964), 43-49.

from the same books printed in t.o. A serious but unavoidable weakness in the design of the study resulted from the fact that participation by the schools had to be entirely voluntary; the administration of each co-operating school decided whether its school would join the experimental or the control group.

Preliminary findings, covering the first eighteen months for a limited sample, show that children in the i.t.a. classes have reached much more advanced books than children in control classes. Relevant data, so far from only a few classes, show that these experimental children read t.o. with greater accuracy and comprehension than children in the control classes, in which t.o. was used exclusively.

John Malone (8) presented another proposed alphabet, UNIFON. This isomorphic spelling system, using a different letter for each phoneme, was designed as a permanent replacement of traditional orthography. UNIFON uses forty capital letters (twenty-two of them from the traditional alphabet), all of which have the same maximum height and width, but lower case letters are also available. Apart from regularizing English spelling, a number of other advantages are claimed for this system: that it is effective for electronic reading and writing devices, that it facilitates the learning of English as a second language, and that with minor additions it could be used as a phonetic alphabet for many other languages. The system has been tried informally as a transitional orthography for beginning readers who, according to Malone, shift easily to t.o.

Edward Fry (3) presented a third scheme for beginning readers that makes use of diacritical marks to indicate how each of the letters in traditional orthography is pronounced. The orthography uses only characters found on a standard typewriter and provides for an almost perfect correspondence between letters and sounds. After the young reader attains a certain proficiency, he shifts to materials in which diacritical marks appear on fewer and fewer words. No empirical evidence has yet been obtained.

Considerable surprise was apparent among the conference participants at the ease with which children reportedly moved from the transitional alphabets to t.o., and a number of questions were raised in discussion, among them the following: Does experience with a more regular alphabet lead the child to conceive of writing as a code and thus help him to attack even traditional orthography more effectively? Is an i.t.a. experience helpful simply because it allows the child to produce the sound of the word for himself without waiting for assistance? Should there not be a careful empirical study of the discriminability and utility of all letter forms proposed for a new orthography before the system is tried out? When the experimental group is called upon to engage in writing and spelling later, will interfering effects of exposure to i.t.a. be revealed? Were the reading passages in the criterion tests restricted to a narrow range of English words with regular spellings, thus failing to expose possible inadequacies of the experimental group?

How much do phonetic methods of teaching help when the written language already has the desired amount of regularity? Frederick Davis (1) reported a study conducted with Emperatriz Tensuan in Luzon in teaching beginning reading in Pilipino, a language that exhibits a high degree of one-to-one grapheme-phoneme correspondence.* The experiment compared two methods of teaching reading. One of these, the cartilla method, is essentially a phonic approach. After learning to "sound" out each letter, the child develops skill in blending the sounds, thus pronouncing unfamiliar words. The second approach, called a combination method, involves having the child associate written words or phrases with their counterparts in speech. The pupil then identifies these familiar written words in the reading material. He subsequently examines the correspondences between graphmes and phonemes in the context of visually familiar words, and then learns to pronounce unfamiliar words.

Efforts were made to equate the two groups, involving thirty-nine classes in all, with respect to school, teachers, and reading materials. The workbook exercises related to the two methods were, of course, different. After two years of instruction in grades 1 and 2, children were given

*The Pilipino study is reported in this issue of THE READING TEACHER.

the Philippine Achievement Test battery. Data were available for a thousand pupils. On no section of the test was there a significant difference between the two groups; what small differences did appear tended to favor the combination method. The results also suggested that the phonic method might be less effective for pupils of low mental ability.

A variety of questions were raised about the Davis report. Did the teachers in the two groups actually conduct their classes very differently? Is it possible that the criterion test tapped semantic and syntactic levels that had not been adequately exploited in the cartilla method?

Linguistic and Perceptual Approaches to Reading

Linguists have consistently pointed out that the correspondence between written and spoken English is weak only if one attempts to relate individual letters and sounds. If the graphemic units chosen are letter patterns, words, and word groups, a high degree of correspondence may be found. This suggested to some participants that the teaching of beginning reading is unlikely to be advanced by attempts to bring about individual letter - to - sound correspondence through modification of the alphabet system. It was argued that the beginning reader should instead be helped to use the correspondence rules already present in English.

Can children make use of such higher-order correspondence rules as they learn to read? Or are such rules merely a convenient way for adult scientists to describe structural relationships between speech and written language? What behavioral processes on the part of the child are involved as he begins to read? Useful answers to questions about the acquisition of reading skill may be found in the directions suggested by Eleanor Gibson, who summarized a series of her investigations (*4, 5, 6*). She analyzed the reading process in terms of three kinds of learning tasks to be mastered more or less in sequence: learning to differentiate graphemes, learning to decode graphemes to phonemes, and forming higher units.

Learning to discriminate one letter from another is not an automatic process. Children at the age of four begin to respond to critical dimensions of letter-like shapes; by eight they easily discriminate between unfamiliar letter forms differing on these dimensions. Part of the child's task appears to be the discovery of what the critical dimensions of difference are, such as "curve-straight" and "obliqueness."

Decoding may be studied by observing the behavior of skilled readers as they attack an unfamiliar language. In one investigation half of the subjects learned the sounds of individual Arabic letters without ever seeing them in words; the other half learned to say words composed of the same letters without being told how the individual letters sounded. When subjects were required to sound out new words constructed with the same letters, the "letter" group was on the average superior to the "word" group, but those of the "word" group

who had spontaneously learned constituent correspondences showed excellent transfer.

Do readers actually behave in accordance with grapheme-phoneme correspondences as formulated by a linguistic analysis? The prediction that readers do not proceed on a letter-by-letter basis is supported by empirical evidence on visual perception of both skilled and early readers.

The smallest unit of encoding can be termed a spelling pattern, a unit of one or more letters which is related to a specified pronunciation. For example, *ck* at the end of a word always has the sound found in *duck*. These spelling-to-sound correspondence rules have been defined for all vowel and consonant clusters up to five letters, in part as a result of recent analyses carried out by computers. In one experiment it was found that first grade children showed a significant difference in in their visual perception of pronounceable and unpronounceable three letter words but not longer ones. The evidence supports the notion that as children mature they perceive as a unit longer and more complex spelling patterns. Little is known about the formation of higher units in reading. Both syntactic and semantic structure as well as spelling patterns undoubtedly determine to some extent the nature of the larger perceptual units so important in the reading process.

Joachim Wohlwill pointed out that reading is essentially a transfer problem: the child has to learn to give to a new set of stimuli verbal responses already in his repertoire. Reviewing the literature on transfer in children, he noted that transfer processes could be conceptualized as varying along a continuum from those fairly specific in nature to altogether nonspecific ones, such as perceptual sets, concepts and rules, and learning sets.

Harry Levin (7) viewed beginning reading as a process of learning and using a code, suggesting that children be introduced to reading by first teaching them the nature of codes in writing systems; children, for example, might invent a coding system of their own before they start formal reading instruction. Since a single grapheme is often associated with more than one phoneme, should the beginning reader, as Bloomfield suggests, master one association thoroughly before coming across a conflicting one? Or is it better to have the child, early in his schooling, encounter graphemes with alternative pronunciations? According to Levin's experiments, it is more difficult to teach variable or conflicting associations in the first place, but on new tasks there is greater transfer. This suggests that the child should be exposed early to a certain amount of irregularity in the correspondences between written and spoken forms of the language, though not necessarily the total range of variation.

Leo Postman, while agreeing with the need to analyze what is learned and how the essential skills are acquired, questioned the basic assumption that success in reading depends on rules or principles more than on specific stimulus response associations. General transfer, as contrasted with specific transfer, involves a range of stimulus and response equivalence that cannot be predicted on the basis of identical elements. However, specific associative processes in the form of horizontal and vertical mediational chains may be responsible for general transfer effects.

In the discussion of these papers a difference in the definition of reading was apparent. Is it effective to regard beginning reading as a decoding process by which appropriate verbal responses are transferred to printed materials? Or is it more fruitful to view beginning reading as a process of gaining meaning from the printed page and applying it? Both definitions could be translated into operational terms which might yield quite different results when used as criterion tests. Does the first definition clarify an important intermediate objective in initial reading instruction, or is it better to focus on the long-range goals from the start?

What is the most useful way of talking about grapheme-phoneme correspondences? Should these rules be treated as a spelling-sound dictionary, or should they be viewed as information which permits the reader to generate appropriate responses in new reading contexts? More important, apparently, is the question of functional stimulus-response units in describing the code. Many considerations, including that of difference in dialect, led one participant to suggest that the most appropriate response unit may be the morpho-phoneme rather than the phoneme.

Some doubt was expressed regarding the value of spelling patterns in the teaching of reading. On the other hand, it was pointed out that there has been no empirical test of the utility of properly teaching such grapheme-phoneme correspondences in reading instruction. Field tests of linguistic approaches, as distinct from "phonic" methods, are currently being conducted in the schools of Philadelphia and Miquon in Pennsylvania. The view was expressed that even the linguistically oriented reading materials which are now becoming commercially available may not reflect the recent advances in the field of linguistics. Perhaps important variables will be found in the prompting and reinforcement conditions provided during reading instruction. It was suggested that it might be fruitful, for example, to focus attention on having the pupil produce appropriate verbal responses under effective reinforcement conditions.

Research in the Teaching of Reading

On the final day of the conference a panel, consisting of Arthur Staats, Jeanne Chall, Ruth Weir, and Lee Cronbach, considered the directions in which research in reading might profitably move. It was pointed out that studies in reading have not been closely related to form a cumulative systematic attack. In many experiments, treatments have been given labels, such as the "phonics" method, without an adequate description of what teaching procedures are in-

volved. Investigators have failed to define reading in measurable terms, and comparisons have often been made between results from studies in which the definitions of reading were quite different. Controls have often been so poor that superior teachers or more advanced books have been assigned to one teaching method. Commercial aspects frequently have overridden what is known about reading; for example, pictures frequently are included in readers not to serve an educational function but to sell the books to adults.

Many deplored the cleavage that has existed between those interested in classroom investigations of reading and those concerned with basic theory and experimentation. Since it is difficult to generalize from the usual short-range laboratory studies to classroom practices, there is a need for well-controlled intermediate-range studies of several weeks' or months' duration. Laboratory methods may be adapted to study various facets of the more complex classroom teaching conditions. The behavioral processes of children in reading need to be studied under different instructional sequences.

Every investigation of a reading system should involve an analytic description of behavior so that points of difficulty and failure can be identified. Long-term follow-up is essential not only because findings from short-range studies are frequently reversed in time, but because a new approach may require modifications in subsequent grades to capitalize on its effects.

The interaction of teaching method with individual differences deserves attention. There is no single method which is likely to work best for all children. Furthermore, different methods are likely to require quite different materials and training of teachers.

In summarizing the three-day session, John Carroll indicated wide interest in the efforts of those who are attempting to introduce transitional alphabets in spite of the fact that linguistic innovations, historically, have always met considerable resistance. The reports that children move easily from reading in the modified alphabet to traditional orthography should cause us to look at our theories of transfer more closely.

Criticism of research in the field of reading should be tempered by the fact that studies in the 1920's and 1930's were carried out with a minimum of resources. Some of the research was of excellent quality even though misquoted and misapplied in practice. Resources now available offer opportunities for far better research in reading. Among the questions which deserve far more study is the relevance of grapheme-phoneme correspondence for the teaching of reading, especially in the light of the reports that young children have been taught to read with little regard for such rules. Research must explore more fully the relative importance of the functions of synthesis and analysis in reading. Far more remains to be learned about how a beginning reader enlarges his apprehension of higher units, from spelling patterns to words to syntax.

References

1. Davis, Frederick B. "The Phonic Method vs. the Combination Method in Teaching Beginning Reading." In Ralph C. Staiger and Culbreth Y. Melton, *New Developments in Programs and Procedures for College-Adult Reading.* Twelfth Yearbook of the National Reading Conference, Milwaukee, Wisconsin: National Reading Conference, Inc., Marquette University, 1963.
2. Downing, John. "The Augmented Roman Alphabet for Learning to Read," *Reading Teacher,* 16 (March 1963), 325-336.
3. Fry, Edward. "A Diacritical Marking System for Beginning Reading Instruction," *Elementary English,* 41 (May 1964), 526-529.
4. Gibson, Eleanor J., Gibson, J. J., Pick, A. D., and Osser, H. "A Developmental Study of the Discrimination of Letter-Like Forms," *Journal of Comparative and Physiological Psychology,* 55 (1962), 897-906.
5. Gibson, Eleanor J., Osser, H., and Pick, A. D. "A Study in the Development of Grapheme - Phoneme Correspondence," *Journal of Verbal Learning and Verbal Behavior,* 2 (1963), 142-146.
6. Gibson, Eleanor J., Pick, A. D., Osser, H., and Hammond, M. "The Role of Grapheme-Phoneme Correspondence in the Perception of Words," *American Journal of Psychology,* 75 (1962), 554-570.
7. Levin, Harry, and Watson, John. "The Learning of Variable Grapheme - to - Phoneme Correspondence; and The Learning of Variable Grapheme - to - Phoneme Correspondence: Variations in the Initial Consonant Position." In *A Basic Research Program on Reading,* Cornell University, 1963 (Cooperative Research Project No. 639, U. S. Office of Education).
8. Malone, John R. "The Larger Aspects of Spelling Reform," *Elementary English,* 39 (1962), 435-445.

Word Recognition Practice: Basal vs. Phonics Programs

GEORGE E. MASON*

THE TEACHER'S manuals and work-books for eight leading series of basal readers and seven well-known sets of phonics-teaching publications were studied in order to compare suggested practices. The level at which each understanding of phonics, structural analysis, or dictionary usage was first introduced, as well as the amount of practice suggested, was recorded. The information was then tabled or depicted in figures for comparisons. The original plan was to compare basal reading series, to compare phonics materials, and finally compare the two types.

Findings

The differences in level of introduction and sequence of introduction of skills and understandings were more numerous than anticipated. The major findings of the study were the extensive *differences among programs of either type*. Few generalizations could be drawn. Therefore comparison of the *two types* of programs was limited to a very few areas.

The following list incorporates those generalizations possible:

(1) Some phonics programs were more similar to basal reading programs than they were to other phonics programs, and vice versa.

(2) Basal reading programs were more apt to teach discrimination of rhyming and alliteration prior to introduction of sound-letter relationships than were phonics materials.

(3) Consonant letter-sound relationships were more apt to be taught first than were vowel letter-sound relationships in all the programs studied. However, in many phonics books isolated letters and sounds are presented, whereas in basal reading series the sounds are usually presented within spoken words and the letters within printed words.

(4) Initial consonant substitution and syllabic division were the only techniques suggested for teaching by *every* basal reading series. Phonics programs teach most commonly (a) the finding of letters (in printed words) representing dictated sounds, (b) writing letters representing dictated sounds, and (c) pronouncing words by "sounding-out" their letters.

(5) The greatest agreement among basal reading series was on the structural skills and understandings. All suggested teaching inflectional endings, compound words, contractions, prefixes, roots, and root changes in derived forms. Phonics programs were completely agreed only on the teaching of prefixes and suffixes (but not on the same ones).

(6) Every basal reading series included a program for developing dictionary skills. No phonics program provided as many activities as any single basal reading series for dictionary skill development.

(7) The phonics programs suggested, in general, more letter-naming. They directed attention to more letters and to more specific sounds than did basal reading programs. The latter presented more total printed and spoken words for practice.

(8) In basal reading series, calling attention to a word's meaning is done by pointing out its use in context, or by providing an incom-

*Improvement of Reading through Classroom Practice, IRA Proceedings, Vol. 9, 1964, 309-310.

plete sentence into which it may be inserted. In phonics programs, the child is usually asked to say or write the word in a sentence.

Summary

Differences exist in levels at which skills and understandings are introduced in basal programs, and in sequences of in- troduction and extent to which practice is suggested. The same differences are evi- dent among phonics and manuals. Pro- grams of either type are different in so many ways that the isolation of the differ- ences in instruction which might be re- sponsible for the differences in achieve- ment seems nearly impossible.

A Study of the Techniques of Word Identification

H. Alan Robinson*

THE PURPOSE of this study was to determine the relative effectiveness of various techniques for the identification of unfamiliar words met in reading. The following hypotheses were proposed:

1. Context clues alone will not be sufficient for the successful identification of unfamiliar words by average fourth grade readers.

2. Word configurations, in addition to context clues, will not add materially to the fourth grader's success in identifying unfamiliar words.

3. Phonic and/or structural elements in initial positions added to context and configuration clues will enable fourth graders to identify unknown words.

4. When context, configuration, and phonic and/or structural elements in initial positions are not of sufficient help, the addition of phonic and/or structural elements in final positions will permit successful identification of the unfamiliar words.

5. When context clues plus configuration and phonic and structural analyses fail, analysis of the words in their entirety will result in successful identification.

A review of the literature indicates that mature readers use context and configuration clues in perceiving words (4). When the words are familiar, these clues suffice, but when the words are unfamiliar more detailed analysis seems necessary (5). It appears that children who are still learning how to read are more influenced by significant parts of words than are mature adult readers (10), although this tendency may be related to the techniques they have learned rather than to natural inclination. According to studies of word perception, when analysis does take place, the first part of the word appears to be more significant for word perception than the end (6).

This study endeavored to discover what the fourth grade reader actually does in attacking unfamiliar words. Toward this end it became necessary to devise two instruments, one for ascertaining the words unfamiliar to a given population, and the other for the presentation of those words in a reading framework in which the subjects would attempt to identify the words through a variety of identification techniques.

Materials

1. *Sight Word Test.* The test words were chosen from those words familiar to 50 per cent or more of pupils in grade six, based on the Dale-Eichholz study (3). This test was designed to screen out those pupils who could identify two-thirds or more of twenty-two test words. The twenty-two test words were randomly scattered through a list of

*With the aid of Carol Hostetter, research assistant.

*The Reading Teacher, 16 (January 1963), 238-242.

forty-five words making up the Sight Word Test.

2. *Test Passage*. Five forms of a selection were designed to measure the ability of fourth grade subjects to identify the twenty-two test words through different techniques of word identification. The passage was below fifth grade reading level excluding the test words, and approximately sixth level including the test words, based on the Dale-Chall readability formula.

Form I of the test passage used blank spaces instead of the twenty-two words in order to assess the subjects' use of context clues alone.

Form II of the same test passage used configurations of the twenty-two words to assess the use of context plus configuration.*

Form III of the same test passage used context and configuration clues plus beginning elements of each of the twenty-two unfamiliar words.

Form IV of the test passage contained context and configuration clues plus beginning elements and final elements of each of the twenty-two unfamiliar words.

Form V of the same test passage contained each of the twenty-two words completely exposed.

Preliminary Investigation

In order to validate the tests, the investigator and a research assistant conducted a pilot study with twenty-five pupils in a private school in Chicago. The tests appeared suitable

---

*In presenting the configurations of words alone each letter in the word was filled in so that the actual letters were represented but could not be identified as such.

for pupils reading at fourth grade levels. The actual study was conducted in May 1962 with fourth graders in a nearby suburban school system where the population was closer to "average" than in a private school.

Procedure

1. The words on the Sight Word Test were presented in rapid succession to each of eighty-eight subjects. Sixty-one subjects failed to pronounce correctly two-thirds or more of the twenty-two test words and, as a result, were chosen as the subjects for the experiment. They returned the following week to read the five forms of the Test Passage.

2. Each of the sixty-one subjects individually read Form I silently, or orally if the subject desired, and stated the words he thought should be placed in each of the twenty-two blank spaces. Subjects were helped to pronounce any words other than the test words if they asked for such help. They were encouraged to think about what they were reading.

3. Subjects were then given the subsequent forms, one at a time. They were asked if they wanted to alter any of their decisions or suggest words for those they had not responded to at all.

4. The number of correct responses for each subject on each of the Test Passages were totaled, and means and standard deviations were computed for forms III through V. Correct responses for forms I and II were so few that statistical treatment would have been meaningless.

5. The number of correct responses for each of the twenty-two words was tabulated, and percentages of words correct on each form were computed.

Findings

Hypotheses one and two may be accepted as valid for this population.

Hypothesis one proposed that average fourth grade readers would not find context clues alone sufficient for the successful identification of unfamiliar words. Through context clues alone about one-seventh of 1 per cent of the test words were identified and only about 14 per cent of the responses were meaningful synonyms. Two of the sixty-one subjects correctly identified one word each, while fifty of the subjects mentioned meaningful synonyms. Of the 1,342 responses possible (number of subjects — 61 times number of words — 22), there were 188 responses, including the two correct identifications.

Hypothesis two stated that the presence of word configurations, in addition to context clues, would not add materially to the fourth graders' success in identifying unfamiliar words. When word configuration was added to context clues, about one-fifth of 1 per cent of the test words were identified, and again about 14 per cent of the responses were meaningful synonyms. Three of the sixty-one subjects correctly identified one word each, although two of them had identified the same words correctly using only context clues. Forty-eight of the subjects mentioned meaningful synonyms; two subjects withdrew estimates they had made using context clues alone. Of the 1,342 possible responses, there were 185 meaningful responses including the three correct identifications.

Hypotheses three through five must be rejected for this population.

Although the subjects were more successful in identifying unfamiliar words when using phonic and/or structural elements and through analyses of the whole word, no single subject succeeded in identifying all the words. Percentages of correct responses for each of the twenty-two words ranged from 0 to 21 per cent (M, 6.4) on Form III (context-configuration-initial elements); 2 to 36 per cent (M, 17.8) on Form IV (context - configuration - initial elements - final elements); 10 to 61 per cent (M, 35.8) on Form V (context and entire word).

Hypothesis three proposed that the addition of phonic and/or structural elements in initial positions to context and configuration clues would enable the fourth graders to identify unknown words. Correct responses on Form III ranged from 0 to 6 per cent with a mean of 1.41 and a standard deviation of 1.66. Obviously, out of a possible twenty-two words correct, the addition of initial elements to context and configuration resulted in little success for this group of subjects or any one subject in the population.

Hypothesis four stated that when context, configuration, and phonic and/or structural elements in initial positions were not of sufficient help, the addition of phonic and/or structural elements in final positions would permit successful identification of the unfamiliar words. Correct responses on Form IV ranged from 0-16 with a mean of 3.93 and a standard deviation of 3.28. Although two subjects were able to identify 50 per cent or more of the words, the addition of final elements did not result in successful identification for the total population.

Hypothesis five proposed that if context clues plus configuration and phonic and structural analyses failed, analysis of the words in their entirety would result in successful identification. Correct responses on Form V ranged from 1-19 with a mean of 7.95 and a standard deviation of 4.58. Approximately one-quarter of the sixty-one subjects could identify 50 per cent or more of the words when viewing the total word in context.

Discussion

An obvious conclusion is that no word identification technique was used very successfully by this group of subjects. No subject correctly identified all the words. On the other hand, the study had certain limitations. The test words were in the listening vocabularies of the pilot population, but this information was not ascertained for the final test population. The school in which the pilot study was conducted is attended by an exceptionally able group of pupils. A limitation might also lie in the test passage, which may not have been constructed well enough to provide the kinds of context clues helpful to fourth grade subjects. Since the results of a study of word identification ought to be cumulative, that is, each word identification technique needs to build on and incorporate the preceding one, another limitation of this study is the single ordering of techniques. This study started with context, added configuration, then beginning elements, then final elements, and finally presented the whole word. Perhaps different results would be achieved if beginning elements were presented before the total configuration of the word, or final elements before beginning, et cetera.

Actually, a case could be built for devoting more attention to any one aspect. It appears that these subjects, for instance, would profit from instruction in the use of context clues. Even when confronted with context clues alone and no word form, the selections of words which could complete meaning were meager and inaccurate. When parts of the word form were presented, most subjects seemed to concentrate all effort on sounding the parts without regard to context. On the other hand, it was impossible to determine the role of context when subjects correctly identified words in the final test passage where the whole word was viewed in the contextual setting.

Nevertheless, it does seem reasonable that these subjects reading at approximately fourth grade level should meet with a greater degree of success in the identification of unfamiliar words than was reflected in this study. Perhaps average fourth grade readers need an intensification of instruction in the synthesizing of word identification techniques. Since it appears that most success in identification occurs when many techniques are used, pupils may need to learn how to marshall these forces.

Perhaps an additional step needs to be taken in the designing of programs aimed at helping pupils identify words. After the pupils have learned to apply the techniques of identification to familiar words, we should not assume that pupils will on their own transfer this skill to unfamiliar words. Probably many pupils similar to the subjects involved in this study need guidance and direction in applying word identification techniques to unfamiliar words.

Further study of average fourth grade readers using the tests of this experiment in a number of permutations could add interesting and valuable evidence to the present results. Additional experimentation of this kind with readers at a variety of grade levels might help to explain the results of this study. This small piece of research only offers a testing method and results for a specific population. Further research along these lines, or even replications of this study, might eventually contribute to the development of significant insights into instructional practices and the construction of instructional materials.

References

1. Anderson, Irving H., and Dearborn, Walter F. *The Psychology of Teaching Reading*. New York: Ronald Press, 1952. Chapter 5.
2. Dale, Edgar, and Chall, Jeanne S. "A Formula for Predicting Readability," *Educational Research Bulletin, Ohio State University*, 27 (Jan. 1918), 11-20.
3. Eichholz, Gerhard, and Dale, Edgar. *Children's Knowledge of Words*. Columbus: Bureau of Educational Research and Service, Ohio State University, 1960.
4. Gray, William S. "Reading" in *Encyclopedia of Educational Research* (edited by Chester W. Harris). New York: Macmillan, 1960. Pages 1098-99.
5. Hamilton, Francis. *The Perceptual Factors in Reading*. Columbia University Contributions to Philosophy, Psychology, and Education, XVII. New York: Science Press, 1907.
6. Huey, Edmund B. *The Psychology and Pedagogy of Reading*. New York: Macmillan, 1908. Chapters 4 and 5.
7. Porter, Douglas. "The Instrumental Value of Sound Cues in Reading." Unpublished paper presented at Annual Meeting of American Educational Research Association, Feb. 17, 1960.
8. Tinker, Miles A. "Visual Apprehension and Perception in Reading," *Psychological Bulletin*, 26 (Apr. 1929), 293-40.
9. Vernon, M. D. *Backwardness in Reading*. Cambridge: Cambridge University Press, 1957. Chapters 2 and 3.
10. Vernon, M. D. *A Further Study of Visual Perception*. Cambridge: Cambridge University Press, 1954.
11. Vernon, M. D. *The Experimental Study of Reading*. Cambridge: Cambridge University Press, 1931. Chapters 5-7.
12. Woodworth, Robert S. *Experimental Psychology*. New York: Holt, 1938. Pages 23 and 28.

COMMENT

Robinson's report is of particular interest in view of the current reassessment of the relative emphasis which should be given to the various aspects of the word recognition program. The study is exploratory and should stimulate further experimentation in the use of various techniques of word recognition.—T.C.

Visual Discrimination of Words and Reading Readiness

Carol Ann Shea*

Introduction

THIS STUDY WAS DESIGNED to develop a test of visual discrimination of words and to determine which of the following tests—*The Metropolitan Reading Readiness Test, Form R*, the *Lorge-Thorndike Intelligence Test,* or the *Test of Visual Discrimination of Words*— was the best predictor of reading achievement at mid-year in first grade.

Failure in first grade is primarily the result of lack of ability to read. This fact suggests that it would be valuable if valid measures of a child's readiness to begin formal reading instruction could be obtained early in the pupil's school life. DeBoer and Dallman (1960) stated that if an attempt is made to teach a child to read before he is ready, many undesirable results may occur. In some cases, a deep seated aversion toward reading may develop. Heilman (1961) contended that when a child is expected to decipher word symbols before he is visually ready to do so, he is likely to fail.

In 1922, Gates made the first investigation of importance that was concerned with visual perception. He concluded that the ability to detect small differences in words showed a fairly high correlation with reading, whereas the ability to see differences in pairs of objects had no association with reading.

Sister Mary of the Visitation (1929) in a study similar to that of Gates, verified many of his conclusions. She concluded that the "ability to discriminate minute details in series of actual words and also in groups of unrelated letters are pre-eminent factors in reading."

Purpose of the investigation

It was the purpose of this study: 1] to develop a test using words that were similar in configuration in order to measure visual discrimination; 2] to determine whether such a test administered at the beginning of first grade would enable teachers to determine more accurately than *The Metropolitan Reading Readiness Test, Form R,* which children were ready for formal reading activities at that time and which children needed more readiness work; 3] to ascertain if the test of visual discrimination of words was a predictor of reading achievement at mid-year in first grade; and 4] to determine which of the following tests: *The Metropolitan Read-*

*The Reading Teacher, 21 (January 1968), 361-367.

ing Readiness Test, Form R, the Lorge-Thorndike Intelligence Test,
or the *Test of Visual Discrimination of Words* was the best predictor of reading achievement at mid-year.

Test construction

A visual discrimination test was constructed by the investigator. This consisted of two sections. The first section was composed of only letters. There were fifty items and two sample items.
All of the upper and lower case letters were used as stimuli. The
second section was composed of actual words that were similar in
configuration and letter components. There were fifty items and
two sample items. The length of the words increased from two⬝
letters to seven-letters. The stimulus word⬝or letter was printed on
individual nine by twelve cards. Each card was held up by the
examiner and the pupils were allowed to look at it. The card was
exposed five seconds for each of the letter items and ten seconds
for each of the word items.

Examples of the Letter Test

1.	P S B R H	Stimulus B
15.	m u n w r	Stimulus m

Examples of the Word Test

4.	pay hay gay guy gap	Stimulus gay
6.	ran sun nun run rut	Stimulus run

The *Visual Discrimination Test,* in its original form, was
administered to 134 kindergarten children in the town of Hamden,
Connecticut. During this same period *The Metropolitan Reading
Readiness Test, Form R* was administered to these children. The
results of these tests were used to establish the reliability and
validity of the *Visual Discrimination Test.*

The difficulty level of the items in the letter portion of the *Visual
Discrimination Test* was computed. Because 82 per cent of the
items on the letter section of the test were in the range of difficulty
of 80 to 100 per cent, it was concluded that information about the
relative differences among the subjects could not be obtained.
Therefore, the letter section was not included in the final form of
the test.

The level of difficulty was computed for each item in the word
section of the *Visual Discrimination Test.* The results showed that
96 per cent of the items were in the range of difficulty of 20 to 89
per cent. It was felt that with this range of difficulty, information

about the differences in visual discrimination among the subjects could be obtained.

In order to establish the validity of the *Visual Discrimination Word Test*, the reading readiness section of *The Metropolitan Reading Readiness Test, Form R* was used as an independent measure of the criterion. A Pearson Product r was computed between the *Visual Discrimination Word Test* and the reading readiness portion of *The Metropolitan Reading Readiness Test, Form R*. The correlation between the experimental test and the criterion measure was .59.

To further establish the validity of the *Visual Discrimination Word Test* the matching section of *The Metropolitan Reading Readiness Test, Form R* was used as a criterion measure. A Pearson Product r was computed between the two tests. The correlation between the experimental test and this criterion measure was .51.

A Kuder-Richardson reliability coefficient was computed for the *Visual Discrimination Word Test*. The reliability coefficient was .91.

Sample and measuring instruments

The first grade children in the Dunbar Hill School in Hamden, Connecticut, were used for the study. There were thirty-four boys and forty-two girls in this group. The ages of the seventy-six children ranged from seven years seven months to five years nine months. The mean age was six years two months.

The *Visual Discrimination Word Test*, the reading readiness portion of *The Metropolitan Reading Readiness Test, Form R*, and the *Lorge-Thorndike Intelligence Test—Level 1, Form A* were administered to the children during the month of September. In January, after approximately four months of reading instruction, each child was tested individually on a word recognition test. The word recognition test included all the words in the pre-primer and primer vocabularies of the Macmillan Company Series and of the Ginn and Company Series.

Statistical procedures and results

1. A frequency distribution was made for each of the following tests: *Metropolitan Reading Readiness Test, Form R* (reading section), the *Visual Discrimination Word Test*, and the *Lorge-Thorndike Intelligence Test*.

2. Quartile points for each of the frequency distributions were found and the distributions were divided into quarters.

3. The scores of each pupil for each of the three tests were

analyzed and classified according to quarters. Tables 1, 2 and 3 show the total number of cases for each quarter in the row designated "number of cases predicted."

4. Quartile points were found for the frequency distribution of the word recognition test and the distribution was divided into quarters.

5. The scores of each pupil on the word recognition test were analyzed and classified according to quarters.

6. A comparison was made for each pupil to determine if their respective scores on each of the three tests designated were in the same quarter as their scores on the word recognition test. If their score on the word recognition test was in the same quarter as originally predicted by either *The Metropolitan Reading Readiness Test,* the *Visual Discrimination Word Test,* or the *Lorge-Thorndike Intelligence Test,* they were included in the total number of cases listed in Tables 1, 2, 3 in the row designated "number of cases that agreed with prediction."

7. The relative per cent of accuracy of each test and each quarter was determined by comparing the number of cases predicted by that test for each quarter with the number of cases that fell within the predicted quarter on the word recognition test.

For example: On the *Visual Discrimination Word Test,* there were twenty-one pupils with scores in the lowest quarter of the distribution. On the word recognition test, sixteen of the twenty-one pupils were in the lowest quarter. Therefore, the *Visual Discrimination Word Test* predicted accurately for seventy-six per cent of the cases.

The *Visual Discrimination Word Test* predicted for the high quarter 11 per cent better than the *Lorge-Thorndike Intelligence Test* and 27 per cent better than the Metropolitan reading readiness section.

For the high middle quarter the Metropolitan was the best predictor of word recognition ability. It predicted 35 per cent of the time for the high middle quarter. It predicted 2 per cent better than the Lorge-Thorndike and 10 per cent better than the Visual Discrimination Test.

Chi square with one degree of freedom was computed for the lowest quarter of the Metropolitan and the Visual Discrimination Test to determine whether these results merely reflected the operation of chance or whether their appearance probably resulted from a significant difference. With the hypothesis $H : P_1 = P_2$ if $P_1 = .76$, the percentage of cases predicted accurately for the lowest quarter of the Visual Discrimination Test (see Table 2) and $P_2 = .52$, the percentage of cases predicted accurately for the lowest quarter of the Metropolitan (see Table 1), the hypothesis can be rejected at about the .15 level of confidence.

In comparing the results of the entire group on the Visual Discrimination Test and the Lorge-Thorndike with the hypothesis $H:P_1 = P_2$ if $P_1 = .50$, the percentage of cases predicted accurately for the entire group by the Visual Discrimination Test (see Table 2) and $P_2 = .37$, the percentage of cases predicted accurately for the entire group by the Lorge-Thorndike (see Table 3) the hypothesis can be rejected at about the .10 level of confidence.

In order to determine which combination of tests would provide the best estimate of readiness to begin formal reading instruction, multiple correlations were performed. Table 4 shows the intercorrelations of these tests and Table 5 the multiple correlations.

In an analysis of the intercorrelations, the Lorge-Thorndike and the Visual Discrimination Test had the lowest intercorrelation (.46) but, the combination of these tests had the highest correlation with the criterion, the word recognition test (.76). Therefore, the Lorge-Thorndike and the Visual Discrimination Test measure different aspects of reading readiness and a combination of both would contribute substantially to prediction.

Table 1   Distribution of cases according to quarters for
The Metropolitan Reading Readiness Test

	Lowest quarter	Second quarter	Third quarter	Highest quarter	Total group
Agree—N	10	9	7	1	27
Disagree—N	19	32	20	5	76
% of agreement	52%	28%	35%	20%	36%

Table 2   Distribution of cases according to quarters for
the Visual Discrimination Word Test

	Lowest quarter	Second quarter	Third quarter	Highest quarter	Total group
Agree—N	16	6	5	11	38
Disagree—N	21	12	20	23	76
% of agreement	76%	50%	25%	47%	50%

On the other hand, the Metropolitan and the Lorge-Thorndike had the highest intercorrelation (.86) but, the combination of these tests had the lowest correlation with the criterion, the word

Table 3   Distribution of cases according to quarters for
the Lorge-Thorndike Intelligence Test

	Lowest quarter	Second quarter	Third quarter	Highest quarter	Total group
Agree—N	8	9	7	4	28
Disagree—N	17	27	21	11	76
% of agreement	47%	33%	33%	36%	37%

Table 4   Intercorrelations among four variables,
including one index word recognition and
three predictive indices

Variable	X_2	X_3	X_4	X_1
X_2 Visual discrimination	—	.49	.46	.65
X_3 Metropolitan	.49	—	.86	.61
X_4 Lorge-Thorndike	.46	.86	—	.66
X_1 Word recognition	.65	.61	.66	—

Table 5   Multiple correlations between the three
predictive tests and the word recognition test

$r1.34$	.66		
$r1.23$	.73		
$r1.24$	.76	$r1.234$	.66

1 equals criterion, Word Recognition Test
2 equals predictive test, Visual Discrimination Word Test
3 equals predictive test, *Metropolitan Reading Reariness Test*
4 equals predictive test, *Lorge-Thorndike Intelligence Test*

recognition test (.66). Therefore, the Metropolitan and the Lorge-Thorndike measure much the same thing and the inclusion of both, instead of either one or the other, would contribute little to the prediction achieved.

With an r of .65 there was substantial correlation between achievement on the Visual Discrimination Test and achievement on the word recognition test and with an r of .66 an almost identical relationship existed between achievement on the Lorge-Thorndike and the word recognition test. The substantial relationship existing between achievement on the Visual Discrimination Test and the word recognition test confirmed the theory that the ability to discriminate visually words was an indicator of readiness to begin formal reading instruction when the sight method of instruction was employed. Schools using different teaching approaches might yield different results. In addition the statistical analysis indicated that the ability to discriminate words visually is particularly significant in the upper and lower quarters. It also confirmed the theory of other investigators that intelligence was a factor in determining when a pupil was ready to learn to read. Neither the ability to make visual discriminations between words nor intelligence is the sole factor to be used to determine readiness for formal reading instruction. The multiple correlations showed that the combination of the Lorge-Thorndike and the Visual Discrimination Test was a better predictor of readiness to read than the combination of the Metropolitan and the Lorge-Thorndike or the Visual Discrimination Test and the Metropolitan.

These results lend support to the theory that the lack of capability to discriminate visually between words is a significant factor in retarding or limiting the reading success of children. This in turn leads to the assumption that children in the crucial lower quarters on the *Visual Discrimination Word Test* should be given extensive training in visual perception before formal reading instruction is started.

References

DeBoer, J. J., and Dallmann, Martha. *The teaching of reading.* New York: Holt, Rinehart & Winston, 1960.

Gates, A. *The psychology of reading and spelling with special reference to disability.* New York: Bureau of Publications, Teachers College, Columbia University, 1922.

Heilman, A. W. *Principles and practices of teaching reading.* Ohio: Merrill, 1961.

Sister Mary of the Visitation. Visual perception in reading and spelling: a statistical analysis. *Educational Research Bulletins,* 1929, 4 (1). Washington, D. C.: The Catholic Education Press.

What Do Teachers Know about Phonics and Syllabication?

George D. Spache and Mary E. Baggett*

THE EXTENT TO WHICH teachers can and do teach their pupils various phonics and syllabication skills is, of course, dependent upon their own knowledge of the underlying principles and conventions. Several previous authors have explored this question by administering various phonics tests to groups of teachers and graduate students in education. In general, the results have not been very encouraging. Gagan (2) found that teachers knew about 68 per cent of the items in the informal Rogers Test of Phonic Ability. Ramsey's and Schubert's studies (4, 6) give similar results on their own phonics tests. Aaron's (1) group of prospective and experienced teachers answered only 57 per cent of his 60-item test. He also found that scores tended to increase with teaching experience, implying that the scores of teachers tended to depend on their classroom experience rather than on the adequacy of their pre-service training. Educational assignment was not associated with performance on the test, contrary to the logical expectation that primary teachers, who commonly present this content, would be most familiar with it. Collectively these studies raise grave doubts regarding the adequacy of the teaching of phonics in our classrooms. Despite the emphasis upon these skills in the manuals and guides accompanying basal reading materials, and the claims of teachers that they faithfully follow such guides (3, 5) can we believe that phonics is well taught by teachers who don't understand the basic principles?

Procedures

All students enrolled in the senior author's workshops and classes during the academic year 1963-64 were given a revised version of Aaron's test of phonics principles and informal tests of syllabication and syllabication principles. Aaron's test was modified by grouping all related items in consecutive groups. A sample item of this fifty-item test is:

> 5. The *u* in *dru' mel* has the same sound as:
> (1) *u* in *true*, (2) *u* in *cut*, (3) *u* in urn, (4) *u* in nature, (5) none of these

The syllabication test asked respondents not to mark the syllables but to write the number of syllables present. Samples of the sixty-five items are:

> 2. cyclic............   61. pleonasm............
> 11. lattice............   65. sisal............
> 37. diatonic............

The twelve-item test on rules for syllabication was a multiple-choice arrangement. A sample item is:

> 4. A consonant between two vowels usually goes with the vowel .... it when the vowel in front is accented and short.
> a) before
> b) following
> c) neither
> d) either before or after

*The Reading Teacher, 19 (November 1965) , 96-99.

Subjects

Six of the respondents were full-time graduate students without previous teaching experience other than their internships. The remainder of 93 were in-service teachers pursuing graduate credit in the area of reading. Aaron's groups were composed of 65 per cent of inexperienced teachers in contrast with our group of 6 per cent.

Results

The mean scores of the 99 students on the three tests and the respective ranges of scores were: Phonics Principles, mean 45.0, range 18-60; Syllabication, mean 59.6, range 30-65; Syllabication Rules, mean score 8.21, range 1-11. The range of the present group in the Phonics test is similar to that in Aaron's study, 13-59, but the mean is greater than his of 34.22. Since years of experience were found to be positively related to success in this test, the differences in the means may well reflect the greater teaching experience of our group.

These means indicate that the group answered correctly 75 per cent of the phonics, 91 per cent of the syllabication, and 68 per cent of the syllabication rules tests. Although competent in the act of syllabication, the group appears no more knowledgeable in the principles of syllabication than in phonics. It is questionable whether those teachers, particularly of intermediate grades, who are expected to teach syllabication can do this competently when they are so weak in the underlying phonic and syllabication principles. How

can they teach pupils a skill which they can do well but do not clearly understand?

Aaron made comparisons within his group of prospective and in-service teachers to discover the influence of teaching experience and assignment upon knowledge of phonics principles. Years of experience were found to be associated with performance, but educational assignment was not related. Apparently teachers at various grade levels have about the same proficiency in applying phonics principles, for what they know has been learned gradually in the classroom, not in training. Using the same categories of experience and assignment in our group yielded the data of Table 1 below.

TABLE 1

SCORES ON PHONICS PRINCIPLES TEST

A. According to Years of Teaching Experience

Scores	0 Yrs.	1-5 Yrs.	6-10 Yrs.	Over 10 Yrs.
Mean	35.00	39.5	44.8	45.2
Range	16-55	16-60	26-60	26-60
Number	6	31	22	40

B. According to Grade Groups

Scores	Grs. 1-3	Grs. 4-6	Grs. 7-12	Other Grades
Mean	46.3	47.6	39.6	46.9
Range	16-60	31-60	26-55	16-60
Number	30	27	25	17

Teachers with ten or more years of experience or six–ten years of experience know significantly more about phonics than beginning teachers. These differences are significant at the .01 and .02 levels, respectively. As in Aaron's group, the test was administered early in the graduate course, prior to discussion·or instruction in this area. Thus the scores reflect upon the adequacy of the preservice training of these groups.

In the present study the teachers assigned to junior and senior high school were significantly poorer in knowledge of phonics, at the .01 level, than all other groups. This is in contrast to the lack of differences among such groups in Aaron's study. Several factors such as size of sample, average length of experience, and the nature of the teaching assignments in this deviant group may account for this result. If, for example, a large proportion of our secondary teachers were science, mathematics, business-education teachers, or the like, they might well be expected to be less familiar with phonics principles.

The data on the remaining tests of syllabication and syllabication rules are summarized in Tables 2 and 3 below.

ence or assignment is significant. Apparently, syllabication accuracy is learned before entering teaching, and does not materially improve with classroom teaching experience at any particular level. Some explanation of the failure to improve in syllabication, despite the experience involved in teaching this skill to pupils, may lie in teacher knowledge of the principles underlying this skill, as shown by the data of Table 3.

TABLE 3

SCORES ON SYLLABICATION RULES TEST

A. According to Years of Teaching Experience

Scores	0 Yrs.	1-5 Yrs.	6-10 Yrs.	Over 10 Yrs.
Mean	7.3	8.0	8.6	8.4
Range	4-11	2-11	1-11	4-11
Number	6	31	22	40

B. According to Grade Groups

Scores	Grs. 1-3	Grs. 4-6	Grs. 7-12	Other Grades
Mean	8.5	9.07	7.6	7.47
Range	4-11	6-11	4-11	1-11
Number	30	27	25	17

TABLE 2

SCORES ON SYLLABICATION TEST

A. According to Years of Teaching Experience

Scores	0 Yrs.	1-5 Yrs.	6-10 Yrs.	Over 10 Yrs.
Mean	61.6	60.5	58.2	59.8
Range	55-65	50-63	35-62	30-64
Number	6	31	22	40

B. According to Grade Groups

Scores	Grs. 1-3	Grs. 4-6	Grs. 7-12	Other Grades
Mean	60.0	60.8	59.3	58.3
Range	35-65	50-65	41-64	32-63
Number	30	27	25	17

None of the comparisons between groups according to teaching experi-

Comparisons among the groups according to teaching experience yield no significant differences. Length of teaching experience does not result in increased knowledge of syllabication rules. Comparisons among the grade groups, however, do indicate that the level .of teaching assignment is significantly related to knowledge of such rules. Teachers of Grades 1-3 are more knowledgeable than those of Grades 7-12 at the 5 per cent level, and more knowledgeable than the Other group (a mixed group of administrators, supervisors, reading specialists, and adult educators) at the 5 per cent level. Intermediate grade teachers score significantly better at the 1 per cent level than secondary teachers or the mixed group. Level of teaching assignment does promote greater learning of syllabication principles among those teachers who are commonly responsible for instruction in this area.

Before offering the implications of these results, an evaluation of the interrelationships among these three tests of word skills is appropriate. The correlation between Phonics Principles and Syllabication was .657, a marked relationship, again implying the continuity and interdependence of these two skills. In contrast, the correlation between the Phonics Principles and Syllabication Rules tests was .370, implying that ability to apply phonics principles does not contribute greatly to similar knowledge of syllabication rules. The correlation of .256 between Syllabication and Syllabication Rules raises questions about the value of knowledge of syllabication principles for success in syllabication. This result is confirmed in an earlier unpublished study of these tests by an *r* of .230 among 69 college freshman students.

Implications

The replication of Aaron's study confirms the need for pre-service instruction for primary and intermediate teachers in phonics and its principles. Secondary teachers whose instructional areas touch upon this skill seem in even greater need of such instruction, in Florida at least.

Pre-service training in syllabication is apparently effective and results in reasonable teacher skill in this area. Knowledge of the underlying rules for syllabication, however, is not strong at any teaching level and only comparatively better for primary and intermediate grade teachers. Other studies of the values of syllabication rules (as compared to phonics principles) are necessary at varying educational levels.

If knowledge of syllabication rules does not markedly influence success in applying phonics principles or in actual syllabication, of what value are such rules? Should more training in phonics and its principles be substituted for the time presently spent on syllabication rules?

References

1. Aaron, Ira E. "What Teachers and Prospective Teachers Know About Phonic Generalizations," *Journal of Educational Research*, 53 (May 1960), 323-330.
2. Gagon, Glen Scott. "A Diagnostic Study of the Phonic Abilities of Elementary Teachers in the State of Utah." Doctoral dissertation, Colorado State College, 1960.
3. Purcell, Barbara A. "Methods of Teaching Reading: A Report of a Tri-State Survey," *Elementary School Journal*, 58 (May 1958), 449-453.
4. Ramsey, Z. Wallace. "Will Tomorrow's Teachers Know and Teach Phonics?" *Reading Teacher*, 15 (Jan. 1962), 241-245.
5. Russell, David H. "Teachers' Views on Phonics," *Elementary English*, 32 (Oct. 1955), 371-375.
6. Schubert, Delwyn G. "Teachers and Word Analysis Skills," *Journal of Developmental Reading* 2 (Summer 1959), 62-64.

Developing Advanced Word Perception Skills

Diana Umstattd*

Texas, California, Georgia, Utah, New York, New Jersey, Pennsylvania . . . New Hampster," said Patty as she quickly read a list of the names of the states. To the last response the teacher whispered, "New Hamp*shire*," and hurried on to the next student. Then the teacher stopped. Here it was again, "New Hamp*ster*." The second student, and also a third one, pronounced it the same way. Why the errors? What must the teacher do?

The Need

Boys and girls at the upper elementary level are interested in learning about hundreds of different things. They seek much of their information from printed materials. This, in turn, demands reading skills that are efficient for their many needs and interests. It requires word perception skills which will enable them to read, with ease, about dozens and dozens of topics, in various kinds of materials, and for numerous purposes. It means that the classroom teacher must teach perception skills that will meet these challenges.

A Balance Theory

In Jerome S. Bruner's book, *A Study of Thinking*,[1] he reported that the capable successful subjects in his experiments selected strategies for operation which would enable them to maintain a balance of informational intake, cognitive strain, and risk, commensurate with the task. It seems to us that this is also true of successful, ambitious readers in the upper elementary grade levels. They want to "look at" and to "think about" words just long enough to get that information which, if combined with other available information about the same words, will

enable them to read the material at hand, for the specific purpose of the moment. The amounts of informational intake, of cognitive strain, and of risk will vary with the student, the topic, the kind of material, and the specific purpose. We shall consider this balance of benefits to the students as we discuss the development of advanced word perception skills.

The Advanced Word Perception Skills

An inspection of the teacher's manuals of a few series of basic readers indicates that, by consensus, the major advanced word perception skills are: phonetic skills, structural analysis skills, syllable phonics, dictionary skills, and abilities to use certain contextual clues.

The methods of teaching these several skills and the status given each one varies somewhat from one series of readers to another. In short, the authors plan to use a balance of informational intake, cognitive strain, and risk that is conducive to the development of their major purposes. The ratio of the components of a given program is in agreement with the respective definitions of reading.

The Development of the Skills

It is not our purpose to discuss the skills program of any series of basic readers nor the philosophy of the author(s) of any series. Instead, we want to observe Patty and her friends as they read to meet their numerous needs and interests. Which skills do they use, and under what circumstances? Are certain skills high on their priority lists, or do they shift freely from one skill to the other as the demands change?

First, let us return to Patty and the list of names of the states. She knew California, Pennsylvania, and Utah, but she said New Hamp*ster* instead of New Hamp-

---

[1]Jerome S. Bruner, Jacqueline J. Goodnow, and George A. Austin. *A Study of Thinking*. New York: Science Editions, Inc., 1962.

Reading and Inquiry, IRA Proceedings, Vol. 10, 1965, 30-32.

shire. Why?

Patty recognized the category—states in the United States. She was familiar with the names, but did not recognize them as sight words. She rapidly used a combination of skills to make initial attacks upon the words. Her background of information hastened her completion of the identification of the words, with one exception. Why did she say "New Hampster?" We believe that she had been hearing it that way, and our hunch was supported by her two peers who made similar errors. The balance of benefits of a particular strategy was at work, and the informational intake was insufficient to compensate for an unknown risk, an error in aural perception in an earlier experience. A new strategy had to be selected and a new balance had to be maintained for the identification of New Hampshire. Patty was equal to the task. She knew where to add a step and how to fit it into her sequence of decisions. Her word perception skills were adequate for the identification of the word.

As we observed Patty and her friends from day to day in various circumstances and with many materials we noticed the preparation that went into their reading. They were constantly aware of their purposes. They also took into account all the information which they could bring to the situation. They anticipated words and clues for recognizing them. They considered the type of material to be encountered. Last, but not least, they were alert to the quality of thinking that they must do. They used all the word perception skills as they read, but were versatile in the timing of the use of each. They consistently matched personal strengths and weaknesses with the specific task at hand.

Some children may learn to shift from skill to skill freely, without direct guidance. Others are like Wayne, who needed much help. Wayne's teacher assisted him in reading arithmetical story problems by teaching him at which points precision was essential and at which points generalizations would be acceptable. For example, he substituted names of friends for the proper names but carefully analyzed all other words within the questions.

In Summary

We recognize that children are faced with voluminous amounts of printed materials. There is neither time nor energy for reading all of it. Yet they must learn much of the content. This demands that they encounter many new words each time they shift to a different topic or a different material. New words demand efficient word perception skills. We have discussed efficiency in terms of pupils, needs, materials, and purposes. We have also discussed efficiency in terms of a balance of benefits which the reader receives from the particular strategies he uses. The choice of strategy may well be considered as the foundation of the development of adequate word perception skills at the upper elementary level.